Routedge Revivals

The Power of Shame

First published in 1985, this book provides a stimulating series of inter-connected essays which address the theme of shame, which, unlike the problem of conscience, has been seldom discussed by moral philosophers. The essays focus on the ethical regulation of human action and judgement, examining both its constant and varying elements and concentrating on contemporary types of moral regulation. Professor Heller uses Aristotelian categories, such as the good life, in her discourse to present a new conception of rationality, distinguishing between shame regulation and conscience regulation of moral conduct, and arguing that shame regulation cannot be completely overcome even in an age of rationalism.

The Power of Shame
A Rational Perspective

Agnes Heller

First published in 1985
by Routledge and Kegan Paul

This edition first published in 2018 by Routledge
2 Park Square, Milton Park, Abingdon, Oxon, OX14 4RN
and by Routledge
711 Third Avenue, New York, NY 10017

Routledge is an imprint of the Taylor & Francis Group, an informa business

© 1985 Agnes Heller

All rights reserved. No part of this book may be reprinted or reproduced or utilised in any form or by any electronic, mechanical, or other means, now known or hereafter invented, including photocopying and recording, or in any information storage or retrieval system, without permission in writing from the publishers.

Publisher's Note
The publisher has gone to great lengths to ensure the quality of this reprint but points out that some imperfections in the original copies may be apparent.

Disclaimer
The publisher has made every effort to trace copyright holders and welcomes correspondence from those they have been unable to contact.

ISBN 13: 978-1-138-56116-8 (hbk)
ISBN 13: 978-0-203-71097-5 (ebk)
ISBN 13: 978-1-138-56121-2 (pbk)

Also by Agnes Heller

Renaissance Man
A Theory of History
Everyday Life

THE POWER OF SHAME
A Rational Perspective

Agnes Heller

ROUTLEDGE & KEGAN PAUL
LONDON, BOSTON, MELBOURNE AND HENLEY

First published in 1985
by Routledge & Kegan Paul plc

14 Leicester Square, London WC2H 7PH, England

9 Park Street, Boston, Mass, 02108, USA

464 St Kilda Road, Melbourne,
Victoria 3004, Australia and

Broadway House, Newtown Road,
Henley on Thames, Oxon RG9 1EN, England

Set in Linotron Times, 10/11
by Input Typesetting Ltd, London

This collection © Agnes Heller 1985

No part of this book may be reproduced in
any form without permission from the publisher,
except for the quotation of brief passages
in criticism

Library of Congress Cataloging in Publication Data

Heller, Ágnes.
The power of shame.
Includes index.
1. Ethics—Addresses, essays, lectures.
2. Social ethics—Addresses, essays, lectures.
3. Rationalism—Addresses, essays, lectures.
4. Shame—Moral and ethical aspects—Addresses,
essays, lectures. I. Title.
BJ1581.2.H44 1985   170   84-18195
British Library CIP Data also available
ISBN 0 7100 9922 3

Contents

	Preface	vii
Chapter 1	The Power of Shame	1
Chapter 2	Paradigm of Work – Paradigm of Production	57
Chapter 3	Everyday Life, Rationality of Reason, Rationality of Intellect	71
Chapter 4	Rationality and Democracy	251
Chapter 5	Can 'True' and 'False' Needs be Posited?	285
Chapter 6	The Dissatisfied Society	300
	Index	316

Preface

With one exception, all the essays in this volume were written in the last two years (the exception being 'Can "True" and "False" Needs be Posited?'). After finishing my book on the theory of history, and before starting work on a theory of ethics, the clarification of my own understanding of rationality presented itself as a necessary task, and, from several aspects, as a stringent one.

The last phrase of the book is an invitation to the public. The author repeats the words of the actor in Brecht's play *The Good Person of Setzuan*: 'There has to be an answer', and I hasten to add that there may be more answers than just one. My intention was to leave *open* the practical viability of theoretical solutions. The problem of rationality was not meant to be concluded as an open-and-shut, but rather as an open, case. And I firmly believe that the essay character of the book is a strong *stylistic* indication of the open-endedness of the theoretical endeavour.

Due to this character of the studies, references to contemporary theories are sparse and polemical in nature. Accordingly, I wish to mention here the authors with whom I feel the strongest theoretical affinity. They belong to different theoretical traditions, and their respective theories may have very little in common. Still, I feel an affinity with all of them, if not to the same extent. They are K. O. Apel, H. Arendt, C. Castoriadis, J. Habermas, A. MacIntyre, G. Lukács and J. Rawls. The category of 'regard' and its particular usage has been borrowed from Sartre. Of course, if one casts a glance at this 'short list', what immediately strikes the mind is the conspicuous presence of three 'neo-Aristotelians'. Ever since I wrote my book on Aristotle's ethics (in 1958–9), I

PREFACE

have always tried to reintroduce Aristotelian categories into the moral and political discourse. The emphasis on Aristotle's heritage sprang from the same (or at least from a similar) critical attitude to the status of morals and politics in modernity as is manifested in the works of Arendt, Castoriadis and MacIntyre. However, my interpretation of Aristotle differs nearly to the same extent from that of the above-mentioned authors as their interpretations differ from one another. Contrary to Arendt, and, to a lesser degree, to Castoriadis, I lay a far greater emphasis on the Aristotelian understanding of *techné*. Contrary to MacIntyre, I do not contrast Aristotle, the offspring of Greek Enlightenment, to the philosophy of Enlightenment; he was the first to combine formal and substantive ethics. He never prescribed what exactly men ought to do to be virtuous, as all purely substantive ethics do, but left it to the good judgment of individuals to find out how, when and under what circumstances they were to act so as to become virtuous. I think that the category of *mesotes* (middle measure) is one of the focal points of the Aristotelian ethics, a category completely neglected by MacIntyre's brilliant book on virtues. These differences in understanding Aristotle are not only matters of interpretation, for they are deeply embedded in a differing view of modernity. No wonder then that my theoretical relations to authors such as Descartes, Spinoza, Kant, Hegel or Marx is far more affirmative (if not uncritical) than is the case in contemporary neo-Aristotelianism.

Ab urbe condita of the ancient Rome is nowadays replaced by the statement 'from the emergence of modernity', even though not so much in historiography as in social philosophy. This book is only one from among many focussing on the same problem. Although my theory is far from being 'value-free', and I state my guiding values more than once, as far as the comparison of modern with premodern is concerned, I neither indulge in complaints about the lost chastity of humankind, nor do I share the self-complacency of a theory of evolution. I simply reconfirm the results of my theory of history from another aspect: we do not yet know whether modernity is a stage of progress or regress as compared with previous human histories. Modernity includes both promise and warning. My intention is to strengthen the promise by making a strong case for warning.

This sounds Weberian, but it is not. Like all social theorists (whether they admit it or not), I am also deeply indebted to Marx, Durkheim and Weber. But today we are living in a post-Marxian, post-Durkheimian and post-Weberian age. Since Marx-bashing

PREFACE

became an almost obligatory pastime, and since Weber, in contrast, is being read like the Gospel, it is more appropriate to say a few words about Weber at this juncture. Weber belonged to the existentialist generation, and he mediated between Kierkegaard on the one hand and Heidegger on the other. The necessity to choose between competing deities differs from the Kierkegaardian either–or only in so far as Weber added science to the list of deities. The idea that in choosing one god, we choose ourselves (our demon), is already a solution of the Heideggerian–Sartrean type. Existentialism falls short of providing us with *any* ethics or moral or political philosophy answering the exigencies of our times. The Weberian ethics of responsibility in politics was implemented by Henry Kissinger and the *White House Years* bears best witness to it. The problems which have to be raised transcend Weber as much as Marx.

I should also make two further remarks in advance. The first concerns the short study, 'Paradigm of Work, Paradigm of Production'. It was written a few months before the publication of *Geschichte und Eigensinn* by Kluge and Negt. The latter applies the paradigm of work in an even more conclusive way than Lukács views his *Ontology* as an exemplification of this paradigm. This is how Kluge and Negt arrive at the formulation, 'work thinks'. It must be added that in applying their paradigm to history, they substitute the paradigm of production for the paradigm of work in the same way as I believe everyone would be compelled to do when embarking on this kind of theoretical experiment.

The second remark concerns a question of terminology. In the lengthy study 'Everyday Life, Rationality of Reason, Rationality of Intellect' I undertake the criticism of the Weberian categories of 'value rationality' and 'goal rationality'. However, in some of my former studies I have used the same categories. In order to avoid confusion (the possibility of which became clear to me only afterwards), let me state here that in my book *For a Radical Philosophy*, a work written in 1976 and to which I refer in several footnotes, I defined these categories in the Aristotelian, *not* the Weberian, meaning of the term. An action is value-rational if the end (the good) is included in the action, that is to say, if the action is an end-in-itself. An action is goal-rational if the end (the good) is *outside* the action. As I do not know whether this present book or *A Radical Philosophy* will be first published in English, it is important that I make this clarification.

PREFACE

I wish to express my gratitude to the administrative staff of the Department of Sociology at La Trobe University for typing this manuscript.

As my written English is still badly in need of stylistic revision, all the essays had to be checked and polished. Some of my colleagues and friends spent a great amount of their precious time to put the manuscript in order. Without their kind assistance this book could not have been published. I am very much obliged to Glenn Mulligan, Brett Lockwood and Julian Triado for their help.

The text of the study 'Everyday Life, Rationality of Reason, Rationality of Intellect' is based on the lectures given in my course at the University of Konstanz, Germany, in the winter semester of 1981–2. During my stay in Konstanz I had the opportunity of repeatedly discussing the problems of rationality with Albrecht Wellmer. His remarks have resulted in a significant contribution to the formation of my ideas on the subject, and I am very much indebted to him. I am also very grateful for the critical remarks of Johann Arnason, George Markus, Glenn Mulligan and Julian Triado.

As in all my work and endeavours during the last twenty years, continuous assistance and encouragement has come from my husband and friend, Ferenc Feher. As the first reader and most ardent critic of all my works, he has actively contributed to every page of this book. It is to him that I owe the deepest gratitude.

CHAPTER 1
The Power of Shame

Introduction

The problem of shame, in marked contrast with the problem of conscience, has seldom been thematized in modern moral philosophy, while discussion of shame as a phenomenon has been mainly confined within the frameworks of psychology and anthropology. (In anthropology, the counterposition of 'shame cultures' and 'guilt cultures' has become widespread.) Although it is true that certain advocates of *Kulturkritik* and of anthropology have noticed that consideration of the shame regulation of human conduct has gained ground in our times, the manifold implications of this recognition have been left unexplored. The following study attempts to fill the gap by offering a *general theory of shame*. The main issue under scrutiny will be the ethical regulation of human action and judgment, examining both its constant and varying elements. I am aware of the inherent difficulties in the task I have undertaken. A thorough analysis of the changing patterns in the system of ethical regulation calls for an historical interpretation, whereas a thorough analysis of the system's constant patterns requires a structural interpretation. Should one undertake both simultaneously, one has to work with an historical *typology* inevitably selective in character. I wish to make it clear from the start that my selection is oriented towards the understanding (and the critique) of contemporary types of moral regulation. Such an undertaking implies the criticism of certain ethical theories which express and endorse these types of regulation, and this will be done in the text usually without explicit reference to these theories. I am going to argue that the *over-rationalization* of moral regulation (i) contributes to the erosion of the pillars of that same regulation; (ii) opens the way to the emergence of an irrational external authority; and (iii) that completely *formalized* moral philosophies not only cannot cope with these dangers but, on occasion, even reinforce them. A postulate, combining material (substantive) with formal ethics, will be formulated as a conclusion.

In what follows, I substitute a distinction between shame and conscience for the more usual division of moral feelings into shame and guilt. Certain distinguished scholars of modern anthropology based their counterposition of shame and guilt on a particular interpretation of Freud's psychology, and although not a follower of Freud, I certainly read his analysis of the problem under scrutiny as a corroboration more of my theory than theirs. In *Civilization and its Discontents*, Freud distinguished two types of *guilt*. The historically primary type of guilt was essentially a reaction to the *fear of external authority*, whereas the historically secondary type of guilt was essentially a reaction to the *fear of internalized authority*. In making this distinction, Freud obviously attributed guilt feelings to people whose cultures were later to be misleadingly identified as 'shame' *as opposed to* 'guilt' cultures. I do not wish to disparage the merits of great anthropologists like Margaret Mead or Ruth Benedict. Even less do I wish to test their Freudian 'orthodoxy'. But the truth of the matter is that shame and guilt cannot sensibly be related to the same *genus proximum*. Guilt is the perpetuation of either shame or the pangs of conscience; it is the consciousness of a moral debt which has to be repaid. The less it can or will be repaid, the more tormenting the guilt feeling becomes. Benedict herself describes a traditional Japanese shame feeling as the feeling of 'being in debt', and the German word for guilt, '*Schuld*', literally *means* 'being in debt'. Works of art testify that guilt can (and often does) pertain to shame. Masaccio's celebrated *Adam and Eve* is one example among many. Adam covers his face, Eve her nakedness – both typical gestures of shame – because they had committed a *sin* which had to be requited by both them and the whole human race through the burden of hard work and the punishment of mortality.

I

Both shame and conscience are feelings. As such, they are involvements of persons in the judgments made by the authorities of human conduct. Feeling can be defined as 'being involved in something'. (In my book *A Theory of Feelings*, I have argued at length for this theoretical proposal. As I cannot repeat my arguments here, I simply refer the reader for details to the first two chapters of the book.) As a result, 'involvement of persons' *means* feeling, and the phrase 'in the judgments made by the authorities of human conduct' *qualifies* the feeling. As any 'authority of human conduct' is a *normative* authority, involvement in such an authority can properly be called *moral* feeling.

Shame and conscience differ insofar as the *authority* in which one is involved is different. In the case of shame, the authority is *social custom* – rituals, habits, codes or rosters of behaviour – represented by the '*eye of others*'. In the case of conscience, the authority is *practical reason* which can become manifest as the 'internal voice'. Both authorities can approve as well as disapprove. A clear conscience is not simply an absence of the pangs of conscience. It is also a highly pleasant feeling, and when we are praised in public and blush in modesty, it is a magnificent experience of happy embarrassment.

The disapproval of either authority may elicit feelings which range from simple uneasiness to the torments of guilt. The intensity and quality of the feeling certainly depends on the character of the violated norm, but only partly. The various shades of guilt feeling have been amply analysed in psychology, and I simply cannot enter into this problem within the context of this paper. But what has to be emphasized is the fact that the intensity of guilt feeling does not depend on the particular authority of judgment in which one is involved. The disapproval of the external authority can trigger guilt feelings which make life completely intolerable, while the disapproval of the internal authority may (on occasion) be easily overcome.

To assert that shame is involvement in the judgment of the external authority is not to support the widely held theory that shame is not internalized. For the question as to whether *shame* is internalized becomes irrelevant once it is seen that shame is a feeling and, as such, an internal occurrence. The proper question then is whether or not the occurrence of the feeling signifies the internalization (not of shame) but of the external authority. If not, shame can only be reactive and would not imply the recognition of the validity of the norms of the external authority by the members of the community. But if the members of a community did not consider certain actions and modes of behaviour as 'shameful', the *fear* of being put to shame would not make people avoid transgressing against the external authority of conduct, and no one would be put to shame at all. But different types and levels of internalization are (and have to be) distinguished in every community. A member of a New Guinea tribe explained the different notions of shame to an anthropologist in the following way. Shame is either 'shame on the skin' or 'deep shame'. If urinating or sexual intercourse is *witnessed* by others, the shame felt is 'shame on the skin'; if someone offends ancestral spirits, the shame felt is 'deep shame'. Here it is the character of the norms infringed that determines the intensity of shame, and it is taken for granted that the infringement of norms that elicits 'shame on the skin' is always *unintentional.* In our society, the intensity of shame does not depend only on the norms but also to a great extent on the *individual's* relation to these norms. If two industrialists go bankrupt, one might commit suicide not because of the loss of wealth but because of being unable to face the 'eye of others', while the other may not experience shame at all. When norms are pluralistic, or when they can be interpreted in a pluralistic way, not everyone will be ashamed, or at least not with the same intensity in cases of transgression against the external authority.

Some scholars argue that it is not the lack of internalization but rather the character of the *sanction* (in cases of transgression) that distinguishes shame from guilt. Shame calls for an *external* sanction whereas guilt is an internal sanction. Although the counterposition of shame and guilt has already been rejected, additional comments are appropriate. If sanction means *punishment,* the distinction between shame and guilt on grounds of their respective sanctions cannot be reasonably supported. In some shameful situations there are no punitive sanctions at all, being ashamed *is* punishment in itself. (If one wishes, one can speak of 'internal sanctions' in such cases. Of course, there are people who do not feel shame even if, in terms of the given expectations, they should. But there are also others who do not feel guilty even if they are in fact guilty.) If sanction does not mean punishment but the torments of the self, again the distinction cannot be supported. When we recall situations in which we were ashamed, a burning feeling of mortification or of being ridiculed is still with us even if our conscience is clear. In cases of shame, it is not the sanction but the authority that is external. If the external authority has been internalized, and if we transgress its norms or rituals, *we lose our honour.* Losing honour means losing *face.* The expression 'losing face' aptly describes the *visual* character of shame. As has been mentioned, the violation of external authority is disapproved of by the 'eye of others'. If the norm violated by our actions is highly placed in the value structure of our community, then the sentence of the 'eye of others' is isolation and expulsion. Banished by and from the 'eye' we can no longer look at *others* with disapprobation when *they* fail to conform with the norms of conduct, for we no longer have *face*. If we lose our honour, we feel guilty; the torments of lost honour are the torments of 'shame-guilt'.

Before any further analysis, I wish to argue for the primogeniture of shame over conscience.

The feeling of shame originates in the 'shame affect'. Affects are empirical human universals, inborn in every healthy specimen of our species. They are expressive, communicative, and may be displayed in facial expressions, modulations of voice and in gestures. Basic expressions of affect are not acquired but 'natural' feeling-responses to fairly complex structures of stimuli. However, the stimuli empowered to evoke the affects may change over time. Affect intensity can be diminished by habit and by turning away from the objects of affect. The following belong to the affects: fear (with the expression of fear), shame (with the expression of shame), rage, disgust, curiosity, gaiety, sadness (with their respective expressions). Even though bodily pain is not an affect proper, it belongs to the same family. Darwin, who made a comprehensive study of the affects, concluded that they were the remnants of instincts produced by the erosion of instinct regulation and its replacement by cultural regulation. It is culture that provides the principal objects of affect for humans. However, shame (with the expression of shame) has to be distinguished within the realm of affects. Unlike fear, for instance, shame affect cannot be conceived of *prior* to culture. In fact, shame and culture are coeval. One can corroborate this statement if one considers that shame affect occurs only in domestic (and not feral) animals, in other words, in animals confronted with the norms of human culture (for example, dogs), whereas other affects can be observed in animals living in a natural environment if the instinct regulation is somewhat eroded and complemented by learning and intelligence.

The feeling of shame is the very affect which makes us conform to our own cultural environment. The 'eye of others' triggers the feeling and the expression of shame: it makes us blush and hide our faces; it arouses the desire to run away, to sink into the earth, to disappear. Needless to say, the shame affect, like all other affects, is integrated into cognition (and vice versa) during socialization. It is in childhood and in situations which we are not prepared to face that we can best observe the pure shame affect. If shame affect is already integrated into cognition, it is no longer a 'pure' affect but more or less an *emotion*. Thus shame-guilt is an emotion.

When speaking of the integration of cognition and the shame affect, I have in mind a continuous process. The first step is the division of the affect into 'good' and 'bad' shame. It only seems to be odd that the expression of shame is identical in both cases. Whether someone is acclaimed or reprimanded in public, the spontaneous reaction can be similar – blushing, hiding one's face and the like, particularly if the person in question is taken by surprise. One obvious explanation of the phenomenon is that, over a very long period of time, excelling over one's fellow-men was trespassing to the same extent as falling below the standard, and both were shameful. An analysis of the Greek notion of *hubris* may support this speculation.

The shame affect can be justly called a moral feeling for it is a response of approbation or disapprobation. It is the only inborn moral feeling in us. No wonder then that it has played (and still plays) an enormous part in the process of socialization. Since the emergence of practical reason as an independent authority of human conduct and conscience, the power of shame has become more and more ambiguous. But because of its inborn character, shame affect will never be truly overcome. Whether we should try to overcome it is a question I will try to answer later on.

Of course, it is not shame affect alone, but all our affects that are used as a kind of 'natural material' during the course of socialization. Disgust, eroticism, fear, gaiety and sadness, as well as bodily pain and rage, are not only 'socialized' but serve as *means* for socialization at the same time. They are instruments and weapons of culture, directed and used against each other. Disgust is 'used' against eroticism, eroticism is 'used' against fear, bodily pain against rage, rage against fear and so on. But whichever affects serve as the means for the socialization of others, whether they are used as instruments or as weapons, they are all related to the affect of shame. If a person is not disgusted by something he or she *ought* to be disgusted by, the person will be put to shame. Bodily pain, the other main 'socializer', is mostly effectual only if accompanied by shame.

It is with some hesitation that I describe the shame affect as the moral feeling *par excellence*, as we often respond with shame to types of disapproval which we do not consider to be related to moral issues But in identifying the shame affect with the inborn moral feeling I mean a simple but crucial thing: shame affect is the very feeling which regulates a person's actions and general behaviour in conformity with the norms and rituals of his or her community. Given that we are social beings, yet born into a world in which the norms and values are *external* to us, coming to conform to these norms is identical with becoming human. Of course in societies with heterogeneous norms of conduct, conforming also means 'selecting'. But in all societies with homogeneous norms of conduct – a condition presumably true for 99 per cent of Man's history – it is the shame response which is (and has been) the primary regulator of socialization. For it is the response that expresses that the person has either not acted in keeping with the norms or exceeded others in observing them. The shame affect expresses deviation or deflection from the system of conduct in both cases and feeling the shame affect is (in itself) a recognition of the validity of the system. Ongka, the New Guinean Aborigine who explained the notion of shame to the anthropologist, made the following remark about 'shame on the skin' (pipil): 'All sensible people feel this pipil. If someone does not his relatives will tell him: you have no shame on your skin, you are crazy.' But if deviation from the norms means wrongdoing, the recognition of the validity of customs through shame feeling alone is insufficient to put things right. Shame expresses a debt either to the community or to the gods of the community – according to Durkheim these amount to the same thing – a debt which has to be repaid. What kind of deviation it is that cannot be put right by shame, how great a debt is and how (and to what extent) it can be repaid, are matters not decided by the debtor but by the creditor – by the system of conduct, the embodiment of the community.

External authority can regulate human conduct on its own only if: (a) the norms of conduct are homogeneous – in other words, if the same norms apply to everyone belonging to the same 'cluster' (age, sex and the like); (b) the community is small; and (c) social change is not noticeable for co-existing generations.

Under the above conditions everyone *knows* what proper conduct is and what kinds of conduct apply to his or her 'cluster'. It is action (not motivation) that counts. If these conditions are not met, however, internal regulation must supplement external regulation. And I mean 'supplementing', not 'replacing'. (The development of such a double authority system can be observed in ontogenesis as well. Due to the thorough and fundamental research of Piaget, we now have a considerable amount of knowledge about the moral development of the child in societies which have a long tradition in supplementary internal regulation.)

If the norms of conduct do not encompass all possible social situations which may occur, then some basic norms become more and more abstract. They do not regulate human conduct in invariable, that is to say, *in exactly the same* situations, but in variable, that is to say, in *similar* situations. A person who intends to observe a norm – having internalized it and wishing to avoid shame and punishment – has to acquire the capacity for *applying* the norm adequately in particular (often unforeseen) situations. This process of application presupposes at least some deliberation, and the agency of deliberation is *practical reason*. The need for such moral deliberation is reinforced if the particular norms of conduct are not homogeneous and if social change (and thus change in the normative structure) becomes noticeable for coexisting generations. One can then raise the question of what 'good' really is, of whether the traditional norms of conduct are the only good ones, or even whether the norms are good at all. One can select from among norms, accepting one, rejecting another. Good action will be more and more dependent on good reasoning, on 'phronesis', as Aristotle called practical reason.

External and internal authority have different *functions*, but it would be a mistake to think that they have nothing in common. Internal authority is not an inborn ability; it develops when a social system cannot maintain its ethical integration without it. True enough, internal regulation can become *functionally independent* and turn against external authority. It can even contribute to the destruction of the ethical integration of a social system if the latter is already undermined. But whether or not practical reason becomes functionally independent, it bears the birthmark of the system of moral customs and habits – the external authority – which it has supplemented. I would go even so far as venturing the proposition that the *structure* of the internal authority is always *homologous* with the *structure* of the external authority it supplements and, further, that the homology is due to the fact that they are authorities of the *same* social structure. By 'homology' I do not mean the identity or even the similarity as far as the *arrangement* of various factors within the two authorities in 'social space' is concerned, but the identity or similarity between these structures in the following respects: tight control–loose control; one-dimensional–two-, or three-dimensional; unified–divided; the arrangement of the value categories (good–evil, successful–

unsuccessful, sacred–profane, true–untrue and the like); monological–dialogical; and abstract–concrete. The identity (or the similarity) of the arrangement of the above-described factors ensures (or creates) the *interdependence* of the internal and external authorities. Later, I am going to exemplify this structural homology using the case of modern society. But in order to indicate the generalizability of my hypothesis, some historical exegesis needs to be made. However, as space does not allow me to corroborate the hypothesis with fine historical detail, the following thoughts will be sketches rather than full analyses.

The Old Testament on the one hand, and the Athenian philosophy on the other, testify to two, quite distinct, patterns of external and internal authority. Although these written cultural objectifications of ethical systems – and objectifications at the highest level – do not fully account for the average patterns of moral behaviour in the communities that sponsored them, their testimony is reliable in so far as the moral *ideals* of the two communities are concerned.

In the case of the Old Testament we are apparently confronted with a 'shame culture', with moral judgment being the exclusive preserve of the external authority. This authority was embodied in the laws of the community, formulated and commanded by the living God. But the empirical and particular customs of the community, and the law commanded by (and embodied in) God, were *not* identical. The latter could and were mobilized against the former. Thus the external authority itself was duplicated: the system of particular social norms and the (ideal) system of more or less abstract norms were not the same. The Eye which disapproved of one's actions, was not only the eye of others but above all the Eye of God. No one could hide from the living God. God could see not only what was *visible* but also what was *invisible*. His eyes could penetrate into the depths of the soul. He could see not only the action but its *motivation*. In this unique case of external authority the *reciprocity* of shame was completely lost. For the reciprocity of shame is always based on mutual visibility – when others can see us we can see them; when the gods can see us we can see the gods. In a polytheistic universe gods can mutually disapprove of each other's actions and we can side with one against the other. But the Jewish God was and is invisible. He can see us, yet we cannot see him. He can put us to shame, while we cannot take sides against him without risking excommunication from the moral world. What is shameful before God is *sin*. If we sin we hide our face in vain. We cannot run away for there is nowhere to escape to from an eye that sees everything. The commandments of this (second) external authority are not only internalized – in a way, norms of external authorities always are – but they function as the commandments of *conscience*, as commandments of an internal authority, as the 'internal voice' we have to follow even if the eyes of other *human beings disapprove* of our actions and behaviour. This 'transformation' of the norms of an external authority into an internal one made the Jewish people (although few in number) capable of surviving in an environment with alien and hostile habits and customs. It was this transformation that made the community observe 'The Law' in defiance of foreign values and rules of conduct. But the external authority functioned as an internal one not only *vis-à-vis* outgroups, but also *within* the community. It was possible to *criticize* and *reject* the empirically existing norms of conduct from the standpoint of the Laws of God, a procedure unparalleled in the history of shame regulation. One could contrast the 'true knowledge' of the law with the opinion of the majority. One could tell one's neighbour: not what he thinks and does is good, but that something else is good. True knowledge could be contrasted with opinion in matters of Good and Evil. Moreover, as Weber brilliantly pointed out, moral obligation *was highly rationalized.* The question as to why exactly the Jewish people had to obey the Law was rationally answered. This obligation had been based on the *Covenant* or, in modern terms, on a contract between God and His people. The Covenant implied a *mutual promise.* The prophets could argue: just as God has always kept His promise, so we too are obliged to keep our promise. The demise of shame reciprocity has already been mentioned. In all probability it disappeared gradually. (Jacob had seen God face to face and Moses asked God to let Himself be seen.) But, in the end, the *reciprocity of conscience* was substituted for the reciprocity of shame. The invisible God communicated with words and his decisions could be influenced by words. To refer again to Weber: the prophets *argued* with God. Word was confronted with word, not face with face.

The structural homology between external and internal authority in the case of ancient Israel is striking. Since the Spirit is the word (the Law), the voice of conscience is not negative (as it was in the case of Socrates) but positive; it commands that we obey the Law under any circumstances. The voice of conscience is not listened to in order to make man live at peace *with himself*, but in order to *rescue* the people of Israel against itself. 'Rescuing

THE POWER OF SHAME

Israel against itself' is the mirror image of the duplication of external authority; but the internal authority is just as much divided as the external one. Commitment to God cannot become *completely personal* so long as the commitment to a particular group of people is an intrinsic part of that commitment to God. We should be righteous not only for the sake of righteousness, but also because God can (and will) save the people only if righteous men can still be found.

When Jesus said 'I am the truth' this was a statement of a unified and pure *personal* conscience, on the basis of which all customs, traditional forms of behaviour, laws and opinions could be proclaimed non-valid. But this gesture of 'pure conscience' had grown out of the structure of divided conscience I have analysed above. The commitment to the elected people was replaced by a commitment to all peoples, to humankind, and thus the divided conscience was unified. A person had become God and conscience replaced the Law. But since there is no internal authority without an external one, the embodiment of the internal authority became the external authority for *others*. The invisible God became *visible*. God, once more, had a *face*. He could even be *depicted*. He looks at us in every church, and we can look at Him and ask for forgiveness not only with our words but with our tears.

The Greek enlightenment offers us a completely different scenario. As the prehistory of Greek rationalism cannot be dealt with here, the reader is referred to Dodds' illuminating studies, but with one reservation. Dodds presents the archaic Greek culture as 'guilt-ridden' in contrast with the 'shame culture' of the Homeric period. However, the evidence I have presented suggests that this guilt was more a matter of shame-guilt than of conscience-guilt. *Hubris* against the gods was *hubris* against social norms and vice versa. Once the mundane authority of human conduct was not only violated but 'intellectually' challenged, the authority of the gods, *ipso facto*, was challenged as well. Since, in the golden age of the Athenian city-state, the *body politic* was the only external authority for the citizen, the internal corruption of that same city-state led to an authority crisis and a shift towards both conscience regulation and interest regulation. Different as these forms of regulation are, they have one thing in common: namely, that they assert the *person* as the source and the fountainhead of rational decision and action. In the case of conscience regulation, rationality is value rationality – the person observes values which are proven valid by his reason. In the case of interest regulation, rationality is goal-rationality – the person rationally chooses goals and means which promote his success.

The homology between external and internal authority is as striking in the Greek as it was in the Hebrew case. The city-state as an external authority was also conceived of *rationally*, but this rationality was posited as *man-made*. No Greek Moses mediated between a divine law and the people. There were several lawgivers and all of them human. Athenian law was open to change. Not only Solon, Peisistrathos, Themistokles, Perikles contributed to institutional change, the *demos* as a whole did so as well. Finally, in the period of democracy, citizens obeyed the laws because *they were the law themselves*. If each and every person is the law, then external and internal authority are identical, and the bond of all ensures the good life of all. But if the city no longer ensures the good life of all, the citizen becomes a *person* and, *as such*, the sole moral authority. This is why the voice of conscience is neither prophetic nor messianic but philosophical. If man (and not God) becomes the measure of all things, philosophy has the last word.

Socrates listened to the voice of conscience and he was indifferent to the disapproving eyes in his community. Yet he submitted to the laws of his state. Did he acknowledge external authority nevertheless? What he did accept was not the authority of the existing city-state but that of an *ideal* one to which he felt himself committed. And in this very gesture a new external authority was born of the womb of an internal one: the authority of the *ideas* of Good and Truth – the self-imposed external authority of philosophy. Such an authority is constituted by the reason of the rational person, but it is constituted as something which is *beyond* its originator. The *love* of truth is anything but self-love for the self is humble before its new god. Just as the Socratic *daimonion* was structurally homologous with the old external authority of the city-state, so was the newly created external authority homologous with the structure of practical reason. Once it was lost in reality the external authority of the state was rebuilt in the world of ideas. Each world of ideas became individual and personal. Such worlds are mutually exclusive in the same way that personalities are, and they all constitute in a rational manner the external authority in an idiosyncratic way.

This short historical detour used as exemplars the structural homology between external and internal authorities in the so-called *Binnenkulturen* (Weber). But the *Binnenkulturen* were not future-oriented even though they shaped what followed. Since the

European Renaissance the interplay of various authorities has become more complex. This is not surprising given that external authorities with different structures – and their respective internal authorities – can co-exist at the same time and in the same place. Thus the same person can acknowledge two different external authorities simultaneously, or he can acknowledge one external authority along with an internal one which is homologous in structure with a second external authority. It is in this situation that the 'sense of guilt' (to which Freud refers) emerges. The 'sense of guilt' is not a feeling elicited by any concrete transgression – crime, sin, or wrongdoing – but by a commitment to two (different) external and internal authorities. It stands to reason why the 'sense of guilt' was discovered by a Jew who was a profoundly convinced man of enlightenment – a deserter from the Synagogue but not his tribe. The 'sense of guilt' is not uncommon in such cases, though seldom is it so deeply felt. If a disbeliever is ashamed of not going to church; if someone despises wealth and respects his parents but feels ashamed when (in shabby clothes) he meets them in 'high society'; if someone disapproves of all kinds of violence yet feels ashamed when called a 'coward' – although there is no transgression in any of these cases, we are not mistaken if we trace each 'sense of guilt' to commitments to follow contradictory norms of conduct commanded by different authorities.

Both pure shame regulation and pure conscience regulation are extreme cases hardly discernible in present-day societies. But they need to be analysed separately (and in their purest forms) in order to discuss their co-existence and detect the moral problems involved in them.

II

In shame regulation, the norms, rules and rituals of conduct to which one must conform are *not rational*. They are certainly not irrational either. Their validity has to be (and indeed is) accepted without reasoning; in other words, without their being *proven* rational by those observing them. The fact that the norms have not been rationalized does not mean that their *observance* is not rational. It is a matter of social self-preservation to observe the norms of our environment, and what may be considered irrational is the failure to do so. Even today there are norms of this non-rationalized kind. We do not walk naked in the streets in the heat of summer, although no one can *reasonably* convince us why we should not do so. Anyone who walks naked in the street is considered mad, just as the aborigines of New Guinea who have no 'shame on the skin' are considered mad.

The violation of external authority elicits the desire to disappear, hide or sink into the earth. In cases of more or less internalized shame we attempt to hide ourselves from future exposure; the fear of being 'found out' becomes permanent. Telling a lie as a first reflex when being questioned is a well-known technique for avoiding shame. Peter lied about being one of Jesus' disciples not because he was frightened, but because he was taken by surprise by the representatives of a community whose norms his master had clearly violated. His first reflex was to avoid shame. Herbert Fingarett's proposal that we explain shame as a failure to match the Ego-ideal has only a restricted relevance, as it can only be applied to cases in which the Ego-ideal is shaped according to the norms of an external authority. If our Ego-ideal is shaped according to our conscience, we can be ashamed even if we measure up completely. For should this Ego-ideal contradict the norms of external authority when it is the judgment of the latter with which we are confronted, we will still feel shame. We can even feel pangs of conscience when we have been ashamed *even though we should not have been*. And acting according to our ideal self can induce us to *avoid* the company of those who disapprove of it.

One can be ashamed both of *acting* differently and of *being* different. The first is an obvious matter, the second needs some exemplification. A hunchback can be ashamed of *being* a hunchback, and (symbolically speaking) a young swan of *not being* a duckling. It is not true that we cannot be ashamed of private feelings or desires: we certainly can if, for instance, we desire something which we suppose no one else does. We do not make public the feelings and desires which would show us as *being* different from others. We conceal them with the usual techniques of shame-avoidance. We are, however, not concerned about motivations which we suppose we share with everyone else.

The archaic and prerational character of shame comes even more to the fore when its relation to 'we-consciousness' is scrutinized. We can be ashamed not only of our own actions and being, but of those of our smaller and larger community as well. We can be ashamed if our family members do not live up to the norms or standards of our external authority, of our environment or social group. This is a well-known fact in no need of further elaboration. What has to be emphasized here is that guilt ascribed to we-consciousness involves *liability* but not *responsibility*. If my father has disgraced the family name, I have to put the shame right. I am liable but I am not responsible. The increasing heterogeneity of the norms of conduct and the growing universalization of certain values do not put an end to the already existing discrepancy between responsibility and liability. Wealthy people can be terribly ashamed when confronted with world poverty, and they often feel the guilt of liability even though they are not responsible for being born wealthy or for the impoverishment of those whose imaginary Eyes rest upon them. The wording of the Bible that the fathers have eaten sour grapes but the teeth of their sons are set on edge, expresses the liability, not the responsibility, of the sons for their fathers' deeds.

When analysing a simple shame culture we have to bear in mind that its codes, norms and rituals of conduct not only prescribe how the members of the community should act and behave, but also how they have to put things right if they fail to comply. Even talion law is but the formalization of a shame culture – one knows that one has to pay an eye for any eye, a tooth for a tooth, a life for a life. For minor wrongdoings shame alone is considered to be an adequate punishment. Highly sophisticated practices of 'putting to shame' have outlived pure shame cultures to survive in societies that combine internal and external authorities. In *The Spirit of the Laws* Montesquieu enumerated several types of norm violation which ought to be punished by putting people to shame. However, the last two centuries have brought about changes with which people have had to cope both theoretically and practically. Here are some of them.

(a) Human beings no longer live in small communities. Today, if the father has eaten sour grapes the sons can move to another village or to a city; their teeth are not set on edge unless they decide to return to put things right. But this is more a matter of conscience than of shame. Hiding has become easier than ever before; we can change our social status, our domicile, even our names and start afresh. So the pressure of shame can be more easily alleviated. If the external authority is abstracted from the particular norms of conduct of particular communities and thus embodied in certain universalistic norms, and if the internal authority applies the universal norms rationally to all particular cases – again, these two structures are homologous – then the changes described above lead to autonomy, to liberation from the *oppressive* character of the external authority. However, if only lip service is paid to universalized values, and if the relative moral autonomy of the person does not rest on a strong internal authority, then the moral regulation of human action and behaviour will be eroded. It will be replaced by interest regulation, and irrational behaviour will become widespread.

Law is a rational authority, for each law can be rationally tested. One can bring arguments for and against them, and they can be changed through the pressures of public opinion and private interests. Although there is an obvious interconnection between legislation and certain norms of moral conduct, and although change in the latter can bring about change in the former (for instance, abortion law), individuals do not treat laws as the bearers of norms of moral conduct *unless they accept other* authorities (from conscience to the non-legally formalized authority of the body politic) cognate with the law. In the case of the erosion of all authorities of moral conduct, the law (more precisely, the penal code) can regulate human behaviour only in terms of instrumental rationality and not in terms of value rationality. People will abstain from infringing the penal code not because such action is considered by them as evil, but because it is punishable and it is in their best interest not to be fined or imprisoned. If they are convicted, they do not pay a debt, nor do they regain their honour since the authority of punishment is neither the eye of the others nor the internal voice. But the assertion that the penal code cannot be a substitute for moral values and cannot contribute to the rejuvenation of eroded ethical authorities, does not imply that it has no ethical function at all. It is a sad fact, but nonetheless a fact, that, as things stand now, the penal code is still a stronghold against indiscriminately irrational mass behaviour. Hannah Arendt was right when pointing out that if criminal acts remain unpunished, people untouched by any kind of moral authority would commit crimes which they would not have committed otherwise, and they *would become accustomed* to committing them more and more frequently. And it is not only from Plato that we have learned how dangerous habit can be.

(b) The demise of community and its partner the (real or imaginary) 'eye of other' led to the loss of the Ideal Eye – the Eye of God. Religion has become to an ever-increasing extent a matter of non-committal faith or of the performance of ceremonies. Even the religious revival of the recent decade contributed far more to intolerance against outgroups than to the ethical reformation of ingroups, at least in the so-called first world, although discontent with the erosion of moral authorities might have been one factor which made certain people turn towards neo-fundamentalism. But in so far as the general tendency is concerned, one may risk the hypothesis that even religious persons no longer feel the steady presence of an Almighty who can penetrate to the depths of their souls. The proud conviction of the Enlightenment that, if only conscience were to replace God, the moral perfection of humankind would be easily achieved as Man would no longer need a crutch, was based on an overestimation of our internal rational resources. This overestimation failed to account for the fact that the loss of the Ideal Eye tended to come about *simultaneously* with the loss of the real eye of the community, and it also failed to face the further fact that we need the crutch of an external authority *not in spite* of our being human but *because* of it. The individual can be the sole repository of moral good only in very exceptional cases, and the *quality* of our values (and the rational manner of their application) is far more decisive than the *sources* from which we draw both our norms and our strength to observe them.

But the demise of the communal external authority and of the ideal authority did not lead to the death of shame. We need once more to recall the fact that the shame affect is inborn in every healthy human being. It cannot be circumvented, it can only be shifted. And it has actually been shifted in two directions. The external authority of human conduct has been particularized and homogenized in one-dimensionality on the one hand, and universalized on the other. I will deal with each of these trends in turn.

The particularization of shame has come about within the nuclear family where norms have *lost their impersonality*, while the one-dimensional homogenization of shame has come about within societies (in the plural) in which norms have *lost their hierarchical structure*.

The nuclear family is the only quasi-natural community left in modern society. It is known that shame, as an inborn moral feeling, is the primary regulator of human conduct in ontogenesis as well. For children – before they are capable of rational discrimination, that is to say, prior to the age at which their conscience may develop – mothers and fathers are external authorities of moral conduct. But fathers and mothers are no longer mediators of *generally* accepted human conduct. They are no longer repositories of impersonal customs and habits. They have themselves discriminated between these very habits, and accepted some and rejected others. Thus their authority has become *personal*, as has their attitude towards their children. In a community where all children have to acquire the same habits (and in which all parents practise more or less the same ones) no child takes it as a *personal* offence if he or she is obliged to fit into these common patterns. But should the patterns of behaviour vary, and should the parents expect their children to fit exactly into *their own* behavioural patterns, and should their practices towards their children become personal *in regard to their behavioural expectations as well*, the sensitivity of the child is amplified, and his or her shame is perpetuated. Punishments are then being understood and experienced as a *want of love*, and the outcome may be unconscious hostility towards this personal authority. Sensitive parents suffer because of this anomaly no less than sensitive children. They can try to resign from the role of the personified external authority but, if they do so, they take the risk of bringing up moral monsters if the inborn 'raw material' of their children is not of particularly good quality.

The one-dimensionality of shame – a product of the decline of the hierarchical arrangement of the norms of conduct – is an equally well-known phenomenon. Being *unsuccessful* has become shameful to an increasing extent, while the paths of achieving success are no longer regulated by normative patterns. To be good *at something* has always belonged to the expectations embodied in the system of rules but it has never before been the decisive one. If someone was good at hunting but reluctant to share, the person in question was not regarded as good at all. The gods of shame culture were pleased by a successful warrior, but only if success had been attained in keeping with the code of honour and without *hubris*. In our times, however, being successful is *dissociated* from the totality of behaviour for the simple reason that the latter is *no longer visible*. Only success is visible, therefore (increasingly) it is in this respect alone that the Others' Eye will approve or disapprove of persons. One can be successful at almost anything and the *means* of achieving success matters less and less, for these means, having been stripped of their normative content, have become *means* of goal-rationality. Even if in certain areas and societies the rules of 'fair play' are still to be observed and are generally considered binding, great success can overrule them. And their observance alone does not prevent anyone from being regarded by others as a 'failure'. If women are not loved by their husbands or if they are jilted by their lovers, they hide these facts from society. Not being elected for (or selected for) a position, failing at an examination, being rebuked in a committee, going bankrupt and the like are all considered shameful irrespective of the cause, circumstance or motivation of failure. However, it would be a delusion to think that external authority has lost its homogenizing power. Being *different* remains shameful given that success as the measure of everything is imposed on individuals by the external authority. The homogenization is carried out in *one respect* only, and this is why it can be called 'one-dimensional'. The Freudian distinction between the Super-Ego and the Ego-Ideal accounts for the divided self of modernity. If the universalized values are internalized as the only external authority, then the so-called 'Super-Ego' constitutes the 'Ego-Ideal' as well, and thus the self is undivided. If it is only and exclusively the one-dimensionally homogenized external authority that is internalized, then the Ego-Ideal will be the sole Super-Ego, and thus the self is, again, undivided. But if a person still acknowledges the validity of the traditional external moral authority (or the authority of universalized values) *and* internalizes the one-dimensionally homogenized external authority as well, the division of the Ego-Ideal and the Super-Ego will be perpetuated and the self will be divided. Here again it has to be emphasized that it is only when the moral authorities are in conflict that the *sense of guilt* emerges. Even if the sense of guilt as a mass phenomenon can be dangerous, its presence nevertheless is a *sign* of human resistance to the one-dimensional homogenization of external authority.

The one-dimensional homogenization of the external authority does not eliminate the rigidity of ceremonial and ritual performance; rather, it *particularizes* both rituals and ceremonies. The garments of a nobleman belonged to his *being* a Nobleman, but being dressed formally or casually does not belong to our being. However, we are *keen* to match the 'prescriptions' (not the norms) of proper dressing. If we fail to match these prescriptions, we will be ridiculed or scorned in certain 'circles'. Before we enter a particular social circle, we have to study carefully its habits of dress. This holds true for gestures, facial expressions, modulations of voice and vocabulary as well. We have to follow the *rules* and 'mind our p's and q's'. And if we do, we are generally regarded as 'decent' without having ever been tested by moral perplexities or examined for our ability to make the *right* decisions – except within the family. The *distance* between people has increased. We never confront others with our *whole personality* but only in our capacity as performers of one or other 'role'. We do not even need to *hide* ourselves in order to avoid shame as *our life is hidden anyway*. We wear our 'roles' outside and our shabby incognito inside. No wonder then that *wars* have become the inexhaustible source for novels and movies. It is only at war that a person is *seen* by others as a person *per se* and not as a role-player. It is only at war that the *real* self is put on trial. In war, success is no longer the measure of all things: comradeship, solidarity, braveness, cleverness, goodness of heart – all matter. Luckily, borderline situations are exceptional. Their idealization is telling, for it plays the tune of nostalgia. Even though this nostalgia is expressive of a deep-lying desire for the moral test – for 'proving our soul' – it is dangerous. The more so as the nostalgia for *past* wars is transformed by the media into a false and misleading imagery of possible wars. The imagery is false because the technological armoury of present warfare (which could, and in all probability will, put an end to human life altogether) does not leave *any* ground for 'moral tests' which have been overestimated and idealized in themselves. In addition, this catering for the need for 'testing' makes people *defenceless* against the temptations of 'great happenings' like terrorism, clandestine organizations and the *false* brotherhood offered in neo-fundamentalist practices.

The shift of shame to match our Ego-Ideal – when the latter is defined by being successful and by playing roles correctly – has not meant, however, *a decrease in the power of shame*. We succumb to shame no less than we did before even though we are no longer able to distinguish between 'shame on the skin' and 'deep shame'. And, if we take into consideration the growing complexity of shame within the family, we can conclude that suffering from shame has not been mitigated.

External authority not only prescribes proper behaviour but also offers modes of conduct for persons who have failed to act according to the requirements set by the authority. Repentance means putting things right and everyone knows *how* they can be put right. Shame is a tormenting feeling. It needs outlets, and the meticulous prescriptions for proper 'repayment' serve as such. The mode of 'repayment' can be very painful, but if it is carried out properly the crumbled person regains his or her posture, the disgraced person his or her honour. This kind of ritualization of repayment is in the main preserved within authoritarian families. But since parents are no longer mediators of customs but impose their own chosen values and their own particular system of conduct upon their children, this ritualization assumes a personal character. *Apologizing* is a typical form of ritualized repayment. But if the father's moral code becomes more or less personal, and if it depends on his *mood* when (or whether at all) apologizing is required, shame is not mitigated by ritual. Either ritual is no longer internalized or it becomes excessive and present even when not required. Again, only children with exceptionally good inborn qualities can face this test without being crippled for life, as did Fanny in Dickens' *Dombey and Son* who had to apologize to her tyrannical father for being born.

Outside the nuclear family ritualized outlets of shame have disappeared almost completely. But it has to be emphasized that since positive shame has *preserved* its affect character to a greater degree than negative shame has done, its ritualized outlets have also been preserved, and changed only on the surface. When acclaimed in public we do basically the same things our ancestors did. We react to positive shame which overemphasized modesty, with a kind of self-humiliation, by pointing to the merits of others – the merits of our friends, family, colleagues and institutions. We 'diminish' ourselves by gestures and words such as bowing and acknowledging.

The realm of negative shame had extended considerably the boundaries of the shame affect and this is precisely why the ritualization of 'putting things right' could be increasingly diminished – there was much that could be cut away. The words 'could be' here point to the *condition* and not to the cause of the disappearance of ritualized repayment. It is the one-dimensional homogenization of the external authority that makes the ritualized repayment of a moral 'debt' basically impossible. If we accept the prestige scale of our environment (as most people more or less do), failure in front of others' eyes can only be requited by success. Apart from the fact that all success is relative to that of others – and so one may constantly be in debt without being able to repay – the *reciprocity* involved in the gesture of putting something right is completely gone. Normally, a violation of external authority can be requited with atonement, that is to say, by inflicting some suffering on ourselves (or by accepting suffering inflicted on us by others) which restores *social justice*. In the case of one-dimensionally homogenized external authorities, we can mitigate, or even eliminate, shame through pleasure (achieving further and greater success) or by causing pain to others or through the reinforcement of *social injustice*. In one-dimensionality, no shame experience can be mitigated by any kind of ritualization, for no repayment practice is available. When this is so, the only outlets that remain are aggression and self-aggression. Men can easily kill if put to shame, even though aggression or self-aggression normally take less violent forms. Laughing at our own shame or playing the clown are mild forms of self-aggression, while slapping (or spitting at) the *face* (!) of another, although violent, is a milder form of aggression than killing. It is true that there is a *traditional* ritual outlet of shame which has survived, but it has done so only at the expense of its original function. *Cursing*, once a ritualized speech-act, has become more and more a 'private' form of shame canalization.

This analysis of the erosion of external moral authorities, of the reconstruction of the emergence of a one-dimensionally homogenized external authority and of the loss of the ritualized forms of 'repayment' of moral debts, could give the impression that we live in an era of unrelieved 'moral decadence'. This is far from being the truth since the tendencies which have been under scrutiny, up to this point, have been *counterbalanced* by other tendencies we have not yet examined.

Manufacturing industry and capitalism were born two centuries ago and so was *modern democracy*. Although these three constituents of our society – I speak here of Western democratic societies only – are interconnected, each has a logic of its own. Once the *idea* of democracy was formulated and, later, the institutions of democracy created, certain values became increasingly *universalized*. A claim of universal validity transcends the barriers of any particular system of norms of conduct. Certain universalized norms, which may be called value-ideas, can come to function as a new external authority of human conduct, as a new moral authority *not* identical with any *existing* external authority, for it transcends more or less *all of them*. It would be an *ideal* external authority constituted for and in relation to an *ideal* community: the community of humankind. With democracy and Enlightenment came the possibility of establishing such an ideal external authority, an authority with the greatest *potential* for moral regulation that has ever been conceived. Even as a *potential* it offers immense resources for conscience. Practical reason turned against the validity of a particular system of norms will not find itself in a dangerous limbo. It can be related to the ideal external authority, the validity of which it accepts unconditionally.

But even the greatest moral potential is still only a potential. If universalized values are not *mediated* to everyone through particular value systems, the ideal external authority will bind only an *elite*. Any such elite will not be a social one, even though intellectuals (in the broad sense of the word) will be over-represented in it. Elite or not, the external authority of moral conduct is the 'eye of others', and this eye cannot be completely imaginary. An ideal community without a real one is like God without a congregation. Yet, even if the universalization of certain values through an elite can more or less counterbalance for a while the disappearance of the *visible* moral universe, it is unable to *reverse* the trend towards the one-dimensional homogenization of the external authority.

But democracy has not only brought about the universalization of certain moral values; it has also created new outlets for the mitigation of the torments of shame. I have already discussed the trans-individuality of shame, and I have argued for the distinction between liability and responsibility. Now, if we can be ashamed of the deeds of our family, of our institutions or nation, the same identification can occur the other way round: we can interpret *our own* shame intersubjectively. If we are put to shame, it may be *not us* who are being put to shame but our kinsmen, institutions or nation.

If the external authority which puts us to shame is internalized *and* shame is interpreted intersubjectively, there are the same responses to negative shame that we are familiar with in the case of positive shame: instead of aggression there is humiliation and its expressions. The shame affect may appear in its pure form as well. If external authority is only partly internalized *and* shame is interpreted intersubjectively, the practice of submission can trigger guilt feelings transformed into grudges, resentment or hatred against the authority the subject succumbed to. The interpretation of shame becomes 'ideological' if the actor discharges his or her shame by imputing to the external authority aggression against his or her family, profession, race, class, sex or community. Shame is thus channelled through projection, and resentment becomes projective. The third typical possibility is, to use Sartre's phrase, 'the radicalization of evil'. The judgment is accepted but *reversed*. What was regarded by the 'eye of others' as deviation, is accepted as the norm. The shame falls back on the authority. The shame is no longer experienced as the 'eye of others' for now, *we are the Eye*. We see others through our own eyes. The spell of external authority is broken. But this reversal of shame does *not* mean the substitution of conscience for shame. In reversing the signs we have not chosen an internal authority instead of an external one. The fact that the spell of external authority is broken means only that through our identification we project back our shame. It is no longer our shame but that of others who put us to shame.

In a pluralistic society the intersubjective interpretation of shame is institutionalized and channelled, and self-aggression and aggression are thus *'civilized'*. The more democratic a society is, the more possibilities it offers for a channelled discharge of resentment and for the reversion of shame. Since personal equality is formally recognized, even the *suspicion* that a person was put to shame because of his or her belonging to a 'group' will be sufficient to translate personal shame into a *social issue*. Even those who were *not* put to shame as a result of any kind of discrimination, but only *interpret* their shame in this context, can discharge this shame by *arguing* against social discrimination and injustice whether real or imagined. If everyone is free to join any organization, or to organize support, then everyone can seek some remedy in some sympathetic public reaction. One can write indignant letters to newspapers, participate in various pressure groups and the like. In order to avoid misunderstanding, I do not mean that the institutions and movements in question were created or came about *in order* to discharge shame, but only that they *can serve* as channels for non-ritualized shame-discharge and shame-reversion.

Just as motivation did not count in a pure shame society, so it does not count when shame is discharged through the channels of democratic institutions. What counts in both cases is *overt behaviour*. But in a pure shame society all overt behaviour was meant to observe the particular norms of the system of conduct, whereas in the case under scrutiny it is meant to be in keeping with the *norms of civility*. The norms of civility do not prescribe behaviour in respect to private styles of life. They only regulate the *forms of public performance*. So it is of no relevance whatever whether someone supports a social issue on the grounds of political principles or because the issue serves him as a projective outlet for resentment. What only matters is that the issue must be *presented* in a rational or *objective* way.

The norms of civility in public performance offer a disciplined and rationalized outlet for shame. If these norms are traditional, if public opinion is already 'tuned in' on them, then the eye of others will *disapprove* of public actions infringing these norms. The norms of civility thus function as a *formal external authority* in public performance. Irrespective of their moral quality, people have to learn to keep with democratic norms in public interaction.

The formal external authority, like the ideal external authority, counterbalances the erosion of the external moral authority of human conduct. But it cannot *reverse* the moral decay triggered by the one-dimensioinal homogenization of the external authority, for it is only public performance, and not the way of life, that is regulated by a formal external authority. It stands to reason that it would do no good for the formal external authority to attempt to regulate the form of life as well, as this could lead only to a formal homogenization of ethics incompatible with the modern personality.

All in all we have to come to the conclusion that the ethical quality of the contemporary person is not better and not worse than it has ever been, only different. We can leave the question open whether morality (*Moralität*), as the ethical motivational system of human beings, can be changed for the better at all. But even the sceptical Kant emphasized that *ethics* (*Sittlichkeit*) can be improved. How it is possible and how it can be achieved, will be discussed in a later paper. A detour over, I now return to my starting point – the intersubjective interpretation of shame.

I have discussed the intersubjective interpretation of shame in a value-free manner. The various procedures of shame-discharge have not been evaluated, only enumerated. I could not have proceeded otherwise, given that the evaluation of the projection of shame does not depend primarily on the *structure* of shame discharge but on the *content* of an action for which the person is put to shame. If a person is put to shame because of a *moral* offence, the intersubjective interpretation of shame is a form of rationalization, a sign of the *lack of conscience*, and thus not admissible. Of course, the matter is not so simple as it seems, because the same action can be regarded as a moral offence by one community while accepted as laudable by another. (A hoodlum who denounces his mates to the law can be ashamed of the deed.) In such and similar cases the universality of the infringed norm may be decisive. To mention the other extreme: if a person is put to shame because of his or her *being* so-and-so and not because of his or her action, the intersubjective interpretation of shame is legitimate and also rational (not rationalized).

But there are cases and situations in which human beings are ashamed without being guilty of any kind of transgression *and* the shame *cannot be interpreted intersubjectively*, even less reversed, because it cannot be made public in any form whatever. Aggression or self-aggression are here the only outlets left. People with decency and self-control have no outlets at all. When feeling this shame, we hide our face, we symbolically sink into the earth and feel miserable: it is thus that we pay our debt for being human.

Instead of summing up in my own words what shame is all

about, I would rather let the artist speak who described it in all its complexity. In his novel *Lord Jim* Conrad recounts a conversation between Marlow (who is the personification of the author) and a French captain. They discuss the story of Jim, a mate on the *Patna*, who deserted the sleeping passengers on his overcrowded ship at the moment of mortal danger:

Suddenly his lips began to move. 'That is so', he resumed, placidly. 'Man is born a coward. . . . It is a difficulty – *parbleu*! It would be too easy otherwise. But habit – habit – necessity – do you see? – *the eye of others* – *voilà*. One puts up with it. And then the example of others who are no better than yourself, and yet make good countenance. . . .'

His voice ceased.

'That young man – you will observe – had none of these inducements – at least at the moment,' I remarked.

He raised his eyebrows forgivingly: 'I don't say: I don't say. The young man in question might have had the best dispositions – the best dispositions,' he repeated, wheezing a little.

'I am glad to see you taking a lenient view,' I said. 'His own feeling in the matter was – ah! – hopeful, and . . .'

The shuffle of his feet under the table interrupted me. He drew up his heavy eyelids. Drew up, I say – no other expression can describe the steady deliberation of the act – and at last was disclosed completely to me. I was confronted by two narrow grey circlets, like two tiny steel rings around the profound blackness of the pupils. The sharp glance, coming from that massive body, gave a notion of extreme efficiency, like a razor-edge on a battle axe. 'Pardon,' he said, punctiliously. His right hand went up, and he swayed forward. 'Allow me . . . I contended that one may get on knowing very well that one's courage does not come of itself (*ne vient pas tout seul*). There is nothing much in that to get upset about. One truth the more ought not to make life impossible. . . . But the honour – the honour, monsieur! . . . The honour . . . that is real – that is! And what life may be worth when' . . . he got on his feet with a ponderous impetuosity, as a startled ox might scramble up from the grass . . . 'when the honour is gone – *ah ça! par example* – I can offer no opinion, I can offer no opinion – because – monsieur – I know nothing of it.'

III

When the dying Hamlet asked Horatio to clear his *name*, a man of conscience appealed to the external authority. Juliet said: ' 'Tis but thy *name* that is my enemy . . . What's Montague? It is nor hand, nor foot, nor arm, nor face, nor any other part belonging to a man . . . What's in a name?' Conscience, the voice of practical reason, is basically *nominalist*. Norms, obligations, values, conceptions of the good – what are they? They are not of flesh and blood. One cannot grasp them; they are not palpably *real*. Why obey them? Why succumb to them? They may well be fancies, ghosts, apparitions. But they are not *innocent* fancies or apparitions. They are *coercive*. They are thirsty gods who live on human blood and sweat.

To stand against external authority as Juliet did, involves contrasting a *chosen* value – conceived of as superior, essential, real and rational – with accepted values. Juliet was not a dropout girl who could not resist passion. Unlike Faust's Margaret, she did not care for 'honour'. She cared only for being faithful to her promise; a promise given in the conviction that it was the *right* thing to do.

Internal authority is *autonomy*. To obey nothing but our conscience means that we are the authors both of our *character* and of our *actions*. And, in doing so, we take *full* responsibility for both our actions and our character. As autonomy is always relative, absolute autonomy cannot be but a regulative idea. The person of conscience obliges himself or herself to act *as if* he or she were the sole author of his or her deeds and character.

Practical reason implies both the *will* to act and the *will* to be good. Will is a rational desire and it implies that the means to achieve our goals are at our disposal. Thus the will to be good implies that the means for achieving ends that our conscience approves of are at our disposal. Since internal direction is involved in the case of will as a realization of practical reason, failure to obey practical reason's demands cannot be hidden from the self irrespective of whether others are aware of it. When there is discrepancy, discord or contradiction between our will and our actual behaviour *pangs of conscience* emerge, feelings which are often more tormenting and painful than shame. As practical reason is an internal authority, the pangs of conscience are not signals of any debt we owe to others but of one we owe to ourselves. Thus the forms of the debt's requital are not and cannot be ritualized. We can only ritually mitigate the pangs of conscience *if we transform them into shame via confession* when the Others will tell us how the debt can and must be repaid. But if we confess only *in order* to alleviate the pangs of conscience and not in order to accept the judgment of others as well, the result will be – to use Dostoevsky's term – 'disorderly repentance'. There are two further ways to put an end to the torments of conscience. These are not ritualized but they are common. One is pretending not to know what we in fact know, pushing knowledge into the unconscious. This is *inauthenticity* and often it is accompanied by anxiety and permanent guilt-feeling. The other is 'regaining our posture' by putting our character right. The latter resembles the gesture of requital but the two are not identical. We put our character right if we do not repeat the deed which was interpreted as guilt by our conscience; in short, we reform our character according to the will. We recall bygone guilts and blunders with *intellectual remorse* but without pangs of conscience.

Since practical reason implies the will to act and to be good, and since it is perceived as an autonomous agency, the failure to follow the voice of conscience can be attributed only to one-*self*. Furthermore, the will to act and to be good is a rational will because of the conviction that all the means to achieve good are at our disposal. These together explain the logic of conscience, a logic that is strange from the standpoint of an external authority of any kind. If we act and behave in keeping with the voice of conscience, all our deeds will be experienced as links in a chain of *necessity*. (We could not have acted otherwise.) As Luther put it: here I stand and I cannot otherwise. However, if we fail to act in keeping with the voice of conscience, all our deeds which contradicted the will of practical reason will be experienced as *contingent* ones. (We not only should have acted differently, but we *could* have acted differently.) This is, indeed, the *logic* of conscience for if we said that we *could* not have acted differently, even though we should have, we would simply renounce the autonomy of the internal authority. Kant's famous dictum that whatever we should do, we can do, gives voice only to the intrinsic logic of conscience. Of course, the dichotomy of necessity and contingency is due to the *illusion* of absolute autonomy.

But even if we state that we could have acted otherwise, the deviation from the will of our internal authority has to be explained. The general explanation, as old as conscience, is putting the blame on 'human nature'. Our feelings, desires, emotions, instincts – our supposedly 'natural' propensities – resist the sovereign rule of practical reason. They have to be suppressed, or eventually transformed, by the sovereign rule of practical reason. This contrast is irrelevant in terms of shame-regulation. Adam and Eve sinned by eating an apple from the tree of *knowledge*, not from the tree of *feeling*. In the predominantly shame-regulated medieval culture individual reasoning (scepticism, doubt, heresy) was far more suspect than passion. A sin committed in passion could easily be 'put right' by sufficient repentance. But individual reasoning was considered 'devilish', and the person who fell 'victim' to it, almost incurable. A sharp distinction between 'intention' and 'consequence' resolves the problem in a different way. *Oedipus the King* and *Oedipus in Kolonos*, if compared, testify to the penetration of the Athenian *sensus communis* by a conscience culture. The person was then considered responsible for his or her action only in so far as the action was willed by him or her; whether good was in fact achieved, or whether it turned into Evil, was not his or her responsibility. Even though in itself a reasonable distinction, and a stronghold against moral hysteria, the distinction between intention and consequences may eventually lead to a total alienation of conscience: if the outcome is bad, the fault lies in others (the circumstances, other actors) and not in us. The alienation of conscience resembles certain shame-avoiding techniques but it is not the same thing. For even when others do not accuse us, we still justify ourselves by seeing others as responsible. The dangers of the alienation of conscience increase in direct proportion to the erosion of the moral force power of external authority.

There are various types of internal regulation of human conduct. Here I can offer only a sketchy description of the main types in a quasi-historical sequence. I start with structures of conscience which emerged to cultures that were predominantly shame-regulated and conclude with those appearing in our own culture. It is a 'quasi'-historical sequence because, although structures of conscience that were once present disappeared in certain later periods, it is possible for *all* the structures enumerated here to exist simultaneously. At this point I have to remind the reader that I have defined conscience as the involvement of persons in the internal authority of human conduct or (in other words) as a feeling pertaining to practical reason. Even though from the standpoint of *society* 'external authority of human conduct' and 'shame culture' are interchangeable terms – as are 'internal authority of human conduct' and conscience culture – the same does not hold true from the standpoint of the *person*. The external authority exists even for those persons who do not feel shame, but if a person does not have a conscience then he has no internal authority at all. This is why the typology of conscience that follows here stands for the typology of practical reason as well. The typology will be historical only in so far as I make an inventory of the most general types of conscience ever-present in every 'non-primitive' culture yet continue with other types which emerged only rarely in previous cultures and which became prevalent only in modern times.

The types of conscience referred to are: (a) complementary conscience; (b) conscience as the ultimate arbiter; and (c) conscience as the sole arbiter of practical decisions. I will deal with each in turn.

(a) *Complementary* conscience can be applicative, corrective or interpretative. Applicative and corrective conscience are not perforce interpretative as well, but interpretative conscience is perforce also applicative and corrective. The distinctions between the forms of complementary conscience are as follows:

(a.a) Conscience is called applicative if practical reason has the authority to apply the norms of conduct of the external authority to particular situations. Here deliberation by practical reason means assessing the case from the viewpoint of the external authority and judging which of the accepted norms of the system of proper conduct has to be applied and how. Thus practical reason *mediates* between norms and action through judgment.

(a.b) Conscience is called corrective if practical reason has the authority to *select* one or more of the norms of the external authority for *amplification*, without, however, denying validity to the rest. When amplified, certain norms become supreme obligations far above the standard set by the external authority. Here deliberation aims not only at the proper application of the external authority but (as in the case of Mucius Scaevola) at *perfectionism* as well.

(a.c) Conscience is called interpretative if practical reason has the authority to interpret and re-interpret the *meaning* of the norms provided by the external authority. Practical reason becomes interdependent with theoretical reason, and a distinction between 'opinion' and 'true knowledge' in respect of the interpretation of various values is presupposed. As the differentiation between mere opinion and true knowledge is undertaken by individuals, and as the 'true' interpretation of values and norms raises the claim for universal validity (even though only within the framework of a community), practical reason becomes more individual and more universal simultaneously. But even if resolved to determine rationally the true meaning of values, interpretative conscience never turns against generally held values embodied in the external authority for it accepts their *validity*.

The internal authority called 'complementary conscience' is structurally homologous with an external authority characterized, very roughly, by the following features: (1) the increasing abstractness of certain norms within the system of norms of conduct; (2) a *sensus communis* regarding the validity of these abstract norms, be they supreme virtues of a body politic or commandments of a divine law; and (3) variability and change as far as particular expectations are concerned, together with the knowledge that the changes (both the better and the worse) have been brought about by social actors. This last propensity of the external authority is homologous only with an interpretative conscience. The idea that the moral quality of a community was 'perfect' in the past but, due to selfishness, negligence, 'carnal desire', effeminacy and the like, has deteriorated since, emerges at this stage.

(b) Conscience *as the ultimate arbiter in practical decisions* can be: legislative conscience, sceptical conscience or bad conscience.

Legislative and sceptical conscience have something in common, namely the *devaluation* of the external authority. Both denounce images of 'honour' – accepted values and norms of conduct – as mere 'names'. It is here that the nominalism of conscience clearly comes to the fore. When Hamlet says that there is nothing good or bad in the world, only *thinking* makes qualities good or bad, he sums up clearly and concisely what the nominalism of conscience is all about. Although their starting point is identical, the sceptical and the legislative conscience draw quite different conclusions from it.

(b.a) Conscience is called legislative if practical reason has not only the authority to interpret the values provided by the external authority individually, but also to accept certain values and *reject* others. Values themselves are considered as 'mere opinions' unless thinking can 'make them good'. All *concrete* norms of the external authority are suspended and tested. But – and this is why legislative conscience is only the ultimate, and not the sole arbiter in practical decisions – *not all abstract norms* are equally suspended and tested. The suspension and testing of all concrete norms is undertaken from the standpoint of a few abstract norms which are, for their part, *absolutized* and *universalized*. Precisely these few abstract values and norms function as *revelatory authorities* for practical reason. Legislative conscience is thus not defensive but offensive. It claims the empirical universalization of its chosen values. The man of legislative conscience intends that his revelatory authority should be accepted as the sole and absolutely valid external authority for *everyone*. To label this type of conscience 'legislative' is thus not a figure of speech.

When I referred to the *absolutist* character of legislative conscience, I did not distinguish the two aspects of this absolutism. One can be absolutist in regard to oneself and in regard to others. All men of legislative conscience are absolutist in regard to themselves; but not all of them are absolutist in regard to others. Legislative conscience can be combined with applicative conscience and in this case it is dialogical and dialectical. If it is not combined with applicative conscience, legislative conscience is intolerant and plays the role of an external, coercive authority for others.

(b.b) Sceptical conscience, in contrast to legislative conscience, is defensive. Here the will of practical reason does not transcend the individual's conduct for it does not claim empirical universalization of its chosen and revelatory values. (This is why it is not legislative.) Liberal, permissive and contemptuous in its judgments, lacking zeal and without hatred, it is the purest form of conscience as the ultimate arbiter. It is the purest since it is completely indifferent to the approbation or disapprobation of any external authority. Persons with a highly developed sceptical internal authority cannot be put to shame at all. In spite of all this, sceptical conscience is not the sole but the ultimate arbiter of moral conduct. This is so not only because it chooses certain substantive values from among many (just as legislative conscience does) but also because, even if indifferent to generally accepted external authorities, it is not indifferent to the 'eye of others'. However, it selects its own possessors of the Eye from among the men of conscience who have the *same* substantive values. It accepts their judgment as the approval or disapproval of 'the other part of the soul'. If this 'other part of the soul' disapproves of an action of the man of sceptical conscience, he is not ashamed but feels *pangs of conscience*.

(b.c) Bad conscience (which is not to be confused with the pangs of conscience), so typical in Calvinism and the Counter-Reformation, has been analysed so often that I feel free to describe it in a very sketchy way. I do not need to give any reasons for considering bad conscience as a particular form of conscience which functions as an ultimate arbiter in practical decisions. I prefer to quote Hegel:

> Es ist ein grosser Eigensinn, der dem Menschen Ehre macht, nichts in der Gesinnung anerkennen zu wollen, was nicht durch den Gedanken gerechtfertigt ist, und dieser Eigensinn ist das Charakteristische der neueren Zeit, ohnehin das eigentümliche Prinzip des Protestantismus.
> (G. W. F. Hegel, *Grundlinien der Philosophie des Rechts*, Werke, v.7. Frankfurt, Suhrkamp, 1970, p. 27: It is a great stubbornness, a stubbornness which is an adornment if one does not want to recognize anything in the intention which is not legitimized by thoughts, and this stubbornness is the characteristic feature of new times, and anyhow the principle specific to protestantism.)

Even though 'bad' conscience was not the only form of conscience consonant with the 'spirit' of early capitalism – so were legislative and sceptical conscience – it was a highly representative one which became more general than the other two types of conscience both of which remained idiosyncratic.

In this type of conscience the duplication of the external authority – which was characteristic of Judaism and, to a lesser extent, of medieval Christianity – has not only been preserved but reinforced. However, the external authority of 'this world' is rationally tested and the external authority from the 'other world' is no longer the law-giver of 'this-worldly' institutions. God, the old other-worldly authority, has been 'brought down to earth' and, as an idealized moral person, gives personal orders to the individual who has to obey if he is to live an exemplary life. It is the same structural change that I described when discussing the changing ethical function of parents, even if a reverse one. The other-worldly father is our reified conscience. If we do not obey him then we do not obey our own conscience. *The supreme external authority does not function as an external authority internalized but as an internal authority externalized.* When conscience is *externalized*, and takes the role of an *external authority*, it *coerces* the person who externalized it; but since it is *conscience* which is externalized, the authority does *not* put us to *shame* but is the cause of continuous *pangs of conscience* as a punishment for our unwillingness to obey. Shame can be extinguished; our debt to an external authority can be requited. If this external authority is a deity, we can requite our debts by sacrifice and repentance. If we only confess, we get absolution. The quantity and quality of the requital is fixed either by the community or by the institution which mediates God's will. But no established means of requital is available in the case of an externalized internal authority; it is then that we shall always be in debt, for the debt can never be fully repaid.

The *externalization* of conscience, as Weber pointed out, implied (and implies) the conviction that this-worldly achievement (success) was a sign of a decent way of life. The constituents of happiness, which were once ascribed by Aristotle to 'good luck' and *not* to virtue, became attributed to virtue, and thus instrumental reason became morally evaluated. To have bad luck meant to have bad conscience. But since no one can be called 'happy this side of death' and since in our lifetime every success is fragile and temporary, we have to torture ourselves continually in order to merit success. As has been mentioned previously, conscience cannot blame else but one's 'nature' – one's native feelings, emotions and desires – when one deviates from the royal road of practical reason. In the case of bad conscience, this logic of conscience gives rise to *preventive practices*. Conscience continually has to torture nature not after, but *before* any sin is committed. The existence of our 'nature' is in itself a sin. The belief in 'original sin' is thus not only one belief among many, not only a myth, but one reactivated in daily practices. Thus the torment of steady remorse – the guilt-feeling one cannot get rid of – is a salient characteristic of bad conscience. I would venture the proposal that the man of bad conscience feels guilty because he *is* guilty, because (in his case) the externalization of the conscience *is, ipso facto*, a transgression against conscience as the *internal* authority. A real guilt is felt, but (being intolerable) it cannot remain conscious. Hence it is *rationalized* in various ways and a belief in original sin is only one of many.

The internal authority as the *ultimate* arbiter in practical decisions is homologous with an external authority characterized (again, very roughly) by the following features: (i) the co-existence of various external authorities, no one of which determines a person's allegiance by virtue of his birth; (ii) the disappearance of a fixed hierarchy of norms and values within every external authority and the subsequent loss of a *sensus communis* regarding the supreme virtues; (iii) a division between technical rules and social norms of correct social behaviour; and (iv) the universalization of certain abstract norms *in statu nascendi*.

(c) Conscience as the *sole arbiter* in practical decisions can be formalized conscience, calculative conscience, narcissistic conscience, or good conscience. All four forms refuse to acknowledge *any* kind of external authority – whether secular or divine – or *any* kind of *material value* as binding for practical reasons. The umbilical cord which (ordinarily) connects the internal authority with the external one, has been cut. But how can practical reason continue to be *a moral authority* if no particular moral value is accepted by it as binding? There is only one solution to this problem. I have mentioned that certain abstract values have become increasingly universalized. If the internal authority regards at least one of these universalized values as binding, it is still legislative conscience, in other words, not the sole but the ultimate arbiter in practical decisions. But there is one possibility left, namely not to accept any universalized value as binding and to base morality on the *principle* of universability. If this is not done, conscience as the sole arbiter of practical decisions *ceases to be a moral agency altogether* and becomes an agency of unrestricted self-realization. The internal agency of value rationality thus becomes the internal authority of *goal rationality*. It is here that the *cunning of practical reason* commences. It is appropriate to speak of the cunning of practical reason, for we shall see how conscience, as the sole arbiter in practical decisions, restores the external authority and thereby shame. But there is a price. The restored external authority is either *void* of moral content or *atavistic* or it is *coercive*.

(c.a) Formalized conscience is morality without ethics. It is a theoretical construction rather than a real type of conscience. Kant made a case for it, but even he had to reconcile one formula of the categorical imperative with a material value. Kant's universal maxim, according to which human beings should not serve for each other as mere means, is a universalization and formalization of the material values of humankind – personal freedom, dignity and the like. But even the resolution to formalize conscience itself cuts the umbilical cord with external authority, and thus the applicative, corrective and interpretative functions of conscience are excluded. Phronesis is replaced by deduction. The distinction made by every type of internal authority between 'human nature' – natural desires, feelings and emotions – and practical reason is conceived of as an unbridgeable gap. And the same happens with the distinction between intentions and consequences, and action, itself, is relegated to the realm of 'nature'. But though Kant made a case for the internal authority as the sole arbiter in *moral* practical decisions, he made a case for the *external authority as well*. External authority has nothing to do with morality and its agent, the conscience, but it must regulate *human nature*. *Ethics* – in contrast to morality – deals with the external regulation of human conduct alone. But as we never know whether someone acted according to the voice of the internal authority or according to the norms of conduct of the external one, the restitution of a shame culture is already noticeable in Kant, at least in so far as *judgment* is concerned.

(c.b) Calculative conscience is homologous with the one-dimensional homogenization of external authority which approves of success and disapproves of failure. Just as the modern individual is divided into 'Man' and 'citizen', so, too, is calculative conscience. In the first case, we can write of 'private calculative conscience', and, in the second, 'public calculative conscience'. Contrary to formalized conscience (which is more a theoretical construct than an actual form of conscience) calculative conscience is real and widespread in its purest form. Its religion is just the opposite to that of formalized conscience: it presupposes the use of other human beings as mere means for individual and public goals. Thus practical reason becomes the prompter and the repository of instrumental rationality.

The *Ego* is the only reality (*das Einzige*) for the calculative-private conscience. It is not concerned about the values or the fate of others unless these can serve as means for its breakthrough. Everything which is useful for the Ego is good, and there is no other good but what is useful. Every step taken in the direction of the breakthrough must be calculated cautiously. No false steps are allowed. The contrast between reason and emotion is thus reinforced. Emotions can mislead and this is why they have to be eliminated. Love, empathy, charity and sympathy are treated as 'weaknesses' by the calculative conscience, and so are aggression, jealousy and (eventually) pride. The man of private-calculative conscience is law-abiding if the violation of legal rules amounts to miscalculation. Should he be pretty sure that he cannot be trapped, he will break any law without the slightest remorse. (In the novels by Balzac there is a whole gallery of men of private calculative conscience who made their fortunes in times of legal turbulence.) The man of private calculative conscience normally abides by the *concrete* norms of conduct of his society, for he *uses* them as *means* for his breakthrough. He is keen on social approval, not because he cares for it *per se*, but because he considers it *useful*. Since the goal of the Ego is to achieve success and fortune in the *existing* society – the external authority of which sets the *limits* on his overt behaviour – the man of private calculative conscience cannot in principle raise himself beyond good and evil, often as he might violate the norms of goodness. Calculative conscience has to take into account the popular view about good and evil. It treats this view as relevant, even binding, for *others*, and as an important factor in successful calculation.

The public calculative conscience substitutes a *group* for the Ego. Good is not defined as 'useful to me' but as 'useful for a class, a group, the majority' and the like. But the Ego claims that it can fathom via mere calculation what would be useful (and good) for a group and how the happiness of the greatest number could be achieved. Any value can be devalued – even those accepted and practised by the target-group or the 'majority' – if it is considered 'harmful' from the standpoint of calculative conscience. Human beings can be, and in fact are, used as mere means. But public-calculative conscience does not go beyond good and evil either, first of all because the goal it intends to achieve (via calculation) functions as a value for the calculator. The man of public-calculative conscience can eventually subject his own self to the goal conceived of as a value. To this point I shall return later.

(c.c) Conscience as the sole arbiter of moral behaviour also appears in the form of narcissistic conscience. The emergence of this type of internal authority is due to the *division* of the external authority into two distinct systems of norms of conduct: one for the citizen and another for the 'private' man. This division does not provide any *new* system of conduct for the third realm – the intimate sphere – only for the realm of the one community left intact, the family. But the more problematic the family becomes, the less regulation is left for the intimate sphere. Narcissistic conscience is homologous in structure with the vanishing external authority in the intimate sphere. Being introspective and introverted, it is preoccupied only with its own self-development. It distinguishes between emotion and reason, but practical reason becomes exclusively self-analytic. The analysis of its own 'soul' is the sole preoccupation of narcissistic conscience. Due to the perpetuated vivisection of the self, the 'outer' world, with its activities and 'swarming', is perceived by the narcissistic conscience as the world of 'tedium'. The person of narcissistic conscience can be self-complacent or suffering. But either way, the conduct of life of the person of narcissistic conscience is usually *seen* by others as an 'aesthetic' form of life void of moral content, even though void of calculation as well. Very true, the person of narcissistic conscience does not use others as mere means *on purpose*. The narcissistic person simply notices others *indirectly* – namely through the emotional oscillation of his or her own soul, the imprint of their remote existence. One may object that narcissistic behaviour is a psychological deformation rather than a human attitude and, as such, it cannot be regarded as a particular structure of conscience. But, in actual fact, narcissicism is not a simple 'deviation' from normality, it is an outcome of a *life-strategy* pursued no less firmly and resolutely than other life-strategies are. All life-strategies can be replaced by others, and if they are not conscience takes full responsibility for them. In the case of narcissistic conscience 'taking full responsibility' means *to reject consciously* all responsibility with conscience's usual cry: 'Here I stand and cannot do otherwise.' But in spite of its rejection of all responsibilities, narcissistic conscience does not go beyond good and evil. The person of narcissistic conscience still accepts the relevance of the distinction between good and evil in the 'outer' world to which he or she chooses not to belong. He or she does not claim any prerogative (either ethical or of any other kind) for himself or herself other than the privilege of undisturbed solitude.

At this stage, certain similarities between the various types of conscience as the ultimate arbiter in practical decisions and those of conscience as the sole arbiter in practical decisions become manifest. Legislative conscience emptied of its value content is equivalent either to formalized conscience – if practical reason is value-rational – or to calculative conscience – if practical reason is goal-rational. Sceptical conscience, stripped of the recognition of the 'other part of the soul' as the external moral authority, is equivalent to narcissistic conscience. And bad conscience is the 'precursor' of good conscience. To this point I now turn.

(c.d) The concept of 'good conscience' was employed by Nietzsche in the same way that I employ it now. It seems to be appropriate to adopt Nietzsche's terminology as it reveals the 'secret' of the very conscience it denotes, namely its genealogy. As we know, in the case of bad conscience, conscience is externalized in the form of the God the Father. This God is the God-of-Conscience. He is not only an all-powerful God but also a personal one. His judgments do not presuppose the mediation of communities or institutions. Should it happen, to speak again in Nietzsche's language, that this God dies, all his powers would pass to those who externalized him. *Good conscience is Man deified*. The will of God becomes the will of Man, the will of the omnipotent the 'will to power'. The source of good and evil does not acknowledge any good and evil: it truly is beyond good and evil. Man deified is the Law; there is no Law except his will; thus he abolishes all laws. The monologic character of practical reason – more or less present in every type of conscience as the sole arbiter of practical decisions – becomes absolute. There are no 'partners' left for any kind of dialogue. There is no shame any more, and no fear of being put to shame. The nominalism of practical reason; the devaluation of values and norms as mere 'names'; and the pride and stubbornness of a conscience that accepts nothing unless it can be justified by reason, a conscience emphatically praised and acclaimed by Hegel – together these allow the 'internal voice' to become *destructive*. The internal authority left on its own unmasks itself as the moral Evil. Be the external authority one-dimensionally homogenized, be it particularized, be it divided or be it eroded, it does not matter: if confronted with good conscience, it is still the embodiment of human values, of the Eye of others, and this Eye turns against good conscience and defines it as Evil. If God does not exist, everything is permitted, Dostoevsky said. And if human beings relied *only* on conscience, this might really be the case.

Of course, good conscience is an extreme form of conscience as the sole arbiter in practical decisions. But what about the other forms? What about calculative conscience? Is it not *almost* beyond good and evil? Is the increasing rationalization of practical decision not already a process which, in the end, leads to hell? Is it so obvious, so much beyond *reasonable* doubt, that obedience to an internal authority is always far superior to obedience to an external one? Is our much-cherished individual autonomy not a double-edged achievement? But if the *structure* of the internal authority is always homologous with the structure of the external one, the questions raised above have to be complemented with a further question: does not the structure of the external authority hold the key to the theoretical and practical solution of the dilemma of practical reason? In short, it is only in the context of an answer to this last question that the others should be answered.

IV

My typology of conscience is a simplification, and I have used it to account only for the main tendencies in conscience regulation. Unelaborated, it fails (a) to cope theoretically with the multifariousness of particular structures of conscience, and (b) to yield an analysis of the varying *value contents* within *each* structure.

Furthermore, in my discussion, the *responses* of the external authorities to the challenge of the internal ones were neglected, and the problem as to how internal authorities can reinforce the legitimacy of their external partners was completely ignored.

The analysis of the combination of structures of conscience and their variety, together with the reconstruction of their value-contents, can only be done in a series of historical studies. As a result, I leave this problem open. But the other two questions cannot be relegated to historiography; they have to be answered briefly.

'The power of shame' is not a figure of speech. The spiritual power of external authority is a real power. Where power becomes *domination*, the internalization of shame *legitimates* the system of domination. When the child learns of *what* he or she should be ashamed, he or she learns thereby the legitimation of a system of domination. The more shame is internalized, the less is brutal force needed in order to integrate a social structure. Of course, not only the political system of domination is legitimized by the internalization of shame but dominance in the social sub-systems – like the power old people hold against the young in traditional societies – is legitimized as well. In *dynamic* societies the domination within sub-systems and within the social structure as a whole can provide persons with different external authorities, and the norms of conduct provided by them can even contradict each other. The more heterogeneous the external authority becomes, the less will shame suffice to accomplish the task of social integration. What shame cannot regulate (or regulate only temporarily and in very few respects) are out-group relationships. Here all conflicts must be settled either by naked force or negotiation.

I started the analysis of conscience with the proposition that, from the position of the internal authority, the gods of the external authority are not innocent creatures, for they have an unquenchable thirst for human blood and sweat. Given that a modern individual has to side with conscience, the question is only with *which type* of conscience to side. But it has to be borne in mind that, before the emergence of conscience, the external authorities could not be (and indeed were not) perceived, criticized or rejected as 'bloodthirsty' idols. They were accepted as 'nature', as the soul and body of the community. For the most part, not even complementary conscience queried the 'order of things': Aristotle regarded slavery and the subjection of women as 'natural'.

The response of the external authority to the attitude of

conscience depends both on the *type* of conscience and the severity of its challenge. That applicative or corrective conscience are not disapproved *as such* by any external authority is understandable. Whether the function of practical reason is (a) to mediate between external authority and the particular situation, or (b) to amplify certain values or norms of the external authority constitutive of the person's behaviour, both the validity and the consensual interpretation of external authority are not challenged in either case. Since few norms have to be abstracted in larger communities, the external authority cannot function at all without being complemented by applicative and corrective conscience. But, even then, there can be discrepancy or conflict on *single* occasions. However, interpretative conscience is regarded as at least *suspect*, if not downright *deviant* or *heretical*, in all social structures in which norms of conduct either (1) are considered sacred and the right to interpret them is monopolized (e.g. by a priesthood) or (2) the *sensus communis* in regard to their interpretation is embedded in a mundane power. In both cases the individual reinterpretation of values is in itself a *challenge* to the external authority, even if all the values of the external authority are accepted as valid ones. The person of interpretative conscience is rejected, ridiculed and punished with all available means by the external authority. This is exemplified by the fate of Socrates. If, however, the norms of conduct are no longer regarded as sacred, and the mundane power does not require a *sensus communis* for their interpretation because domination is rationalized, the interpretative conscience *is not censured as such*, though it may be rejected with suspicion within more traditional subsystems. In modern (capitalist, industrial, democratic) societies in which various values have already been universalized, these values can be activated in practice *only if they are interpreted*. Values such as freedom, justice, equality are always interpreted in various (also in contradictory) ways. Since interpretative conscience is now empirically generalized, not only are the few universalized values open to interpretation, but so are the rules of one-dimensionally homogenized external authority. A person may say: *not that* is success, but *this* is success; *not that* (which you normally consider as such) is failure, but *this* is failure. In the Eye of Others this person can in turn be judged as 'stupid', 'inconsiderate', or 'a fool', but he or she will not be *punished*. But whether or not complementary conscience challenges external authority, it *never contributes* in itself to the *emergence* and to the establishment of a *new type* of external authority.

Legislative conscience is always the *agency of revolt* against the dominating external authority(ies). Since it tests all values of the external authority rationally – except those which function as revelatory authorities for its judgments – the person of legislative conscience discredits the system of conduct of the external authority by judging that system *irrational*. Since legislative conscience simply rejects the total regulation of persons by any kind of external authority, and stands for the *freedom of personality* and moral autonomy instead, the person of legislative conscience discredits the external authority as *fundamentalist*. However, from the standpoint of the external authority (as Hegel pointed out) legislative conscience is the embodiment of evil and has to be punished, crushed, and annihilated. But, if legislative conscience is strong enough, it *cannot* be crushed, for the external authority has no hold on it. The immortal words of Socrates, 'Anytos and Meletos can *kill* me but they cannot do me *harm*', formulate the creed of legislative conscience. But as it is not always strong enough, legislative conscience can be humiliated.

However, it happened only in modern European history that legislative conscience not only revolted against traditional external authorities but also contributed to the emergence of new ones. As has been mentioned, legislative conscience can be both dialogical and intolerant. Dialogical legislative conscience contributed to the universalization of a few values, the ensemble of which could, did and does serve as *the external authority* of human conduct for *autonomous individuals*. It also contributed to the emergence of the institutions of modern democracy through the abstraction of norms recognized as binding in public life. Intolerant legislative conscience contributed to the combination of abstract morality and concrete terrorism in Jacobinism – a combination that had been theoretically argued for by Rousseau. This was the first stage of the 'cunning of practical reason': legislative conscience which had challenged its opposite, fundamentalism, became fundamentalist itself.

Sceptical conscience, even though always tolerant and never offensive, is no less a provocation against external authorities than legislative conscience. The person of sceptical conscience challenges external authority with his or her *indifference*. The main agencies of power and domination feel themselves less threatened by sceptical than by legislative conscience, and they destroy persons of sceptical conscience only exceptionally. They seldom need to act at all – public opinion will do the dirty work anyway – for people normally understand and tolerate hatred far more than contempt and indifference. Confronted with the stubborn disdain of sceptical conscience, the popular furore bursts into flames.

Since sceptical conscience is indifferent to external authorities of human conduct, it cannot contribute to the emergence of a new authority to regulate human conduct. But it can contribute, and has in fact contributed, to the emergence of new authorities which do *not* regulate human conduct. Science and art – the first is not to be confused with the theoretical attitude, nor the second with creative artistic activity embedded in daily life – stripped of their moral content function as authorities *per se* in modernity. When Goethe said: 'Wer Wissenschaft und Kunst besitzt, Der hat Religion, Wer diese beiden nicht besitzt, Der habe Religion' (Who has science and art, has got religion, who has not got both, should have religion), he expressed the haughtiness of sceptical conscience. Here the notion 'religion' is substituted for *moral* regulation of any kind. Given that sceptical conscience is always elitist and never claims universalization, it contributed to the emergence of authorities needed by an elite. And it is here that we meet the second stage of the 'cunning of practical reason'. Science, the great challenger of all traditional and ossified external authorities of human conduct, was implemented as technology and it thus created one of the most powerful external authorities in modern life: it has become the creed and the basic tool of domination.

Since bad conscience is the externalization of conscience, the person of bad conscience acts and behaves *as if he or she were* the repository of external authority. Bad conscience does not refuse authority and it does not select among values *individually*. It challenges the modes of conduct of other groups and it judges the norms of out-groups as irrational. Thus it provokes the hatred of these 'others' who, in turn, want to annihilate *as aliens* the *groups* of persons with bad conscience. This propensity of bad conscience to promote reciprocal hatred contributed both to the emergence of the *nation* as a new external authority, and to modern nationalism. As shame could never regulate external conflicts, they were usually settled by wars, and bad conscience provides this traditional way of settling external conflicts with an *ideology*.

Since success is, as we all know from Weber's analysis, the sign of divine grace for the person of bad conscience, and thus frugality and abstinence are the means to achieve it, the response of the 'outgroup' is not only hatred but also contempt for 'industry' which is regarded as the loss of decorum without which life is not worth living. It is needless to retell the story about protestantism and the spirit of capitalism, but it is not superfluous to call attention to the 'cunning of reason'. Bad conscience contributed to the emergence of the one-dimensionally homogenized external authority, an authority the sole norm of which is success. But this success is not the sign of 'grace', it *is* grace. It is not the fruit of daily moral exercise, but simply of good calculation; it does not induce abstinence but hedonism, not decency but permissiveness. Its stronghold is not God but money. Its providence is the market and its prayer is void of devotion.

I have mentioned that legislative conscience cannot be crushed if practical reason is strong and determined and that the same holds true of sceptical conscience. But the average person of legislative or sceptical conscience cannot normally resist the immense pressure of external authorities if the latter are still strong and unchallenged by new external authorities. To be hated, ridiculed and despised by our fellow-creatures is not an easy burden to carry. To be labelled 'deviant' or 'abnormal' is even more difficult to cope with. And if the obstinacy of the legislative or sceptical conscience is broken when confronted with the Eye of Others, this is not only a matter of cowardice or weakness. For it is legitimate to raise the question: how do we know that we and we *alone* are right, and our fellow creatures are all wrong? Does our conscience always tell the truth? When the Other's Eye rests upon us and rejects us, can we be absolutely sure that our internal voice is not the voice of the Devil? There are obviously cases in which this question ought to be answered straightforwardly in the affirmative but usually there is room for doubt. But how about conscience as the *sole* arbiter of human conduct?

All types of conscience that functioned (and function) as the ultimate arbiters of human conduct substantially enlarged the realm of individual autonomy. It is true that they also contributed to the emergence of new types of external authority. But none of the external authorities that were created extinguished *completely* the autonomy they sprang from. Even though some of these authorities became *coercive* and limited autonomy either temporarily or more permanently – and this is why we could speak about the cunning of practical reason in the making – at least one of them, legislative conscience in its dialogical employment, contributed to the establishment of the only external authorities so far with norms to which a truly autonomous conscience can be related.

THE POWER OF SHAME

In what follows I want to show that conscience as the *sole arbiter* in practical decisions not only contributes to the emergence of new external authorities, but that these new external authorities extinguish individual autonomy. Practical reason abandoned to itself produces its mirror-image in *despotic* external authorities of new forms of domination. The 'cunning of practical reason' is thus completed. (I exclude from the analysis the *formalized conscience* which is only a philosophical construct. In practice, formalized conscience is only an extreme version of legislative conscience.)

Private calculative reason in the process of generalization produces public opinion as an external authority. This public opinion cannot be the outcome of unrestricted argumentation (to use Habermas' term) since it is produced by 'monological' goal-directed behaviour. It is an instrumentalized, manipulated public opinion. It directs and guides monological personal behaviour just as much as traditional norms of conduct did, but it is devoid of moral values. Rationality becomes *rationalization,* observance of norms becomes conformity. When Riesman analysed modern 'other-directedness', or Benedict the recurrence of shame culture, they referred to this phenomenon. Being different and acting differently, are not only penalized by rationalized public opinion, they are also mostly prevented. Persons who in keeping with a private-calculative conscience use other persons as mere means, contribute thereby only to their one-dimensionality. But since public opinion is still not 'totalitarian' and does not repress other authorities of human conduct by *force*, it cannot extinguish autonomy completely.

While private-calculative conscience is related both to competition and formal equality, public calculative conscience is related to inequality. Since the goal is conceived of as a 'common' one – the glory of the nation, the happiness of the greater number, the power of a class or a party – yet practical reason is monological, it has to be assumed that only the *few* – namely the 'best' – can calculate correctly. These few establish the goals, choose the means (other human beings as means included) and they either persuade or force all others to serve as means for the purposes, of the 'great man' – the scientist, the brains trust, the elite. The autonomy of the few thus presupposes the heteronomy of others. 'The world spirit on horseback', as Hegel put it, this unforgettable seducer of generations, Napoleon, was nothing but the public-calculative conscience disguised as the redeemer. The pseudo-religion of modern charisma was thus created. The modern 'hero' is different from Mucius Scaevola, the modern 'saint' is different

THE POWER OF SHAME

from Francis of Assisi. The heroes and saints of bygone times acted in keeping with the traditional-normative external authority through corrective conscience, and they surpassed the average in courage and resolution. The modern 'hero' and the modern 'saint' provide norms for others; the honour of others is to obey them. This high-flown and arrogant individualism and its calculative rationality thus creates a new kind of collectivity. It is a sham-collectivity as it has no values of its own but only 'emanated' ones. The source of the value emanation is the great calculator himself. Needless to say, Bolshevism is based on calculative-collective conscience in its extreme form, and Stalin was its 'purest' representation. In *Darkness at Noon* Koestler's Rubashov ponders in his prison cell: 'Must one also pay for the righteous acts? *Was there another measure besides that of reason?*'

Collective-calculative conscience is characterized by the *externalization* of conscience as a *mundane power*. The main slogan of the Bolshevik youth organization was the following: 'The party is our reason, honour and conscience.' But since practical reason as the *sole* arbiter in practical decisions is externalized, the person becomes *defenceless* against any 'reasoning' provided by the externalized conscience. Everything can be proved to be the *right* thing to do by externalized conscience. Nothing is *wrong* any longer, for the great calculator provides the actors with sophisticated arguments to justify rationally even the most unbelievable crimes. Inmates of Stalinist prison cells recall that there was only one way to resist, namely to mobilize the long forgotten *ten commandments*, particularly one of them: 'You should not give false testimony against your neighbours.' This provided them with a *norm* beyond reasoning.

If conscience as the sole arbiter of practical decision is externalized, anxiety is no longer the fear of ourselves but the fear of an external authority whose judgment we accept. However, this external authority is not, as the traditional external authority had been, a system of moral conduct. Thus we *do not know*, and cannot ever know for sure, what our transgressions are; and we cannot be sure when we commit transgressions and how. One can be loyal, yet be judged (and hanged) for being disloyal; one can be obedient yet condemned as disobedient. Shame becomes all-embracing and *permanent*. One has to succumb to the judgment of external authority as if it were one's own conscience (and reason) – but it is not. On the ruins of a crushed conscience, the permanent shame takes the lead victoriously.

But, and therein lies the dialectical twist, the crushed conscience which has succumbed to the power of shame does not 'wither away' completely. The feeling of a 'secondary anxiety' – the faint voice of a crushed conscience – has to be (and usually is) extinguished through even more unconditional loyalty and stricter obedience, and through making atomized human persons accomplices in crimes they have never dreamt of. But occasionally, as a saving grace, this can lead to the 'reconstruction of conscience' as well. Since we have to pay, we may have not acted in a 'right' way, not in the sense intended by the external authority but in that of our crushed conscience, whose faint voice can still be heard. Should this question be raised, the spell of shame is broken, the externalization of our conscience retrieved and our autonomy regained. The recovered conscience will not be the sole arbiter in practical decisions any longer, but at least the recovery of conscience will be accepted as an *ultimate value*, as one beyond reasoning.

Good conscience is not calculative; it is total identification with our *being superior*. It does not imply using others as means for calculated goals but it does imply the *destruction* of others in the process of the self-realization of this being. Private good conscience is an exceptional case, since if an isolated private person acts and behaves according to his or her good conscience, he or she sooner or later collides with the penal code. In spite of this, the persons of private good conscience are increasing in number, from wealthy people who steal from supermarkets because they simply feel the need to do it, to 'refined' intellectuals who 'self-realize' themselves, via the humiliation and destruction of others, without being motivated by any kind of interest. Private good conscience is often characterized as irrational simply for the reason that no usual human motivation can account for the action of the person of good conscience. Neither calculation, nor any kind of human passion, is evident. But this irrationality is only the last step in the process which started when values were first called 'mere names'. The deification of the individual person *means* that there are no *limits*, since limits are not rational; it is the total rationalization of the Ego without a Super-Ego.

But even private good conscience *restitutes external authority* and thus shame. The person of good conscience is seldom solitary. Normally, he has his *entourage*, his admirers. He holds human souls on strings. He calls himself the new Jesus Christ. His flock is characterized by hatred towards external authority and a quasi-religious love towards him. This love is absolute, erotic and hysterical. The flock has no longer a conscience of its own: it externalizes its conscience in the Leader. The Leader's Eye is judgment, and it is the only one. He has no need to rationalize his purposes, no need to have any purpose at all; his will, his desire, each is a command in itself. But there is a certain kind of perverted reciprocity in this externalization. If his conscience is externalized, the follower is reborn in the eyes of the leader. He becomes a man of good conscience himself through obedience. As long as he admires his god and obeys him, he is a superman as well. As long as he is loyal, he need be afraid of nothing. Rubashov's question of whether one has to pay for the righteous deed, cannot even be raised since, on the one hand, the follower will never pay if he is only loyal, and, on the other, 'right' and 'wrong' are exclusively defined as obedience or disobedience. Let me reiterate that good conscience is originally bad conscience 'emancipated' from God in Heaven. Thus externalization of good conscience does arise from the crushing of conscience. Here the unity of internal and external authority is realized as the unity of Ego and Alter-Ego.

In the case of Nazism, millions of miniature 'supermen' went on with the work of destruction. The Führer was the ideal alter-ego for the follower. 'Loyalty is your honour', the Nazi slogan said. The slightest doubt of the Führer meant, at the same time, a doubt of *one's own* superiority. Because of the identity of Ego and Alter-Ego, self-realization became completely identical with obedience to the external authority. Thus external authority became absolute, the Eye of the Other annihilating. The power of shame became impenetrable. Conscience as an agent of internal authority, as a check on and critique of external authority, could only be regained if the Führer was killed *inside*. But since the Führer had to be killed inside, the retrieved conscience could not be good conscience any longer.

As long as prerational (traditional) norms of conduct are observed, with or without selection, human behaviour is rational, even if individual reason is not critical. Acting according to the code of honour means acting according to values embodied in norms. But if the rules of conduct are outcomes of mere calculation or if it is the self-realization (deification) of individuals or groups that constitutes them, the rules of conduct (quasi-norms) themselves cease to be prerational and become irrational. The rules of conduct (quasi-norms) thus institutionalized *cannot be rationally observed* and the Others' Eye becomes the 'evil eye'.

If conscience as the ultimate arbiter of human behaviour challenges the norms of the existing external authority, there is always room for doubt as to whether we were *really* right. But if external authority becomes the externalization of public calculative conscience or of good conscience – that is to say, if observing external rules or obeying commands becomes irrational – one cannot raise the slightest doubt as to whether the protest of the internal voice is right. In this case the 'internal voice' becomes a value-in-itself and for-itself, the only value left resisting the irrational externalization of conscience. Let me quote Koestler again: 'Proof disapproved proof, and finally we had to resort to *faith* – to *axiomatic faith* in the rightness of one's own reasoning.' In this case, and in this case alone, the feeling of 'I am right (and everyone else is wrong)' ought to be chosen with the *gesture of ultimate faith*, since it is only faith that can endow us with value for our conscience and thus for our conduct.

V

Traditional systems of conduct have not completely disappeared in our liberal capitalist democracies, but they are in a state of continuous decomposition. And even if private calculative conscience has become paramount, different types of conscience exist alongside as well. Moral deliberation taken before action is, however, very sporadic. Such deliberation is not so much needed now as in earlier times since, outside the family, we rarely meet our fellow creatures except within institutional frameworks where the rules of the game are set, and where, if we play in a fair way, our duties are exhausted. In short, moral behaviour has become highly pragmatic. But this pragmatism, which suffices for the routines of daily life, makes us very vulnerable in borderline situations. This is an incipient danger for it paves the way for irrational actions whenever there is social instability. The fact that the usual conflicts between the two authorities are (in our society) mostly trivial is also an alarming sign; all the more so since the changing fashions in public opinion do not correct, but rather reinforce the external authority's identification of the successful with the good. If basic values cannot be gained from the norms of conduct, conscience becomes incapable of questioning the rules of the game and is prevented from contributing to the emergence of alternative external authorities.

Let me reiterate the conclusion of the second section: morally, we are neither better nor worse than previous generations, only different. This statement may be insulting to those who believe in theories of universal progress or of universal regress but I think it is a true statement. But it could not be denied that we have the chance either to score higher or no score lower in ethics than our ancestors did.

When the types of conscience were analysed, the *sequence* of their development was established. This sequence implies simply that the historically *later* types of conscience logically presupposed the existence of the former ones. Speaking of the logic and the history of the development of conscience simultaneously does not assume that history *has to follow* the logic, even if it has done so up until now. It has to be borne in mind that only the history of modern Europe has followed this logic, no other history did, and thus the coincidence of logic and history can be regarded as an empirical contingency. Besides, whether one describes the sequential logic of the development of conscience as progressive or regressive depends mainly on the value-position taken.

I also suggested in the second section that we should accept the theory that our modern society – born around the time of the French Revolution – has not one social logic but three: those of capitalism, industrialization and democracy. All those who stress democracy at the expense of the two other components of modernity with the resolve to contribute to democracy's radicalization, have to regard the emergence of conscience as the *sole* arbiter in practical decisions as a *relapse*. And this they have to do in spite of the fact that this type of conscience was the *last* step in a logical sequence of development. It is simple to describe the emergence of irrational external authorities as a *regression*, but it is too simple to be true. As I have argued, irrational external authority is constituted by conscience as the sole arbiter of practical decision, a type of conscience which is anything but old or traditional. Not every relapse (from the value-position taken by us) is regressive, and not every progress is the 'latest', 'the most recent', 'the last thing'. But, except for conscience as the sole arbiter in practical decisions, the developmental sequence of the form of conscience has to be perceived as a *tendentially* progressive development by all those who further the logic of democracy. Thus the emergence of the internal authority to complement the mere external regulation of human conduct was progress in this way. And so were (1) the emergence of interpretative conscience as against solely applicative and corrective forms, and (2) the breakthrough of conscience as the ultimate arbiter of human conduct. But in the latter case we have to start to select. Since it was only legislative conscience in its dialogical employment that contributed to the crystallization of democratic norms, it stands to reason that, if we take the position of democracy, we must regard this type of conscience as an ultimate arbiter in practical decisions as only one of many that are *unconditionally progressive*. Democracy presupposes the relative autonomy of conscience; it implies that practical reason has to make the ultimate decisions in matters of human action and behaviour. The deed of the Enlightenment, the release from our self-imposed tutelage, is precisely this non-complying with the external authority as if it were nature; to unmask its *concrete norms* as 'mere names' and to test them with our own reason. But we have to recall that only theoretical reason can test everything, not practical reason as the ultimate (but not the sole) arbiter in human decisions. And conscience as the sole arbiter in human decision was denounced as a 'relapse' (even if not a regression).

The autonomy of conscience can be only *relative*, and this relativity is not only the *limit* but also the *well* of practical reason. We cannot have Duty without having duties. But duties are no longer an impenetrable forest of prohibitory signs; they are rather indications of the direction we have to follow while cutting our own path.

In the conclusion of the preceding section three questions were raised: (1) whether the increasing rationalization of practical decisions is not already a process which will finally lead to hell; (2) whether our much cherished individual autonomy is not a double-edged achievement; and (3) whether the external authority holds the key to the theoretical and practical resolution of the dilemma of practical reason. It is now time to return to these questions.

The dilemma of practical reason was further elaborated in this section, and it became clear that it can be conceived of as an antinomy. On the one hand, the norm of practical reason induces us to decide all practical matters solely in accordance with our own reason. On the other hand, if all practical decisions are made solely in accordance with our own reason, then *no* practical decision will be (or could be) rational any more. In order to solve this antinomy we should not renounce the inducement of practical reason: should we do so, we would not solve the antinomy but simply reject practical reason or conscience as the internal authority of human conduct. Here I have to come up with an answer to the third of the questions I raised. I indeed believe that the external authority holds the key to the solution of the antinomy.

But first a remark is necessary. Even though I am indebted to Durkheim's analysis of the *conscience collective*, I avoided the use of his term in this discussion for understandable reasons. External authority is 'collective' in the sense that it is shared by more or less everyone in a society due to the fact that it is the very system which integrates the person into the social structure and, thereby, into the form of domination. But I would not call this phenomenon a *conscience collective* as the term is misleading. A 'collectivity' has no mind, nor can it have a conscience or be conscious. Theoretical and practical knowledge together with norms of conduct are embodied in a system of objectivations. This system is collective in so far as the members of the society have to acquire and mediate it if they are to survive. Persons are thus the 'bearers' of the system of objectivations, but the latter is never identical with the sum total of beliefs – in the case of the external authority of human conduct, normative beliefs – held by the sum total of persons in the given society. Conscience contributes to *change* in the normative system of objectivations by contributing to change in the content, interpretation or structure of the values of the system.

Even though conscience is personal, it is always *intersubjective*. Practical reason is never 'pure', for two reasons. First, it is in constant dialogue with the norms of conduct of the external authority. But external authority is not a 'thing', given that the normative structures of objectivation are acquired and mediated by persons, and that their judgment is the judgment of persons whose Eyes rest upon you. The men and women of internal authority carry on a dialogue with these persons whenever they give reasons as to *why* they refuse to comply with the norms the other persons comply with. 'Giving reason' does not mean providing a theoretical argument (even though this too can be the case) but interpreting the norms of external authority as contradictory ones and mobilizing one against the other. However, no dialogue could come about if the interlocutors did not share some beliefs and some values. There is no possible dialogue if the 'others' could not put the person of conscience to shame. Of course, shame can be reversed. But if all shame is reversed, then, even if the Eye of the other persons of conscience is accepted as the external authority, intersubjectivity ceases to be dialogical.

The second reason why practical reason is never pure is because it is always 'affected' by feelings. Internal authority is not 'inborn', it develops in *life experiences*. The emotional depth of life experiences is constitutive of the resoluteness of the internal authority. Besides, there are types of feelings which particularly 'affect' practical reason. So do the sense of justice (emotional involvement in justice), empathy and sympathy. If the latter two are predominant, the reversal of shame can hardly occur: you cannot see the others when blinded by tears.

Since practical reason is never 'pure', shame and pangs of conscience do not exclude each other. It is a common human experience that if we already feel pangs of conscience, then these feelings can be *amplified* if persons, who more or less share our values, see us. And this is true the other way round: the disapproval of such persons can play on the instrument of our conscience and produce its *voice*, silent as it has been beforehand.

The authorities of human conduct are intrinsically interwoven with a system of beliefs. The internal authority challenges this system of beliefs (from one aspect or another) and replaces it with *another* system of beliefs. It was Kant's wisdom to distinguish sharply between theoretical and practical reason in this respect. To substitute new beliefs for old ones can bring about *more theoretical knowledge* but never more knowledge for reason in its practical employment. Reason in its practical employment has always *the same* task to fulfil and needs exactly *the same* knowledge in order to fulfil it: it has to distinguish between good and evil in order to act according to the first and to avoid the second. Instrumental reason cannot fulfil this function. Here we come back to the *regression* character of conscience as the sole arbiter in practical decisions. Since (when formalized) it is but a theoretical construct, and since all other types of conscience are involvements in instrumental reason, conscience as the sole arbiter of practical decisions ceases to provide us with the *only knowledge* on which the employment of practical reason rests.

Our species is open to change. But we cannot change our species. Moreover, we should not change it even if we could. Since in the process of our 'self-domestication' regulation via social norms replaced instinct regulation, we cannot get rid of normative regulation without getting rid of ourselves. Only the God of our imagination can live without external regulation, even he is involved in a dialogue with us, otherwise what good would prayer do? And he is immortal and we are not. The intention of becoming similar to the God of our imagination is *hubris* in the old meaning of the word; a *hubris* which can only lead (as was proven) to the re-establishment of an external authority but this time an irrational one.

Here I have to return to the suggestion that even though we are neither better nor worse than our ancestors, only different, we probably can score either higher or lower than they did in the future.

Instrumental reason devoid of the only knowledge integral in practical reason – the knowledge that distinguishes good from evil – could push our world into a nuclear catastrophe, the self-destructiveness of which our ancestors could not dream of even in their worst dreams. But even if this does not happen, discontent with the lack of value-regulation could induce people to accept a remedy which may kill the patient: the remedy of *fundamentalism* could be adopted and the modern individual with his or her painstakingly acquired relative autonomy might perish. Neo-fundamentalism (whether it has recourse to traditional beliefs or constructs new ones) proposes the reintroduction of fixed and hierarchical *concrete* norms of behaviour which every person has to obey. A traditional type of external authority re-established in this way would function as a coercive authority of domination. This means to fall short of enlightenment in a process of a de-enlightenment. Even if some aspects of private life and behaviour were still organized in keeping with religious morality, democracy in all its forms has always emerged together with an increasing rationality in public conduct and increasing individual autonomy. Democracy is already victimized by the preponderance of instrumental rationality, but it cannot survive at all under the auspices of a homogeneous and pre-rational external authority. Returning to this kind of authority would mean both relapse and regression. But one cannot dismiss the fundamentalist claim as absurd simply because it contradicts the main trend hitherto observed in modern European history. Having no knowledge of the future we are not entitled to exclude the possibility of a fundamentalist regression although we may opt against it. Yet even if we have no right to depict derisively the prospects of neo-fundamentalism as sheer absurdity, we do have the right (and solid grounds) to assume (1) that the vicious circle of coercive external authority – rationalized internal authority – coercive external authority is by no means inevitable, and (2) that revelatory external and internal authority can meet and reinforce each other.

But to repeat: the key to solve the antinomy of practical reason is held by the external authority.

If only the external authority ceased to be the agent of domination, if we only recognized the ideal Eye of humankind as the eye of others, if only the supreme values were shared by all humankind, and if only these values could become revelatory authorities for every internal authority, then conscience could be again *interpretative*. All value interpretations could be related to the supreme values which would function as binding norms, but as norms-for-conscience validated by every act and judgment regulated by practical reasons. Thus the external authority would be acquired and mediated only by persons of conscience, and only a person of conscience could put another person to shame. Since we already have a few values that have been universalized, the transformation of the external authority into a revelatory one stripped of the coercive character of previous external authorities is not completely out of reach. But this can only happen if at least *one material value* of the already universalized ones is accepted as *ultimate*, as the one which is beyond individual reasoning, which cannot be questioned, cannot be tested, cannot be denounced as a 'mere name', and to which all arguments, interpretation, judgment and action should be related.

Dostoevsky's *Crime and Punishment* is the immortal story of a breakout from the vicious circle. At the beginning of the novel we see Raskolnikov *in shame*. He hides in a dirty hole, turning his face from the Eye of Others. The Others represent the external authority of tradition. They are his mother, sister and friend. They are pious. Their charity is traditional and so are their values. Raskolnikov did not live up to this authority: he feels guilty and he *is* guilty. He cherishes the idea of revolt against this authority in his soul, the ideas of calculative conscience. Two types of authority live together in one person. Conscience as the sole arbiter in practical decisions clashes with the acceptance of any external authority. The collision of the external and internal authority usually leads to neurotic anxiety, to the perpetuation of the sense of guilt. In order to get rid of this anxiety, Raskolnikov decides to renounce all binding values of external authority and listen only to the voice of calculative conscience. His calculative conscience is a combination of private and public calculative conscience: it is not only for his own benefit but also for the benefit of humankind that he plans to murder the usurer. (Of course, the archetype of calculative conscience is Napoleon.) However, Raskolnikov's calculations fail by chance. But this chance is representative since all calculations can fail and often do: at least one of the victims had nothing to do with either Raskolnikov's benefit or with that of humankind. The persecuting law is an external authority but not an ethical one: it is the external authority constituted by instrumental reason. Raskolnikov and Porfiry fight with basically the same weapon, and this is why the law could never become a revelatory authority for Raskolnikov. But Sonia could. Sonia is the *opposite* pole of calculation for she sacrificed herself for others. But at the same time Sonia is the *opposite* of the traditional norms of conduct as well. She is the one who took shame upon herself willingly. The prostitute is the symbol of shame, the embodiment of lost honour. Sonia's religion is personal and so is her God. It is thus that she becomes a revelatory authority for Raskolnikov who bows to her, not as a person, but as the embodiment of the *suffering of humankind*. Humility before this suffering was a material value revealed by Sonia, a value which annulled all the temptations of mere calculative conscience. Raskolnikov accepted this value by *a gesture*. What we accept with a gesture is *beyond reasoning*: it cannot be questioned, it cannot be called a mere name, it is *ultimate*. Raskolnikov did not return to the hearth of traditional external authority and he did not renounce conscience either. The repentance came from within, although the revelatory material value was embodied in the Other. The Eye of the Other judged, and the judgment was voluntarily accepted, since the agency of the judgment was not coercive but *liberating*.

The young Lukács said that Dostoevsky's novels belong to a world not yet born. On the level of artistic parable this may be true. But even if practical reason should take recourse to an ultimate gesture – to the gesture without which the children of Adam and Eve cannot distinguish between good and evil, to the gesture without which we shall not blush and hide our faces before our fellow-creatures in cases of wrongdoing, to the gesture which makes us say 'I am sorry', and makes us forgive others if they say 'I am sorry' – theoretical reason cannot and should not. Theory has to *argue* for the acceptance of this ultimate gesture.

CHAPTER 2

Paradigm of Work – Paradigm of Production

Both in Marxist literature of the last hundred years and in the various attempts at refuting the Marxian theoretical legacy, the paradigm of production and the paradigm of work have mostly been understood as if they were interchangeable with one another. True enough, as we shall see, Marx himself cannot be completely acquitted from the charge of being the source of confusion. In what follows, I wish to make a clear-cut distinction between the two paradigms. I am going to argue that both imply perfectly different reconstructions of society and that the theoretical attempts at falsifying the paradigm of production have not even affected the paradigm of work, and vice versa. Furthermore, I wish to show that both paradigms run into various difficulties and need to be supplemented by various auxiliary principles in order to be maintained if they can be coherently maintained at all.

The paradigm of work is the application of a *structural model of work-activity* to all other kinds of human activity. In this way, work is presented as an anthropologically primary human universal. The emphasis on structural primacy of work does not imply the theory of its historical and social primacy with any kind of necessity. It goes without saying that the structure of work can be reconstructed in several ways and this circumstance accounts for the variety of the theories affiliated with the paradigm of work.

In order to simplify my task, let me start with a brief analysis of the *Economic-Philosophical Manuscripts*, the opus of Marx's youth in which the paradigm of work had not yet been replaced by the paradigm of production. Here, work is described as the

PARADIGM OF WORK – PARADIGM OF PRODUCTION

'life activity' of man, as the free, conscious and universal activity *per se*. The product of work is the objectification of human essence. Thus the model of work encompasses all constituents of our humanness. Non-alienated life, self-creative life is homologous with non-alienated labour. And by contrast, if work is alienated, whole life is alienated as well. The model of alienated labour is the model of alienated life. The latter is completely homologous in its structure with alienated labour:

> As we have found the concept of *private property* through *analysis* from the concept of *alienated, externalized labor*, so we can develop all the *categories* of political economy with the aid of these two factors, and we shall again find in each category . . . only a *particular* and *developed expression* of these primary foundations. (*Writings of the Young Marx on Philosophy and Society*, edited and translated by Lloyd D. Easton and Kurt H. Guddat, New York, Anchor Books, 1967, p. 299.)

Economic categories are, then, *expressions* of the structure of alienated work in capitalist society. In the same fashion, the categories of communism are expressions of the structure of non-alienated labour. The structural dichotomy of 'genuine human species life' and 'alienated species life' is based on that same dichotomy of work.

As a detailed Marx-analysis would go beyond the framework of this study, I venture to oppose the conception of *Capital* to the theoretical proposal of the *Paris Manuscripts*, in full awareness of the coexistence of both paradigms in the major works by Marx in the intermediary period. The anthropological analysis of the structure of human labour re-emerges in *Capital* although it does not occupy the central role as it did in the early opus. What is, however. more important is the slight but basic modification of the reconstruction of the process of labour. In both reconstructions, human work is contrasted to similar activities of animals. In the *Paris Manuscripts* the argument reads as follows:

> It [the animal] produces in a one-sided way while man produces universally. The animal produces under the domination of immediate physical need while man produces free of physical need and only genuinely so in freedom from such need. . . . The animal builds only according to the standard and need of the species . . . while man knows how to produce according to the standard of any species and at all

times knows how to apply an intrinsic standard to the object. (*Writings of the Young Marx on Philosophy and Society*, p. 295.)

In *Capital* the same problem is formulated as follows:

But what distinguishes the worst architect from the best of bees is this, that the architect raises his structure in imagination before he erects it in reality. He not only effects a change of form in the material on which he works, but he also realizes a purpose of his own that gives the law to his modus operandi, and to which he must subordinate his will. . . . An *instrument* of labour is a thing, or a complex of things, which the labourer interposes between himself and the subject of his labour, and which serves as the *conductor* of his activity. (Karl Marx, *Capital*, translated by Samuel Moore and Edward Aveling, New York, International Publishers, 1970, vol. I, pp. 178–9. My italics.)

It has often been pointed out that the first part of Marx's train of thought had simply been taken over from Aristotle's description of *techné*. Contrary to the emphasis on freedom and universality in the *Paris Manuscripts*, here work is described as goal-rational activity *per se* characterized by the subordination of will to the instrument. Needless to say, that 'conscious activity' and goal-rational activity are not interchangeable with one another. *Techné* had already with Aristotle been opposed to *energeia* (embracing both theory and praxis). But in that case a *different* structure of activity prevailed, the patterns of which cannot be described by the triad: subject – means (instruments) – object, the rationality of which is not dependent on the successful choice of means and the realization of goals. However, Marx modified the Aristotelian reconstruction of *techné* in that he overemphasized (as compared to Aristotle) the function of instruments in the above-mentioned triad. The real protagonist of the labour process is the instrument in its capacity as the conductor of human activity and, at the same time, as subservient to human aims. But this structure of the labour process cannot serve as a model of every kind of human activity even in societies based on domination, exploitation and hierarchy, that is, in a type of intra-human relationship in which human beings serve for other human beings as mere means. But, as we shall see, in the above-quoted passage Marx described not alienated but non-alienated labour. He described the structure of

PARADIGM OF WORK - PARADIGM OF PRODUCTION

concrete labour and not that of abstract labour which becomes obvious from the conclusion: 'The process disappears in the product; the latter is a use-value . . .' (*Capital*, vol. 1, p. 180).

The universalization of this structure as the model of all non-alienated human activities and forms of communication could not have been fitted into the whole framework of Marx's philosophy either. Thus the reduction of the structure of work to goal-rational activity conducted by instruments opened the way to the distinction of *techné* and *praxis* on the one hand, and to the identification of labour with the socially necessary production of material wealth on the other. The new analysis of the work process serves as the anthropological basis for the replacement of the paradigm of work by the paradigm of production, a switch Marx has already accomplished and argued for in the clearest way both in the Preface and in the Introduction to the 'Critique of Political Economy'.

Contrary to the paradigm of work, the paradigm of production does not involve the conception of structural homology of all human life activities with the 'model' of work. But it does involve the conception of the (historical and social) *primacy* of production as against all other forms of human interaction and communication. On the other hand, as I have already suggested, the paradigm of work does not imply the notion of historical or social primacy of work as against other types of human action and communication. The structure of all the various forms of human life are deduced *logically* from, and constituted *analogically* through the model of work, without even raising the question of 'what was first?' or 'what is the motivating force?' or 'what is the "encompassing moment"?' Further, within the paradigm of production the individual subject becomes an epiphenomenon whereas within the paradigm of work the individual work process (the work process of the individual subject) serves as a structural model. The social character of work is founded anthropologically. The individual actor acts according to the species essence, and the same species essence is expressed in all individual activities. Apart from other factors, this is the reason why the paradigm of work is not easily applicable within the framework of a philosophy of history. The attentive reader of the *Economic-Philosophical Manuscripts* cannot miss the point that the question of *why* human work became alienated, and *why* it will be de-alienated, has not properly been answered by Marx, even though he had already started to complement the paradigm of work by the paradigm of production at this stage. But the paradigm of production can easily

PARADIGM OF WORK - PARADIGM OF PRODUCTION

be applied within a philosophy of history, although it can also exist independently on any such philosophy.

Since the application of the paradigm of production within the framework of a philosophy of history by Marx is common knowledge, it is sufficient to enumerate the problems solved thereby and disregard for the time being the new problems created through this theoretical suggestion.

(a) Production has been identified as the 'encompassing moment' of the economic structure of all societies within the trinity of production, distribution and consumption. It is only the wisdom of common sense that has been reaffirmed by the theory of the 'encompassing moment', namely, the thesis that something has to be produced in order to be distributed and consumed.

(b) Production has been singled out as the motivating force of human history, that is to say, as the independent variable of historical development.

(c) The development of the forces of production has thus accounted for the *continuity* of human history. Continuity can be understood as a chain of progression with eventual setbacks.

(d) The theory of clash between the development of the forces of production and of the relations of production has accounted for the *discontinuity* in human history.

(e) The unity of the forces and relations of production served as the principle of periodization. Five subsequent modes of production could be distinguished. They could be compared to each other through the application of the stage of development of the forces of production as the indicator of progress.

(f) Last but not least, the paradigm of production has served as the vehicle of a guaranteed future, as the continuous development of production was to lead to the collapse of capitalism and the realization of classless society.

Even from this simplified description it becomes clear that the paradigm of production does not only differ from the paradigm of work but that these two paradigms logically contradict each other, especially as far as their application to history is concerned.

It has already been mentioned that the paradigm of production does not involve the emphasis on the structural homology between production and other forms of institutions and actions. Marx has always emphasized just the contrary. In his conception, there is a contradiction between the process of production and the process of valorization, a contradiction between the division of labour in society and within the factory, a contradiction between social production and private appropriation, and so on. The categorical distinction between production on the one hand and all other human activities and forms of communication on the other, becomes even more clear if we take Marx's image of future into consideration. Although the *Capital* and the *Grundrisse* present two different models incompatible in this respect, both are unanimous in regard of the above-mentioned aspect. In *Capital* Marx describes the coming communist society in terms of a complete duality: the realm of production will remain the realm of necessity whereas all other spheres of life will realize human freedom. He similarly separates the management of things from the self-management of men. Needless to say, the realm of necessity within the framework of which every member of society performs simple labour and the realm of freedom within the framework of which all human abilities develop, are completely dichotomic in character, as far as the structure of activity is concerned. In *Grundrisse* Marx solves the problem in a different way. He argues that future man will 'step beside production'. If this were so, the forces of production would no longer be composed of two elements (worker plus instrument), since the first would be reduced to nil. It is interesting to note that the paradigm of work reappears in both suggestions, but work is not only distinguished from production, it is rather contrasted to it: free, conscious, universal work is performed *outside* production. In so far as it is performed outside production (in leisure time), work, once again, becomes the main *model* of non-alienated human activities, of praxis as such.

The paradigm of production can be conceived of very easily without several other components of the Marxian theory. To mention only the obvious one: the distinction between basis and superstructure, the primacy of the former as against the latter are by no means necessary theoretical implications of the paradigm, and vice versa. But I strongly disagree with the opinion that the basis–superstructure distinction did not belong to the core of Marx's theory. Even if one disregards the strong version of this theory (that in the Preface to the 'Critique of Political Economy'), it remains undeniable that the primacy of economic (property) relations as compared to the political and legal forms of intercourse and the ideological forms of self-expression is the very essence of the Marxian historical materialism, even to a far greater extent than the paradigm of production itself. Marx's philosophy of history rests on the combination of these two components. No matter whether they are in harmony or in contradiction with the forces of production, the relations of production *mediate* between production and all other forms of human intercourse, and this mediation accounts for the variety of structures of action within the same social totality. Those interpreters of Marx who apply the concept of production to all spheres of human interaction not as a figure of speech but in the sense of homology (speaking of 'production of art' or 'production of ideas') merge two different paradigms into one, that of work and that of production, without being clearly aware of the switch of paradigms. At the same time, one can quite consciously use the model of production as the model of all human activities, but this operation requires a total break with the Marxian philosophy of history. This is precisely Foucault's method in that he distinguishes between three types of technique (the technique of production, the technique of power, the technique of self) while establishing a homologous understanding of the productive, political and interpersonal forms of intercourse.

Let us now return to Marx's analysis of the structure of work in *Capital*. Work has been described there as goal-rational activity *per se* conducted by the instruments of work. As a result, praxis could no longer be understood as a version of the work-model. Consequently, the process of alienation and the perspective of de-alienation had to be grasped in two different ways as well. Although the first traces of such a conception could already be found in the earlier works, it is easier to understand it on the basis of *Capital*.

If work is goal-rational activity *per se*, the alienation of work is primarily the alienation of goal-rationality. In analysing modern factory work, Marx emphasized the *second* division of mental and manual labour: they had become divided *within the same work process*. This means that although the whole process of production is highly rationalized the labour of the workers is no longer rational from the workers' own standpoint. The workers do not raise the outcome of the work 'in their imagination', and the adequate means of realizing the goals (the instrument) is not chosen by them either. The work process thus becomes *senseless* from the viewpoint of the workers. The Weberian idea that the increase in rationalization goes hand in hand with the decrease in rationality (from the viewpoint of the individual actor) is already present in Marx. Lukács, in *History and Class Consciousness*, was perfectly justified in combining the theories of his master and his friend. The question raised by Marx, and not raised later by Weber, was as follows: how can work once again become goal-rational in the case of rationalized social production? And the answer was unambiguous: the workers (the producers) themselves have to raise the goal of production and choose the instruments adequate to the realization of goals. The collective control of production *is* goal-rationality regained. It stands to reason that the concept of 'associated producers' has not been taken over uncritically from Saint-Simon. Only individuals can associate. Every individual has to participate in raising goals and choosing means (instrument) in order to regain goal-rationality now distorted and alienated as mere rationalization. But since at this stage Marx distinguishes between work activity and other human activities according to their different structure, since the structure of praxis was for him not homologous with the structure of labour, it is obvious that the project of restoring goal-rationality proper in production does not imply positing goal rationality as a general feature of all other forms of human activity (interaction, communication). Just the contrary is the case. One has only to glance at the Marxian description of valorization of capital, for it to become obvious that all single capitalists act in a goal-rational way: the profit is the goal and the production is the means to it. The activity of the individual workers is no less goal-rational: subsistence is the goal, work is the means to it. Goal-rationality in the realm of social intercourse is calculation. It implies competition and the alienation of needs as interests. Whereas *within the realm of production* rationalization leads to the loss of goal-rationality, within the framework of social relations mere goal-rationality generates anarchy. Thus goal-rationality becomes exclusive in a sphere in which it should not become exclusive and it is absent from a sphere in which it should be present. Goal-rationality is fetishistic in the sphere of human interactions because, even though it is not confronted with nature but with other human-social beings, it conceives of them as if they were nature (things). In this manner, goal-rationality becomes alienated into rationalization, and communicative rationality (relations between human beings) becomes alienated into goal-rationality. Needless to say, the self-emancipatory deed of the proletariat does not follow the patterns of goal-rationality: it is conceived as a rupture with calculative reason. As long as workers act in keeping with goal-rationality, they remain inside the logic of capitalist society.

But it would be too easy to read Max Weber into Marx and describe praxis (as contrasted to *techné*) as value-rational action. The Marxian conception was rather bound up with the Hegelian distinction between *Verstand* and *Vernunft*. Hegelian *Vernunft* develops towards self-consciousness of history as freedom. The supreme rationality of communism in Marx implies that man becomes the author of all his actions and human contacts (different in types and structures); as a result, man is liberated from all compulsions and develops his/her personality in a manifold way. The development of universal human wealth was the supreme value for Marx. But he posited this value as a *fact* in a communist future, so that the same value could not maintain an 'Ought'-character in this future. The romantic feature of the work of his youth, the unity of individual and species, had never really been renounced by Marx.

When I referred to the re-emergence of the paradigm of work in both *Grundrisse* and *Capital outside* the sphere of production I emphasized that it is understood again primarily as 'free', 'universal' and 'conscious' activity. Now I should add that the assertion of work (in this understanding) as the model of praxis, referred to work on the level of *Vernunft* and not to that of *Verstand*. But here the differences between *Grundrisse* and *Capital* have to be emphasized. In *Grundrisse*, in which production as work disappears, the distinction between *Verstand* and *Vernunft* disappears as well. But in *Capital* this distinction prevails, even in an imaginary communist future.

I contended at the beginning of this study that both the paradigm of work and that of production run into difficulties if pursued in a conclusive way, and that the difficulties are of different provenance. It would be going too far to develop all logically possible variations of the two language games. For that reason, I shall restrict my analysis to two theoretical proposals that anyone can check.

It was in his old age that Lukács undertook the task of revitalization of the paradigm of work, in his *Ontology of Social Being*. The basic idea of the book consists precisely of the outspoken and conclusive application of this paradigm. The reconstruction of the structure of social being starts with a lengthy chapter on work. The following chapters ('Reproduction', 'Ideology', 'Alienation') analyse the various forms of human intercourse as expressions, and eventually as modifications, of the fundamental pattern of human action: of work.

The Lukácsian reconstruction of the work model is basically Aristotelian. The main constituents of the analysis are, on the one hand, the above-quoted passage by Marx from *Capital*, and, on the other, the Aristotelian conception of *techné* based on Nicolai Hartmann's thorough reconstruction in his *Theological Thinking*.

Work is, then, described as the combination of final nexus and causal nexus. The social actor first 'raises the image' of the goal, hence the point of departure of work is 'teleological positing'. Once the means adequate to the realization of the goal has been selected, the same social actor touches off a chain of causal determinants which, in its turn, leads to the actual realization of the goal. Both teleological positing and unleashing of causal determinants are of course attributed to individual persons, single actors. All other human relations are structurally homologous with this 'one-man-show'.

Of course, all human actions are teleological in nature. More precisely, if human behaviour is *not teleological*, it cannot be called an 'action' at all (for example, 'being afraid' is not an action). The question is why precisely work, as one type of teleological positing, should be regarded as the basic model *par excellence* of all other, similarly teleological, acts of positing. Aristotle, the inventor of the model applied by Lukács, adopted an entirely different position. For him, striving for goals was a universal characteristic of rational human behaviour and, within this realm, he distinguished various types of goal-directed actions. The various types of teleological action had been distinguished from each other not only *formally*, but also as far as their *content* was concerned. With Aristotle, *the character of the goal itself* was co-constitutive of the structure of action. Whether the goal is the good of the state or the happiness of the individual, it touches off mechanisms of action different from those triggered when a new object of general use is posited as goal. The process of finding the adequate means of triggering casual determinism and of realizing the goal is, in this purity, only attributed to *techné* within the realm of various teleological activities. In this manner, Lukács narrows down the Aristotelian paradigm of teleology to a paradigm of work.

But here the following remark is appropriate: even though this narrowing down of the paradigm of teleology led to theoretically fallacious consequences, it was, at the same time, an attempt at 'modernizing' Aristotle, and as such, highly justified. As I have mentioned, the paradigm of teleology involved, with Aristotle, the hierarchization of goals in keeping with their contents. This hierarchy had not been arbitrarily invented by the Stagerite: he established their order following the idealized consensus of his polis and his age. To construct a *substantive* hierarchy of goals in modern society, without any real life foundation for it, would have meant the superimposition of the theorist's own value hierarchy on the real historical agents. In so doing, the theorist would have placed himself outside the society to which he belonged. Lukács intended to avoid this pitfall through a certain amount of formalization: choosing the paradigm of work in order to accomplish this formalization was an attempt of great format even if it failed.

Obviously it was not only Marx's concept of work that induced Lukács to switch the Aristotelian paradigm. Max Weber's notion of goal-rationality could equally have had its share in the change. It was Max Weber who formalized the types of action separating them from the particular content of the individual goals in a conclusive way. It was Max Weber who described all goal-oriented human actions as goal-rational ones, at least in each case in which rationality depended on the successful realization of goals. Even though in his later years Weber made efforts to distinguish value-rationality from goal-rationality, the former remained in large measure a partial element within the all-encompassing goal-rationality. But should the notion of goal-rationality replace that of teleological positing, work will serve as the paragon of all human activities (except the residual ones). Of course, *work* is meant here, not the process of production: work as a 'one-man-show'.

What are the difficulties presented by the paradigm of work?

First of all, all social actions and relations have to be explained by the analogy of an *individual action*. Society has to be built up by *Cartesian* elements. True, the single element with Lukács is no longer a *cogito*, not even Husserlian intentionality. It encompasses the whole man: mind and body. The same element establishes relation between man and nature (teleology and causal nexus). To put it simply, this is a materialistic version of *cogito*, nevertheless a version of cogito. Intersubjectivity is not prior to it, it has to be deduced from this materialistic cogito (intentionality).

Secondly, the conception is *reductionist*, since one particular type of teleological positing has to account for *all* types. Thus Lukács is compelled to describe the activities of human intercourse, ideology and the like as *modified versions* of the structure of work. He too struggles with the problem of values, and suggests several (sometimes contradictory) procedures to deduce value-oriented behaviour from the structure of work.

Thirdly, Lukács' main concern is to reaffirm the Marxian philosophy of history. As I have already mentioned, neither the paradigm of work alone, nor that of teleology, can perform this task. Max Weber discarded philosophy of history completely, and in this way he needed no auxiliary paradigms. But Lukács did. If the structure of work is an ontological universal, and if all human actions can be understood through the application of this very model, no laws of development in history can be established. Lukács solved this problem by introducing the distinction between 'species-essence-in-itself' and 'species-essence-for-itself'. Work always embodied 'species essence' but only 'in itself'. The universal progress in history is 'pushing back the limits of nature' towards 'species-essence-for-itself'. This process has three constituents: production (pushing back the limits of 'external' nature), denaturalization of the individual actors (pushing back the limits of 'internal nature'), and, last but not least, the universalization of integrations. Within this threefold process production is the motivating force. So in order to reassert the philosophy of history, Lukács reintroduced the paradigm of production as if it were the simple conclusion of the paradigm of work, which it is not. This is why *The Ontology of Social Being* becomes an inconsistent and self-contradicting attempt at reshaping Marxism on the basis of the paradigm of work.

If the paradigm of work does not allow for a proper distinction between *techné* and *praxis*, the paradigm of production reduces the latter into a secondary, non-autonomous phenomenon. In order to exemplify this reduction, we have to return to the *Capital* and to all those writings of Marx in which the paradigm of production is basically substituted for the paradigm of work. As I have already mentioned, the patterns of social intercourse due to this switch of paradigms, are no longer shaped after the structure of work. But even though the emancipatory deed of the proletariat is not described in terms of the work model either, it becomes completely dependent on the development of production. The revolutionary subject (the repository of praxis) is but the executioner of a historical necessity, of the quasi-natural forces embodied in production. As we know, the subject of world-historical transition is capable of abbreviating the pangs of delivery or of shortening its process, but it is a subject without alternatives (because 'relapse into barbarism' is not a real alternative).

Further, the paradigm of production brings about a decisive distinction within the realm of work. By accepting it, Marx was compelled to make a sharp distinction between productive and unproductive labour. The primacy of productive (as against unproductive) labour had to be emphatically stressed. It has often been pointed out that this distinction proved to be wholly inconclusive and confused as far as the economic reproduction of society as a whole was concerned. But the anthropological conception of work became even more ambiguous: qualitatively similar work activities

PARADIGM OF WORK – PARADIGM OF PRODUCTION

had been put in two different clusters, and qualitatively different ones in the same. The ontological structure of work had been historicized, and its historical characteristics ontologized. Let me add, however, that at one stage of his activity Marx did find a resolution of this contradiction: in *Grundrisse*, where he reflected on the paradigm of production *historically* as well. Here he restricted the validity of his paradigm to the so-called 'prehistory'. Space will not allow me to say more than that the rejection of the validity of the paradigm of production in the future also had a retroactive effect on the analysis of class societies. The emphasis on the individual subject, this basic characteristic of the paradigm of work, is prevalent in *Grundrisse*.

If we consider the two paradigms in their pure forms and refrain from attempts to combine them in a theoretically contradictory and inconsistent manner, we can reach the following conclusions:

(1) The paradigm of production qualifies for a proper paradigm of a philosophy of history, whereas the paradigm of work does not.

(2) The paradigm of production is able to differentiate between *praxis* and *techné* in structure, whereas the paradigm of work does not.

(3) The paradigm of production constitutes intersubjectivity as the mere expression of the development of a quasi-natural force; the paradigm of work constitutes intersubjectivity from the individual acts of teleological positing. The former is historicized positivism, the latter is materialistic Cartesianism.

(4) The paradigm of production reconstructs societies as structured, mediated and contradictory wholes. The paradigm of work constitutes a relation between two wholes: individual and species (humankind), or individual and cultural world (as a whole) in all spheres of interaction and communication.

It is not surprising, then, that the unification of these two paradigms constantly fails. But this statement does not exclude their unification in a third paradigm which is not identical with either of them. Let me posit a suggestion for a solution from among several possible ones. We could accept *a structure of objectivation* as a paradigm, a complex which constitutes the core of social life present in all societies but completely variable as far as their particular content is concerned. It may be called 'the sphere of objectivation-in-itself'. This is a structure of objectivations that all human beings have to appropriate in order to survive in a given cultural environment. It has three components: the use of man-made objects, observing the culturally defined ensemble of customs, and the use of ordinary language. Since these three components can only be appropriated together, one is justified in speaking of one structure of objectivation. This sphere of objectivation embodies intersubjectivity, but, as already mentioned, it is appropriated individually and allows for more or less individual (personal) alternatives. At the same time, it can be considered as the basis of all social actions, and forms a communication in a given historical period and cultural context. But this is not to say that it defines their structure as well. It only means that these various structures might be translated back into the sphere of objectivation-in-itself. Beyond doubt, this paradigm does not qualify for the paradigm of a philosophy of history, simply because the sphere of objectivation-in-itself produces only the needs for change and not the actions which bring it about or affect its direction. But it has one advantage which cannot be denied: if it is accepted, all paradigms accepted hitherto in this-worldly philosophies (those of work, production, intercourse, communications, life and culture) could be meaningfully united.

CHAPTER 3

Everyday Life, Rationality of Reason, Rationality of Intellect

Preface

In the present study I seek to systematize, albeit briefly and from one perspective only, the principal ideas already elaborated over the past two decades in the following books of mine: *Everyday Life, Towards a Marxist Theory of Value, On Instincts, A Theory of Feelings, A Theory of History*, and several other writings. A summary, almost by definition, must be laconic and straightforward. It does not permit digressions and detours, however attractive or desirable broader philosophical inquiries into or reflections on major issues might be. This is why I must abandon almost entirely the analysis of all those theories related to my main problem. To succumb to such temptations would only lead me away from the question which no philosophical discourse can today avoid. The problem of rationality has come of age as the focal point *par excellence* of contemporary philosophical and sociological discourse. Yet this centrality has not produced unanimity: theoretical proposals for the solution of the problems are many and varied. In a different way and for different reasons an absence of unanimity also characterizes the problem of everyday life.

Amongst the answers to the problem of rationality and everyday life, Jürgen Habermas' recent two-volume work, *A Theory of Communicative Action*, is deservedly prominent. In line with his usual mode of theorizing Habermas develops his position through reflections and comments on the most important central contemporary theoretical discourses. My study is not so ambitious, constrained as it is by both its form as a synthethis and a desire for brevity. I acknowledge that these self-imposed constraints carry the risk that I may be charged with ignorance.

I The category of rationality, the category of everyday life, and what these terms refer to

The historical reconstruction of the emergence of the categories of 'rationality' and 'everyday life' (or 'life-world') will be carried out here through the application of those same categories the emergence of which is to be reconstructed. To properly accomplish this task, the following two statements must be accepted as simultaneously valid:

(a) In various human histories (or at least in the majority) the notion of rationality and the notion of everyday life are nonexistent, at least in the generalized and generalizable content in which they are today being claimed by every theory of rationality and of everyday life. It is precisely for this reason that an inquiry into the *when* and *how* of their emergence is a legitimate enterprise.

(b) The categories (or notions) of rationality and of everyday life can and should be applied to every human history. Were this not the case, these categories could not raise their claim to generality and generalizability.

At the outset I should note that a similar procedure has been justified by Habermas with his reintroduction of the Marxian notion of 'real abstraction', which, it will be recalled, Marx had summarized in the well-known formula that the anatomy of man serves as a clue to the anatomy of ape. However, *within the framework of my theory of history*, the notion of 'real abstraction' alone does not justify the application of the philosophical categories of rationality and everyday life to human histories prior to the birth of these categories, for I would argue that where a *consciousness* of a social phenomenon is not yet present, the phenomenon itself cannot be accepted as present either. In order to substantiate my assertion that the categories of 'rationality' and 'everyday life' may legitimately claim generality, I must show that the consciousness of rationality and the consciousness of the distinction between 'everyday' and 'non-everyday' are both empirical human universals. It is also necessary to show that the categories of rationality and everyday life emerge at junctures where the consciousness of rationality and of the distinction between 'everyday' and 'non-everyday' lose their 'taken for grant-edness' and become problematized.

Before addressing these questions I will focus on the problem raised in complex (a) above and then move on to examine complex (b) in the sections which follow.

Within complex (a) the discussion of the emergence of the category of 'rationality' has priority over that of the emergence of the category of 'everyday life'. In discussing emergence one must proceed historically, and the notion of 'everyday life' surfaced along with the category of *rationalization*, and not with the notion of rationality, which has a far longer record.

Preliminary considerations on rationality

Good–bad, good–evil, true–false, correct–incorrect, useful–harmful, holy–profane, beautiful–ugly, successful–unsuccessful are all categories of value-orientation. In every society, *what* is good or evil, true or false and the like, is usually defined by a system of objectivations (which I will analyse below). Categories of value-orientation are empirical universals, as least in so far as they are implicated in the all-embracing category of good and bad. They inform us about valid norms and proper rules, as well as about the ways and means by which they can or should be observed. It is clear that the pair of categories 'rational' – 'irrational' does not belong to the realm of empirical universals. Ordinary language users are still reluctant to employ the word 'irrational' when referring to people and actions that they regard as incomprehensible or unreasonable. Instead, they prefer the words 'mad' or 'crazy'. The question 'are you crazy?' refers to the irrationality of an action, forbearance or emotional report of the interlocutor: the inquirer *imputes* irrationality but does not say so, which in itself indicates the lack of empirical universality of the term. On the other hand, it needs to be emphasized that the distinction between sane and mad is both the archetype of the categories of rational–irrational and is empirically universal.

Sane and mad are indeed empirically universal notions, but they do not belong to the categories of value-orientation. They refer to the human capacity or incapacity to *distinguish* between good and bad (good and evil, useful and harmful and the like) in accordance with the valid customs of a particular community. If someone is capable of making a proper distinction but chooses instead to transgress a valid custom, he or she is not considered to be 'mad' but to be bad or evil. Of course, 'madness' is often not regarded negatively but positively, as a quality not below but beyond the 'normal' human ability of discrimination. 'Madness' can even be interpreted as a sign of divine grace and ranged within the scope of the supreme value, the 'holy'. Nevertheless, this fact does not annul the suggestion that the distinction between sane and mad can be regarded as the archetype of the distinction between rational and irrational. 'Holy madness' can only be exceptional, its distinguished role presupposing the sanity of the bulk of the community. This suggests that the distinction between everyday and non-everyday behaviour also belongs to the realm of empirical human universals. The 'holy mad' can be considered as simultaneously holy and mad precisely because he or she is beyond the scope of everyday life.

Let me now turn to the question of rationality and offer my own definition of this category, one which will be preliminary and fairly abstract at first but which I hope to concretize sufficiently as I progress.

By *rationality* I mean 'acting according to reason'. By *reason* I mean *'bon sens'*, that is to say, the faculty of discriminating between good and bad (good and evil, true and false, useful and harmful and the like). One can act 'according to reason' if one abides by at least *one* positively discriminated category. The categories of value-orientation are ordered hierarchically. The supreme pair of categories applying to all members of the community are *good* and *evil*. By *practical reason* I mean *'bon sens'*, the faculty of discriminating between good and bad whilst operating according to the *hierarchy* of the categories of value-orientation. In what follows I will argue that rationality, or 'acting according to reason', means in the *last instance 'acting according to practical reason'*.

The *problem* of rationality arises when and where the external authority regulating human behaviour and action (the world of customs) loses its efficacy and thus its ability to define, in specific cases, the 'what' and the 'how' of good actions (this is discussed in detail in 'Power and Shame'). As a result, individuals have to *deliberate* and *make* a right decision. Good and proper judgment is no longer identical simply with the ability to discriminate; it now includes a deliberative moment in which interprettation and the *application* of discrimination are raised. In this context, knowing what good is involves the determination of how and when it applies. Theoretical and practical reason, thus far undistinguished, must now be differentiated in order to be interrelated once again: good actions should be based on true knowledge.

The differentation of theoretical and practical reason *plus* their conscious combination are thus related to the birth of *morality*. By morality I mean individuals' *conscious and practical relation to their world of normative customs*, in other words, the relation between the *two authorities*, the internal and the external, which function in the judgment of human conduct. Practical reason, as the ability of discriminating, according to their hierarchy, between the categories of value-orientation, can thus discriminate between 'true' and 'untrue' opinions regarding right or wrong norms as well. The latter use is identical with *practical reason proper* as against *practical reason in nuce*.

True knowledge in the service of practical reason has been and still is referred to as 'truth'. The exclamation 'I want to know the truth' is not equivalent to the statement that 'I want to know whether X is or is not the case'. (For further details on this point see my *For a Radical Philosophy*, forthcoming from Basil Blackwell.) It means instead that I desperately want to know what the case is in order to know how to act in harmony with moral goodness (or in order to make up for a former action of mine in penitence). The pursuit of truth thus means acting according to practical reason (that is, rationally) under the guidance of the *double authority* of the judgment of human conduct.

The emergence of practical reason proper and of the double authority of the judgment of human conduct laid the groundwork for the *invention* of the category of rationality. I use the word 'invention' deliberately, in order to emphasize that the former (the emergence of practical reason proper and of the double authority) does not necessarily bring forth the latter (the notion of rationality). Moral religions (I apply here Weber's concept) can cope with this novel phenomenon and dispense with this notion. Only in cases where traditional religion was insufficiently equipped for legitimating individual conscience and the world of norms simultaneously by conferring the attribute of 'truth' upon the deity; that is, only in cases where the question of 'what truth really is' had to be raised, could the potential be present for the discovery and the invention of 'rationality'.

It was Socrates who invented (and thus discovered) the category of rationality simultaneously with the invention and discovery of the 'internal voice' of conscience. Like all great discoverers, he pushed his case to the extreme. With the dictum that virtue can be taught, he imputed not only omnipotence to practical reason but identified the will to be good with the knowledge of 'truth'. But what kind of truth was singled out here? Truth itself has to be constituted in order to be taught. And the constitution of truth, which should be substantiated by means of valid arguments in order that it may be taught, is the *procedure sui generis* of philosophy. *The invention of rationality thus became the invention of philosophy.* The category of rationality was born and remains a *philosophical* category.

It is not possible to analyse here the various difficulties modern philosophies have had to surmount to satisfy the claims of their ancient founding father. In one important way the nature of the respective tasks is different. Whereas the inquirers of classical antiquity could determine their own 'truth' on the basis of the validity of certain values and norms attaching to their small city-state, the philosophers of modernity have had to establish their claims to 'truth', and thus prove the validity of their values themselves by deducing those values from true statements about certain facts (from self-evident statements) on the basis of good argument. However, for my present purposes, and despite certain difficulties and the modifications which these might require, I would argue that *all* philosophies *equally* raise claims to *truth* and each of them offer a *different* one.

Every philosophy deserving of the name argues for its own truth rationally. Every philosophy reflects too upon the category of rationality. Whether reason is understood as omnipotent or limited, whether rationality is acclaimed or rejected, which types of 'reason' or 'rationality' are being distinguished and which of these attains 'primacy'; all this depends on the particular truth of the given philosophy. The belief that a definition or typology of rationality can be offered free of any kind of evaluation or reference to truth is delusory, arbitrary or empty.

I have not excluded irrationalistic philosophies from the sphere of 'philosophy proper', but I would point to the self-contradiction intrinsic to such enterprises. Arguing rationally against reason proves one's own case by contradicting the very case which has to be proven. Irrationalist philosophers cheat in the game we call philosophy. This charge does not apply to religious philosophies which have their referential basis in God as the Supreme Intellect. All philosophies rest on at least one statement which is 'taken for granted' (self-evident), and the statement about the existence of a Supreme Intellect is only one among many.

I have pointed out that (a) 'rationality' was discovered (and the category invented) by philosophy; (b) that philosophy constitutes its 'truth' and argues for it rationally; (c) that philosophy reflects upon 'reason' (whether it is conceived of as omnipotent or impotent); and (d) that every philosophy constructs a particular truth of its own. If one combines all the above elements into one construct, one could conclude that, in the final instance, philosophy is the self-consciousness of *morality*. Morality has been defined here as the conscious and practical relations of individuals to their world of normative customs, as the relation between the internal and external authorities for the judgment of human conduct. Morality presupposes the differentiation of practical from theoretical reason. These are then combined again under the guidance of practical reason. The supreme truth of philosophies is the unity of the true and the good, and any rational argument must prove this truth. Various philosophies constitute various truths because they express the *individual's* relationship to the world of normative customs, and thus they must seek recourse to intersubjective norms or values, or at least to intersubjective 'evidence', to be able to relate to those external authorities in the judgment of human conduct. In this way the notion of 'rationality' is in the last instance a *moral category*. (When Habermas remarks that the notion of 'functional reason' is meant *ironically* in the philosophical discourse of today, as was the notion of 'instrumental reason' by Horkheimer and Adorno, he proceeds along similar lines.) Irrespective of its particular interpretation, wherever the notion of rationality arises, it always carries with it a preference for one form of life as the *good* life.

I have offered a preliminary concept of rationality. I have further suggested that all philosophies involve the notion of rationality while arguing on behalf of their respective truths in a rational way, and that their interpretation and understanding of reason depends on their respective truths. There are as many truth claims and as many interpretations of rationality as there are philosophies. My definition of reason and rationality is obviously one possible definition among many and I believe that I am able to argue on behalf of it and verify it. I wish also to make it clear that my definition of reason and rationality is a *commitment* to this very definition and to the form of life it implies.

Preliminary considerations regarding everyday life

The category of 'everyday life' emerged in both philosophy and sociology after the First World War, though certain basic problems bound up with this category had been under discussion from the mid-nineteenth century onwards. Everyday life (life-world) had to become *problematic* in order to be *problematized*.

Yet one might object that if everyday life *sensu stricto* was not a matter of concern in various philosophies, everyday thinking certainly always has been. Possible examples would include the juxtaposition of *doxa* and *epistheme* in ancient Greece or the juxtaposition of good common sense (right reason) and 'prejudices' in the seventeenth or eighteenth century. But any analysis of depth clearly shows that these alleged prototypes have very little in common with the modern distinction between everyday and scientific thinking. Taking the ancient juxtaposition first, we can see that in Greek philosophy 'mere opinion' meant unreflected thinking in all societal spheres or institutions (household, politics, religion, morals, arts or the images of the universe), whereas true knowledge meant reflected thinking in exactly the same spheres. Friendship, the everyday relation *par excellence*, was considered to be based alternatively on true knowledge of virtue and on mere opinion. Turning again to the seventeenth or eighteenth century, we can see that 'good common sense', to which philosophy could resort, was *not* tantamount to 'everyday thinking'; it was rather a philosophical construct of a type of human intellect which remained *unspoilt* by the false imageries of traditional world-views or religions, unaffected by false and 'unnatural' customs and the like. Everyday thinking did serve as a background or contrast in this regard without becoming an object of theoretical concern in its own right.

Everyday life and thinking started to become thematized simultaneously with the discovery of 'rationalization' or 'reification'. The latter two categories express the same trend (or phenomenon) in social life, but within the framework of different social theories that of the Weberian theory on the one hand and the Marxian-Lukácsian theory on the other. At this stage of the analysis it will suffice simply to state that it is under the conditions of rationalization that everyday life becomes problematic. I emphasize that 'conditions of rationalization' is not synonymous with 'sufficient cause'. Even if we try to explain and not merely interpret the problematic character of contemporary everyday life, we must operate with a multifactoral model. At any rate, the simultaneous emergence of the thematization of everyday life and thinking and that of rationalization indicates the intrinsic interconnection of these phenomena. And even if we leave open, for the moment, the question of *why* and *how* life became problematic, we cannot

fail to notice the signs which indicate a common problem in various realms of life.
Perhaps the most noticeable sign in this respect is modern art. (I do not want to enter here into the discussion of so-called postmodernity. This is a matter extending far beyond my present problem.) For the purpose of demonstration I will focus upon painting, though any other art form would also suffice. European painting from the early Renaissance period to the twentieth century flourished on the basis of a *self-evident* unity of everyday life and 'what is beyond'. The histories of Jesus, those non-everyday histories *par excellence*, were transposed into and depicted in a "natural' everyday setting. The bourgeois or the peasant *intérieur* or the human habitat as landscape in the various Dutch schools exude the atmosphere of a way of life which might be merry or sad, simple or complex, lofty or ridiculous, but which is always worth living. When looking at these pictures up until the period of Impressionism it is difficult to resist the desire (and under such pictorial influence even the chimerical *possibility*) to walk in the streets, to bathe in the rivers, to console the people, to touch the garments depicted; in short, we simply long to be there. Rilke, who said that while Chardin's apples can be eaten, those of Cézanne can no longer be, was the chronicler of a dramatic change that came about at the turn of our century. No one feels the desire to climb Cézanne's hills, just as no one falls in love with the women on the canvases of Picasso. Modern painting does not exude the atmosphere of a way of life, rather the contrary: it is good art *precisely in that it no longer does so.* Modern art is a gesture of revolt against a *life without form*, and it can become form only through this gesture. (This is a reconstruction of the trend, not of the history, of the arts. Life often became problematic before our century as well. Painting reacted to this mainly by contrasting ancient histories in a theatrical mise-en-scène, to present life, as in the work of Tintoretto, Greco or Poussin, for example.)

It may appear difficult to accept that the rupture with everyday life carried out by the arts and the thematization of everyday life in modern social theory signal exactly the same process. Yet this argument can be supported by singling out even a few twentieth-century philosophies and social theories. From the young Lukács, through Heidegger, up to Adorno or Neo-positivism, there were several important thinkers who adopted exactly the same attitudes as the arts did. Turning away from a formless, empty, repetitive and meaningless everyday life thus became a philosophical programme. Everyday life came to be thematized from the standpoint of a 'truth' which then defined this life as void of truth. The kinds of 'truth' counterposed to life varied. They ranged from the model of a pure and quantified science, the language of which can no longer be translated into ordinary language, to the model of pure subjectivity of Life (with a capital L), the depths of which cannot be discerned, but are obscured by the shallowness of everyday intersubjectivity.

It was to sociology's credit that it adopted a new approach. Sociology did not turn away from the social life of the present to find refuge in de-anthropomorphized science or in mere subjectivity. It became sociology precisely by accepting the challenge, before it became incorporated into philosophical paradigms. All this shed new light on everyday life and thinking. Given that everyday life and thinking became the foundation of intersubjectivity, in turn this life and thinking had to be analysed in its own right. Furthermore, the action of addressing social life in order to understand it did not allow the rejection of everyday life and thinking as spheres of inauthenticity. When conducting a survey and drawing certain conclusions from questionnaires filled out by randomly selected people, one must assume that the everyday consciousness and knowledge contained in the questionnaire can provide information relevant to the problems we are concerned with. Of course, 'opinions' should not simply be collected and presented as some sort of 'aggregate' truth: they should be treated critically. But even if they are thus treated, they cannot be taken as mere items of information about the fetishistic and inauthentic mind alone, but should also be taken as items of information about a kind of proper knowledge. It goes without saying that the fact that everyday life has become problematic is never concealed in any sociology worthy of its name. But sociology has a dual approach to this constellation. On the one hand it explains this process via understanding the transformation of macrostructures. On the other hand it views problematic everyday life as a critic of this very transformation of macrostructures, independently of the basic acceptance or rejection of the macrostructural development. The word 'basic' is important here. Neither *total* acceptance nor *total* rejection of this process can constitute a good sociology. What is totally rejected cannot be understood in its own right; what is totally accepted cannot be analysed critically. And every sociology is perforce critical, because it is, to reiterate, a theory which reflects upon a *problematic* everyday life.

Even though the new approach to the problematic nature of

everyday life was first taken by sociology, philosophy rapidly followed suit. But to do this philosophy too had to become *social theory*. One need only think of the transformation of Wittgenstein from *Tractatus* to *Philosophical Investigations*, or the transformation of Husserl from *Logische Untersuchungen* to *Krisis*, to comprehend how this happened. Everyday life and thinking has become the starting point and concern of modern philosophy, and so constitutive of various paradigms (mainly the paradigm of ordinary language).

Still, every philosophy reflects upon the category of rationality, and all interpret rationality from the standpoint of their respective truths (which are the unity of good and true) constructed by the philosophers themselves. As the intersubjectivity of everyday life and thinking have become constitutive of the paradigms of modern philosophy, one way or another these paradigms have to derive rationality from everyday action, thinking, reasoning. It is no longer possible simply to counterpose the rationality of science to irrational or prerational everyday thinking. It sounds paradoxical but is nonetheless true that it is precisely the 'problematic' character of everyday life which induces philosophy to reflect upon it as upon the *foundation* of all human knowledge, action, of all types of rationality.

It might be wondered why I have not here offered a preliminary definition of everyday life when I did so in the case of rationality. The reason is very simple. Everyday life is taken for granted; everyone knows *what* everyday life is. The *interpretation* of everyday life and its relation to what lies beyond it, from the perspective of rationality, will be a general goal of this study. A preliminary definition of everyday life is unnecessary: its preliminary interpretation is impossible.

II The paradigm of the sphere of 'objectivation in itself'

To establish my theory of everyday life and rationality I will employ the paradigm of 'the sphere of objectivation in itself'. I will show that the 'sphere of objectivation in itself' represents a distinctive approach – a new paradigm, if you like – to the contemporary problem of rationality and everyday life. It is distinctive for a number of reasons. This sphere is *evidently* an empirical universal of social life in general: it is the backbone of contemporary everyday life in particular, and it embodies and explains the intersubjectivity of our knowledge, action and communication. It is of course true that certain other paradigms qualify equally well for the accomplishment of this threefold task. There is the paradigm of language, the paradigm of communication, the paradigm of work and the like. But I have not developed my own paradigm merely in order to present a more complete and coherent theory than these others. My intention has also been to present at least an *equally good theory* from the standpoint of a value, of a *truth*. The value directing me in this theoretical task is the *'human being as a whole'*, or more precisely, *the unity of the human personality*.

The sphere of objectivation 'in itself' as the social a priori *of human experience*

The sphere of objectivation 'in itself' is the social *a priori* of *human* experience. It has three constituents: ordinary language, man-made objects (with the rules for their use, including the *use* to which the natural environment is put), and customs. These constituents can only be separated in and by philosophy or social theory. Those observing the 'norms-and-rules' of the sphere of objectivation in itself never separate them; if they did, they would no longer observe the 'norms-and-rules' of this sphere. One cannot use man-made objects (within this sphere) without observing customary norms and without being competent in the rules of ordinary language usage. One cannot be competent in the use of ordinary language (within this sphere) without being able both properly to use man-made objects and observe customs. Again, within this sphere one cannot observe customary norms without being competent in ordinary language and in the use of man-made objects. This does not mean that all three types of competence have to be acquired simultaneously. It means more than this, namely that there is no action at all, speech acts included, which would not *entail* actions related to the other two constituents of the sphere of objectivation in itself. In this sense each constituent is inherent in the other two, and vice versa. Rules and norms cannot be separated.

A newborn is thrown by fate into a world of a *particular* sphere of objectivation 'in itself'. 'Growing up' means the transformation of this accident into a defined 'being in a particular world'. This happens via the appropriation of the objectivation 'in itself'. To be a 'grown-up' means the end result of this process of appropriation. A 'grown-up' is a human person who has acquired complete competence in using the 'norms-and-rules' of the sphere of objectivation 'in itself'. (See in detail my *Everyday Life* (Routledge &

Kegan Paul, 1984) and *A Theory of Feelings*, (Van Gorcum, Assen, 1979).)

I have just referred to the sphere of objectivation 'in itself' as to the social *a priori* of human experience. I also mentioned the accident of birth. The sphere of objectivation 'in itself' starts to transform the accident of birth into a defined 'being born into a particular world'. This transformation is already occurring at the moment of birth, and often even in the prenatal period. Furthermore, several societies determine whether the newborn *may grow up* at all, or whether it should die. 'Growing up' to a 'particular' world is a process that cannot even start if the biological constitution of the newborn shows signs of incapacity for accomplishing the tasks of the appropriation of the given set of 'norms-and-rules'. The 'accident of birth' does not refer to the social *a priori*, but to the generic *a priori*, to the simple fact that all children of humans are born with *a body* programmed for social existence. This programme, which entails the computer called 'mind' being able to perform various symbolic actions simultaneously, is ready to be fed with social information of *any kind*. No newborn can become human without being led by a *particular* sphere of objectivation 'in itself', this social *a priori* of human experience; but, let me repeat, it could be led by *any particular* existing sphere. The 'accident of birth' means that this sphere is not predetermined.

The two *a priori* of human existence are by no means identical with 'nature' on the one hand and 'culture' on the other. Even though we do not know (and indeed might never come to know) how the threshold between nature and societal nature was crossed several million years ago, we can and we do know that it took place via the successive substitution of social regulation for instinct regulation. 'Social regulation' meant primarily the regulation by a sphere of objectivation providing safe rules for repetitive action; by a forebear of the sphere of objectivation 'in itself'. The biologically 'unprotected' character of the human newborn, a fundamental fact of the human condition discovered and expressed in various mythologies, is due to this process. This biological shortcoming which alone made possible (for it made necessary) the establishment of human power via higher intelligence, is not only a 'natural' product, it is a social product as well. The *human* newborn, this late product of self-domestication, is not only the offspring of nature, but of culture as well. The problem of nature and culture reappears in a similar light if we look at the sphere of objectivation 'in itself'. On the one hand, culture has to function for a very long period as if it were nature: as organic and self-evident, and it was only from the neolithic revolution onwards (whenever and wherever it took place) that a firm distinction between culture and nature became possible at all. On the other hand, human relation to what is now called 'external nature' is a cornerstone of this system of objectivation. And, of course, culture is *not* identical with the sphere of objectivation 'in itself' either.

'To be grown up' *means* to acquire full competence in following without fail the 'norms-and-rules' of the sphere of objectivation 'in itself'. One cannot have human experiences, cannot act, cannot speak, cannot think, without undergoing this process of appropriation. And given that humans are 'programmed' to this appropriation (by birth), the process is carried out *intentionally*. Still, there are always *cultural spheres* (certainly in all cultures we are familiar with), the appropriation of which *does not belong* to the prerequisites of mere competence in social life.

All societies produce *cultural* and *cognitive surpluses* which are not fed back into the sphere of objectivation 'in itself'. They are absorbed and practised in cultural spheres *distinct* from the former. I will return to this later. All that I wish to make clear at present is that the *a priori* of generic essence is not identical with 'nature' and that the *a priori* of the sphere of objectivation 'in itself' is not identical with 'culture'.

Given that the 'know-what' and 'know-how' embodied in the 'norms-and-rules' of the sphere of objectivation 'in itself' have to be appropriated equally (even if not equally well) by everyone who is 'thrown' into a particular sphere of objectivation 'in itself', as the latter is the social *a priori* of human experience, then *intersubjectivity is primary as against subjectivity*. On the other hand, the *a priori* of generic essence does not exhaust the 'programme' of the newborn. Each human newborn is generically unique and the 'melting pot' of the sphere of objectivation 'in itself' does not obliterate this uniqueness. While appropriating 'norms-and-rules' equally, human subjects have never become uniform. In this respect they do not differ from their animal ancestors, who were characterized by a similar biochemical individuality. But since humans are born only with a 'mute' generic essence, and appropriate generic essence 'in itself' via the appropriation of intersubjectivity (see *A Theory of Feelings*) and because they do this intentionally, the process of appropriation is a simultaneous process of subjectivation *and* objectivation. As a result, the product is not simply a more or less 'perfect' version of the species, it is a *subject* with the *consciousness of its own subjectivity*, of its being a particular 'I'. This subject is not the residuum of a never fully completed 'socialization'; but is the driving force of socialization itself. Moreover, subjects can become the bearers of a cultural deficit or surplus in any given culture. In the case of a deficit it is legitimate to speak, with Durkheim, of 'deviance'. In the case of 'cultural surplus', subjects go *beyond* the appropriation of intersubjectivity presented by the sphere of objectivation 'in itself'. (Later I will look at 'cognitive surplus', which is not a 'subjective surplus' [as a cultural surplus is].) This can happen in personal experience, where no rule or norm applies, and/or in taking recourse to another (higher) sphere of objectivation, or, incidentally, even in constituting such a sphere. Even though intersubjectivity is primary as against subjectivity, it is still true that because both objectivation and subjectivation come about in the process of appropriation of this same intersubjectivity, a 'subject' is not simply intersubjectivity confined to one body/mind. The appropriation of the *a priori* of human experience makes *human* experience possible in the first place. Even so, this does not mean that human experience is identical with being familiar with the 'norms-and-rules' of the sphere of objectivation 'in itself'. The appropriation of this sphere accounts not only for the intersubjectivity of knowledge and of the patterns of action but also for the uniqueness of the experience of every 'I' within a given life-world.

We can thus describe the sphere of objectivation 'in itself' as the *foundation* of all knowledge and experience in social life. It is at once the foundation of every higher type of objectivation, and of every subjective experience. The appropriation of the higher types of objectivation already presupposes a competence in following the 'norms-and-rules' of the sphere of objectivation 'in itself'. And several of these higher types of objectivations 'absorb' the cultural surplus of subjective experience as well.

The sphere of objectivation 'in itself' and everyday life

The sphere of objectivation 'in itself' has been and still is the sphere of objectivation *sui generis* of *everyday life*. By this I do not mean that the sphere of objectivation 'in itself' defines *exclusively* the patterns of action and the scope of knowledge of the life-world, but only that everyday life presupposes the appropriation of this sphere of objectivation in the first place – put otherwise, it is in everyday life that humans appropriate the sphere of objectivation 'in itself'. This is precisely why everyday life and knowledge is the foundation of every kind of knowledge and institution existing beyond it, even if these forms of (institutionalized) knowledge are eventually fed back into everyday life. But neither the intensity nor the scope of this feedback should hamper the adequate appropriation of the sphere of objectivation 'in itself'. If it did, the society in question would fall apart and disappear. The appropriation of the sphere of objectivation 'in itself' is the precondition not only of individual survival in any given society but of the survival of the particular society as well.

At this point it is appropriate to repeat that the three constituents of the sphere of objectivation 'in itself' are ordinary language, man-made objects (with adequate rules for their use), and customs. These intertwined constituents provide humans with the necessary 'know-what' and 'know-how', that make possible adult survival and self-reproduction in the given social environment (*Umwelt*).

'Norms-and-rules' are not simply 'instructions for use'. If they were, they could not function as 'norms-and-rules'. They provide humans with *meaning* in a threefold manner. First, they themselves are meaningful. This is a tautological statement, since the use of ordinary language is a constituent of this sphere. Secondly, as 'norms-and-rules', they embody or represent the *positive* 'side' of the general category of value-orientation (good–bad), namely, the 'good'. They also represent *at least* the positive 'side' of *one* secondary category of value orientation (sacred–as against profane, good–as against evil, useful, true, correct and the like); normally, however, they represent more than one, and certainly good as against evil. This is why the categories of value-orientation (and definitely those of good–bad) are empirical universals. 'Sacred', 'good', 'useful', as against 'profane', 'evil', 'harmful', *stand for*, at least initially, an inducement to act 'according to the "norms-and-rules" of the sphere of objectivation "in itself" '. Thirdly, 'norms-and-rules' are meaningful because they are legitimated as such by a meaningful world-view. As all world-views are meaningful, the category of 'meaningful world-view' appears tautological. Yet this term stands for *Weltbild*, and not for *Weltanschauung*, and the adjective 'meaningful' simply denotes that the world-view provides the sphere of objectivation 'in itself' with the meaning of 'sacred order', or at least 'proper order'. To put it bluntly, in a very broad sense of the term, meaningful world-views *legitimate* the sphere of objectivation 'in itself'. They legitimate through *genesis* (the mythology of genesis, later being occasionally replaced by history, see *A Theory of History*, Routledge and

Kegan Paul, 1982). Knowledge about gods, the spirits of ancestors and the like, or for that matter even knowledge about the 'universe', is mediated by the sphere of objectivation 'in itself' as self-legitimation as well. One cannot become a 'grown-up' in a particular society without being introduced to this kind of knowledge. But in most societies not everyone is initiated into the subtleties of the meaningful world-view. (In view of my limited anthropological knowledge I would hesitate to expand this statement to embrace *all* societies.) The problem of exclusivity affected even those societies without an established 'priesthood' as the bearer of a secret knowledge. On the basis both of the above and of the assumption that a cultural surplus is normally absorbed by another kind of objectivation (I refer to this as objectivation 'for itself'), one can conclude that even if the sphere of objectivation 'in itself' *mediates* all kinds of knowledge sufficient for a person to become a 'grown-up', it cannot be said that this sphere *engenders* the sum total of this knowledge. One is thus entitled to assume that both the following statements are true: (a) the appropriation of the sphere of objectivation 'in itself' is the backbone of everyday life; (b) one cannot understand and explain everyday life from the vantage point of the sphere of objectivation 'in itself' *alone*.

The sphere of objectivation 'in itself', as well as everyday life and thinking (we have seen that the latter is more extensive than the former), encompasses both *historically static* and *historically variable* elements. Static elements in everyday life and thinking are either *identical with* or *stem from* the static elements of the sphere of objectivation 'in itself', this 'backbone' of everyday life and thinking. The ratio between static and variable elements in everyday life depends on two factors: on the ratio between static and variable elements of the sphere of objectivation 'in itself', and on the ratio between everyday action, thinking and communication governed by the appropriation of the sphere of objectivation 'in itself', and everyday action, thinking and communication *directly* related to other kinds of objectivation.

It is a commonplace that the *content* of the 'norms-and-rules' of the sphere of objectivation 'in itself' belongs to the variable elements. However, this content, whatever it may be, *is taken for granted* by the members of any particular society. Should the 'norms-and-rules' be questioned, they cannot be questioned *from within* or *from the standpoint* of the sphere of objectivation 'in itself'. This is why the understanding of the content of this sphere by members of another society is so enormously difficult. Anthropologists have gone to excessive pains to understand all particular spheres of objectivation 'in itself' in their own right. It is doubtful whether they can succeed at all in this endeavour, or succeed to any large extent. Further, the degree of regulation by the sphere of objectivation 'in itself' can vary from very high to very low. The character and complexity of the other coexisting spheres of objectivation are to a high degree responsible for the 'tightness' or 'looseness' (degree of regulation) of the 'norms-and-rules' of the sphere of objectivation 'in itself' in general, and for the tightness or looseness of its *various* 'norms-and-rules' in particular (they may tighten some and loosen others). The emergence and growth of the social division of labour (termed by Durkheim 'the organic division of labour') is tantamount to the *splitting* of the sphere of objectivation 'in itself' into various and coexisting spheres of objectivation 'in itself'. From this time onwards the 'accident of birth' means not only to be 'thrown' into a particular culture but also into a particular social stratum, class, position and the like. The 'norms-and-rules' presented by the sphere of objectivation 'in itself' are, in content, different for the members of different social classes or strata, notwithstanding that the latter share elements of these contents, particularly those provided by meaningful world-views. (For instance, the 'untouchables', take their 'norms-and-rules', legitimated by the Brahmanic faith which is *common* to all members of society, for granted. Complying with these 'norms-and-rules' increases their chance of being reborn into a higher caste.) The social division of labour and the 'splitting' of the sphere of objectivation 'in itself' does not perforce lead to the loosening of the 'norms-and-rules' presented by the different spheres of objectivation 'in itself'; the less so, considering that they entail 'norms-and-rules' which regulate intra-class behaviour. In tribal societies certain 'norms-and-rules' can be extremely loose. In what follows I will concentrate on the analysis of everyday life within societies with highly differentiated spheres of objectivation 'in itself', and a social division of labour where these spheres of objectivation are relatively 'loose' and where the knowledge mediated (and not engendered) by these spheres is proportionally high. Clearly, the presence of a high proportion of mediated knowledge does not falsify the assumption that the sphere of objectivation 'in itself' is the foundation of all human knowledge and action. Indeed, the high proportion of mediated knowledge verifies this assumption given the fact that a kind of knowledge which has not been engendered by the sphere of objectivation 'in itself' *has to be mediated by it*. This reinforces the initial thesis that the 'know-what' and the 'know-how' that every member of the social environment has to appropriate should be presented to these members as 'norms-and-rules' of the sphere of objectivation 'in itself'. As the ultimate objective of this study is the understanding of rationality in *modern* everyday life, the objectives, as it were, define the emphasis as well.

To illustrate the constant elements in everyday action, one has to examine the constant elements of the sphere of objectivation 'in itself'. I wish to argue that these constant elements shape *almost all* our everyday actions; that they shape, not only actions aimed at the appropriation of the 'norms-and-rules' of the sphere of objectivation 'in itself', but *also* actions aimed at the appropriation of the 'norms-and-rules' of *another* sphere of objectivation, namely that of institutions. I say *'almost* all' everyday actions (speech-acts included) because people can, and generally do, have more or less *direct* access to types of knowledge and to values which are *not* mediated by the sphere of objectivation 'in itself'. Their actions (and speech-acts) can thus be governed directly by those 'norms-and-rules' of objectivations other than the objectivation 'in itself'. I will argue later that these two attitudes imply two different uses of reason as well.

The basic constant element of the sphere of objectivation 'in itself' has already been presented in the definition of this sphere. I have pointed out that each of the three constituents of this sphere (the use of man-made objects, the use of customs, the use of ordinary language) is inherent in the other two. Thus the basic category to be applied to the sphere of objectivation 'in itself' is *inherence*, and this applies to *all possible* spheres of objectivation 'in itself'. Inherence does not mean identity. If in a traditional society mother and daughter discuss the dinner they are going to prepare, they observe certain customs (by the simple fact of preparing the meal for the male members of the family), they use ordinary language (in discussing the matter, referring to the ingredients as 'salt' or 'beef'), and adapt to the rules of technology when using man-made objects (stove, knife, forks and the like). Each of these, of course, is not reducible to the other. Discussing the dinner, for instance, is not identical with cooking it well.

The second constant element of every sphere of objectivation 'in itself' has also been mentioned; that its 'norms-and-rules' are normally taken for granted. This simple fact has several connotations, one being that acting according to the 'norms-and-rules' of the sphere of objectivation 'in itself' *never calls for explanation*, whether causal or motivational. This can be formulated the other way round: if one acts according to the 'norms-and-rules' of the sphere of objectivation 'in itself', one's action is completely transparent to all members of that same social environment. This is precisely why it is so difficult to translate these 'norms-and-rules' into the language of a different culture. It is hard to explain to aliens patterns of actions which would otherwise not require explanation at all. Further, the 'norms-and-rules' of the sphere of objectivation 'in itself' are not reflected upon. We can think *in conjunction* with something we do within the sphere of objectivation 'in itself' but within this sphere we do not think *about* something we do. Eventually, we can even be completely unaware of *doing* something (within this sphere). We can thus observe various 'norms-and-rules' of the sphere of objectivation in itself, simultaneously thinking on conjunction with some, but not with others.

Much has been said about the indexicality of language in contemporary social discourse. I believe that the motion of 'indexicality' can be applied to the sphere of objectivation 'in itself' in two different, if related, contexts. First, all three constituents of the sphere of objectivation 'in itself' are 'indexical', in so far as they point at each other. Secondly, all 'norms-and-rules' of the sphere of objectivation 'in itself' function more or less as *Wegweiser* (Wittgenstein) for everyday action and thinking.

The indexicality of ordinary speech acts is the manifestation of the inherence of the sphere of objectivation 'in itself'. Speech acts are situated in the use of man-made objects and in following customs. But man-made objects indicate customs as well. If they did not, it would be absurd even to try what archaeologists normally do, namely to reconstruct at least *some* of the customs of an extinct culture from the available man-made objects they leave. If I say 'goodbye' to someone, it is not only my speech-act that is situated in my intention to leave; my intention to leave is situated in my saying 'goodbye' as well, since, in keeping with custom, I cannot leave unless I say so. All three constituents of the sphere of objectivation 'in itself' signalize their use *in interconnection with the other two*. Using one constituent *in isolation* means that *the action is no longer taken for granted*, but has to be accounted for. Should someone leave without saying 'goodbye', the action calls for an explanation ('Was he angry?' 'Was he offended?' 'Was he simply rude?'). The proper use of a kitchen knife is cutting food. 'What do you do with this kitchen knife?' is a relevant question only if the kitchen knife is used in a 'non-customary' way.

EVERYDAY LIFE AND RATIONALITY

At the same time, all 'norms-and-rules' of the sphere of objectivation 'in itself' function like an 'index' for everyday human behaviour, thinking and action. They indicate the direction, the basic contents and the 'limits' of proper actions and speech acts within a given life-world. The adequate appropriation of the sphere of objectivation 'in itself' means that one is familiar with the 'road signs' (one can 'read' them) and one follows the direction indicated by them. Since road signs only indicate the proper direction and do not define the particular character of each action completely, there is always a 'playground' for different, if similar, actions (speech acts included), all of which more or less meet the requirements set by the 'norms-and-rules' of the sphere of objectivation 'in itself'. The width of this 'playground' depends on the looseness or tightness (degree of regulation) of the 'norms-and-rules' of the sphere of objectivation 'in itself', and while it can never be nil, this width is always limited. The limit of such a playground can be called the 'critical limit' of the application of 'norms-and-rules'. Transcending these limits can be an act of madness (irrationality) or a criminal act, or can simply lead to certain 'catastrophes' of everyday life. The effects engendered are related either to the nature of the particular 'norms-and-rules' transgressed or to the concrete character of the act of transgression. (If I fail to maintain the man-made object called 'car' and miles from nowhere the car breaks down, it is a catastrophe of everyday life; if I drive into someone because of a similar failure, it is a criminal act; if I try to drive knowing that there is no petrol in my tank, I act irrationally.) Finally, transcending the 'critical limit' of any 'norms-and-rules' of the sphere of objectivation 'in itself' *might* also be the outcome (and indication) of a person's *direct* relationship to objectivations other than the ones within the sphere of objectivation 'in itself' within everyday life. To this problem I will return later.

All actions encompassed by the 'norms-and-rules' of the sphere of objectivation 'in itself' are shaped by the sphere of objectivation 'in itself', even if the 'norms-and-rules' are fairly loose. In my book *Everyday Life* I examined in detail all these action patterns – pragmatism, probability, overgeneralization, the use of typological images, analogy, the 'rude treatment' of singularity. As all these patterns derive from the static elements of the sphere of objectivation 'in itself' and from the appropriation of the 'norms-and-rules' of this sphere, they are also static. Without these action patterns there is no everyday life and thinking, and so no life and thinking at all. Even though in what follows I concentrate on the changing elements of everyday life, and in particular on the everyday life of the present, one should not disregard those constant elements representing our ineradicable ties with human histories, of which ours is but one.

The human person-as-a-whole

Everyday life is *not* a system. Apart from the fact that its backbone, the sphere of objectivation 'in itself', is not a system either, it entails more or less the direct cognitive or practical relation to other spheres of objectivation as well. But the statement that the sphere of objectivation 'it itself' does not constitute a system needs further elaboration.

The sphere of objectivation 'in itself' guides humans in *all types* of action, understanding and belief. There are absolutely no 'systemic' connections between taking a train, saying a prayer, dressing, making love, gardening, taking a drug, etc. These heterogeneous activities have only one thing in common, that they are guided by the sphere of objectivation 'in itself'. Precisely because of the heterogeneity of this sphere, all of its 'norms-and-rules' have to be equally taken as granted. Accordingly none of them should be used as an *explanatory* device for the justification of any other. (You cannot justify taking a train by explaining why you took a drug.) This is why even the legitimating world-views do not need to be logically consistent systems of beliefs in this sphere. Occasionally, *different* world-views can be offered by the same system of objectivation 'in itself' without hampering the 'taken-for-grantedness' of heterogeneous activities. (For instance, if the wife of X becomes sick, he can send immediately for an ambulance *and* go to church to pray for her recovery.)

Everyday life is not a system, but it is not an institution either. However, there is one institution which has been and remains the institution *par excellence* of everyday life: the family. In all its various historical forms the family is the main agent of the 'melting pot' of spheres of objectivation 'in itself', in so far as it performs the task of developing the competence in following 'norms-and-rules' required by every member of a society in the process of 'growing-up'. The emergence of the institution of 'family' is coeval with the emergence of the sphere of objectivation 'in itself'. The obvious explanation of this is that sexual regulation is the first social regulation. But the longevity of this institution cannot be accounted for by its genesis alone. I would ascribe the longevity of the family institution (though not wholly) to its natural propensity to counterbalance the accident of birth. What is socially 'accidental' is not biologically accidental. Family ties also being biological, this makes the social accident appear naturally determined. By being the biological offspring of parents (and ancestors), by being tied biologically to relatives (and the ancestors of these relatives), one is already defined as a member of the culture one is born into (by accident). Despite the loosening of organic ties in modernity, they are still present, and play a decisive role in *national* identity.

Apart from the family, the core institution of everyday life, those other institutions in the framework of which we must learn to act and think in everyday life are highly heterogeneous. It will suffice at present to emphasize that no matter how many institutions participate in making us comply with the 'norms-and-rules' of the sphere of objectivation 'in itself' (church, school, to mention only two important ones), the appropriation of the 'norms-and-rules' of this sphere does not take place exclusively through institutions. However, it is equally important that the 'know-what' and 'know-how' presented in institutions of everyday life is the 'know-what' and 'know-how' *for* the appropriation of the 'norms-and-rules' of the particular sphere of objectivation 'in itself', and *not* for the appropriation of the 'norms-and-rules' of institutions. The everyday churchgoer is not informed about theology and will not learn to 'move' within the institution of the church. Elementary school became obligatory, and thus part and parcel of everyday life, because writing, reading and counting were supposed to belong to the 'norms-and-rules' of the sphere of objectivation 'in itself'. (No one could become a proper 'grown-up' without the appropriation of these skills.) These institutions further contribute to the stabilization of knowledge about a meaningful world-view, and to the legitimation of the 'norms-and-rules' the person has to appropriate as a way of life. Schools can offer the meaningful world-view 'religion' and/or the other meaningful world-view 'science'. But even now, education is only obligatory so far as the meaningful world-view 'science' is concerned. Education immediately becomes *optional* when it comes to *sciences*. If someone learns by singing folk-songs it is not the institution 'art' that has been mediated; if someone learns by recognizing the constellations in the night sky, it is not the institution 'science' which has been mediated. More will be said about this in the next chapter.

It was Georg Lukács who first pointed out that the acting, thinking and feeling subject of everyday life is the *human being-*

as-a-whole, in contrast to 'human wholeness', the subject of higher objectivations. Given that everyday life is heterogeneous, one can only be competent in it if one develops at least to some degree the most heterogeneous human propensities and abilities. Abilities like manipulation, discussion, self-control, discrimination, love, sensitivity, decision-making and so forth have to be equally and simultaneously developed in order to cope with all the 'norms-and-rules' of the sphere of objectivation 'in itself', let alone the practical and/or theoretical reception of other objectivations. Here we return to the assumption that the sphere of objectivation 'in itself' is the foundation of all other objectivations, as well as of the cultural surplus of subjective experience. There are absolutely *no types* of abilities which one would not acquire, at least *in nuce*, through the appropriation of the sphere of objectivation 'in itself', via the twofold process of objectivation/subjectivation. Everyday life provides humans with all their propensities, on the basis of which everyday life itself *can be transcended* (by developing some of these propensities in preference to others).

Cognitive surplus, cultural surplus

Observing the 'norms-and-rules' of the sphere of objectivation 'in itself', like following road signs, requires three distinct types of thinking, all three embedded in, or related to, actions. These are inventive, repetitive and intuitive thinking. Should the everyday subject have direct access to objectivation spheres other than the sphere 'in itself', these three types are by no means necessarily embedded in, or related to, actions. But since everyday performances are mostly actions, and most actions are related to the sphere of objectivation 'in itself', even the briefest analysis of everyday thinking must begin with the *how* of the observance of the 'norms-and-rules' of the sphere of objectivation 'in itself'.

For the sake of the non-professional reader I should add that the category of *reason* and the category of *thinking alias* cognition (perception included) are *not* identical. Reason is a philosophical category, an evaluated one, and 'what reason really is' is defined departing from the definition of truth of respective philosophies. On the other hand, the category of thinking is empirical and value-free, and terming it 'cognition' in no way alters its status. Of course, one *could* identify one type of thinking with reason (for instance, problem-solving) and *evaluate* it accordingly. Even so, I will be arguing here directly against such an identification. It will be recalled that by reason (*ratio*) I mean the faculty of discriminating between good and bad (good and evil, sacred and profane, true and false, useful and harmful, and the like), and by practical reason the faculty of discriminating according to the hierarchy of the categories of value-orientation (with good coming first). Undoubtedly, this faculty presupposes cognition (including perception), even if it is *not identical* with it. Let me briefly illustrate. If someone stops at a red light, he or she acts according to reason, in other words, rationally. However, on the one hand, acting irrationally in this respect, that is to say, not stopping at the red light, equally involves cognition; on the other hand, the act of discriminating between red and green has nothing to do with discriminating between good and bad. Rationality does not necessarily imply good thinking (making a mistake in a mathematical equation does not imply irrational thinking). Similarly, there are cases to which no rule or norm applies, and there are various options none of which infringe any 'rules-and-norms' (for instance, whether or not we should put our overcoat on). One could dismiss all this by arguing that in keeping with the roles of language (and logic) one in fact inevitably acts according to rules (that is, rationally) in each of the above cases, and accordingly that no other rules (or norms) have to be presupposed to understand what reason is all about. However, language itself disproves this claim merely in distinguishing between good and bad. That language has rules is a very late discovery. But that language *has to be used according to rules other than the grammatical rules of language* is empirically universal knowledge. The same criticism applies to the Habermasian version of speech-act theory. If every speech-act raises claims to truth, rightness and authenticity, then *what* is true, right, and, for that matter, authentic, must be presented by the sphere of objectivation 'in itself', of which language is only *one* constituent. That good thinking is not perforce in harmony with *practical reason* is therefore a far more acceptable proposition. One can solve the problem of destroying humankind with good (logically correct) thinking, that is to say, one can use cognition in the service of an effect which can only be seen as absolute irrationality. In this regard the notion of 'instrumental reason' only serves to blur irreducible differences separating the categories of thinking and reason. Whether *instrumental thinking* can legitimately be called instrumental *reason* is a problem to which I will return.

Having made this detour, I return to the brief analysis of the three types of thinking through which the sphere of objectivation 'in itself' is appropriated. Given that this sphere consists of several 'norms-and-rules', albeit heterogeneous ones, to learn 'how to think' is, both philogenetically and ontogenetically, a process which takes place 'according to reason'.

Inventive thinking (and action) and intuitive thinking (and action) are both future-oriented and past-oriented, that is to say, *teleological* and *reconstructive*. The third type of thinking (action), the repetitive, is present-oriented (though it involves aspects of both future – and past – orientation).

The sphere of objectivation 'in itself' is embodied in and mediated by the adult population of a given life-world. Since 'becoming a grown-up' *means* accomplishing the appropriation of 'norms-and-rules' of the objectivation 'in itself', embodied and mediated by a preceding adult generation, this statement is self-evident: 'Collective consciousness' is the shared knowledge of these 'norms-and-rules'.

Collective consciousness is the consciousness of the *repeatable*; moreover, it *is* the repeatable. The 'norms-and-rules' of the sphere of objectivation 'in itself' are 'norms-and-rules' precisely because they have been repeatedly observed, they can be repeatedly observed and they should be repeatedly observed. And everyday action or thinking appropriating the sphere of objectivation 'in itself' can be called 'repetitive' in so far as it keeps alive and reproduces a sphere which *embodies* repetition. But this kind of repetition (reproduction of the sphere of 'what has been repeated') encompasses not only repetitive thinking (action) proper, but also inventive thinking (action) and intuitive thinking (action).

Inventive thinking (action) is, first and foremost, *problem-solving*. There are three levels of problem-solving in everyday life. Without the first two, human life could not be reproduced under any circumstances, while without the third, it cannot be reproduced under specific circumstances.

The first level of inventive thinking (action) comprises the *learning process*. In order to appropriate the 'know-what' and the 'know-how' embodied in the sphere of objectivation 'in itself', humans have to *intend* to appropriate them. Even if the intention is *imposed* on the subject (by inflicting bodily pain or by bringing shame on a person), an internalized intention must be present: humans cannot be socialized by mere 'training'. Learning how to control one's body and mind, how to channel the demands of each into socially necessary action, is a process of inventive thinking (action). Even though the problem to be solved has already been solved by others, and presented as such, every new

'I' must personally solve it *again*, with and in respect of his/her body and mind. Due to the rapid transformation of the 'norms-and-rules' of the sphere of objectivation 'in itself' in modernity, adults have to relearn repeatedly. It takes no special effort to understand what this problem is all about. We are told how to use an elevator, which does not mean solving the problem of the use of an elevator in general, but we solve in fact *a* problem if *we* learn to use it. In such a simple case, goal and means are not distinct, but even if they become separated by inserting a further, mediated, goal between them (learn to brush your teeth *in order* to keep them healthy!), both *goals and means* are simultaneously induced by the sphere of objectivation 'in itself'.

The second level of inventive thinking is reached when the means appropriate to achieving a particular goal have to be selected or found by the actor himself. Given that 'norms-and-rules' provide a 'playground' for different, if similar, actions, the second type of inventive thinking is utilized all the time (for example, I have to and intend to disclose some bad news to another person, and I ruminate over the best, the least offensive, approach). In the case of an unforeseen event this particular level of inventive thinking becomes predominant (I have left my key at home – and how to open the door?). On the second level of inventive thinking the goals themselves are fixed by the sphere of objectivation 'in itself', and the means selected must not infringe its 'norms-and-rules' either. The third level of inventive thinking (action) within the framework of everyday life consists of *raising new problems*. Raising new problems might, though not always, imply the transcendence of the authority of the sphere of objectivation 'in itself' (still within everyday life). I will return to this problem shortly.

Repetitive thinking is quasi-instinctive. It is the *habitual* thinking (action) that we perform in everyday life *without deliberation*. In it, teleology (intention) is relegated to the background. The grammar of ordinary language is similarly relegated: we act according to its rules without necessarily knowing them. One must remember that because repetitive thinking (action) is thinking (action), it *is* teleological, even if this teleology is present only in the background. Indeed, whenever we are hindered in implementing an act of repetitive thinking (action), this teleology comes to our awareness. In short, without repetitive thinking (action) we would be unable to reproduce ourselves.

To appropriate 'norms-and-rules' of the sphere of objectivation 'in itself' is not an easy task, but it is always more or less accomplished. Yet to know the 'norms-and-rules', and to comply with them, specially according to their hierarchy, are two different aspects of the same process. Unless we allow this differentiation the sphere of objectivation 'in itself' could only consist of rules without normative power. One should not forget that humans are 'thrown' into a particular sphere of objectivation 'in itself', into the 'melting pot' of a collective consciousness, by accident of birth, and that all humans are born with a highly idiosyncratic bio-psychological endowment. 'Fitting into' the 'norms-and-rules' of the sphere of objectivation 'in itself' might mean pleasure for one and suffering for another. The normative elements of rules might be infringed because of the suffering they inflict, even if not for that reason alone. Suffering triggered by the appropriation of rules is counterbalanced by other suffering, primarily by suffering from shame in the case of failure to appropriate (see 'The Power of Shame'). In any societal environment, however, humans have the capacity to appropriate their sociocultural world at a level over and above that of the primary appropriation of the sphere of objectivation 'in itself'. They can produce a *cultural surplus* and a *cognitive surplus*. I have already mentioned that a 'cultural surplus' arises in personal *experience*. Even though the sphere of objectivation 'in itself' serves as the social *a priori* of all experience, the experience of each 'I' is unique. This personal experience cannot be adequately expressed in ordinary language, and eventually it cannot be translated into this language at all. But what is 'unspeakable' in terms of ordinary language can still be expressed in *another* language; in the 'language' of art, of the sacred, and the like. Personal experience, which is *subjective* within the sphere of objectivation 'in itself', can be *objectified* and eventually becomes *intersubjective* if absorbed into the sphere of objectivation 'in itself'. This is why the subjective surplus can be legitimately called a 'cultural surplus'.

'Cognitive surplus' (or surplus knowledge) has a quite different origin. This surplus can be produced not only in everyday life, but also in and by various institutions already disconnected from the sphere of objectivation 'in itself'. Still, to simplify my task I am going to illustrate the way in which a cognitive surplus is created in a society (tribe or clan) *prior* to the separation of the sphere of institutions from everyday life, or in one having only a low degree of separation.

A 'collective consciousness' entails and mediates an amount of cumulated knowledge sufficient for the unobstructed reproduction of a particular way of life. Individual knowledge (of 'know-what' and 'know-how') cannot surpass the knowledge presented and mediated by the sphere of objectivation 'in itself'. But the aggregate of the knowledge of individuals can and often does surpass the knowledge embodied in the 'norms-and-rules' of this sphere. In the case of an unobstructed social reproduction, a cognitive surplus can only find expression in the 'enrichment' of existing 'norms-and-rules', even if occasionally it might be put to use in the sphere of objectivation 'for itself'; for instance, in sacred ceremonies. If, however, social reproduction is impeded, the 'cognitive surplus' can be put to use in a manner bringing about *substantive changes* in the 'norms-and-rules' of the sphere of objectivation 'in itself'. There is no reason to assume that the amount of cultural surplus created in a life-world, and the amount of cognitive surplus created in the same life-world, are proportional. There is even less reason to assume that the amount of cultural surplus and the amount of cognitive surplus created in a society as a whole are proportional. Today, for instance, the amount of cognitive surplus is immense. Even if only a small part of it is put to use in everyday life, this will suffice to alter the content of the 'norms-and-rules' of the sphere of objectivation 'in itself' very rapidly. On the other hand, the amount of cultural surplus created has considerably shrunk, at least relatively, if not absolutely.

Everyday life, and its backbone, the sphere of objectivation 'in itself', is the territory of both freedom and bondage. The relative proportions of each may vary, but both must be present. Bondage alone would mean no alternatives, no possibility for inventive and intuitive thinking (action), no 'playground' for similar actions, no evil, with its inevitable counterpart of good, no cultural or cognitive surplus; in other words, no human life. Freedom alone would mean no learning processes, and, even taking the adult population alone, would mean no repeatability, no stability, no 'taken-for-grantedness', no norms, no rules, no good, with its counterpart of evil; in other words, no human life also. As these alternatives are merely speculative, we must turn to those possibilities which more genuinely approximate tendencies pointing in one or the other direction. It is legitimate to assume that certain ancient cultures broke down because they failed to maintain a proper balance between 'freedom' and 'bondage'. Should the sphere of objectivation 'in itself' become ossified, should it reduce subjects to mere automatons, no cognitive surplus can be created, and this culture would then be vulnerable to unforeseen events (changes in the natural environment, enemies of a new type and the like).

Alternatively, the other extreme may eventuate from either exogenous or endogenous causes. The former situation (that is, the one which is not due to the organic development of the culture in question) would arise where, for instance, an adult population, the bearer and mediator of the 'norms-and-rules' of the sphere of objectivation 'in itself', is destroyed in great number (by war, by mass enslavement, or by plague). The latter, on the other hand, would arise with a simultaneous loosening of the strictest 'norms-and-rules' of the sphere of objectivation 'in itself' and the weakening of the legitimizing meaningful world-view (even to the point of complete loss of stability). This is the phenomenon to which ancient historians referred as 'old age', the senility of a culture preceding its near or total extinction. Obviously, the patterns of everyday life have become increasingly unstable in the modern Western world, although this lack of stability is balanced to some degree by the (relative) stability of institutions, and by the situation where science has succeeded in becoming the legitimating and meaningful world-view. On the other hand, relatively stable institutions and the legitimating world-view (science) not only counterbalance the increasing instability of the life-world, but they also contribute to this instability via a process termed by Habermas 'the colonization of life-world'. Discovering the symptoms of 'senility' in our culture, however, does not imply any prediction of its extinction: indeed, the immense cognitive surplus created in this culture *can* be utilized to establish a proper balance between freedom and bondage, with the balance overwhelmingly in favour of freedom.

Rationality of reason

The expression 'rationality of reason' sounds odd. Moreover, at first glance it seems tautological. In terms of my initial definition of rationality, rationality *means* 'acting according to reason'. This definition was of a preliminary nature and thus open to further qualifications. In order to clarify the meaning, and justify the introduction, of the construct 'rationality of reason', I need to distinguish at this point between *two attitudes* of reason. Reason has been defined as the faculty of discriminating between good and bad (good and evil, sacred and profane, true and false, useful and harmful and the like), the practical reason as the same faculty of discriminating according to the hierarchy of the categories of value-orientation (with good coming first). But the faculty of discrimination can be applied in two different ways. Reason can discriminate according to the 'norms-and-rules' of any particular societal environment by taking the 'norms-and-rules' themselves for granted. On the other hand, reason can discriminate according to one norm (or a few norms) by which all 'norms-and-rules' of the societal environment can then be questioned and tested. Clearly, any 'norms-and-rules' tested and questioned can no longer be taken for granted and the mere fact of their existence or their being observed will not suffice to establish their *validity*. From the vantage point of this latter attitude of reason, only those norms validated by reason can be accepted as 'true'; that is, they have to be *proven* to be good and true. I refer to this latter attitude of reason as 'intellect'. The choice of 'intellect' is arbitrary, although it is informed by certain philosophical traditions in which 'intellect' is viewed as a faculty higher than *ratio*. Even if what I have in mind is not two distinct faculties, but two attitudes of the same faculty, these traditions provide a firm basis for such a categorial distinction. It should be further remembered that the employment of reason as intellect *means rationalism*. I could thus have termed 'acting according to reason' rationality, and 'acting according to intellect' rationalism. I have *not* done so because in modern discourses the notion 'rationality' normally stands for 'rationalism'. What I wish to emphasize by employing the term 'rationality' *both* in the case of 'acting according to reason' and in that of 'acting according to intellect', is rather that the notion 'rationality' applies in the former case *no less* than in the latter. I will return to this distinction and *analyse it* in depth. For now, let me point out that by rationality of reason I mean the *competence* to observe the 'norms-and-rules' of the sphere of objectivation 'in itself', and the *competence* to observe the 'norms-and-rules' of any other objectivations *as if they were* the 'norms-and-rules' of the sphere of objectivation 'in itself'.

Rationality of reason (acting according to reason as *ratio*) involves learning how to perform repetitive actions (via teleological positing and self-control), exploring the 'playground' for the application of 'norms-and-rules', the propensity of choosing the proper means to goals (both in human interaction and in the use of objects), replacing one means by another (a functionally equivalent one if necessary), giving reasons for one's actions both prospectively and retrospectively, deliberating in a logically consistent way, making true statements and revoking others if they have been proved to be false, passing judgments and revoking others if they have been proved to be wrong, recalling and interpreting past inventive and intuitive actions, and constructing

EVERYDAY LIFE AND RATIONALITY

thereby in all of this a personal *identity*. I have not included intuitive thinking (action) among the principal expressions of performances of rationality of reason because here no 'norm-and-rule' applies. However, intuition is not pre-rational but post-rational: one cannot have intuition without a previous competence in observing 'norms-and-rules' of exactly the same level on which intuition 'occurs'. Moreover, reinterpretation and recollection of intuition is a performance within the range of rationality of reason. Intuition is 'good' if it can be *retrospectively* fitted into the framework of observing a 'norm-and-rule'. Neither have I included the act of 'raising new problems' in the performances of rationality of reason. One can acquire competence in observing the 'norms-and-rules' of the sphere of objectivation 'in itself' *without* raising new problems at all. Yet 'raising new problems' can belong to the performance of rationality of reason if the new problems are raised in, and engendered by, the sphere of objectivation 'in itself', or in any other sphere, the 'norms-and-rules' of which are observed as if they were the 'norms-and-rules' of the sphere of objectivation 'in itself' (that is, as if they were taken for granted). As long as the cognitive surplus is not used as a body of knowledge in which the truth-claim and the validity-claim of the 'norms-and-rules' should be tested, the production of cognitive surplus is still the performance of rationality of reason. Moreover, should the cognitive surplus engendered by the sphere of objectivation 'in itself' be used for testing the 'norms-and-rules' of this sphere, it would cease to be a 'surplus'.

Rationality of reason is the all-embracing form of rationality. Firstly, it is a 'cultural constant'. There is no societal life without 'rationality of reason', whereas 'rationality of intellect' is rather exceptional if one considers the number of human societies in which it actually operates. Secondly, rationality of intellect presupposes rationality of reason in *every* society.

To be competent in the 'norms-and-rules' of the sphere of objectivation 'in itself' *means* to be human. It follows that the motto of the Enlightenment, 'every human being is born with reason', is a statement of fact. Of course, this fact lends itself to many possible interpretations. In my interpretation the motto means that every human being is preprogrammed by an already socialized nature *for* the appropriation of a sphere of objectivation 'in itself', *for* the competence in following 'norms-and-rules'. It means, and this amounts to the same thing, that all adult human beings in all human cultures think and act rationally. They can think and act irrationally (which they do time and again) only because they are competent in following 'norms-and-rules', that is, only because they are rational.

But that which *is* rational from the standpoint of the rationality of reason is *not* necessarily rational from the standpoint of the rationality of intellect (and vice versa). *This is why the statement 'every human being is born with reason' does not contradict the statement that 'humans are irrational beings'.* The first refers to the rationality of reason from the viewpoint of the same rationality of reason, whilst the second statement is formulated from one possible perspective of the rationality of intellect. The notion of rationality alone does not refer to the same element of reason in the two statements, and its dual usage here illustrates the necessity to distinguish the two attitudes of reason.

III The sphere of objectivation 'for itself'

'absolute spirit' and 'objective spirit' reconsidered'

The sphere of objectivations 'for itself' consists of various types of objectivations, all of which have something in common, namely, the function of providing human life with *meaning*. More precisely, it is the function of providing human life with meaning that *defines* those objectivations belonging to the sphere 'for itself'. In terms of my hypothesis, the sphere of objectivation 'for itself' is a precondition for 'social life' to no less an extent than is the sphere of objectivation 'in itself'. (Since the publication of *Everyday Life*, I have changed my view on this problem.) This is so not only because it is invariably the sphere of objectivation 'for itself' which renders meaning to the heterogeneous 'norms-and-rules' of the sphere of objectivation 'in itself', and thus establishes their unity, but also because it is this sphere that absorbs the 'cultural surplus' of subjective experience. Durkheim made a strong case for the unifying function of the objectivation 'for itself' being exemplified in one type of objectivation 'in itself', that of religion. He argued that, as the symbol of ideal community, religion constitutes real community (which largely amounts to the same thing: the two merge into one form of collective consciousness). But he never gave any account of the other function of the objectivation 'for itself', that of absorbing the cultural surplus of subjective experience. Such experience was regarded by Durkheim as a mere epiphenomenon. My argument differs from this in that I attribute empirical universality to the sphere of objectivation 'for itself' on the grounds of *both* functions.

The empirical universality of the sphere of objectivation 'for itself' is stressed here to highlight its contrast with the empirical particularity of the sphere of objectivation 'for and in itself'. The latter consists of various *institutions* (economic, political, cultural and the like) creating together the *identity of a particular social structure*. In societies where the sphere of objectivation 'in itself' confronts everyone with *the same* 'norms-and-rules' (apart from the sociobiological division of labour between the sexes and age groups), this sphere *is identical* with the social structure. However, when the sphere of objectivation 'in itself' becomes diversified due to the social division of labour, and when people must appropriate different 'norms-and-rules' according to their position in this division of labour, no single sphere of objectivation 'in itself' can function as the repository of structural identity. Any reconstruction of human histories will show that the 'differentiation' of various institutions entailed the institutionalization of domination. The social structures whose identity was established by the sphere of objectivation 'for and in itself' were structures of domination, in contrast to preceding structures whose identity was established by both the sphere of objectivation 'in itself' and meaningful world-views. But historical trends cannot be equated with sequences of logical necessity. There is no reason for excluding the logical possibility of a society characterized by a broad sphere of objectivation 'for and in itself' which does not institutionalize domination. But in this case the content of the 'norms-and-rules' of various spheres of objectivation cannot be constituted according to the social division of labour. This is another problem to which I shall return.

Whilst I rely heavily on Hegel's categories of 'objective spirit' and 'absolute spirit' – the distinction between them is, to my view, a particularly important one – very little else of Hegel remains in my conception of rationality. The triad of objectivations offered so far differs substantially from the Hegelian one (subjective spirit, objective spirit, absolute spirit) because the sphere of objectivation 'in itself' is *not* identical with 'subjective spirit', even though its appropriation is the precondition for the emergence of subjectivity. Further, I do not accept Hegel's notion of 'world-spirit', or any of its substitutes (see *A Theory of History*). To clarify my own conception I will give a more detailed exposition of the two (higher) spheres of objectivations.

The objectivations 'for itself'

Objectivations 'for itself', which all provide human life with meaning, are: religions, sciences, arts and philosophy. Two elements of this statement call for explanation. Firstly, the qualifying phrase '. . . provide human *life* with meaning' is not synonymous with '. . . provide humans with meaning'. All 'norms-and-rules' of the sphere of objectivation 'in itself' provide humans with meaning, but the unity of this heterogeneous sphere is established and secured by meaningful world-views, and whether human life is provided with meaning hinges on the interpretative and explanatory power of a particular world-view. Naturally, the sphere of objectivation 'in itself' is normally appropriated together with its unifying and meaningful world-view. Viewed from the perspective, the distinction between the sphere of objectivation 'in itself' and the sphere of objectivations 'for itself' seems to be very problematic. Nonetheless, to take recourse to a previous argument, the *whole* content of the sphere of objectivation 'for itself' is not mediated by the sphere of objectivation 'in itself', not even in small and lightly stratified communities. The more stratified and complex a society becomes the greater is the gap between the contents of the sphere of objectivation 'for itself' and the proportion of content mediated by every particular sphere of objectivation 'in itself'. This gap increases if *various* objectivations 'for itself' are ready to provide human life with *different* meaning, even if they reinforce one another, and even more if they implicitly or explicitly compete with one another. This competition may eventually lead to the loss of unifying meaning mediated by the sphere of objectivation 'in itself', and/or to an increase in individual freedom, to the emergence of rationality of intellect.

The second element of the introductory statement calling for explanation is the use of the *plural* in the case of three types of objectivations 'in itself' (religions, sciences, arts), and of the *singular* in the case of philosophy. Religion, Science, Art (capitalized and in the singular)* are categories which first surfaced in the high Renaissance, though various forms of these objectivations 'for itself' can be traced back to all human histories. The notion of 'philosophy' (in the singular) was invented in ancient Athens,

---

* In the case of sciences, arts and religions the use of the singular was introduced from different perspectives and for different reasons, and these disciplines embraced different phenomena. However, the use of the singular signalized, in all three forms of expression, the tendency to universalization. On this, see my *Renaissance Man* (Routledge and Kegan Paul, 1980).

and the type of objectivation it refers to was created and invented together with the label (it has no predecessors in earlier human histories). I have already hinted at the significance of this difference and I will return to the problem.

Even if the various objectivations 'for itself' can be almost undifferentiated, they never are *completely*: We know of no human society in which each dance and song had a ritual-religious message, nor do we know of one in which every kind of theoretical attitude to cumulated knowledge (and the excellence in it) would have been explained by superhuman forces within the framework of inherited mythological-religious belief. *All* churches were *equally* institutions of religious devotion in the Middle Ages. Nevertheless, ecclesiastic or lay authorities would hardly have gone to the lengths they did to retain the services of the most famous master builders, had they considered all buildings to be of equal aesthetic value. I cannot analyse here historical details, important as they are in understanding the development of culture. I can only analyse the different types of objectivations 'for itself' in their pure form.

The *common* characteristic features of the objectivations 'for itself' are the following:

(a) They all provide human life with meaning. No further elaboration of this statement is needed because of its tautological character: this was the definition of the sphere of objectivation 'for itself'.

(b) They can all fulfil two vital social functions, not only alternatively, but also simultaneously. One is the legitimation of social structure (legitimation of the sphere of objectivation 'for itself' included). The second is just the reverse; the '*desubstantialization*' of (denying substance from) the sphere of objectivation 'in itself' (and eventually whole social structures) from the standpoint of a 'higher order'. This is a *critical* function, even if the criticism is not necessarily explicit.

(c) All particular objectivations within the sphere of objectivation 'for itself' are *homogeneous*. Certainly, this homogeneity would sometimes be only relative (as compared to the heterogeneity of the sphere of objectivation 'in itself'), but it is a major characteristic of the *ideal type* of an objectivation 'for itself'. Homogeneity functions on two levels. The first refers to a particular objectivation 'for itself' (the religion, the architecture, the philosophy of a historical period). All actions within a particular sphere of objectivation 'for itself' become meaningful (within this sphere) by being connected with all other actions (again within this sphere). While taking a bus is a meaningful action independently of paying a visit to a friend, going to school, or making a tour, taking holy communion is a meaningful action only in its interrelation with the whole body of belief of Christianity. Within the sphere of the 'sacred' a language different to that prevailing within the 'profane' is spoken, and systems of symbols operate within the context of the 'sacred' which are interrelated. The same applies to 'poetry'. At the second level, homogeneity refers to one single action performed or a single work created in this sphere (*a* prayer, *a* novel, *a* philosophical work).

(d) All objectivations 'for itself' have their own 'norms-and-rules' (otherwise they could not be even relatively 'homogeneous'). These 'norms-and-rules' are *intrinsic* to each kind of objectivation 'for itself', and they are not interchangeable with the 'norms-and-rules' of *other* spheres of objectivations, nor with each other's 'norms-and-rules'.

It follows from (c) that all 'norms-and-rules' of these objectivations are homogeneous. Norms alone or rules alone do not comprise an objectivation 'for itself'. The momentary disconnection of norms and rules which is possible, as we have seen, within the sphere of objectivation 'in itself', is not possible at all in the sphere of objectivation 'for itself'. Of course, the 'norms-and-rules' of this sphere can be severed, and this is precisely what has occurred in modernity. But in so doing we do not move in this sphere of objectivation any longer. Techniques of this sphere of objectivation can be disconnected from its norms, and if this is done, one moves and acts within the sphere of objectivation 'for and in itself'. Contrariwise, norms can be disconnected from rules, and if this is done, one subscribes to values which are heterogeneous, open to several interpretations without offering concrete 'norms-and-rules' for their application. Certainly, if norms (values) have been abstracted from the sphere of objectivation 'for itself', they then have a great potential for both legitimation and criticism. No longer embedded in the homogeneous 'norms-and-rules' of sciences, religions, arts and philosophy, they function as *moral* values (and principles) for action. However, morality itself is not an objectivation (even if it has a few objectivations in the form of ethical virtues); it is not a sphere, but rather the relation of subjects to the normative content of all three spheres of objectivation where this relation is constituted and expressed by action (speech act included).

(e) Objectivations 'for itself' absorb and embody a cultural surplus and this 'occurrence' has various aspects. Some of them at least can be mentioned here:

(ea) They offer outlets for a subjective surplus because the individuals of a particular society can appropriate their homogeneous 'norms-and-rules' in addition to the heterogeneous 'norms-and-rules' of the sphere of objectivation 'in itself'.

(eb) They embody and express every mortal's desire for immortality. This desire, expressed in all myths, can be satisfied through the 'immortalization of mortals' (communities and individuals alike). The mind-soul-body triad is immortalized in trinities such as those found in stories which, however much they are modified, can never be totally changed, in gigantic symbols created from lasting materials (stone, precious metals), or through the 'fixation' of meanings, rites, stories and deeds (hieroglyphs, paintings, carvings). If myth is the sole expression of historicity, myth will be 'immortalized'. If, on the contrary, it is history, then history will be 'immortalized'. Spinoza's remark about philosophy, that it is created and valid *sub specie aeternitatis*, unveiled the secret of all types of objectivation 'in itself'. From this perspective it is of secondary importance whether present and eternity are conceptually distinguished or not. If they are, immortality is viewed as the survival of not only the individual but of the social body as well. Up until the present, where it has become one of the major tenets of modernity, the latter has been the exception in history rather than the rule.

(ec) It follows from (eb) that objectivations 'for itself' can survive the social structure which they 'immortalize'. They can do so because of their homogeneous composition. Homogeneous objectivations can be interpreted, and so understood in their own right, without any knowledge of the social structures they immortalize. Their meaning can be mediated (through reception/adoption) by actors of a later or different social structure on the basis of *their* life experiences. For this to happen a consciousness of history is required but 'immortalized' symbols contribute to the emergence of such a consciousness. It appears paradoxical that it is precisely the immortalized symbols of social structures that inflict the feeling (and consciousness) of transience. Germanicus standing before the ruins of the temple of Karnak was gripped by a gloomy premonition: if the empire creating this marvel had disappeared without trace, he ruminated, the same could happen to Rome.

(ed) The structure of those generations following ours will determine *which* immortalized body of meaning will be received by successive cultures. But it should be noted that the immortalized bodies of meaning appropriated by the members of these successive structures do not belong to these structures. This is why the 'present historical age' is always broader than the 'historical present'. (The first encompasses all meaningful objectivations 'for itself' available for reception-appropriation; the second the social structures and objectivations created in it: see *A Theory of History*.) The greater the difference in volume between them, the more the 'subjective surplus' can be absorbed via the reception of past and immortalized objectivations 'for itself'. Here we come to a second paradox. Objectivations 'for itself' which at the time of their 'immortalization' served as legitimating world-views, can have an immense *criticial potential* through reception. (This holds true not only for the arts, but very often also for religions, and in the most recent debates, for the sciences as well.)

How we learn 'moving' in the sphere of objectivations 'for itself': the 'human wholeness'

I reiterate that all objectivations 'for itself' have their own intrinsic and homogeneous 'norms-and-rules'. One must appropriate them to be capable of 'moving' within one of these homogeneous spheres. This process implies a degree of learning not less than that involved in appropriating the heterogeneous 'norms-and-rules' of the sphere of objectivations 'in itself'. Learning of the first type can occur in everyday life, even if it is not a precondition for the reproduction of adult life, yet it occurs in specialized institutions as well. The demarcation between everyday appropriation of 'norms-and-rules' of an objectivation 'for itself' and the specialized/institutionalized non-everyday appropriation of the same type can be very elastic or very strict. But elasticity between the everyday and the non-everyday does not imply that the demarcation between the sphere of objectivation 'in itself' and that of objectivation 'for itself' is also elastic. Even if the recital of a poem or hymn is an everyday action which everyone can perform, there is a strict demarcation between ordinary language and the language of this poem or hymn. Changes of voice, of modulation (singing, chanting), of rhythm, facial expression and gestures, belong to 'reciting a poem or hymn'. The language of prayer would be 'unnatural' for profane use. Painting a portrait is not identical with 'painting pure and simple', even if painting belongs to the activities of everyday life. In all cultures there are strict 'norms-and-rules' specifying what a 'painting' (a portrait or any other image) should look like, even in our age, where spontaneous self-expression is so highly valued. Irrespective of whether one is aware of it or not the appropriation of any objectivation 'for itself' does not imply learning in general, but rather a particular kind of learning – learning how 'to move' in a homogeneous medium.

Within the homogeneous spheres of objectivation 'for itself' things, events, and so on can be regarded as 'natural' even when they are clearly not so, in the body of knowledge presented by the sphere of objectivation 'in itself'. The hunter who recites with artistic ease the fairy tale of Little Red Riding Hood, giving details of the opening of the wolf's belly in order to free a devoured granny and girl, can make it sound perfectly natural, even though he would never entertain anything like that in 'real life', that is to say, within the sphere of objectivations 'in itself'. We move in three dimensions, but we paint in two. It is 'natural' that the iconic statue of a warrior is five times his real size although of course we do not expect warriors to attain such dimensions. This discrepancy in our knowledge (between the two spheres) is not only manifest in the 'know-what' but in the 'know-how'. Using holy objects in a lay manner is sacrilege.

Subjects (individuals or groups) ascend to the homogeneous medium of objectivation 'for itself' from the springboard of the sphere of objectivations 'in itself' in a manner which Lukács has described in detail in his *Aesthetics* (see also my *Everyday Life*). These subjects 'suspend' their heterogeneous everyday activities, concentrate all their faculties on one task, and 'surrender' thereby to the homogeneous 'norms-and-rules' of the particular objectivation 'for itself'. By so doing the human-as-a-whole (the subject 'moving' in the sphere of objectivation 'in itself') transforms himself into 'human wholeness' (the original German terms in Lukács are *der ganze Mensch – der Menschenganz*). All of the subject's mental, spiritual and manual abilities developed and practised in pursuing several distinct activities are thus unified, expressed and objectified in and through a homogeneous medium. This objectivation is simultaneously a new form of subjectivation:

the subject 'for itself' is born from the subject 'in itself'. But the subject 'for itself' thus created (self-created) must be retransformed into a subject 'in itself'. If this did not happen the subject could not survive. But the subject 'in itself' thus reborn can *differ* from the subject 'in itself' that existed prior to the experience, though this is not necessarily so. Put simply, if the 'subjective surplus' can be absorbed by the sphere of objectivation 'for itself', the nexus can be formulated the other way round as well: the sphere of objectivation 'for itself' reinforces the production of subjective (cultural) surplus.

I cannot deal here with the various *psychological* states (or techniques) which serve to accelerate the ascent to a particular objectivation 'for itself'; for instance, a trance, or 'blocking' sensual experiences other than those of the appropriated mediums (shutting our eyes when listening to music, silence, darkness, and the like). There are virtuosi of such techniques: Weber even speaks about religious virtuosi. More importantly, there is the fact, in itself perhaps not so astonishing, that even if the techniques are quite different, the characteristic features of the 'ascent' into one homogeneous medium of an objectivation 'for itself' are exactly *the same*. In scientific or philosophical discourse, we in fact suspend the heterogeneous activities (and types of knowledge) of the sphere of objectivation 'in itself' no less than in the case of the mystical experience or artistic creation or reception (and we concentrate all our human powers on one task and homogenize them thereby).

The relationship between intuitive, repetitive and inventive thinking (action) within the sphere of objectivations 'for itself' differs substantially from their interplay with the sphere of objectivation 'in itself'.

If objectivations 'for itself' are meaningful homogeneous objectivations (systems of implicit 'norms-and-rules'), they must embrace repetition. Apart from the virtual self-launching of a particular form of objectivation 'for itself', they exist precisely because they 'have been repeated'. One can write a poem because poetry exists (writing poems has been repeated), and so on. But no activity (or thinking) related to an objectivation 'for itself' can be *mere* repetition. The repetitive element always present, is enmeshed as *one factor* in the performance as a *whole* which, as such, is unrepeatable. Against this it can be argued that one never takes the same bus in exactly the same manner either. Yet it is important to understand that it would not matter if one did. Besides, I have mentioned already that the various repetitive elements embodied in and induced by the sphere of objectivation 'in itself' are not interrelated in any particular place or time, whereas those embodied in and induced by any particular objectivation 'for itself' are necessarily interrelated: they are repetitions within the same homogeneous medium. For example, if a repetitive element is modified, all other repetitive elements are to some degree modified as well (e.g. the use of new materials in sculpture).

One *learns* repetitive thinking (action) within the sphere of objectivations 'for itself' via inventive thinking (action), just as is done within the sphere of objectivation 'in itself'. But inventive thinking (action) cannot completely disappear in repetition. Also, the ratio between invention and repetition can alter markedly. For instance, in modern creative art inventive thinking (action) is preponderant, whereas prior to the clear distinction between arts and crafts repetitive action (thinking) predominated, though invention was never absent.

Intuitive thinking (action) is decisive in the process of both 'ascent' into and 'moving within' the sphere of objectivation 'for itself'. We may recall that the appropriation of 'norms-and-rules' in the sphere of objectivation 'in itself' is the precondition for good intuition in this sphere. We may also recall that we are capable of self-reproduction and of observing the 'norms-and-rules' of objectivation 'in itself' *without* intuition. But the same intuition resulting from the appropriation of the sphere of objectivation 'in itself' *can become* the starting point for our 'ascent' into a sphere of objectivation 'for itself'. This is called 'inspiration'. Intuition may come first both in creation and reception; it can also be exclusive. But if it is exclusive and not combined with repetition (repeatability) and invention, it remains a subjective experience and/or a gesture. This subjective experience or gesture (for example, mystical experience) can be embedded in the objectivation 'for itself' only if the subject of experience can insert his or her experience retrospectively into this sphere through repetitive and inventive thinking. (For instance, if the subject can at least circumscribe what is unspeakable.)

But even if the starting point of the 'ascent' into the sphere of objectivation 'for itself' is not intuition but inventive thinking (problem-solving or raising new problems) or repetitive action (psychological techniques), one cannot 'move' within this sphere without intuition. When we learn and practise 'moving' within any homogeneous medium we develop a 'secondary' intuition, one functioning *only* within this particular medium. Baudelaire's Albatross is the paradigm of this 'division of labour' of intuition; the sublime bird flying freely in one medium and inept and helpless in the other. That intuition is 'needed' in the sphere of objectivation 'for itself' is an understatement: it is intrinsic to this sphere, not something 'added' to it.

Fantasy, imagination and good judgment are combinations of inventive and intuitive thinking (action). But they must not run amok or go astray. They have to be checked, controlled and led by the 'norms-and-rules' of any particular objectivation 'for itself'. It should again be made clear that 'moving' within an objectivation 'for itself' *means* observing homogeneous 'norms-and-rules'. Without fantasy, imagination and good judgment they cannot be followed (nor, for that matter, could one eventually contribute to their change, as opposed to their mere 'variation'). But even if one creates a *new* type of objectivation 'for itself' (just as Aeschylus created tragedy), one still cannot do it without observing certain basic 'rules-and-norms' of a previous form of objectivation.

At this point we must distinguish between various types of objectivations within the sphere of objectivation 'for itself', though here I can only take into account their present forms. Three aspects of all objectivations 'for itself' have to be accounted for: (a) creation or re-creation (objectivation); (b) the objectified body of meaning; (c) appropriation (total or partial) and reception (total or partial) retrospectively. It does not depend on the 'norms-and-rules' of a particular objectivation 'for itself', whether inventive, repetitive or intuitive thinking plays the decisive role in the *creation* or *re-creation* of this objectivation. It may in fact depend on several factors, which are usually historical but sometimes individual in nature. There were times when, for instance, intuition played a far greater role in medicine than in musical performance. That today the converse is true, is due to the perfected 'technology' of diagnosis, on the one hand, and to the individualization of the musical performance, on the other. But whatever the proportions, all three types of thinking are present, even now, in the process of creation or re-creation of every type of objectivation 'for itself'. If they are not, it is an unmistakable sign that not the sphere of objectivation 'for itself', but the sphere of objectivation 'in itself' or – and this is also frequently the case – the sphere of objectivation 'for and in itself', has been created (for instance, not science but the institutional application of science).

If we examine the *objectified body of meaning*, we come to an entirely different conclusion. There are objectified bodies of meaning (first of all science, but most of philosophy as well) which must be 'purged' of intuitive thinking even if intuition has predominated in the process of creation (discovery). Intuitive thinking is post rational and thus has to be eliminated from the results of the discovery of all objectivations 'for itself' where rational verification is normative. If someone makes a new observation by intuition, it has to be controlled by repeated experiment. If someone has an intuitive insight into a new solution to a problem, the problem is not solved in fantasy or imagination. It is solved, and can be presented as such, only if the discovery can be logically deduced and all the steps of this deduction checked, repeated and controlled by all those who are competent in following the same 'norms-and-rules'. If a physician recounts all his good intuitions this will not yield a book on medicine, but rather the intellectual autobiography of a scholar. On the other hand, in art works intuition is not eliminated, but rather is made explicit. Even where a work of art is created with the lever of inventive thinking (for example, raising and solving problems such as which idea has to be expressed, which material has to be used and how, how to achieve the best effect, etc.), or even where the final version of the work is preceded by numerous 'experimental' versions, inventive thinking, at least in its pure form, has to disappear from the objectivation. The work of art needs to be 'purified' of the marks of 'problem-solving' to become what it should be. The art work has to be presented as a combination and unity of repetition and intuition. Inventive thinking is thus 'absorbed' by intuition (in imagination, fantasy and so on). Repetition stands for observing the 'norms-and-rules' of the genre in question; intuition stands for uniqueness, for the wholly non-repeatable. The complete reconstruction of this uniqueness is thus impossible (intuition is not rational), in contrast to the scientific discovery, where complete reconstruction is not only possible but mandatory. I cannot provide a detailed analysis of religion as an example in this context, because certain religions resemble art, certain others philosophy, and yet others science. It suffices here to refer to Max Weber's brilliant studies (with regard to philosophy, I have analysed the problem in *For a Radical Philosophy*).

The comprehensive appropriation (reception) of the objectivations 'for itself' confronts us with a series of combinations of the three types of thinking (action). As the objective of this study does not permit lengthy theoretical excursions of this kind, the discussions will be rather preliminary and sketchy.

The comprehensive appropriation (reception included) can be

total or partial (with regard to philosophy, I have analysed this problem as well in *For a Radical Philosophy*). Not even total reception or comprehensive appropriation requires a complete knowledge ('know-what' and 'know-how') about the whole sphere of objectivation 'for itself' in question. It simply means that the subject (or subjects) can move freely within the homogeneous medium of one type of objectivation 'for itself'. Total (comprehensive) appropriation (or reception) of an objectivation 'for itself' can never be made imperative by the sphere of objectivation 'in itself'. But since the heterogeneous activities of the sphere of objectivation 'in itself' must be unified by a meaningful world-view, and only objectivations 'for itself' provide human lives with meaning (the first constituent of the definition of the sphere of objectivation 'for itself'), the *partial* appropriation (or reception) of at least one of these objectivations is normally made imperative by the sphere of objectivation 'in itself'. If this were not so, life would not be given meaning: deviance, and finally the self-destruction of a way of life, would follow. And even those objectivations 'for itself', the partial appropriation (reception) of which is not made imperative by the sphere of objectivation 'for itself', can be, and in fact are, partially comprehended or appropriated within the different institutions inherent to the sphere of objectivations 'for and in itself'. If partial appropriation or reception of an objectivation 'for itself' is made imperative by the sphere of objectivation 'in itself', the relations of intuitive, inventive and repetitive thinking (action) to one another by the comprehension and reception of the sphere of objectivation 'for itself' is tantamount to their relation in the appropriation and application of the 'norms-and-rules' of the sphere of objectivication in itself in general (see section II). If partial appropriation or reception of an objectivation 'for itself' becomes constitutive in the sphere of objectivation 'for itself', then the relation of intuitive, inventive and repetitive thinking (action) will follow the particular pattern of the same relation in so far as it is adequate to the appropriation of any specific objectivation 'for and in itself'. (For instance, 'moving' within the institution of the 'market' requires a greater amount of good intuition than 'moving' within the institution of the 'supermarket'.)

Partial appropriation (or reception) can be individual as well. In other words, it can neither be rendered imperative by the sphere of objectivation 'in itself' nor institutionalized. This is a very important factor in everyday life, particularly in certain historical periods such as ours. I have already mentioned that in everyday life we may have *direct* access to knowledge and experience offered by higher objectivations which have not been mediated by the sphere of objectivation 'in itself'. Art and philosophy best qualify for this individual reception, whether it be total or partial. There is a constant oscillation between everyday life and objectivations 'for itself'. Moreover, a cluster of individuals, situated in similar 'life-worlds', in similar need-structures and with similar life-experiences, are very likely to 'recognize' their own problems in the same message embodied in objectivations 'for itself', provided they have access to them. Artistic taste (in a period where organic *sensus communis* has already disappeared) and public discussion (in the same period) derive from this continuous oscillation.

Re-acting, reception and understanding of the objectivations 'for itself'

Drawing up the typology of reception is a relatively simple task if one considers total reception alone. Important as it is, it is not possible to analyse partial reception on its own, though it can be comprehended from what follows.

Intuitive, inventive and repetitive thinking (action) can be largely thinking or largely acting. If it is largely action, then the distinction between the three aspects of our relation to the objectivations 'for itself' is a distinction *in nuce* (it is not explicit). In this case, repetition plus intuition *leads* invention; more precisely, inventive thinking (action) can never lead the other two. Since re-acting is creation and appropriation simultaneously, reception (or understanding) as a distinct stage does not appear. I am going to term this kind of creating–appropriating (re-acting) of an objectivation 'for itself' *magical*.

If the proportion of thinking and acting is different in the process of creation and of appropriation of any objectivation 'for itself', and the difference is apparent, the following ideal types can be distinguished:

(a) Action (as creation) is *objectivation* (carried out by repetition and imagination): appropriation of the created objects happens via 'doing something meaningful' with these objects. (This happens when a sculpture used in a religious ceremony is afterwards dumped as henceforth useless.) I term this kind of creation and appropriation of objectivation 'for itself' *magico-mystical*. If objects of magico-mystical creation and appropriation are eventually 'immortalized', they can become triggers of pure reception for another culture. (For example, the painting in ancient Egyptian tombs trigger pure reception in us.) In the case of pure reception, of course, the objects lose their magical aspect.

(b) Creative action is objectivation (unity of repetition and imagination), but thinking becomes preponderant as against action at the stage of appropriation (intuitive thinking, or, eventually, inventive thinking 'leads' imagination). Appropriation thereby becomes reception. This kind of creation and reception 'for itself' I term *mystical*.

(c) Creative action is objectivation, but *inventive* thinking leads in the act of creation and in reception as well. I term this kind of creation and appropriation 'for itself' *intellectual–mystical*.

(d) Creative action is objectivation of knowledge and not objectivation of collective or individual experience. Thinking is the action. Appropriation does not happen via reception. It is comprehensive understanding. The creation and appropriation of an objectivation 'in itself' of this kind I term *intellectual*.

Here a few additional explanatory remarks must be made. I have already mentioned that societies can reproduce themselves without a differentiation of the sphere of objectivations 'for and in itself', but they cannot do so without the sphere of objectivation 'for itself' (which absorbs and creates cultural and cognitive surplus). To what extent this sphere of objectivation 'for itself' is distinct from the sphere of objectivation 'in itself' is another question. In some societies one can easily move from one sphere to the other (switching from ordinary language to chanting ritual songs and hymns); in others the total reception of certain objectivations 'for itself' requires special 'cultural training', and in others a total comprehensive understanding requires a long specialized education (our society is a case in point). In certain societies only one type of objectivation 'for itself' renders meaning to the lives of all members, whilst in others more than one such objectivation competes for the 'souls' of its members, even if they do not compete on the same level and with equal success.

If the sphere of objectivation 'for itself' is not yet differentiated, it presents as one unity all the elements of magical, magico-mystical, mystical, intellectual–mystical and intellectual action, creation, reception and understanding. Only the differentiation within one type of objectivation plus the differentiation between various types of objectivation 'for itself', a process taking place in different ways and in various historical periods, brings about relative specialization in all types of creation and appropriation mentioned above according to the particular 'norms-and-rules' of particular objectivations 'for itself'. But to repeat: this differentiation is always relative, even though the degree of 'relativity' is greater in certain objectivations 'for itself' than in others. This can be clearly exemplified in the arts, if we take into consideration only the historical period in which the notion of 'Art' has already been invented. A ceremonial peasant dance (for instance, at a wedding) is magical in character, rock music is magico-mystical, the 'peak experience' of the reception of a painting by Rembrandt or of listening to a Mozart concerto is purely mystical, reading *Ulysses* is intellectual–mystical (one cannot attain reception without a certain degree of intellectual understanding). Only pure comprehensive understanding is excluded from the total appropriation of the homogeneous medium of any work (or act) of art. The natural sciences are less elastic, at least since they became, in the process of 'intellectualization', a separate objectivation 'for itself', distinct from religion and philosophy. (I refer the reader to Weber in this respect.) Present-day science is a purely intellectual objectivation. But our relation to science has not completely lost its 'mystical' element: the expression 'the miracles of science' is not merely a figure of speech. And if one considers the popularity of astrology or parapsychology, one may add that the need for a magico-mystical reception of science has not died out completely, even if the satisfaction of this need has become marginalized. However, far more important in this respect is that simultaneously with the intellectualization and growing independence of modern natural sciences, a secular and mystical human relation to nature has developed. The emphatic relation to nature (a purely mystical experience) has become private. It is only art which expresses and reinforces this mystical experience which does not belong to art (or any of the arts). For Kant, the 'starlit sky' was still one of the two major miracles of life, and the 'starlit sky' is not simply a problem for the natural sciences to 'solve' – it is also the symbol of nature as the object of mystical experience. To sum up: the loss of 'elasticity' in the modern natural sciences has, in the main, been a substantial gain, creating a free zone for an entirely subjective (and mystical) experience. It is subjective because it does not imply the 'ascent' to any particular objectivation 'for itself' (the experience of the 'starlit sky' is not a religious experience if it is not embedded in a religious world-view; it is not a scientific understanding, it is not the reception of art or the reception of philosophy). There is only one other experience similar to it: self-surrender to the beloved.

And so all objectivations 'for itself' provide human lives with meaning (this is part of their definition). All of them are open to partial reception (and understanding) and to total reception (understanding). Partial reception (understanding) of at least one objectivation 'for itself' is normally made imperative by the sphere of objectivation 'in itself'. Partial reception (and understanding) of all objectivations 'for itself' can occur within everyday life (including the reception of objectivations 'for itself' which are not embedded in and mediated by the sphere of objectivation 'in itself'). As far as total reception is concerned, it may be (a) a non-everyday occurrence embedded in everyday life; (b) a non-everyday occurrence, the accomplishment of which requires everyday knowledge together *with both* experience and subjective surplus; (c) a non-everyday occurrence, the accomplishment of which requires cultural training or additional knowledge but not specialization; (d) a non-everyday occurrence the accomplishment of which requires specialization, a kind of knowledge accessible only to a few; and (e) the same type of knowledge as required by one's profession, and part of everyday life in this capacity.

It stands to reason that the types of objectivations 'for itself' which can be received (understood) totally according to points (a) and (b) can never become institutionalized as legitimating world-views of domination, and that the types of objectivation 'for itself' which can be appropriated (understood) totally according to point (c) do not qualify for the function of a 'dominating world-view' (only as an accessory legitimating world-view of institutions). As a result, only objectivations 'for itself' characterized in point (d) can be institutionalized as dominating world-views, and only two kinds of objectivation 'for itself' qualify for this function: *religion* and *science*.

In all this I do not mean that religion and science cannot but legitimate domination. All objectivations 'for itself' have both a legitimating and a critical function, and this holds true for religion and science too. I mean that they, and only they, qualify for the institutionalization of legitimation, because they alone qualify for the institutionalization of cumulative knowledge.

IV The sphere of objectivation 'for and in itself'

Institutions and social structure

I tried to show in section II that the sphere of objectivation 'in itself' is not an institution, even if it includes an institution, that of the family. By contrast, the sphere of objectivations 'for and in itself' consists wholly of institutions. All these institutions are characterized by a relatively homogeneous system of 'norms-and-rules'. But the seemingly contradictory notion of relative homogeneity calls for explanation.

Institutions are subsystems of the social structure. More correctly, I would define social structure as the conglomerate of such subsystems (institutions) as produce and reproduce *social identity* through mutual support. According to certain system theories (a proposition taken over by Habermas as well) we have to reckon, at least in modernity, with two 'general' subsystems, state and economy (power and money), and with their autonomous logic of self-reproduction and expansion. I would challenge this conception on several grounds, though at this point I can only enumerate them. Firstly, it excludes Eastern European societies from the notion of 'modernity', for these societies cannot be understood within this categorial framework.* Secondly, it is unable to distinguish between industrialization and capitalism. Thirdly, it is unable to distinguish between the different types of political rule (democratic and non-democratic). Fourthly, as far as the dynamic of modernity is concerned, it excludes alternatives (alternative versions of development of the systems). Even if I concede that Western European societies can to some extent be understood according to whether they are dominated by the system of 'economy' or that of state, I would add that an essential change in one institution (or in a few) could change the 'social identity' completely. (For instance, self-management might implement such a change.) It is for this reason that I define social structure as the conglomerate of mutually interconnected and mutually supportive institutions (as subsystems).

Without entering into historical analyses or an account of the

---

* For a different interpretation see Feher-Heller-Markus: *Dictatorship Over Needs* (Blackwell). A. Arato, who tried to apply Habermas' conception to Eastern European societies (see his 'Critical Sociology and Authoritarian State Socialism' in *Habermas Critical Debates*, Macmillan, 1982), had to change the original content of the two 'subsystems' in order to incorporate the Eastern European material.

various combinations of subsystems (studies which can only be performed in historiography), it should be noted that subsystems (institutions) can only be relatively homogeneous. This is so for the simple reason that their 'norms-and-rules' are embedded in a social structure; in other words, they are interconnected with all *other* institutions which are equally subsystems of the same structure. Furthermore, each particular institution is embedded in a conglomerate of mutually interconnected institutions. Consequently, because their intrinsic 'norms-and-rules' are mutually interrelated, institutions have to be at least relatively homogeneous, and no one can follow any rule of any institution without some familiarity with others. It follows that 'moving' within the sphere of objectivation 'for and in itself' requires the homogenization of human abilities to no less a degree, even if differently, than does the ascent into the sphere of objectivation 'for itself'. A useful analogy here would be 'following the rules of the game'. It would not suffice to know how to make a move with a pawn in order to play chess; to that end, one has to be familiar with all the rules of 'playing chess'. And when we sit down to play chess, we shift our thinking and adjust it to the purpose of 'playing chess'. Also, we suspend other heterogeneous activities (including perception and feeling) in order to play chess correctly. Wittgenstein's analogy between playing chess and ordinary language games is not convincing. We play ordinary language games without concentration, without homogenization, simply because speaking ordinary language is a constituent of the sphere of objectivation 'in itself'. On the other hand, 'playing chess' is no analogy for the appropriation of the objectivations 'for itself' either. 'Playing chess' hardly provides us with a meaningful world-view, nor for that matter, do we transform ourselves into whole humans by playing chess. This is why 'following the rules of the game' is a good analogy only for following the 'norms-and-rules' of the sphere of objectivation 'for and in itself'. But even here, analogy is only analogy; it does not give a complete account of the behaviour (and expectation) implied by following the 'norms-and-rules of an objectivation for itself'. The rules of chess are entirely homogeneous, whereas – and I have hinted at this already – the 'norms-and-rules' of the sphere of objectivation 'for and in itself' are not. There is another difference between 'minding the rules of the game' and 'minding the norms-and-rules of the objectivation for and in itself', a difference indicated in my substituting the notion of 'norms-and-rules' for that of rules in the case of every objectivation 'for and in itself'. The normative element in playing games is simply identical with 'minding the rules'. To put it simply, in playing games, the only expectation A has of B is that he will not cheat. But it is only as a result of a most recent development (more a tendency than a *fait accompli*) that following the 'norms-and-rules' of objectivations 'for and in itself' could, and should, be reduced to merely 'minding the rules'. The exclusive emphasis on the norm of 'fair play' signalizes the main trend, even if this norm might be interpreted (and observed) more broadly than simply 'minding the rules'. It was symbolic interactionism, and Goffman in particular, which drew our attention to the intrinsic network of ceremonial behaviour within an institutionally patterned matrix of action. Goffman offered a fairly Durkheimian explanation of the phenomenon, to which I subscribe conditionally, suggesting that the 'mana' of society is expressed by every individual who performs these ceremonies. For instance, the organization and arrangement of space within an institution is not simply a rule which should be minded. Should someone fail to arrange space, he or she infringes a norm in a way having nothing at all to do with 'cheating', and which is not due to ignorance of rules either. Of course, ceremonies can become means of cheating as well, but using them in this way means infringing the norm. For example, defending a client in court is a 'norm-and-rule' which every lawyer must observe. If this is regarded as a game, the game cannot be played without observing certain ceremonies inherent in institutionalized court procedures, let alone without certain moral 'norms-and-ideas' of the barrister as a person; ceremonies which might play a decisive and positive role in the defence unless they contradict the rules of the institution. However, ceremonies can be misused even if rules are kept: lawyers who commit such transgressions can be despised but not disbarred. Only in the case of an all-embracing bureaucratization of an institution can the normative content of the 'norms-and-rules' of an objectivation 'for and in itself' shrink to almost nil.

The specialized human

The human being-as-a-whole is the subject of the sphere of objectivation 'in itself', but it can never be the subject of the sphere of objectivation 'for and in itself'. Every institutionalized form of acting, making (something) or speaking requires a special education or training to develop and activate various human capacities, including the capacity to suspend heterogeneous everyday activities within the framework of an institution. Special education or training is not identical with specialization (professionalization); (in ancient democratic Athens every free citizen went through an education of this kind), yet the tendency towards specialization is unmistakably inherent in the sphere of objectivation 'for and in itself'. On the other hand, the subject of the sphere of objectivation 'for and in itself' is not the 'whole human' either, since not every human ability is absorbed by and concentrated in one single task if one observes the 'norms-and-rules' of an institution. Not only are heterogeneous everyday activities suspended, as happens in the appropriation of an objectivation 'for itself', but several human abilities are excluded. Should these abilities 'intrude' in the performance, the subject cannot mind the 'norms-and-rules' of the institution in a proper way. If we compare with one another (a) the use of man-made objects, (b) work within an institution of production, and (c) the creation of art works, the difference between suspension and exclusion of human abilities becomes very clear. The use of man-made objects (within the sphere of objectivations 'in itself') is not the type of action, nor is it various types of actions, yet it encompasses one aspect of all possible actions heterogeneous in character (eating, wedding, sleeping, giving a present and so on). Work, within the institution of production, excludes heterogeneous activities on the one hand (when we eat we do not work, even if in eating we use man-made objects), the mobilization of several abilities on the other (for instance, persuasion, anger, the sense of justice). The excluded capacities are always of great importance because the criticism of institutionalized actions normally mobilizes just these capacities (this holds true of all institutionalized actions). The creation of art works excludes heterogeneous activities, but it implies the concentration of all human abilities (none of them is excluded *ex principio*).

When I term the subject of the sphere of objectivation 'for and in itself' 'the specialized human', I do so on the grounds explained above. It should be repeated that 'the specialized human' is not necessarily a 'professional', and that special or even extraordinary talents do not make a 'specialized human'. (The subject of the sphere of objectivation 'for itself' is not a specialized human.) Moreover, institutions can only be well-established, mediated and able to survive if being the specialized human of a particular institution does not require any special talents, but can be continuously reproduced by training and education. The specialized human is the subject of reproducible know-how and know-what.

Accordingly, the sphere of objectivations 'for and in itself' can properly function without a cultural (subjective) surplus. It does not absorb cultural surplus directly but it can absorb it indirectly. I will now address this problem.

I emphasize once again that the unity of the heterogeneous sphere of objectivations 'in itself' is provided by meaningful world-views, while objectivations 'for itself' provide human life with meaning. Collective imagination is the soul of the social body, this is more than a figure of speech, since imagination stores past experiences together with their explanation, and shapes the patterns of self-creation and self-understanding of individual subjects. I call this collective imagination 'historical consciousness'. All different types of objectivations 'for itself' engendered or modified by the same social structure (including the appropriation of ancient, 'immortalized' ones) express the same stage of historical consciousness (see *A Theory of History*). There is only one exception to this: our own, modern, age.

If meaningful world-views provide the unity of heterogeneous activities related to and led by the sphere of objectivation 'in itself', the differentiation of the sphere of objectivation 'for itself' (institutions, subsystems) from the sphere of objectivation 'in itself' cannot prevent this unity from coming about. If it did, activities related to and led by the sphere of objectivation 'in itself' would lose their unity, and the life of man as a whole would become void of meaning. This is why the know-what and know-how of the specialized subject not only presupposes specialized education (training) for abiding by the 'norms-and-rules' of an institution, but this specialized education must be related to a meaningful world-view as well. Institutions draw their legitimacy from meaningful world-views to no less a degree than the sphere of objectivation 'in itself'. They can draw this legitimacy from all objectivations 'for itself'. But 'drawing legitimacy' does not suffice to make these institutions run smoothly and continuously. It has to be repeated that institutions can only be reproduced if the specialized human being (*its* subject) can be reproduced irrespective of the presence or absence of any 'cultural surplus'. This constellation has five consequences. First, one particular meaningful world-view has to be institutionalized in order for the specialized human being to be reproduced. Second, this world-view should provide for the continuous cumulation of knowledge. Third, it should provide for specialization. Fourth, the specialized knowledge provided by the world-view (minding the 'norms-and-rules' of the institution) should be taught. Finally, this meaningful world-view, thus institutionalized, should qualify for continuous legitimation of the social order (domination). The world-views which accomplish these tasks are those dominating any given historical epoch. They may have exclusivity or they may be contested by other meaningful world-views. If they are contested, all the contesting world-views are critical. I have already stated that there are only two objectivations 'for itself' which qualify for institutionalization, as only they satisfy all the prerequisites listed above. These are religion and science. Until the dawn of modernity, religion was the institutionalized objectivation 'for itself': since modernity, science has followed suit. Science has had a critical function as long as it contested religion as the main (dominating) institutionalized objectivation 'for itself'. Now it is the turn of religion (in the form of still institutionalized or non-institutionalized belief) to criticize science.

It is easy to understand why art does not qualify to become the leading institution of an epoch. I have already argued that 'Art' is a modern category, whose emergence was coeval with that of purely mystical (or later intellectual-mystical) reception. Mystical reception is antithetical to specialization: the mystical recipient is never the specialized thinker or actor. In earlier periods the arts were embedded in everyday life and/or in religious institutions, and occasionally even in those political institutions mainly shaped by religious or philosophical world-views. In addition, art never cumulates knowledge continuously, or if it does, this knowledge is technical in character, and not the type which generates art work as a meaningful objectivation. But what of philosophy?

I argued in the first chapter that philosophy is the very objectivation which systematizes knowledge from the viewpoint of practical reason, and this is why it was precisely philosophy which invented the category of 'rationality'. It is philosophy which raises questions concerning the validity of our norms and the truth of our knowledge. Indeed, this 'query' is the quintessence of philosophy; this is why it cannot take any existing practice or knowledge for granted. Given that it is, by definition, de-legitimizing, philosophy cannot be institutionalized as a legitimating world-view. In this regard it is perhaps superfluous to point out that the official doctrine of Diamat (Dialectical Materialism) is not a philosophy. Of course, philosophy can function in the service of other legitimating world-views (for instance, both religion and science). Whether or not philosophy could become the leading world-view for institutions in a society *without* any kind of domination, the problem of ideology as a kind of partial reception of philosophy cannot be discussed here; see: *For a Radical Philosophy*.

One could object to all this by referring to the increasing institutionalization of both art and philosophy. However, I would argue that any increase in *the number of* institutions which exist *for* art and philosophy does not imply the institutionalization *of* art and philosophy. (For a critique of the theory of the 'institutionalization of art', presented first of all by Peter Bürger in *Theorie der Avantgarde*, 1973, Frankfurt, see F. Feher, 'What Is Beyond Art?' *Thesis Eleven*, Melbourne, No. 5, 1982.)

In my brief analysis of art, I touched upon creation and reception. As far as creation is concerned, almost no increase in institutionalization has come about. The only specialized learning process in the arts involves the appropriation of its cumulative knowledge, its technique. But given that the knowledge of technique is specialized, creation has always been mediated by craft institutions. Being an art academy student is functionally equivalent to any apprenticeship; it is only the type of institution that differs. By contrast, creative literature has very few technical requirements, so its production has never been institutionalized as such. (How the creation of literary works can be embedded in religious or political institutions is a problem I cannot deal with here.) And what applies to creation, applies to reception as well. Reception can be public or private. There have always been institutions for public reception, and they exist now as well, but all of them are institutions for, and not of, reception. People are always free to reject, to criticize, or to remain indifferent to, a work of art. In other words, their reception *sensu stricto* cannot be entirely institutionalized, even if it takes place within an institutional framework. The difference can be illustrated by the following example. Those seeking advice from the oracle of Delphi had to believe in the institution and act accordingly, otherwise the exercise made no sense at all. But the viewers of the the tragedies of Euripides could either be affected or remain unaffected by them, like them or dislike them. Similarly, no one could possibly say that the acceptance of a scientific discovery is a matter of taste, although it is entirely legitimate to say this about the reception of an art work. In modernity the reception of works of art has tended to become more private, rather than increasingly institutionalized.

It is neither creation nor reception, but the distribution of art that becomes increasingly institutionalized in modernity. Yet the problems pertaining to this cannot be used as arguments to support the thesis of the institutionalization of art, given that the distribution of art does not belong to art proper, but rather to the institution of the market.

The institutionalization of philosophy provides a more clear-cut example. Although the education of philosophers has always been characterized by a fairly loose master–apprentice relationship, philosophical schools do *not* institutionalize philosophy, its creation or its reception. Instead, they provide individuals with the capacities necessary for independent inquiry and rational discourse. The appropriation of cumulative knowledge inherent in philosophy would be one such capacity. However, knowledge of this kind could never constitute the objectivation 'for itself' called philosophy, in respect of either its creation or reception. Only practice in independent inquiry and rational discourse can accomplish this. Indeed, should philosophy become entirely learned, and thus exclusively practised within an institutional framework, it would be philosophy only in name; at best, it could only be a type of science termed philosophy. Little wonder, then, that with the institutionalized professionalization of philosophical training, philosophy proper is created mostly by those who have been marginalized from institutions. Philosophy thus circumvents its own institutions, and lives against them, not from them (see *For a Radical Philosophy*).

The dominating world-views and the institutions

At this stage, I can perhaps repeat my previous statement with more emphasis: among objectivations 'for itself', only religion and science qualify for institutionalization in every respect. This propensity accounts for the historical fact that religion, and in recent times science, have become dominating world-views in so far as they permeate all institutions and the sphere of objectivation 'in itself'. Obviously, the statement that religion and science have become institutionalized does not mean that all institutions are either religious or scientific in nature. Political and economic institutions, and several cultural institutions, are not institutionalizations of either religion or science. But since they are permeated by the dominating world-view, their intrinsic 'norms-and-rules' imply substantively, or at least structurally and functionally, the spirit of this dominating world-view. I have repeatedly argued here that it is normally the dominating world-view which provides for the unity of heterogeneous activities related to and led by the sphere of objectivation 'in itself'. It is easy to understand why this is so. The dominating world-view legitimates the social order, and thereby legitimates the 'norms-and-rules' of the sphere of objectivation 'in itself'. Legitimations of this kind are more necessary in societies with a developed social division of labour, because here the dominating world-view has the double task of reinforcing the division of the sphere of objectivation 'for itself', and reinforcing it in respect of the dominating as well as of the dominated. If the dominating world-view performs this task successfully, life will be provided with meaning, but the meaning has to be taken for granted. If it cannot perform this task successfully, the 'norms-and-rules' of the sphere of objectivation 'in itself' will not be taken for granted, at least not by a considerable minority. In this case the following alternatives are left: (a) life without meaning (anomie); (b) taking recourse to another meaningful world-view which provides life with meaning without challenging the dominating structures; (c) taking recourse to another meaningful world-view which provides life with meaning by challenging the dominating structures which are no longer taken for granted. If the latter alternative is taken, not only will the sphere of objectivation 'in itself' be tested and queried, but so will institutions. I will examine this more closely below. For the time being, religion and science have to be compared with respect to their performance in legitimating the 'norms-and-rules' of the sphere of objectivation 'in itself'.

In this comparison certain differences are striking, even at first glance. Whereas religion has scored very well in providing life with meaning, science is far behind in the competition. Whereas, again, religion has scored very well in the 'norms-and-rules' of the sphere of objectivation 'in itself' accepted as 'taken for granted', science has certainly scored very well where *rules* are concerned, but not with *norms*. Science strips 'norms-and-rules' of their holiness and transforms them, even if never completely, into mere instructions for use. Not eating pork is a 'norm-and-rule' for Jews and Muslims: they abide by it because it represents part of their meaningful world-view. On the other hand, to avoid saturated fats because of the danger of heart attack is an instruction for use. The latter has nothing to do with a meaningful (good) life, only with life pure and simple. Similarly, cleanliness can be a ritual or a mere technique of avoiding infection and disease. Both fiction and social theory have often featured the dangers implicit in the trend of turning 'norms-and-rules' into mere instructions for use. The horrors of a 'brave new world' are extrapolations of the intrusion of science, as the dominating (and institutionalized) world-view, into everyday life. But extrapolations of this kind do not account for the emancipatory potentials equally implicit in the *failure* of science to legitimate 'norms-and-rules' of the sphere of objectivation 'in itself' where the emphasis is on the normative character. This 'failure as emancipation' can be accounted for in the following way. As long as the appropriation of all 'norms-and-rules' of the sphere of objectivation 'in itself' is an ethical issue (as long as customs are holy), it is difficult to escape the pressure of internalization (anomie is the way out). When 'norms-and-rules' are no longer holy, or only so to a limited degree, the pressure of internalization is low, and it is precisely this lowering of pressure which I call 'emancipation by failure'. Of course, this can lead to the generalization of ethical barbarism simultaneously with social conformity, but it can also open the way for a highly individualized form of life. For this latter scenario to eventuate, one would have to seek recourse in non institutionalized objectivations 'for itself'.

At this point I would like to reach back to Habermas' notion of the 'colonization of everyday life', and apply it in a slightly modified way. Science, the dominating (and institutionalized) objectivation 'for itself', permeates all institutions (via the rationalization of institutions). It intrudes, directly or indirectly, into everyday life (as ideology of science and as the 'rationalization' of everyday life). While I accept Habermas' terminology and subscribe to the description of the phenomenon in question, I would add that *everyday life has by and large always been colonized*. There have only been a few exceptional 'moments' in human histories when this was not the case, mostly during those times when religion lost control because it had been replaced by another religion or because competing objectivations 'for itself' had challenged the dominating world-view. A glance at the only institution of the sphere of objectivation 'in itself', the family, will suffice to show what I have in mind. Women have a long record of suffering due to this 'traditional type' of colonization. Nonrationalized institutions can colonize everyday life just as well as rationalized ones. A relative independence of everyday life had first to come about in order that the warning 'It must not be colonized!' could be formulated. This relative independence was created by the relative separation of state from civil society at the dawn of modernity. Prior to this, with a very few exceptions, the rule was that everyday life had not been colonized in a tortuous process, but rather was the colony, pure and simple, of a particular institutionalized meaningful world-view. The family was a colony of religion and its institutions throughout the Middle Ages. Science and rationalized institutions cannot therefore colonize it *more*, only in a *different way*.

A possible objection to this is that everyday life having already been a colony, it could not be colonized. Yet this speaks more in favour of modernity, because it suggests that 'colonization' is not yet a state beyond the point of no return. A second objection is that religion performed the task of 'colonization' properly because the 'norms-and-rules' of the sphere of objectivation 'in itself' had been legitimized precisely in their capacity of 'norms-and-rules', and not simply as instructions for use. This, of course, is very true. Even so, as I have pointed out, the change may comprise a gain as well as a loss, and whether it is finally a gain or loss depends on several other factors. But perhaps the most serious objection is that the previous types of colonization of everyday life have left intact at least the basic structural patterns of the spheres of objectivation 'in itself', whereas modern colonization disrupts these very patterns and prevents this sphere from functioning properly. This objection needs to be answered in detail.

I mentioned in Section II that the sphere of objectivation 'in itself' contains structurally constant and structurally variable elements. Inventive, repetitive and intuitive action (thinking) ensure *together* the appropriation of the 'norms-and-rules' of this sphere of objectivation, and the adult generation must be able to *mediate* fairly firm 'norms-and-rules' to their successors. The proportion of the three types of thinking (action) is elastic and prone to change, while the content of the 'norms-and-rules' can also change within a generation, if proper relearning is still possible and if relearned thinking (action) can become routinized up to a certain point.

Clearly, the colonization of everyday life by science (and rationalization) has not changed the constant features of the sphere of objectivation 'in itself', nor those of their appropriation. Had it done so, the features would not be constant, or we would not survive. At this point certain questions should be raised as to how, firstly, the intrusion of rationalized institutions into everyday life has shaped the variable (and elastic) elements of this sphere, and, secondly, whether these new patterns *might* transform the *relation* between the sphere of objectivation 'in itself' and the sphere of objectivation 'for and in itself'. Historically, the sphere of objectivation 'for and in itself' emerged from the sphere of objectivation 'in itself' in which it was previously embedded. Could an increase in institutionalization and in the rationalization of institutions result in the opposite effect? Could it happen, or is it likely to happen, that various rationalized institutions might simply *take over* the socializing function of the sphere of objectivation 'in itself'? If this did occur, the colonization of everyday life would lead to the disappearance of the *subject* of the appropriation of the sphere of objectivation 'in itself', to the disappearance of human being-as-a whole. But the latter is the source of cultural (subjective) surplus absorbed by the objectivations 'for itself', and science, like religion, is an objectivation 'for itself'; it cannot survive and flourish without absorbing cultural surplus. Of course, if science is institutionalized, the *institutions* are reproduced *without* absorbing cultural surplus. But if the institutionalized meaningful world-view loses its ability to provide meaning, it loses vitality also, sooner or later becomes *inapt* for institutionalization. What I want to argue, therefore, is simply this: if the specialized human replaces human being-as-a-whole, the 'whole human' cannot emerge either, and the dominating world-view (in this case science) will be weakened by the lack of a sufficient amount of absorbed cultural surplus. Should this happen, the breakdown of the entire social structure would be inevitable.

One could object that although the human person-as-a-whole is alone the source of cultural surplus, he or she is *not* the source of cognitive surplus. Thus, if the specialized subject operating within the framework of institutions could produce a cognitive surplus, the ability of science (as the dominant world-view) to generate meaning could be unlimited, rendering our conclusion of an eventual breakdown of the social structure as at best premature. In reply to this objection I would propose that institutions (and specialized subjects within institutions) do not produce a cognitive surplus. Institutions may have a greater or lesser *learning capacity*, they may go through *learning processes*. However, the learning capacity of institutions is tantamount to their ability to absorb and implement cognitive surplus produced either by everyday life or by the objectivations 'for itself'. Cognitive surplus is thus not produced by institutions, but is utilized and absorbed by them, and indeed ceases to be a *surplus* once it is so absorbed. Science produces a huge cognitive surplus, but *not* as an institution, only in its capacity of an objectivation 'for itself'. Even if today scientific research occurs within an institutionalized framework, this research does not involve simply minding the rules of the game of scientific institutions, but observing the 'norms-and-rules' of the particular objectivation 'for itself' called 'science'. The subject of scientific research is not the specialized subject, even if this subject is specialized in one of the various fields of science. 'Human wholeness' presupposes the 'human being-as-a-whole'. The scientist's self-abandonment to science, self-surrender to science, presupposes passion, an inquietude of spirit, curiosity, the concentration of all energies for the solution of the task, intuition, and so on, and requires these things to just the same extent as does the self-abandonment practised by the artist. No discussion of the paradigmatical case of Einstein is necessary to exemplify what this means. One could object that all of this is only true in the case of 'revolutionary science', and not in the case of 'normal science', to use Kuhn's distinction. But even if this were so, it would still be safely stated that without revolutionary science the 'energy resources' of 'normal science' would soon run dry. Consequently, after this digression, I reassert that if the rationalizing process of institutions triggered by modern scientific development was to progress unimpeded, then such a tendency could only be self-defeating also for science as a dominating world-view. There can be no human wholeness without a human person-as-a-whole.

The dominating world-view of 'science'* and everyday life

The cumulation of cognitive surplus is not a matter of pure chance, even if factors incidental to the sphere of objectivation 'in itself' may contribute to its direction or acceleration, and even if such factors hinder it completely. The dominant meaningful world-view which permeates all institutions and legitimizes the 'norms-and-rules' of the sphere of objectivation 'in itself', both creates avenues for, and sets firm limits to, the growth and implementation of cognitive surplus. This is why a cognitive surplus alone cannot bring about any change in dominant meaningful world-views. A cultural surplus absorbable by *any* objectivation 'for itself', and not exclusively by the dominant one, can be 'midwife' to a cognitive surplus, by setting it free from the dominating world-view. The term 'midwife' used by Socrates, expressed adequately what happened in the short period of Greek enlightenment. Philosophy, a new objectivation 'for itself', was invented as a midwife, not simply in order to offer a novel type of knowledge, but to liberate the cognitive surplus of everyday life from its imprisonment by traditional 'opinion'. The denunciation of Anytos was based on realistic considerations. Socrates was an atheist not because he

---

* The inverted commas indicate that, the notion of 'science' does not stand for sciences proper but for 'scientificity', science as ideology.

did not believe in God or gods (this was of secondary importance), but because he refused to accept the mastery of the dominant world-view over the cognitive surplus. Though there was a different outcome, something similar happened during the Renaissance. This time, it was both art and philosophy (and their various combinations) that performed the function of the 'midwife'. They liberated the accumulated cognitive surplus from the control of religion and all the institutions permeated by it. Yet here the midwife was akin to the magician's apprentice who released a far more powerful genie from the bottle than intended. This is true even though a long period of time elapsed before the new dominating world-view became comfortably institutionalized and started to permeate all institutions (via their rationalization), after which, eventually, its spearhead intruded into everyday life.

Of course, science is not a completely novel objectivation 'for itself'. Irrespective of whether it was embedded in religion, or, occasionally, in philosophy or in arts, it had a specific function: to harness and systematize the cognitive surplus scattered around in the heterogeneous activities of the sphere of objectivation 'in itself'. This was done mainly for speculative, though occasionally for pragmatic, purposes (for instance, in religious institutions or in warfare). Conversely, modern science produces knowledge of a quality and quantity and with a rapidity which surpasses the ability of the human being-as-a-whole to grasp it in a manifold way. The cognitive surplus created by science 'pours into' all institutions permeated by the dominating world-view and also into everyday life. No cognitive surplus can be produced any longer by the sphere of objectivation 'in itself', or by its subject, the human person-as-a-whole.

However, a *cultural surplus* is still engendered now within everyday life. If absorbed by the objectivation 'for itself' called science, it becomes the 'fuel' of revolutionary science. If absorbed by competing objectivations 'for itself' (art, philosophy, religion), it can fuel the *criticism* of our social structure and of the dominating world-view. I repeat here what has been said about the emergence of the 'public domain' in modernity. The ratio between the dominating world-view *mediated* by the sphere of objectivation 'in itself', and the objectivations 'for itself' to which humans have direct access, has altered in favour of the latter. Moreover, humans have direct access to norms and values originally created by objectivations 'for itself' but which became severed from these objectivations, and increasingly behave like objectivations 'for itself' in their own right. (I have in mind here universalized norms and values.) As a result, a cultural surplus is no longer simply the objectivation of subjective experience, but implies *reflection upon* the subjective experience itself from the viewpoint of an objectivation 'for itself' or of certain universalized values. Thus the public domain (and taste), as the meeting point *par excellence* of everyday experience and objectivation 'for itself' (universalized norms and values included), becomes a new source for the creation of a cultural surplus. By all this I do not mean that the objectivation of subjective experience (without reflection) ceases to be an energy source for cultural surplus. I will return to this problem below.

The consequences of this situation where a cognitive surplus is no longer produced by everyday life are so well-known that it suffices to mention only a few of them. The change in the variable structures of the sphere of objectivation 'in itself', together with the transformation of its rules, comes from 'outside': they are implementations of scientific discoveries either direct (popularized science) or indirect (ever-newer technologies). This tendency is all-embracing. It affects all activities (household, dressing, cooking, child-rearing, healing, entertainment, sexuality and so on). The speed at which rules change is increasing, so that one has to relearn more and more frequently. Thus life experience amounts to next to nothing. (In this new era old people are helpless rather than wise, because the elasticity of relearning is lost in old age.) Knowledge is decreasingly mediated in personal human interaction. Face-to-face interaction (everyday communication) is no longer the basic source of information, of advice, of know-how and know-what. The tension, richness and density of primary human contact is thus imperilled. Some contend that emotional intensity might redress this loss, yet this can only be true if human contact is sought as an end in itself. The centrality of *amour passion* in modern life signals the need for this remedy. But *amour passion* alone cannot substitute for all human contacts, and is short-lived if it draws its strength only from itself (from emotional intensity). The enhancement of emotional intensity in parent–child relationships is also sought as a remedy against the loss of the primary functions of this relationship (in order to transform the accident of birth into the 'necessity' of living precisely here and now). Given that birth is still accidental, and the mediating function of parents has been taken over by various institutions, biological ties no longer suffice to make us accept our world as, of necessity, ours. Children need their parents only in order to be fed and sheltered, and once grown up they need them no longer. The growing emotional intensity in the family can therefore only establish lasting human contact if the accident of birth favours this contact.

The colonization of everyday life by science is thus characterized by the following features: (1) the unity of the 'norms-and-rules' of the objectivation 'in itself' is disrupted, so that rules contain a decreasing proportion of normative elements; (2) the content and character of rules (in their capacity of instructions for use) are 'fed into' everyday life by science, directly and indirectly; (3) the sphere of objectivation 'in itself' cannot produce cognitive surplus; (4) personal human contacts lose their richness, intensity and their function in social reproduction, and are maintained only by emotional intensity. But do these changes in the variable elements of the sphere of objectivation 'in itself' prevent their constant elements from being reproduced? And further, is 'disruption' in the sphere of objectivation 'in itself' indeed the foreseeable consequence of the tendency described?

I wish to argue that in contemporary everyday life the constant features of the sphere of objectivation 'in itself' remain completely intact, and that there is absolutely no indication that they will be disrupted. All types of thinking (action) in everyday life follow the same patterns they have followed in all human histories. The sphere of objectivation 'in itself' has never become a system or institution. The heterogeneity of this sphere has remained its basic feature, and its subject has remained the human being-as-a-whole. The intrusion of science and of rationalized institutions into everyday life not only does not impede this heterogeneity, but rather reinforces it. This is because the rationalized institutions and scientific 'results' are of a varying nature. A certain type of institution requires a certain type of thinking (action), another type a different one, yet these actions are not related in any meaningful way. This follows from the fact (and vice versa) that science as a dominating world-view cannot provide for the *unity* of the heterogeneous sphere of objectivation 'in itself'; it cannot provide life with meaning. This creates a void which, in conjunction with the decrease in the meaning and intensity of personal, face-to-face contacts, creates a *steady tension* in everyday life. The source of this tension can be located precisely in the circumstance that while the constant features of the sphere of objectivation 'in itself' are *intact*, there is no meaning in life. To put it more correctly, the appropriation of the heterogeneous constituents of the sphere of objectivation 'in itself' is no longer identical with the appropriation of a *way of life*. A tension is felt by the human person-as-a-whole: he or she can only be a whole in so far as he or she has to perform heterogeneous activities, but again, he or she can only be a 'whole' if those heterogeneous activities are combined in such a way as to secure the continuous identity of the person. If only the first condition is met, the human person-as-a-whole cannot emerge. This tension could be called the feeling of alienation. The sombre feeling that our heterogeneous actions are 'puppet-like' that they are directed by a faceless and soulless 'externality', and thus neither by the tender hands of our fellow creatures nor by a living God, is not prompted by the failure of the agency of socialization, but rather by its success. However, this feeling, this tension, produces a great amount of *cultural surplus*, which undermines the stability of everyday reproduction. This cultural surplus can be left unabsorbed by objectivations 'for itself' and can backlash as (individual or collective) hysteria; in other words, it can function as if it were a *cultural deficit*. It can also be absorbed by higher objectivations as the potential for a change of life (individual and collective).

Let us now look briefly at the constant elements of the objectivations 'in itself', and at our relations with them in contemporary everyday life. All rationalized institutions inserted into the sphere of objectivation 'in itself' are simply taken for granted. First of all, it is the belief in the omniscience and omnipotence of science that is taken for granted, a belief having absolutely nothing to do either with scientific knowledge or with the appropriation of the relatively homogeneous 'norms-and-rules' of any rationalized institution. We believe in the healing effect of the doctor's prescription without having the slightest knowledge of medicine. If an item of information is labelled 'scientific' we believe in its being true in the same way as people once believed in the truth of divine revelation. To learn how to shop belongs to the appropriation of the sphere of objectivation 'in itself'. And we need not know how the market works (we need not be familiar with the relatively homogeneous 'norms-and-rules' of the institution 'market') in order to perform the task of shopping repeatedly and successfully (granted that we have the money to pay). The fact that children must go to school is taken for granted no less than that we get a picture if we switch on the television, or that we are governed by a prime minister or a president or by both. We can perform repetitive, inventive and intuitive actions led by the sphere of objectivation 'in itself', and we can perform many actions simultaneously. When we relearn (for example, how to use man-made objects), we can easily appropriate new skills because technology and the market act to simplify procedures. Both technology and the market take the *constant patterns* of the sphere of objectivation 'in itself' into consideration when they produce for households.

With this sketchy outline I have sought to make it clear that in spite of all our socio-structural changes we are still 'primarily' socialized by the sphere of objectivation 'in itself', that our everyday life is still built around the appropriation of *heterogeneous* 'norms-and-rules', and that we still appropriate and apply them with the proper combination of repetitive, intuitive and inventive thinking. Further, I have sought to prove that science, as the dominating world-view of modernity, fails to combine the heterogeneous 'norms-and-rules' into a meaningful whole as a 'way of life', and that I consider this failure to be not only a loss but an asset, or at least a *potential* asset.

I pointed out in the second chapter that in societies characterized by the social division of labour, the sphere of objectivation 'in itself' is divided as well. The members of various castes, estates and strata have quite different 'norms-and-rules' to appropriate. The dominating world-view has normally succeeded by legitimating why this *should* be so. Simultaneously with the development of the capitalist mode of industrialization and the emergence of socioeconomic classes in Western Europe and the United States, science took over the function of a dominating world-view from religion (see F. Feher-A. Heller: 'Class, Democracy, Modernity', in *Theory and Society* (12) 1983). But since science, contrary to religion, is unable to combine the heterogeneous 'norms-and-rules' of the sphere of objectivation 'in itself'', and thereby sanctify them, it can only *technically, not morally*, legitimate domination. (This was one of the reasons for the failure of legitimation via 'substantive rationality' in Eastern European societies. See F. Feher-A. Heller-G. Markus, *Dictatorship Over Needs*, Basil Blackwell, Oxford, 1982.) That the son of the serf has to learn the handling of the hoe, while the son of a landlord has to learn the handling of the sword, was something explicable by religion. It was presented not as an isolated 'norms-and-rules', but in interconnections with all the others. The division between the sphere of objectivation 'in itself' could be, and in fact was, explained as a divinely ordained moral order. If the meaningful world-view was internalized (and on the whole it was), the serf could not perceive the division of the sphere of objectivation 'in itself' as unjust. But no science can *morally* legitimate the social differences between skills and the social manners which have to be appropriated; in particular, no science can contend that there exists a legitimate necessity for these social differences. Furthermore, no science can legitimate the sexual division of labour (in behaviour, skills to be appropriated and so on), especially not a necessity for it. Consequently, all those who experience class, sex and race discrimination will perceive the division of the sphere of objectivation 'in itself' as *unjust*, or at least they will tend to do so. This is why it is a potential asset that science, as a dominating worldview, fails to provide life with meaning. Other conditions must be met before it can be regarded as a real asset.

The tendency of certain values to become universalized

'Rationality of reason' has been defined as the competence to follow 'norms-and-rules'. We follow the 'norms-and-rules' of our sphere of objectivation 'in itself' to a degree *not less* and *not more* than our ancestors did. This statement is formulated polemically against two diametrically opposed assertions. According to the first, in everyday life we act and think *more* rationally in modernity than we did earlier on, *because* the leading and dominating worldview of our age is a *rational* objectivation 'for itself' (science), and *because* our institutions are *rationalized*. In this view, rationalized rules are followed *more* rationally than pre-rational ones. Instead of analysing at this stage whether we really act and think (or, more precisely, whether we *can* think and act) more rationally now than earlier, I wish to emphasize the following. The fact that certain rules are set by a rationalist world-view or by rationalized institutions *does not imply* that we *follow* these rules *more* rationally than we earlier followed prerationalist ones. At least, there is no indication whatsoever that the appropriation of the 'norms-and-rules' of the sphere of objectivation 'in itself', a process which simply mediates the entirely heterogeneous results of different sciences and institutions which we cannot comprehend, became more rational. According to the second assertion, we have become *less rational*, since our heterogeneous everyday activities are no longer knotted together in a comprehensible 'way of life'. Yet this latter position is no more convincing than the first. Beyond doubt, the 'norms-and-rules' of the objectivation 'in itself' has become more technical than normative; I have pointed this out repeatedly. But if it is indeed so, then following the *rules* (and displaying competence in following these rules) completely satisfies the criterion of the 'rationality of reason'. The sphere of objectivation 'in itself', with all its heterogeneous 'norms-and-rules', is thus appropriated, maintained and mediated by rationality of reason. The question of how rational is this 'rationality of reason' can only be raised if the yardstick of 'rationality' (its 'norms-and-rules') is *external* to the sphere of objectivation 'in itself'.

Here I return to a problem that has been often touched upon but not yet answered: the tendency of certain values to become universalized (see: 'The Power of Shame', 'Rationality and Democracy', 'The Dissatisfied Society', in this volume).

I distinguish between three types of norms: concrete norms, abstract norms, and universal norms.

The 'norms-and-rules' of the sphere of objectivation 'in itself' are concrete norms: this is precisely why they are called 'norms-and-rules'. 'What is to be done' and 'how it is to be done' are posited simultaneously. Also posited simultaneously are the questions 'what is to be preferred' and 'how it is to be preferred'. The above are imperative and optative 'norms-and-rules' (see *Towards a Marxist Theory of Values*, Telos Press, 1973). Given that the three constituents of the sphere of objectivation 'in itself' (use of ordinary language, use of man-made objects, use of customs) are interwoven in every type of thinking (action), even if in different proportions, the notion 'concrete norms' applies to the entire sphere. The intracultural proportion of 'optative' and 'imperative' concrete norms varies enormously according to cultures, but neither of them can become exclusive. There is still a great number of concrete norms in modern life, and parents give a high priority to inducing children to observe them (how to greet adults, how to eat and drink 'properly', which words are 'improper' for public use, and so on).

Abstract norms are *moral* norms, and they entail several concrete norms. If persons are to observe abstract norms, they have to be familiar not only with the abstract norm itself but also with the interpretation of this abstract norm through concrete ones. Further, they have to determine *which* interpretation of the norm applies to a particular situation, and how it applies. Whether the abstract norm refers to actions ('You ought not to kill') or to behaviour ('You should be generous or courageous'), in the last instance it is practical reason (conscience) that makes the right (or, incidentally, the wrong) decision. If observing abstract norms only requires finding out which particular (concrete) interpretation of this norm applies to any situation, practical reason is *complementary conscience*, and the rationality of practical reason is still 'rationality of reason'. However, as happens mainly (though not exclusively) in periods of increasing *rationalism*, abstract norms are observed as against their interpretations through concrete norms (for instance 'You ought not to kill in war either'). If observing abstract norms involves a shift away from observing the concrete ones that they entail; in other words, if observing the abstract norm turns against the interpretations in the given societal environment, the rationality of practical reason is no longer exclusively 'rationality of reason', but also 'rationality of intellect'.

In contrast to the very long history of abstract norms, universal norms have only a short record. Without the tendency of certain abstract norms to become universalized, science could not have displaced religion as the dominating world-view. I have already pointed out that a great amount of cultural surplus (absorbed by art and philosophy) played the role of a catalyst in setting a cognitive surplus free from the embrace of religion. This could only happen because this cultural surplus, both in quantity and in character, possessed a tendency to universalization. Even though a 'cultural surplus' is always produced in everyday life, it is normally absorbed by traditional objectivation 'for itself'. But if objectivation 'in itself' cannot perform smoothly the task of reproduction for indigenous reasons, the amount of cultural surplus can increase, and it can pour into *critical* objectivation 'for itself', unintentionally creating new ones. If a further cumulation of cognitive surplus is impeded by the dominating world-view, this can also result in an overproduction of cultural surplus, if other conditions are met. During the Renaissance, the expansion of the market, the monetarization of the economy and the accumulation of a cognitive surplus led to a devalorization of 'norms-and-rules' of the various spheres of objectivation 'in itself', and of the unifying (dominating) world-view. Since money is a general (universal) equivalent of wealth (Marx), monetarization disrupts the smooth functioning of particularistic concrete 'norms-and-rules' of life-worlds. The increased cultural surplus engendered by this tension was so substantial that it is no wonder that when it was absorbed by the sphere of objectivation 'for itself', it shifted all these objectivations towards universality. Thus universal values first announced their emergence within various objectivations 'for itself'. Art (capitalized and in the singular) is a product of this universalization. Of course, the first basic reaction was absorbing this cultural surplus in a traditional way (for instance, substituting new religions for old ones or adjusting the old to new requirements). But even if Protestantism expressed the 'spirit of capitalism', it could not become the new dominating world-view simply because no religion ever speaks a universal language, there always being competing religions. However, science does speak a universal language. It invented a symbolic language which is the common medium of communication between all scientists, irrespective of their religious beliefs, race or nationality. No life-world, no particular way of life, is expressed in this language. But this universality of science implies something else as well. Speaking *this* universal language properly has nothing to do with proper behaviour, with being a good or a bad person, an honest or a dishonest friend, a stoic or a philanderer, greedy or generous, magnanimous or petty, and so on.

The universal language of science could only be discovered in a time when the universal equivalent was set on a course for the destruction of all particularistic barriers of particular life-worlds. It also bears the hallmark of its birth: moral indifference. I certainly do not regard monetarization as a negative phenomenon (neither did Marx), even less the emergence of the common-universal language of science. Nor would I deny, that from the moment of its conception, science (and technology) possessed an independent logic of its own. My thesis is simply this: just as money 'doesn't stink', science 'doesn't stink' either. True enough, there is one particular moral norm intrinsic to science: the pursuit of *true knowledge*. The scientist must not *cheat* in scientific research but must present knowledge believed to be true not only 'beyond reasonable doubt', but according to the proper rules of procedure of the given science. But the scientist, of course, can cheat or lie outside the scientific pursuit without losing credibility as a scientist. In modern science, then, theoretical reason submits practical reason to itself, and the morality of science is reduced to observing the 'norms-and-rules' of a purely theoretical pursuit. Thus modern natural sciences speak a universal language and are of universal value without providing humans with *universal norms*.

The statement that science is a universal value is, however, not the statement of science, but a statement about science. Scientists have always pursued the elaboration of their universal language and their discoveries without pondering much upon the universality of their endeavour. The prompters of great scientific revolutions (from Newton to Einstein) were often personally attached to religions, to mysticisms of various kinds or to popular philosophies. Their attitude often had much in common with the 'naivety' of everyday men, namely with the wish to 'intrude' into the 'miracles of nature' or 'the miracles of creation'. It was left to philosophy, from the late Renaissance onwards, to declare the value of science universal. In this respect it should not be forgotten that philosophy was a midwife to the birth of science, nor should we forget that the statement that values have no truth claim is definitely not a scientific 'discovery', but a philosophical proposition about science.

Science with its scientific truth and scientific rationalism was not the only universal value brought to light by philosophy. The values of freedom, humankind, personality, were similarly brought to light as universal values. Philosophy not only served as a midwife at the birth of the sciences but also at that of *democratic institutions*.

I did not start this analysis with the concept of 'value' but with that of 'norm'. I have distinguished between concrete, abstract and universal norms. It is perfectly clear what abstract and concrete norms are and how they are observed. But what is a 'universal norm'? Are universal values norms? Can they be observed, and if so, how?

All norms are related to values. The interpretation of abstract norms varies historically, according to cultures, social classes and the like. The change in the (interpreted) content of abstract norms is due to the change of values to which the norms are related. For instance, the moral postulate of being loyal is an abstract norm. But whether our loyalty goes first to our 'master', our friend or an idea, whether the first type of loyalty (governed by a master) or the last (governed by an idea) is a possible or admissible interpretation of the abstract norm of loyalty, depends on whether 'living according to social hierarchy' or 'living according to chosen ideas' is an accepted value or not. If we examine premodern histories, it will immediately occur to us that the *interpretation* of abstract values is highly authoritative. All the various interpretations were legitimated by religions, and the differing interpretations of the same 'virtue' were attributed to different social classes (estates). The universalization of a few abstract norms occurred through the breakdown of authoritative interpretation and allocation of virtues. The individual interpretation of abstract norms challenged the 'world order' and accelerated the tendential disappearance of authoritative interpretations (see 'The Power of Shame' for my view of conscience as the ultimate arbiter in moral decisions). But it was precisely this authoritative interpretation that ensured the normative character of abstract norms, even if only a small group accepted it as binding, mostly in times of transition (for example, early Christian interpretation of values as against traditional Roman ones). If we presuppose the existence (and the validity) of *universal norms*, we should be able to prove that not only *universal values* are accepted but something more as well, namely, the assumption that at least one interpretation of universal values induces every human being to act so that these values are observed. In short, at least one universal *virtue* has to be accepted and practised (the lack of 'universal virtues' was rightly a matter of grave concern for Hannah Arendt). Otherwise, universal values have no universal *normative* power. And quite obviously this is not the case. Accordingly, universalized values are not universal norms, or, more precisely, there is no universal norm related to any of the universalized values. From all this the conclusion has to be drawn that the third type of norm, the universal, figures only as a logical and historical possibility.

Abstract norms were already to be interpreted in an authoritative way in order to function as norms proper. It stands to reason then that universal norms could not function in a proper (normative) way without some degree of authoritative interpretation. But who could, and should, be the authority of this interpretation?

For the moment I shall defer any reply to this crucial question. Still, one thing is certain. The dominating objectivation 'for itself' of our times, science, cannot provide an 'authoritative interpretation' of universal values, despite the fact that it speaks a universal language. Some reasons for this have already been discussed. Yet it is also true because science constructs the world as a world of objects. Objects can be understood, influenced, and changed, but they cannot be invoked. The dichotomy of facts and values, *created* rather than *discovered* by science, is both the cause and the effect of this limitation. (Philosophies which generalize this dichotomy serve as ideologies of legitimation for the dominating world-view.) But the statement that science creates the dichotomy of facts and values is one-sided. Science simply constructs theories and interprets facts within these theories without having recourse to any value other than its own, the value of scientific truth. But in speaking of 'dichotomy' we implicitly assert the existence of 'validity' of values engendered *not* by science, but *outside* the competence and 'territory' of science. Where do these values come from? There are, firstly, certain 'vestiges' of values belonging to earlier historical periods. Religions, which still institutionalize 'belief', even if they no longer institutionalize knowledge, have remained fountainheads of certain values. Other objectivations 'for itself', like philosophy or art, engender values independently of science. The fact that the various objectivations 'for itself' have an intrinsic set of values of their own, is a modern phenomenon, and above all it indicates that science is not the dominating world-view of our epoch in the way that religion had been in previous ones. It was this fact that led Weber to believe that we choose values irrationally. In Weber's terms the selection of one deity from the 'warring gods' of the modern world is an option not grounded in the observation of values of any kind, but rather, at best, in a proper assessment of the suitability of our talents for a particular vocation.

But the fact that science, as a dominating world-view, 'sets free' values, norms, ethical action and judgment (in contrast to religions), is above all what makes possible only in modernity this cultural Olympus of independent deities. This is, of course, tantamount to an acknowledgment that the *dominating world-view of modernity is self-restricted as far as its domination is concerned*. This world-view can only be all-embracing if other objectivations *cease to produce* values for the life-world and for institutions.

It may appear that I have manoeuvred myself into a serious self-contradiction here. I have argued that only *two* objectivations 'for itself' can be institutionalized: science and religion. From this, I proceeded to discuss the possibility of other objectivations producing values for the life-world, as well as for institutions. Of course, I could have in mind the revitalization of religions as a principal world-view which institutionalizes values. This cannot be excluded as a future possibility, though it seems an unlikely one. However, historically, certain universalized values have become separated from the objectivations 'for itself' which produced them, in the main from philosophy. These now function as *value ideas* (the definition of which is that their opposite cannot be chosen as a value: for an analysis of value ideas see *For a Radical Philosophy*). They are ideas exactly because they 'float' in our historical consciousness: everyone can have recourse to them without being at all familiar with any objectivation 'for itself'. They function *as if they were* an objectivation 'for itself', which they are not (as they have no homogeneous 'norms-and-rules' of their own). These 'free-floating ideas' are not meaningful world-views, but all meaningful world-views engendered by modernity must take recourse to them. No concrete virtues are derived from value ideas, but the latter can function as *regulative* ideas for an ethical conduct of life. Moreover, they share the propensities of religion and science in so far as they can be *institutionalized*. The constitutions of political democracies based on 'human rights' are conceived of precisely as institutionalizations of universalized values. If we hold that all human beings are born free and equal, and are endowed with reason, we anchor the institutions in these universalized values.

Science is *not based* on any universal value. As I have said, true and false are categories of value orientation, and in this sense they are *transcultural*. What is new in modern science is not the pursuit of true knowledge but the specific procedures through which scientific 'true knowledge' can be achieved. But *universalization* is the foundation of modern science. The modern interpretation of what true knowledge is implies the *universality* of true knowledge. It would be now absolutely inadmissible to talk about scientific truth in the way Saint Paul talked about the truth of Christianity: that it was nonsense to the pagans, scandalous to the Romans, and true precisely thereby.

My assumption has been that the universal language of science could only have been invented because the universal equivalent (money) had pulled down the barriers of particularistic ways of life. But if universalization is the foundation of modern science, and if modern democracy is based on a few universal values, the idea of the self-regulating market is a utopian extrapolation of the modern market mechanism. The idea of a self-regulating market conceives of the market mechanism as an institution which implements the values of freedom and equality unwittingly in other words, irrespective of the will of individuals to observe and implement them as universal values. (This idea is contained in Adam Smith's famous conception of the 'invisible hand'.) However, this correctly observed tendency of a market mechanism could never reach the state of 'self-regulation' (for details of this see K. Polanyi's classic book, *The Great Transformation*), because from the outset it was counterbalanced by the institution of science and the institution of democracy, even if in two different ways. To be brief, political democracy, where it had come about, was only able to *delimit* the independent mechanism of market, whereas science *intruded* into it. True enough, at the beginning, scientific research had not aimed at its own implementation as technology. However, the development of *technology*, as a *conscious* project progressively channelling new techniques into industrial production, would have been inconceivable had science not already been established as the leading meaningful worldview. It was only the very early implementation of the 'spirit of modern sicence' that made the market mechanism *expand*. Marx had precisely this phenomenon in mind when he suggested that only the production of relative surplus (as against absolute surplus) led to the *real* subjection of labour to capital. The market could not expand due to mere egoistic motivations: the deliberate implementation of new technologies became the cornerstone of competition. These days, the intrusion of science into market mechanisms has gone a long way. Given that the forms of this intrusion are common knowledge, this brief reference to them will suffice. However, the observation above, that democracy only delimits the scope of a market mechanism, whereas science has deeply intruded into it, is another expression and reconfirmation of the thesis that science is the *de facto* dominating world-view of our age. (To see this contrast in another form, we can refer on the one hand to Marx's remark that democracy stops at the factory gate, and on the other hand to the equally well-known fact that science had first been implemented *within* the factory gate before it was implemented *outside* it.) Moreover, science has deeply intruded into the political sphere of modern democracy. The specificity of modern bureaucracy, its rationalized structure as described by Weber, follows the patterns of modern, institutionalized science with its principles of optimization and instrumental action. And modern democracy prompted rather than impeded the growth of rationalized bureaucracies, both in volume and in influence. At the same time, this very bureaucracy sets limits to the overall implementation of the universal values established by constitutions. It follows that the only institution based on universal values is delimited as well as obstructed by the universalized and institutionalized dominating world-view which, for its part, is not based on universal values. It is also most important to add that whilst universal values are empirical universals, their implementation within the institution of democracy is far from being empirically universal: states with democratic constitutions are fairly exceptional. On the other hand, science and scientific technology are empirically universalized. The concept of 'modernization' *does not mean* the implementation of universal values in democratic institutions, but it does mean the implementation of sophisticated new technologies. Thus, science as a dominating and institutionalized world-view is a double-edged achievement: we enjoy its benefits and we are threatened by its destructive power, and the potential of the latter ranges from the destruction of the 'good life' to the destruction of life altogether.

All the same, these destructive powers do not necessarily follow from the existence of the meaningful world-view called modern science. It should not be forgotten that science contributed to the

EVERYDAY LIFE AND RATIONALITY

weakening of the binding character of particular 'norms-and-rules' of the system of objectivation 'in itself', and that it had, and still has, a liberating effect on our life. Nor should it be forgotten that, so far, science speaks the only universal language that exists and is thus *shaped* by universal values, even if it is *not based* on them. Further, it cannot be denied that even the institutionalization of science and its application as technology has had beneficial effects, primarily because it has set time free. But all these benefits have been overshadowed by the intrusion of science into every institution and into everyday life, an intrusion that has not been counterbalanced by the entry of democracy into the same spheres. Even the institutions of democracy, where they exist at all, are increasingly permeated by science, and it is assumed that 'expertise' keeps them moving. In this situation people cannot make decisions in matters of the greatest concern, not only because of the absence of proper channels of such a decision-making, but increasingly because the items of information available for decision-making speak a scientific language 'incomprehensible to the man in the street'. This is equally true in respect of armament, fiscal policy or court procedure. A jury composed of men of good common sense *should* be able to decide whether a defendant is guilty or not guilty, but it often *cannot*: the 'scientific language' of sophisticated psychology is beyond them. No democratic decision-making is possible within the framework of bureaucratized–rationalized institutions. People who, in their majority, are employed by these institutions, *cannot learn to practise democratic procedures* and cannot channel the practice of these procedures into other everyday activities already deeply permeated by science (directly or indirectly).

Learning to follow the 'norms-and-rules' of an *institution* has increasingly become a prerequisite for 'earning a living'. The appropriation of the sphere of objectivation 'in itself' had embraced 'earning a living' not only in so-called 'primitive societies' but in the estates, including those of peasants and craftsmen. This is no longer the case for factory workers, hospital personnel, civil servants, academics and so on. The separation of habitat and work place, already analysed by Sombart, which takes place in the form of the division of 'working hours' and 'leisure hours', are well-known consequences of this development. It is a 'norm-and-rule' of the the objectivation 'in itself' that one has to work (one has to earn a living), but if one performs this task within rationalized institutions, the 'norms-and-rules' one must thereby appropriate are *not* the 'norms-and-rules' of the sphere of objectivation 'in itself' (see *Everyday Life*, (Routledge and Kegan Paul 1984), especially my distinction between 'labour' and 'work'). Those who do not go through this division of the personality into human being-as-a-whole on the one hand and the specialized subject on the other, appear as nonworking members of society even when they toil from dawn to dusk (for instance, women). How this development was fed back into everyday life, in particular into the only institution of the sphere of objectivation 'in itself', the family, is a story, too long to be retraced here (see my 'Women, civil society and family' and 'The emotional division of labour between the sexes'). But several other types of feedback into everyday life are worth mentioning. The 'norms-and-rules' of the specialized objectivation 'for and in itself' are experienced both as burdens and narcotics. The radius of action for the human being-as-a-whole is shrinking to the point where humans can no longer survive if they cease to be specialized beings. (For example, the pensioners who do not know what to do with their time.) The attitudes required for action within the specialized institutions will be internalized. The scope of personal contacts will be reduced to those with people in the same profession. Occasionally, a deep involvement in an institution may develop, a substitute 'meaning of life' of a kind which makes a person a bore to those not sharing the same involvement. A simultaneous and increasing institutionalization of the sphere of objectivation 'in itself' can be noted in so far as the surface of this sphere will be so reduced as to be identical with the only institution in it, the family.

Competence in following the 'norms-and-rules' of the sphere of objectivation 'in itself' has been called the 'rationality of reason'. In the last chapter I briefly enumerated the main features and the main accomplishments of rationality of this kind. Should one turn to the sphere of objectivation 'for and in itself', one will immediately realize that in order to observe the 'norms-and-rules' of any institution *the same features suffice* and *the same accomplishments are required*. The assertion that the same features 'suffice' does not imply that other features are necessarily excluded. It simply means that one *can* follow the 'norms-and-rules' of any objectivation 'for and in itself' without transcending the structures and boundaries of the rationality of reason. The 'norms-and-rules' of the objectivation 'for and in itself' can be taken for granted by the specialized subject. Moreover, normally they *are* taken for granted. Of course, when one proceeds from following the 'norms-and-rules' of the sphere of objectivation 'in itself' to following the rules of any institution, one must suspend, as it were, the 'norms-

and-rules' of the former to be able to follow those of the latter. But a suspension of this kind is rather pragmatic, and is neither epistemological nor ethical; in other words, it is *not practical*. Accomplishing this 'switch' does not involve querying the validity of the 'norms-and-rules' of the sphere of objectivation 'in itself'. But the same holds true the other way round: if one 'switches back' from following the 'norms-and-rules' of an institution to following the 'norms-and-rules' of the sphere of objectivation 'in itself', one normally would not query the validity of the 'norms-and-rules' of the objectivation 'for and in itself' one has observed so far. The feedback of the objectivation 'for and in itself' into the sphere of objectivation 'in itself' happens unwittingly and not via a conscious–practical process of evaluative criticism and selection. And to repeat, in all this I do not suggest that a conscious selection of this kind cannot be the case, nor do I suggest that suspending the following of the 'norms-and-rules' of the sphere of objectivation 'in itself' in favour of following 'norms-and-rules' of the objectivation 'for and in itself' *cannot* have epistemological and ethical (and therefore practical) implications. But for these to happen the subject must *transcend* the relatively homogeneous structure of 'norms-and-rules' of an institution and relativize its homogeneity by taking recourse to one objectivation 'for itself' or to a universalized value.

Everyday life is not exhausted by the appropriation of the 'norms-and-rules' of the sphere of objectivation 'in itself'. Men and women have *direct access* to the objectivation 'for itself', at least to their partial reception and understanding. I have analysed the oscillating character of the interchange between everyday experience and higher objectivations (in taste and in the public domain). But institutions are relatively homogeneous subsystems, and it thus seems very unlikely that men and women could, while keeping with the 'norms-and-rules' of an institution, also have direct access to objectivations 'for itself' within the framework of these institutions. How can any person transcend the relatively homogeneous system of institutions? The reply to this is simple enough. From the perspective of the *person* working within a rationalized institution, 'acting within the framework of an institution' is an *everyday* experience, it belongs to everyday life. 'Factory' or 'office' are rationalized institutions, but working in a factory or in an office is, with all its implications, part of the everyday life of a worker or clerk. The experience of this work, with its 'hidden injuries', can be related, just like all everyday experiences, to objectivations 'for itself'. People can then ask questions as to whether the *roles* allotted to them in 'observing the rules of the game' of the institution are just or unjust, and further, whether the rules of the game themselves *should be* what they are. This can and does happen because science (in contrast to religion) can only legitimate technically, and cannot normally decree that things *should be* as they are. Another reason is that several universal values (freedom, equality, humaneness and the like) can be interpreted in different ways. Moreover, justice can be interpreted in terms of the freedom and equality of all (which was not the case in previous societies). But if this happens, we are no longer dealing with rationality of reason but with *rationality of intellect*.

Rationality of intellect has been identified with the attitude of rationalism. But the attitude of rationalism does not necessarily imply the *procedure* of rationalism, even if in the final analysis it usually does. Thus, even though I will only elaborate on this problem later, I must state in advance that 'rationality of intellect' is *not* identical with the culture of critical discourse.

V Rationality of reason, rationality of intellect

The vivisection of rationality

At this stage I must return to the point of departure of the present essay: the centrality that the problem of rationality has acquired in contemporary sociology. In the wake of the words (not necessarily the spirit) of Max Weber,* one tendency has become predominant, if not exclusive, in this discourse. I call it the 'vivisection of rationality'. The term denotes the attempt of drawing up a typology of 'rationalities' on the grounds of *formal* propensities of *actions* abstracted from the context of these actions in their life-world and from the social structure in general, and also abstracted from the concrete content of the actions in question and the meaning of this content as it appears in the historical consciousness of actors. It is generally held that it was Weber who *defined* the category of rationality when he distinguished between goal-rational and value-rational actions. Yet to make this definition more conclusive it is necessary to further subdivide these types to 'obtain' a particular 'type' of rationality for each structur-

---

* J. Arnason takes a more resolute stand. He argues that the procedure I named the vivisection of rationality 'has absolutely nothing to do with the Weberian project'. See John Arnason, *Praxis and Interpretation*.

ally distinct type of action. A well-known division is that of a goal-rationality, instrumental rationality, strategic rationality and communicative rationality. Even if this and similar kinds of formal subdivisions of all human actions were to be accepted as relevant, it would not mean that the definition of various actions could be treated as if they were the definitions of various types of rationality. Weber could easily dispense with any definition of rationality because in terms of his theory of history, rational action proper emerges only in modernity, or, conversely, modernity is the period distinguished by rational actions. For Weber, 'traditional action' is neither rational nor irrational; at best, it is 'relatively rational', which is why it appears 'irrational' from the perspective of modernity (see Weber's *Wirtschaft und Gesellschaft*, Tübingen, SCB Mohr (Siebeck), 1972). Weber was thus theorizing via the historical consciousness of modernity, where the *interpretation* of rationality, as far as its exact meaning and substance are concerned, has a 'taken for granted' character. This 'taken for granted' interpretation is undertaken by the dominating worldview of science, or the philosophy of science, and eventually by universalized values as well. But not even a giant like Max Weber could completely avoid certain confusions surrounding his restricting the scope of relevance of the sphere of rational action proper. In his sociology of religion Weber occasionally applies the notion of rationality and of rationalization to traditional societies also, and in a way not wholly consistent with his concept of rationality as elaborated in his purely theoretical studies. (For instance, Weber speaks of the 'rationality' of the Pantheon of gods based on the *rational* 'sense of order'. But what is this 'rational sense of order'? And why are stereotyped religious rites rational? They are traditional, so in terms of Weber's own theory, they should not be *called* rational.) Notwithstanding such inconsistencies, Weber was at least not guilty of committing the theoretical fallacy of defining forms of action and believing thereby to have correspondingly defined the different types of rationality. However, this cannot be said of the contemporary 'vivisection of rationality', which is thoroughly guilty of this fallacy, and in addition even amplifies the hidden inconsistencies of the Weberian conception. For if we subscribe to the Weberian distinction, we are only entitled to make the hypothetical assertion that if an action is rational, then it can be either goal-rational or value-rational. If, on the other hand, we subscribe to the distinction made by K. O. Apel, we are only entitled to make the hypothetical assertion that 'if an action is rational, then it can be either goal-rational, or instrumentally rational, or strategically rational, or communicatively rational'. But all this hardly answers, the question of when an action can be called rational at all, be it goal-oriented, instrumental, pragmatic or communicative. This is a relevant question because all these actions can be rational as well as non-rational depending on the content of such actions. I would not deny that by the above statement I contrast my own concept of rationality to a purely formal approach. But in what follows I will show that my definition of rationality – acting according to reason either by competence in minding 'norms-and-rules' or by competence in observing a norm of a given particular historical epoch – eliminates theoretical confusions and logical contradictions which cannot be eliminated by a merely formal treatment of rationality.

It is beyond doubt that the contemporary 'vivisection of rationality' serves a respectable purpose. If forms of action are, by definition, forms of rationality, then rationality must be ascribed to all human beings regardless of their social context, world-views and the like, for the actions themselves are conceived of as human universals. In this way the celebrated thesis of the enlightenment, that human beings are born endowed with reason, is reconfirmed. This is even more so in theories where 'communicative rationality' is conceived of as a human universal. Notwithstanding the obvious sympathy I have for contemporary analyses of rationality, certain criticisms are warranted.

I take to be representative of the procedure of the 'vivisection of rationality' a recent paper by Karl-Otto Apel, 'Three dimensions of understanding meaning in analytic philosophy; linguistic conventions, intentions and reference to things', *Philosophy and Social Criticism*, No. 2, 1980. This paper has the considerable merit of offering a *definition* of rationality (an infrequent gesture on the part of the 'vivisectors'), and of performing vivisection in a very dense way (in less than two pages). Apel argues thus: 'It seems to me that, on the human level of possible interaction by speech, it is possible to make the following distinction between *types of actions* in general (and, for that matter, *types of rule-following competence or rationality*' (my italics). In other words, types of action are here identical with types of rationality, and rationality is defined as 'rule-following competence'. At first glance the reader may wonder what difference it makes if one defines rationality as 'rule-following competence', as Apel does, or 'competence in following "norms-and-rules" or observing norms', as I do. However, the difference is enormous. First of all, Apel's definition is tautological. Actions of all types have their intrinsic rules. Indeed, they are *defined* and *distinguished* by Apel precisely on this basis of having intrinsic rules. Since actions of all types are so defined, and the types of actions are conceived as of types of rationality, the procedure of distinction already *implies* that rationality is 'rule-following competence'. Very simply, the Apelian definition of rationality cannot determine whether an instrumental action is rational or not, because the very fact that the action in question belongs to the 'type' instrumental action already defines it as rational. In the definition of rationality (of reason) as competence in following 'norms-and-rules', there is no such tautology, or even anything similar. The assumption here is that the rules of actions are embedded in norms-for-action, and if a rule is followed in a manner contrary to the normative expectations of a given life-world, institution and the like, then an action can be irrational or non-rational whereas if it is followed in line with these expectations, the same type of action will be rational, even if the *form* of action is identical in both cases. As a consequence, my definition of rationality introduces historico-substantive elements into the understanding of rationality. But my definition, in contrast to that of Apel, implies something else as well, namely that the rationality of an action (or of an action-type) *does not depend* on the character of a single action (or on types of actions) alone. All types of actions are embedded in a 'conglomerate' (or series) of actions, and an action (or a type of action) is rational or non-rational if the entire 'conglomerate' of actions makes it such.

The terror of prostitutes and the case of rationality

I wish to illustrate the foregoing argument in two ways. First, I will examine a possible case of a bizarre individual action. Later, I will show that the same model can be applied to social actions typically performed within a social structure.

Let us suppose that X decides to strangle prostitutes because they contaminate society. He intends to 'purify' society and acts accordingly. (The *form* of this action could be called 'value-rational'.) Let us suppose that he also argues before his friends that 'prostitutes contaminate society', and that they accept the *principles* of his intended action. Let us further suppose that he can find at least *one* person who *agrees* with him that the best solution to the problem lies in strangling the prostitutes. It is possible to fulfil all of these conditions, and these speech-acts in their totality, as far as their *form* is concerned, can legitimately be called 'communicative rational'. Let us then suppose that our man chooses the proper means for the goal (adequate rope and correct timing and deployment of physical strength), and that he realizes his goal. He strangles the prostitutes of his city, and even manages to escape the authorities. The *form* of *these* actions could be called goal-rational or pragmatic-rational. Yet the spontaneous reaction to these killings, given a minimum of common sense, will inevitably be that X acted *irrationally*. People with no knowledge of theories of rationality would cry that 'He must have been *mad*.' But why mad, and why irrational? During each stage of his plan, X acted in harmony with one or the other formal criteria of rationality, didn't he? Nevertheless, it can easily be shown that our man acted irrationally, even 'madly', and for the following reasons.

(1) All human actions are related to other human actions; single actions are set within a series of actions. No action can be called 'rational', even if it meets the formal criteria of one or the other 'types' of rationality, if the series of actions of which it is part infringes the *'norms-and-rules'* of the given life-world (the word 'norm' requires special emphasis here). The converse is also true: no action can be called 'irrational', even if it does *not* meet *any* formal criterion of 'rationality', if in the entire series of actions the 'norms-and-rules' are being observed. Drinking wine at a party does not contradict the 'norms-and-rules' of being a 'sociable' person, but rather belongs to the series of actions which make someone 'sociable'. In this sense it cannot be called irrational, even if it is *not rational* according to *any* formal criterion of rationality. Even people who do not usually drink wine might do so in order to keep with the 'norms-and-rules'. Drinking wine is not a rational action, *but it may be a rational action all the same.* The crucial factor is the action context.

(2) Further, the rationality of action is *substantively* defined by *accessible knowledge* ('know-how', 'know-what'), the knowledge of norms included. If someone does not acquire the accessible knowledge of a particular life-world or institution, their actions will be *regarded* as irrational, irrespective of whether or not these actions meet any formal criteria of 'rational action'. People who in their adult life move to another country having different cultural traditions will soon discover that some (and perhaps all) of their actions which hitherto had been regarded as completely rational are now regarded as irrational. One might object that those actions *regarded* as irrational in a new culture *are in fact* rational.

However, in this respect I would argue that the rationality of action is *constituted by the regard*. Although I have not yet analysed 'rationality of intellect', this statement follows from the definition of 'rationality of reason', the foundation of the rationality of intellect. If rationality of reason means competence in observing the 'norms-and-rules' of the sphere of objectivation 'in itself', then everyone who has appropriated the 'norms-and-rules' of this sphere in a culture or class different to the one in which he or she now has to act, will act irrationally unless he or she appropriates the 'norms-and-rules' of the new one. I will return to this question later and generalize (from one perspective only) the thesis so far formulated, that *no action* is either irrational or rational *per se* (as no action stands for itself), it is only *regard* that makes it such.

(3) The 'vivisection of rationality' dissects the related series of actions into separate forms of 'rationalities'. In so doing it dissects the human person-as-a-whole. The question of whether a human person *is* indeed rational and *to what extent* he or she is rational cannot even be raised. But, this is precisely the question which we raise in everyday life, a question of utmost importance. I wish to mention but one implication: the rationality of our actions might depend on the right or wrong judgment concerning the more or less rational *character* of another person. In (1) I have already argued that the rationality or irrationality of a single action depends on the cluster of actions of which it is part. Whether a person is rational to a greater or lesser degree can be better decided on the grounds of *many* clusters of action indicative of a human person-as-a-whole.

(4) I concur with the main tenet of the theories of the 'vivisection of rationality' in so far as I attribute rationality to action. This is clear if one recalls the conclusion of the first chapter. I stated there that the category of rationality was discovered by philosophy, in conjunction with the discovery of practical reason. In defining rationality of reason as competence in minding 'norms-and-rules', and not, as Apel defines it, as competence in minding rules, I have done no more than live up to my introductory hypothesis. Of course, I have extended the relevant application of the category of 'rationality of reason' to the human species as a whole (with the statement that all humans are born with reason). In other words, I have also applied this category to human cultures in which practical reason had not yet been discovered and formulated, since it had not yet been 'individualized'. I made this extension on the grounds of the assumption that practical reason *in*

nuce (acting according to the hierarchy of categories of value orientation) is an empirical universal.

(5) If actions are invariably embedded in *clusters* of actions, each of which implies minding certain 'norms-and-rules', feelings cannot be exempt, from being divided into rational–irrational either. More precisely, it is only precognitive feelings that remain unaffected by this division (drives, pain, and so on). (For a typology of feelings, and for an analysis of the unity of feeling, thinking, acting, see *A Theory of Feelings*.) In my book on feelings, I have sufficiently argued on behalf of the thesis that there is no action without feeling (without involvement in the goal of action or in the process of action), so I need not repeat my arguments here. I will restrict myself to a brief analysis of affects and emotions, irrespective of whether they are related to particular actions or to behaviour in general. In both cases it holds true that emotion (or affect) is rational if it evolves and becomes manifest *according to 'norms-and-rules'*. Should someone feel grief at the funeral of one of his parents or a friend, this is a rational feeling because one *should* feel it, and because people normally do. No one will say 'You're crazy' because you feel grief on this occasion. But should one start laughing instead, most people would regard your emotional response as irrational. Of course, if someone does not accept the norm that parents should be respected and loved, but instead accepts the norm that 'good persons should be respected and loved', and at the same time does not consider his parents to qualify as good persons, the situation could be entirely different. Indeed, should he feel grief at their funeral, he might well assess his own grief as an irrational feeling. If an emotional response is not in harmony either with the 'norms-and-rules' of external authority or with the norms (values) of internal authority, *then* it is an irrational emotional response (see 'The Power of Shame'). The same holds true of action proper (and not of behaviour). In my view, Weber had precisely this problem in mind when he distinguished emotional actions from traditional goal-rational, and value-rational actions. No action is *less* rational *because* it is emotional. Emotional actions are *only* irrational *if* emotions make us act such that the action *contradicts* the 'norms-and-rules' accepted by the actor. Of course, there is a marked *moral* difference between an irrational emotional response or irrational action if the infringed norms are of *equal* moral content (if they are both imperative, among others). However, this most important moral issue has no bearing on the distinction between rational and irrational affects or emotions.

EVERYDAY LIFE AND RATIONALITY

I am fully aware of the sketchy character of this analysis. Since rationality of intellect has not yet been analysed, certain questions simply have to be left open and these loose ends will be dealt with at the end of this chapter. To date I have sought only to give a persuasive answer to the problem why X, the strangler of prostitutes, acted irrationally, despite the fact that each of his actions could have been described as rational in terms of one or another *form* of 'rational action'.

According to point (1) above, the rationality of any form of action depends on the rationality of the 'cluster of actions' in which it is embedded. The rationality or irrationality of the 'cluster of actions' depends, again, on the all-encompassing action (this can be the 'final' act of the series of action, though not necessarily so). The rationality or irrationality of all the actions of X depends on the judgment as to whether 'strangling prostitutes' was an irrational act or not, since it is precisely this that was the all-encompassing action in his cluster of actions. In itself, killing can be legal and illegal, rational and irrational, even moral and immoral (depending on the legal system, the concrete norms of a societal environment, and the interpretation of abstract norms).

Now, when X killed the prostitutes he acted not only against the law but also against the 'norms-and-rules' of our life-world. However, this fact alone would not make his act irrational. One can infringe 'norms-and-rules' of a social environment *voluntarily*, either from the standpoint of another norm which is being observed, or by the withdrawal of consent to the validity of these 'norms-and-rules', or simply because it seems to serve our interest. In the latter cases the act is criminal or illegal but not irrational. It is obvious that X did not take recourse to any *norm* counterposed to the 'biases' of his social environment. On the contrary, his point of departure was a bias that he shared with others ('prostitutes contaminate society'). One should not forget that he discussed this subject with friends who concurred with his view about prostitutes. X did not withdraw his consent from the general normative judgment of his society: from the premise of despising prostitutes, regarding them as 'base creatures', even as people who *must* be eliminated, he acted on these maxims to the extreme. It was not his idea but the action taken in conformity with the idea that contradicted the 'norms-and-rules': the action of strangling the prostitutes. Thus X acted against the external authority of judgment (general opinion about 'norms-and-rules') *on the ground* of an assumption *drawn* from the external authority. If it is true, as stated earlier, that an emotional response is rational in so far as it is adequate to 'norms-and-rules', in this particular case the emotional response to the shared assumption ('prostitutes contaminate society') was *intemperate*, and in that sense *inadequate* (in terms of these 'norms-and-rules'), and therefore irrational.

At this stage the reader may object to all this as a sterile theoretical exercise. What has the solid problem of rationality to do with the case study of an obviously mentally ill person who has run amok? Was not this analysis supposed to be a study of a social phenomenon? Yet I believe that while giving this account of X, I have also given an account of the *modus operandi* of modern totalitarian systems.

If one dissects various actions in Nazi Germany or the Soviet Union, the yield obtained will be actions which, according to their *form*, are goal-rational, value-rational, or, if you like, goal-rational, instrumental-rational, pragmatic-rational and communicative-rational. However, should one take the *cluster* of actions, and apply the previous specifications to it, one must conclude that all actions within the cluster are *irrational* because of the irrationality of the overall action. My case study of X is a simple analogy of *one* cluster of actions in Nazi Germany. 'The purity of race' as a selected value and the thesis that 'Jews contaminate the purity of society' as a fairly consensually accepted statement are to be understood from the perspective of Auschwitz, this factory of extermination which was run according to the *form* of goal-rationality. Here, as well as in the case of X, the means adequate for the goal were selected and implemented and the goal was achieved. And just as the irrationality of the strangler's actions is not diminished by the fact that, in our hypothetical case, he was not apprehended the irrationality of the cluster of Nazi actions would not have been diminished either, had the Nazis won the war. (Unless, of course, the victory had been total and all representatives of the earlier universal 'regard' had been exterminated in the wake of this victory.) It follows from this that the longevity of the Bolshevik system is far from being any proof of its 'rationality'.

Certain 'vivisectors of rationality' blame all the ills of modernity on 'instrumental rationality'. The crux of the matter is that *instrumental action* can be rational in relation to its *form* and irrational in relation to its *content*. Instrumental 'reason' can be blamed for the invention and implementation of sophisticated technologies for social action. But the rationality or irrationality of social action does *not* depend on the possible degree of sophistication of the technology applied. Using gas chambers to achieve mass extermination is not irrational to a greater or lesser extent, but to exactly the same degree, as using rope to strangle prostitutes. In both cases the term 'instrumental *action*' can be applied, but not the term 'instrumental *rationality*'. Could we even for a moment attribute instrumental *rationality* to an action which, however 'rationally' implemented in a formal sense, would destroy humankind, and, in all probability, life itself (and with it the only framework within which the question of rationality can be raised)? The answer is obviously in the negative, and this only substantiates the theoretical suggestion that the rationality of any action does not solely depend on the form of action, for it can be conceived as rational only in conjunction with other actions. Only from the perspective of the overall action can its rationality be determined.

It is appropriate here to return to my thesis (brought forth in point (2)) that the rationality or irrationality of actions is constituted by the *regard*. The regard is that of 'norms-and-rules' (or norms), or more precisely, that of people who accept the validity of 'norms-and-rules' (or norms). I already argued that the dominating world-view of our epoch is science, and that universalized values, as consensually accepted value ideas, have become the highest (free-floating) values that humans can have recourse to. It stands to reason that in our age the regard which *renders* actions rational or irrational is, in the last instance, the regard of science and that of universalized value-ideas. It is exactly *this* regard that ultimately renders all actions of Nazism irrational, that 'irrationalizes' them, simply because the theory and practice of racism contradicts both the dominating world-view *and* the universalized values. In the case of Bolshevism, both universalized values and the dominating world-view (science) were (theoretically) reasserted, and even hyperbolically laboured. This accounts for the confusion of the regard. Even if the regard put the system on display as spectacularly irrational, 'irrationalized' it, it could not give a proper account of the grounds on which it did so. More precisely, various 'regards' from the perspective of various 'norms-and-rules' and of various interpretations of rationality emerged, based on entirely different reasons. (One could mention the Trotskyites who exposed the regime as irrational on the ground that it fell short of its revolutionary promises, while still essentially approving of it.) Despite all the confusion and the variety of regards, 'irrationalizing' the Soviet system involves two elements common to all regards, and the same ones as I have hinted at in the case of X, the strangler. To repeat them, it was not the statement that 'prostitutes contaminate the purity of society' which violated any 'norms-and-rules' (as I assumed that a bias of this kind was accepted by many as a valid statement), but the fact that this statement served as an 'ideology' for strangling prostitutes; in other words, that the same commonsensical 'norms-and-rules' which was violated by the final act served as ideology. In Soviet society, the idea of observing certain universalized values (allegedly for the first time in a genuine way) was realized by *violating all* universalized values, in a violation the type of which and the extent of which surpassed several times any violations committed by the social agents they wanted to 'purify' society of.

Not only in respect of totalitarian societies, but in respect of all social actions (clusters of actions), it is the *regard* which renders a cluster irrational, which 'irrationalizes' it. In our epoch, the supreme 'regard' can be the 'regard' of universalized values, the 'regard' of the dominating world-view, or the regard of both. Why do we believe that peace is rational, or that wars are irrational (a 'regard' which is no longer the exclusive property of sophisticated idealists but also that of the 'man in the street')? Why do we regard mass epidemics due to lack of vaccine as irrational? Epidemics are natural disasters, like earthquakes, and in themselves are neither rational nor irrational. It is we who 'irrationalize' them on the basis of an action that could have taken place (vaccination). Moreover, we deem that such an action not only could have but *should* have taken place (on the one hand because of knowledge provided by science, on the other hand because of norms provided by science and universalized values). Forbearance too is an action, and can be 'rationalized' and 'irrationalized' accordingly. Thus, in 'irrationalizing' epidemics, we do not 'irrationalize' a natural event (which would be a pan-rationalistic transgression), but the forbearance in its prevention.

A further criticism of the 'vivisection of rationality'

The last example serves as an introduction to a further criticism of the 'vivisection of rationality'. If the 'regard' defines vaccination as 'rational', *what kind* of rationality is at work here? Is it instrumental–rational, strategic–rational or communicative–rational to employ the forms of rational action differentiated by Apel, or is it, along with Weber, rational, or value-rational or goal-rational?

It will prove useful here to analyse Weber's notion of goal-rationality more carefully. At first glance the category seems rather illuminating. Yet on closer scrutiny certain weaknesses are apparent. Alfred Schutz undertook a thorough investigation of Weber's use of the concept of 'goal rationality', and he concluded that Weber failed to differentiate between act and action. Apel made this Weberian concept slightly more substantive, and in doing so he used it less ambiguously than Weber in one respect, but more ambiguously in another. (I have in mind here his distinction between instrumental and strategic action.)

One can define goal-rational action as *goal-oriented* action. This definition is tautological. Action *means* goal-oriented human activity, so that behaviour which is not goal-oriented is not action. (A tantrum, for instance, would not be an action.) Should we take this definition seriously, it could mean that each and every action is rational. An *action theory* would then be unable to differentiate between rational and irrational (as every action is, by definition, to be understood as rational). But 'rationality' is, following Hegel, a 'reflexive category'; it only *means* something *in contrast* to irrationality or non-rationality or a-rationality. Therefore, if every action is to be understood as rational, then no action can be defined as rational; if we define goal-rationality as goal-oriented action, then no action is rational.

A narrower definition of goal-rationality is that an action is goal-rational if the actor chooses the *proper means* to achieve a goal. Rationality of action is not attributed to goal-orientation, but to the means-goal relationship. Here, we must first consider what the term 'proper means' is all about. 'Proper' can be understood, firstly, as meaning adequate to the 'norms-and-rules' of the objectivation 'in itself', or, for that matter, to the 'norms-and-rules' of *any* objectivation. Should we subscribe to this interpretation, the notion 'proper' stands not only for *means* but for the *goal* as well. To refer back to the case of X, we saw that proper means failed to make his action rational because the goal was improper. Let us momentarily assume that only the goals of an action are more or less 'prescribed' by the respective objectivations, and not the means. The means could then be chosen 'properly' by the actors to achieve a given goal. But how can we know that the means were chosen properly? Can we say that *if* the goal was realized, *then* the means must have been chosen properly (rationally)? Let us take the case of two armies locked in war, obviously, only one can win. Is it reasonable to assume that the generals of all the victorious armies in history, up until now, have acted goal-rationally (in that they won), whereas the generals of all the vanquished armies have not acted with goal-rationality (in that they lost)? This is clearly an unreasonable assumption, for victory depends on a *cluster* of factors, of which the 'proper' selection of means is but one among several others – strength, population size, current level of military technology, natural events, topography, and so on. Goal-realization is, then, at best partial, and certainly not conclusive, evidence of the rationality of action based on the proper selection of means, as the goal can remain unrealized for another actor selecting the same means and employing the same action. Further, we know from Kant, Hegel and Marx (and even from our own personal experiences), that actors, especially in modernity, very often choose proper means for their goals, only to achieve an end which *they did not at all intend*. Since no social actor acts in limbo but always in conjunction (and sometimes in conflict) with other actors and actions, the outcome of an action does not depend solely on the choice of 'proper' means. Both individual and collective purposes intersect other individual and collective purposes.

Weber provides a limited and relative solution to the problem. Within the framework of his theory, the losers can be seen as having acted rationally all the same, if not in terms of goal-rationality, then in terms of value-rationality, because the latter kind of rationality can be recognized 'irrespective of the consequences'. But certain contemporary 'vivisectors of rationality' have thrown this life-belt away.

Let me briefly enumerate the types of rational action elaborated by Apel in the paper I referred to above. They are the following:

(1) 'Pure instrumental rationality of purposive-rational actions', which characterizes man's relation to inorganic nature.

(2) Instrumental purposive-rational action 'in treating human behaviour like that of nature', which can only succeed 'to a certain extent'. (What, we might ask Apel, of human relations to organic nature?) Actions of these two kinds of instrumental purposive rationality do not imply communicative rationality.

(3) Strategical action as purposive-rational action characterized by the interaction of the game (for instance, in war or business negotiations). This type of rational action implies 'reciprocity of the rule-following actions and thus . . . equal status of the partners'. This type of action already implies a measure of communicative rationality, but it is not yet communicative rationality proper.

(4) Communicative rationality proper as coming to an agreement about, and thus the sharing of, the meanings, also the 'occasion meanings', of linguistic utterances by communication.

EVERYDAY LIFE AND RATIONALITY

Before going further with his 'vivisection of rationality', Apel states: 'I suggest that there must be special *communicative actions*, i.e. actions of sharing *linguistic meaning*. These actions must be different from purposive-rational actions in that their conditions of success (or felicity) are not satisfied by somebody's fulfilling the rules of *means-end-rationality* solitarily . . . i.e. independently of fulfilling the rules of agreement with other persons.'

This statement has several implications. First of all, it implies the astonishing opinion that purposive rational action (identified by Apel with means-end-rationality) means 'rule fulfilment' as a solitary enterprise. This would imply the conclusion that man's relation to (inorganic) nature and man's relation to other men as mere objects or means is a 'solitary' undertaking, a conclusion I believe to be completely wrong on the level of both individual and social action.

Let us look at individual action. What is fundamentally wrong with Apel's statement is the identification introduced by his 'i.e.'. He speaks of fulfilling the rules of 'means-end-rationality' solitarily, *i.e.* independently of fulfilling rules of agreement with other persons. It is obvious that I can fulfil 'means-end-rationality' solitarily, that is to say, when I am alone. I can also fulfil the 'rules' of pure communicative rationality when I am alone. When I am pondering on a moral matter, and I enumerate all the relevant arguments and counter-arguments to myself, I act according to 'communicative rationality', even if I am completely alone. But in *neither* case can I fulfil a 'rule' *independently* of fulfilling rules of agreement with other persons. By 'agreement' I mean virtual agreement, in so far as both 'means-end-rationality' and communicative rationality depend on my observing consensual norms as well. And if we speak about *social* action, then nothing is less 'solitary' than production and domination.

Actions of domination and production are the types of actions which have to be most strictly appropriated by every newborn thrown into any world, and they are the ones most powerfully legitimated by a meaningful world-view. Whether 'agreement' is granted (as suggested in the quote from Apel) in respect of successful legitimation, or whether it is not, and whether the fulfilled rules are the rules *of* agreement or not, they are indeed rules *by* agreement, that is to say, intersubjective rules. Apel wants to avoid this dichotomic dilemma in relation to social action (even if not in 'our relation to nature'), and this is why he introduces the special case of purposive rationality, namely, 'strategic action'. Strategic action is not 'solitary', and it cannot be, since it presupposes 'partners' who observe 'the rules of the game'. Equally problematic here is the use of 'and thus' (to requote the relevant passage: strategic rationality implies 'reciprocity in the rule-following actions and *thus* . . . equal status of the partners'). It may be evident that the second statement does not follow from the first, irrespective of whether we have in mind war or a business relationship (Apel's examples), or innumerable cases of other actions which are reciprocal. Most of the 'norms-and-rules' of the sphere of objectivation 'in itself' and *all* the 'norms-and-rules' of *any* institution imply reciprocity of some kind. (The father gives bread, the child obeys; if I make mistakes, I will be chastized; if I work, I get food and shelter; if I work hard, I will be awarded a day off, and so on.) But reciprocity in following 'the rules of the game' *does not necessarily imply* 'the equal status of the partners', and usually in fact does not do so at all. Though 'the equal status of partners' is *formally* implied, in reality this is usually not the case (e.g. in war). The ancients knew all about this 'rule of the game', as the classic story of the wolf and the lamb testifies. So does the famous motto *Vae victis!*

Further, as we know, Apel restricts the form of rationality conceived of as proper means-goal relationships to actions aimed at objects or quasi-objects. However, it is obvious that actions of this kind encompass a wide range of actions related neither to nature nor to the use of others as mere objects. Disclosing bad news to a friend requires *deliberation* about the proper means of doing so. Similarly, we can deliberate upon the proper means of memorizing a poem, of delivering a speech and so on. Good judgment in action involves first of all the *moral* propensity to find the proper means to a goal we accept as 'good'. When we speak about the perlocutory effects of the speech act, we conceive of this act as a 'means' to the effects. *But it is far from being true that the perlocutory effect of a speech act equals the instrumentalization of the person we intend to influence.* If I ponder on *how* to ask a favour of someone, I obviously want to achieve a goal external to the speech act (I want the favour to be granted). But if the means (the way in which I ask the favour) are in harmony with the 'norms-and-rules' of my life-world, one could hardly describe this means-goal relationship as a case of 'instrumental rationality'. Whether the action can be described as 'instrumental' or not depends on the goal, not on the means-goal relationship alone.

In all this I have not denied that using the proper means to an end *is* one of the propensities of rationality. Indeed, I have listed this propensity among the characteristics of 'rationality of reason'. I wanted instead to raise doubts about the relevance of a separate *form* of rationality distinguished and isolated from other forms as 'purposive rationality'.

However, one could also interpret Apel's theoretical proposal in the following way: that the subgroup of purposive rationality is not based on the assumption that it is *only* instrumental action that implies a proper means-goal relationship, but rather on the assumption that this form of action implies *only* a proper means-goal relationship. Apel, then, could have in mind the process of *optimization within rationalized institutions*. This would mean that rationalized institutions of production imply instrumental rational action, whereas rationalized institutions of social intercourse can imply, alternatively, instrumental-rational and strategic-rational action. Though I do not think that this was what Apel did have in mind, I cannot simply ignore this interpretation.

This reading implies that Apel's 'instrumental rational' actions exist only in modernity and cannot be detected in prior histories, at least not in their pure forms. But instrumental-purposive rationality as a separate cluster of rationality *means* our relation to inorganic nature. Accordingly, our relation to nature can be rational only within the framework of rationalized productive institutions. But within the rationalized institutions of production the producers normally have no idea about the goal of production and cannot choose the means to achieve the goal. In such a situation, when does goal-rationality, understood as the proper selection of means to a goal, arise? And if those working in production conceive of their own production as means, this is identical with production being means for the goal of 'reproduction of the worker as a human being'. From this aspect, goal-rationality is 'relation to nature' only in so far as humans are also biological beings. Consequently, rather than being its proper field of action, productive activity within rationalized institutions involves (so far) a substantial curtailment of goal-rationality. Of course, one could suggest that at least the upper level of the rationalized institutions of production acts according to the form of purposive-instrumental rationality. Yet the goals determined at the 'top' can hardly be described as the 'transformation of nature'. The 'transformation of nature' (relation to 'nature') serves rather as the *means* for *another end*. (In capitalism, the 'end' is profit, in the dictatorship over needs which calls itself 'real socialism', the 'end' is control.) This leaves us with the natural scientists, whose goal is indeed the understanding and transformation of nature. But science has become the dominating world-view of our epoch, and its universal language gained momentum simultaneously with the universalization of certain values. As Weber put it, science is one deity from among many in our pluralistic Pantheon. *The natural scientists do not* follow simply technical rules, but also 'norms-and-rules'. Their objective is not optimization (selection of proper means to a 'given' goal) but also *observing the norm of scientific research and inquiry*. Thus purposive-instrumental rationality, in Apel's interpretation of the category, does not exhaust their action pattern either.

To all this one could object that even if within rationalized institutions of production no single actor acts according to the scheme of 'purposive rationality', such institutions are still goal-rational in that they 'optimize' production. This interpretation of Apel's 'purposive rationality' differs substantially from the one I have just criticized. To this point it has been assumed that, according to Apel, we can *act* in terms of the scheme of purposive-instrumental rationality only within rationalized institutions. Now it is being assumed that rationalized institutions *function* in terms of purposive-instrumental rationality. Adopting such a position would mean *substituting system theory for action theory*. But if we think in terms of a system theory, the following must be borne in mind. (a) The last type of rational action on Apel's list (communicative rationality) cannot be conceived of in terms of a system theory, thus the ground upon which the division of various forms of action is made is heterogeneous. (b) Even if there are institutions (subsystems) or rationalized production, they are reproduced not only by 'purposive-instrumental actions' but also by 'strategic actions'. (c) 'Optimization' is a relative category. Certainly, the notion of 'optimization' has not been used by Apel, but I have already argued that the *definition* of pure purposive-instrumental rationality as man's relation to nature, justifies attributing 'optimization' to 'instrumental rationality' within a system-theoretical framework. 'Optimization' is undoubtedly one of the propensities of rationality of reason, but whatever the optimal solution may be, or even the optimal output, it depends on the 'norms-and-rules of objectivation 'in itself', objectivation 'for and in itself', and objectivation 'for itself'. 'Optimal' may mean the best proportion (in terms of the category of 'good', 'beautiful', 'useful'), the best result (in terms of the same categories), and so on. So for the sake of simplicity let us confine the term to the category of 'useful'. The optimal conquest of nature is 'optimal' only within the framework of, and in relation to, 'norms-and-rules' of a particular society. 'Useful'–'harmful' are categories of value-orientation, and so orient us in regard to values. If we regard the conquest of nature per se as useful (if we do not specify or delineate certain areas of it as useful), then 'optimal' will come to mean maximum conquest. Should it be otherwise, then maximum conquest will not be identical with 'optimal'; moreover, it could be 'irrationalized' by the dominating regard. Only if the principle of 'production for production's sake' is an uncontestable value in society can *maximal* and *optimal* coincide. A regard which challenges this identification is gaining momentum today, and is increasingly irrationalizing the 'maximum conquest of nature'. Thus within contemporary institutions of production, maximal and optimal coincide, whereas this coalescence is questioned outside these institutions. Of course, one could speak of 'optimization' in a restricted sense (optimal from the viewpoint of norms, values and the like). But optimization of this kind does not characterize rationalized production alone; it has characterized productions of all kinds throughout human histories. Beside, if 'optimal' is understood in relation to '*norms*-and-rules', one has to completely renounce Apel's definition (and restriction) of instrumental rationality. (d) Finally, if man's rational relation to nature is tantamount to the rationalization of production, then all other human actions related to nature are by definition irrational, or at least non-rational. Caring for plants or animals merely in order to enjoy their being and beauty does not fit into *any* form of rationality enumerated by Apel.

Here I rest my case against the 'vivisection of rationality'. Later I will analyse the problem of rational communication, which I regard as a very important asset of the theories of Apel and Habermas.

Unleashing of the critical potential of objectivation 'for itself'

Rationality of reason has been defined here as competence in minding 'norms-and-rules', and rationality of intellect as *competence in observing norms* (or at least one norm) while *confronting* these norms (or this norm) *critically* with the 'norms-and-rules' (or with at least one 'norm-and-rule') of the sphere of objectivation 'in itself' or any other objectivations. The reader may remember my statement that objectivations 'for itself' have both a legitimating *and* a critical potential. The norms observed by the rationality of intellect are provided by one or another objectivation 'for itself' ('free floating' universalized values included). Rationalism (rationality of intellect) implies unleashing the critical potential of these norms. This can happen through the simple confrontation of the 'utopian form of life', embodied in one or another type of objectivation 'for itself', with real life. It can also happen with the interpretation or reinterpretation of values inherent in the same objectivations 'for itself'. The reinterpreted and thus observed values serve as yardsticks for the good and the true, and the 'norms-and-rules' are criticized because they do not measure up to this yardstick, or, eventually, because they contradict the optative and/or imperative norms required by the prevailing value standards. These two forms of unleashing the critical potential of objectivations 'for itself' are not always distinct (although they can be). I must add that the statement that rationalism implies the unleashing of the critical potential of objectivations 'for itself' (universalized values included) is not interchangeable with the obverse assertion, namely, that unleashing the critical potential of objectivations 'for itself' constitutes rationalism. Unleashing the critical potential of objectivations 'for itself' is the *precondition* of rationalism, but is not identical with it. Accordingly, I suggest that we speak of 'rationalism *in nuce*' as functioning in all cases, and about 'rationalism proper' when referring to distinct cases.

When a criticial potential is unleashed *en masse*, this indicates an *unstable equilibrium* in the social structure in question. It indicates that 'norms-and-rules' hitherto 'taken for granted' are being eroded. It also indicates (in conjunction with this erosion), the emergence of needs which can no longer be satisfied in the existing life-world or by the institutions which have given birth to them. These and similar tendencies were evident in premodern societies (for example in Athens, at about the end of the fifth century BC, or in imperial Rome). However, modern (capitalist, democratic, industrial) society is a special case in that an unstable equilibrium is its essential constituent (see *A Theory of History*, Part 4). Little wonder then that the critical potential of objectivations 'for itself' is continuously unleashed in modernity, and, moreover, that this critical potential played the role of a midwife at the very birth of modernity (see my discussion of legislative, sceptical and bad conscience in 'The Power of Shame'.) I should add that rationality of intellect is not bound up either with exceptional circumstances or with modernity. It can make its appearance in every relatively complex and conflict-ridden society. But before a critical potential appears *en masse, specific* types of conflicts have to gain momentum.

In order to analyse further 'rationality of intellect', let me first

reiterate certain features of the specific qualities of various objectivations 'for itself', and also of the appropriation of the sphere of
objectivation 'for itself' in everyday life and beyond.

(1) Objectivations 'for itself' are empirical (human) universals.
(2) These objectivations absorb cultural surplus and can 'store' cognitive surplus.
(3) They also involve the tendency (and the possibility), to immortalize cultures, so the latter can be 'resurrected' by the subjects of any subsequent culture.
(4) Precisely because of this possibility, the 'present age' is not identical with the historical present or present history. Rather, it entails all available objectivations 'for itself' created by previous cultures but resurrected by the present one.
(5) Objectivations 'for itself' have a homogeneous system of 'norms-and-rules' of their own, adequate to their homogeneous medium.
(6) In order to appropriate any particular objectivation 'for itself', one must ascend into the homogeneous medium of this very objectivation and suspend the 'norms-and-rules' of the sphere of objectivation 'in itself'.
(7) This can happen within the scope of everyday life, but it may require rising above everyday life.
(8) Irrespective of whether this suspension and ascent into the homogeneous medium takes place via action (for instance, via an ecstatic dance), reception or creation, the experience (emotional–intellectual) is always fed back into everyday life.

It follows from these points that the rise into the sphere of objectivation 'for itself' does not necessarily presuppose a switch from
rationality of reason to rationality of intellect. True enough, the
suspension of the 'norms-and-rules' of the sphere of objectivation
'in itself' indicates that the subjects do not feel completely at ease
within the framework of rationality of reason, or at least that they
need a 'second home' in order to do so. But the suspension of
rationality of reason can take the course of an at least partial
suspension of *rationality altogether*. The liberation of impulses
checked and controlled by the concrete 'norms-and-rules' of
rationality of reason can make this 'ascent' very powerful. Of
course, only a *relative* suspension of the rationality of reason
is possible. Normally, the 'liberation of impulses' has to follow

established rules and techniques, and it is possible to perform well in any type of objectivation 'for itself' if one liberates impulses *in conformity* with the 'norms-and-rules' of these objectivations (for example, in a trance). Should one suspend rationality of reason without following the usual techniques and rules established for such a 'rise', one's manner of action is *irrationalized* by the dominant regard. Societies can put a premium on this irrationality (they can refer to it as superhuman, or even conceive of it as a manifestation of divinity), as well as dismiss it as evil or simply insane; again, it all depends on the particular 'norms-and-rules'.

After this digression it has to be emphasized once more that the rise from the objectivation 'in itself' to the objectivation 'for itself' is often performed relatively irrationally. Since one ceases to observe the 'norms-and-rules' of the sphere of objectivation 'in itself' while suspending them, the act of rising cannot be seen as completely rational by *any* regard of *any* life-world. To repeat, the *regard* of the rationality of intellect does not necessarily 'rationalize' rises of all kinds. However, some of them can be completely 'rationalized'. In section III I distinguished between intellectual (and intellectual-mystical) types of reception or understanding, and other types of reception or action within the sphere of objectivation 'for itself'. The use of the notion 'intellectual' must now be clarified. I refer to certain kinds of objectivations and/or understanding and reception as 'intellectual' because rationality of intellect is able to 'rationalize' the rise of these objectivations 'for itself', even if this rise is (relatively) 'irrationalized' from the standpoint of rationality of reason. Clearly, it is these (intellectual) objectivations that are best qualified, for the purposes of intellect proper (the 'organ' of rationalism), for the unleashing of the critical potential of the sphere of objectivation 'for itself'.

Here I must return briefly to the liberation of impulses (checked and controlled by the 'norms-and-rules' of objectivations 'in itself') which occurs through the rise into the sphere of objectivations 'for itself'. With certain modifications, the Freudian notion of 'sublimation' provides a model for this liberation. By the accident of birth we are 'thrown' into one particular sphere of objectivation 'in itself' and must appropriate particular types of 'norms-and-rules'. It is only thus that we become humans. All our emotive, cognitive and conative abilities are shaped by our life-world. But the 'accident' of birth and the 'norms-and-rules' of the given life-world do not 'fit together' unproblematically. As the subjective potential which cannot be wholly articulated in the framework of the 'norms-and-rules' of the objectivation 'in itself', cultural surplus is a *subjective* surplus. It is precisely this subjective potential which is unleashed via the suspension of rationality of reason, in the process of the rise into an objectivation 'for itself'. This is why the rise is always accompanied by a heightened feeling of satisfaction, pleasure or happiness. Satisfaction, pleasure and happiness are quasi-erotic feelings, and this is what makes the application of the Freudian theory of sublimation so plausible. Since a sexual impulse is a drive and thus not codetermined by sociality, whereas the modes of its satisfaction are always regulated by 'norms-and-rules', accounting for subjective surplus through creative activity as sublimation makes the empirical universality of the sphere of objectivation 'for itself' accountable as well. Even so, what is not explained by the theory is the multifarious types of objectivation 'for itself', from ecstasies to pure speculation. If only the sexual impulse is sublimated, why does this sublimation take such different forms, all of them requiring and absorbing entirely different human abilities? The first to address this problem was Plato, who explained this heightened feeling of happiness by the theory of 'the recollection of ideas'. In Plato, the quasi-erotic feeling has purely intellectual resources. And this served not only the explanation of the pleasure of intellectual speculation (philosophy) but also the feeling of pleasure triggered by beauty or by 'non-sexual' love. Contrary to both Plato and Freud, I would rather suggest a pluralistic explanation. All subjective impulses and abilities which cannot be completely absorbed by the sphere of objectivation 'in itself', even if they are shaped by it (from sexuality to pure speculation), can become a 'cultural surplus' and be absorbed by the sphere of objectivation 'for itself'. We are all born with a genetic code, and each aspect of this code makes us to a greater or lesser degree fit for the appropriation of the 'norms-and-rules' of the world we are born into. The tendencies curtailed by a particular set of 'norms-and-rules' can be impulsive and emotional as well as intellectual. To liberate any of these tendencies from the Procrustean bed of 'norms-and-rules' of any objectivation 'in itself' is pleasurable because *living to the utmost limit of our impulses and/or abilities is pleasurable*. This theoretical suggestion might account for both the heightened feeling of satisfaction in the process of the 'rise' and the great variety of objectivations 'for itself'.

I must now return to the problem of the rationality of irrationality of the 'rise', and I repeat that the rationality of intellect can 'rationalize' the rise to the *intellectual* objectivations. In the last section I briefly dealt with *two* intellectual objectivations: philosophy and science. However, science is institutionalized as the dominating world-view of today, whereas philosophy is not. Science as the dominating world-view intrudes directly and indirectly into everyday life. This is why the rise from everyday consciousness to 'normal' science is today a purely cognitive process. One simply *learns* to speak the language of science and to suspend ordinary language, ordinary perception, ordinary use of objects, ordinary customs. This rise is completely *'rationalized'*, not only by the rationality of intellect but also *by the rationality of reason*. This is why, *irrespective of the regard*, we can speak of the rationality of the 'rise'. But since this rise does not, within the framework of rationalized institutions of science, imply living up to the utmost limits of our impulses, emotions, abilities and the like, it is not accompanied by any heightened feeling of satisfaction, of pleasure, or of happiness. To *learn* how to speak the language of any science, to become competent in minding its 'norms-and-rules', is pleasurable only in the same way as it is pleasurable to succeed in appropriating any 'norms-and-rules' of the sphere of objectivation 'in itself'. But pleasure and satisfaction decrease to the extent that routine sets in, in the same way that it does when we have already acquired competence in minding 'norms-and-rules' of objectivations 'in itself', and repetition has been substituted for invention. When Weber warned the students of science not to wait for 'inspiration' but to do hard work instead, he too had in mind this propensity of modern science.

Of course, Kuhn's distinction between normal and revolutionary science should also be borne in mind at this point. Revolutionary science absorbs cultural surplus no less than other objectivations 'for itself' do. The rise to revolutionary science *should* be 'rationalized' by the rationality of intellect as well. But, *to some extent*, rationality of reason 'irrationalizes' this rise. For instance, explaining revolutionary science in terms of the 'genius' is fairly widespread.

Rationality of intellect was first defined as competence in minding norms (or one single norm) by confronting them (or it) with the 'norms-and-rules' of any objectivation. This was an *interim* definition. I have also mentioned that objectivations 'for itself' (free-floating universalized values included) *provide* norms for the rationality of intellect. Yet, this *does not mean* that *minding the 'norms-and-rules'* of an objectivation 'for itself' is a task performed by the 'rationality of intellect'. While moving freely in a homogeneous medium of an objectivation 'for itself', one certainly still minds 'norms-and-rules', and the latter are intrinsically interwoven. In static societies the 'norms-and-rules' of any objectivation 'for itself' are *not less* 'taken for granted' than the 'norms-and-rules' of the sphere of objectivation 'in itself'. One rises from the sphere of heterogeneous 'norms-and-rules' to a sphere of homogeneous ones, but does not test or query the 'norms-and-rules' of the latter at all. In dynamic societies one can question the 'norms-and-rules' from the vantage point of *another* type of objectivation, the 'norms-and-rules' of which are, however, taken for granted (for example, the conception of *'perception confuse'* of art criticized from the standpoint of rational science, or that of the 'godforsaken world' of science criticized from the position of religion). Even if one can also distinguish, at least in modern times, between 'concrete' 'norms-and-rules' and 'abstract' 'norms-and-rules' within certain objectivations 'for itself', and even if the first can be changed while the second is observed, this change often remains unreflective, at least for those who make it. (It is mainly philosophy that performs the act of reflection.) One could conclude that the rise from the sphere of objectivation 'in itself' to the homogeneous medium of an objectivation 'for itself' does not necessarily imply the switch from rationality of reason to rationality of intellect. Normally, the same attitude of reason is at work in the medium of the latter as in the sphere of the former (minding 'norms-and-rules' which are more or less 'taken for granted'). But the free movement within the sphere of objectivation 'for itself' cannot be accounted for by rationality of reason alone. Imagination and fantasy are also at work, and in a proportion greater than in the appropriation of the 'norms-and-rules' of the sphere of objectivation 'in itself'. But more important than the heightened proportion of imagination and fantasy at work in objectivations 'for itself' is the fact that both imagination and fantasy are *homogenized* and *thus* heightened by the 'norms-and-rules' of any objectivation 'for itself'. The proportion between rationality of reasons and homogenized imagination depends on the type of objectivation, on the strictness or tightness of the 'norms-and-rules', on whether they are more concrete or more abstract, or on their density. These propensities are historical variables. Finally, the 'proportion' varies, and the more abstract the 'norms-and-rules' of an objectivation 'for itself' are, the more they vary, and the more they do so *individually*, both in respect of the creative and the receptive subject.

However, there is only one type of objectivation 'for itself' in which the rules are completely *defined by the norms*, and this is philosophy. I have already mentioned that philosophy constructs the supreme idea of truth (as the unity of true and good), and that it confronts this idea *critically* with the 'norms-and-rules' of the sphere of objectivation 'in itself', and occasionally with 'norms-and-rules' of institutions and those of other objectivations 'for itself' as well. Thus observing the norms of philosophy means thinking and acting according to the rationality of intellect. *Philosophy is rationality of intellect incarnate.* In philosophy, intuitive imagination and fantasy are transformed into the 'aura' of rationality of intellect. This is why the category of rationality was discovered *and* constructed by philosophy. Rationality of reason could be discovered because rationality of intellect had been constructed.

The suggestion that the rules of philosophy are completely defined by its norms was something of an understatement, the rules of philosophy having no *technical propensities*. Since the truth of philosophy is critically confronted not only with any concrete belief which is 'taken for granted' but with 'taken-for-grantedness' as such, its validity has to be proved. And it can only be proved if this truth is inferred via rational argumentation.

But rationality of reason is the foundation of rationality of intellect. Philosophy cannot cut the thread on which its own rationality hinges; this would be suicidal. To be able to argue rationally, philosophies must ultimately have recourse to something 'taken for granted' (self-evident). This is how even irrationalist philosophies proceed. Rationalist philosophies, empiricist ones included, differ from irrationalist ones in so far as the former accept at least one propensity of rationality of reason as their self-evident point of departure, whereas irrationalist philosophies take certain non-rational human motivations or propensities 'for granted'. This is really an enormous difference, for even if irrationalist philosophies do not break with the *procedure* of rationality of intellect, they apply this procedure in order to complete the break with rationality of reason. It is not the procedure of having an (ultimate) recourse to a measure of self-evidence that alone binds rationality of intellect to rationality of reason. (In my theory of rational argumentation I rely heavily on the theories of Apel and Habermas. However, the final elaboration of the theory is mine, as is the responsibility for it.) Further on I will return to the elaboration of the different uses of rational arguments from the perspective of rationality of reason and of rationality of intellect.

But even if philosophy is the only objectivation proper of rationality of intellect, it is far from being the only objectivation 'for itself' which can provide *norms* for the rationality of intellect. I repeat that all objectivations 'for itself' can be 'used' for this purpose irrespective of whether they were *created* for this use or not. Both Adorno and Lukács emphatically pointed to the *defetishizing* function of art, the crucial divergences of their respective theories notwithstanding. Due to these divergences, Adorno attributed a defetishizing function to modern art alone, whereas Lukács attributed such a function to all great works of art (and with some exaggeration it could be stated that it was to modern art alone that he did not attribute such a function). According to Lukács, great art works are 'work individualities' (*Werk-individualitäten*) which embody the 'generic essence' of humankind. This is why they dismantle, by their very existence, all particularistic ways of life. Lukács refers to the famous line of Rilke's poem on archaic Apollo-torso: 'You have to change your life.' The cathartic reception of art, so Lukács argues, is tantamount to self-identification with the generic essence. The regard of the recipient immaterializes, and desubstantializes the routine activities of everyday life and of institutions which (hitherto) have been 'taken for granted', and the fetishistic life discloses its hollowness. Of course, after the catharsis in reception one can return to the routines of everyday life and of institutions as if nothing had happened. But if it was an inquietude of spirit and a vague feeling of emptiness and dissatisfaction that prepared the cathartic reception, there will be no returning to self-indulgent particularity. The regard of generic essence will not dissolve into the thin air of a faint remembrance, but will remain with the subject as the *norm*, critically confronted with the 'norms-and-rules' hitherto taken for granted. In my terminology, rationality of reason will be replaced or complemented by rationality of intellect. Adorno went so far as to assert that the fetishism of modern life had become so inscrutable and all-pervasive that not even authentic philosophy could take off from life. Rather, it had to seek recourse in art, the only non-fetishized enclave left in modernity. Once again, in my terminology, this means that philosophy can be the objectivation of rationality of intellect only as a philosophy of art. I do not subscribe to Adorno's 'negative dialectics', nor to his conception of philosophy. Nonetheless, I have referred to his theory (and to that of Lukács, which I sympathize with) mostly to corroborate the thesis that art works too can provide actors with norms to be observed and critically employed, as opposed to the 'norms-and-rules' of the regular routine of institutions and everyday life. The attitude of rationality of intellect is to adopt the position of norms provided by art works, and to *devalue* 'norms-and-rules' as void and meaningless if measured with the yardstick of these norms. I repeat that religions can also provide norms for the rationality of intellect. This is true given one proviso: they do so only as world-views, and not within the framework of 'institutionalized beliefs'.

Preliminary remarks on rational argumentation

Since rational argumentation plays a crucial role in the phenomenology of rationality of intellect that I am now going to present, a few words should be said about rational communication (and argumentation) within the precursive sphere of competence of rationality of reason. Obviously, all persons observing the 'norms-and-rules' of the sphere of objectivation 'in itself' communicate rationally with one another in conjunction with the understanding and application of these very 'norms-and-rules'. Of course, non-rational elements are always present to some degree in everyday interaction. These elements can be prerational or post-rational. Only drives are completely prerational, whereas affects are relatively prerational. There is also another type of prerationality (an equally relative one). This becomes motivational only in relation to one (or a few) 'norms-and-rules', and not in relation to all of them. However, it is a misreading of everyday life to assume that prerational elements make communication necessarily *less* rational from the perspective of rationality of reason. This becomes true only *from the standpoint of rationality of intellect.* Literature, our inexhaustible source of knowledge about human character, offers plenty of evidence to the effect that people with strong prerational impulses often tend to adhere more rigidly to certain 'norms-and-rules' than do others. Clearly, prerational impulses *can* diminish the rationality of communication, even to the point where communication ceases to be rational (and becomes 'irrationalized' in relation to the rationality of reason). On the other hand, post-rational elements in human intercourse tend to increase the rationality of communication. In this respect we may recall the analysis of intuition in the previous chapter. Still, if the 'norms-and-rules' of the various types of communication are observed, communication is rational (from the perspective of rationality of reason) irrespective of the prerational and post-rational elements that may enter into communicative action. The Freudian notion of 'rationalization' denotes precisely the process in and through which persons fit their prerational impulses into the framework of rationality of reason.

Moreover, it is also true that rational communication *includes rational argumentation*. In respect of the rationality of reason, argumentation is rational if the argument takes recourse without self-contradiction to *any* 'norm-and-rule' which is taken for granted and which applies to the case argued for. Explaining *why* a particular 'norm-and-rule' which is taken for granted *does not apply* to the particular case in question is a form of rational argumentation within the framework of rationality of reason as well. But no rational argument ('of reason') can question the *validity* of the 'norms-and-rules' of the objectivation 'in itself', or of any objectivation for that matter.

This is why rational argumentation is by no means the precondition of the establishment and the continuity of rational communication in respect of the rationality of reason. Rational argumentation is mainly needed when an action (or forbearance) calls for an explanation (justification) because it is exceptional or inscrutable, and thus contrary to, or deviant from, expectations. The more deviant a particular action (or forbearance) is, the more the interlocutor is inclined (be it a single person or a group of persons) to attribute prerational 'motivations' to the actor in question (on motivation, see *A Theory of Feelings*). But if the person whose actions are preliminarily explained by prerational motivations is able to justify his or her action by rational argumentation, simultaneously fitting this action into the framework of any 'norm-and-rule' which is taken for granted, and doing so without contradiction, then the action (or forbearance) will be accepted as 'rational' with respect to the rationality of reason. One can rationalize one's actions (in the Freudian meaning of the notion) via rational argumentation, but this doesn't mean that all arguments of rationality of reason are of this nature. If a person flees the battlefields, the first and 'natural' explanation is that of fear. But if this person can show (through rational argument) that he *didn't* run away, but that his action was a tactic that had contributed to a subsequent victory, it will be regarded as in keeping with the 'norms-and-rules' of military conduct. In a case like this the argument has nothing to do with the Freudian 'rationalization'.

Rational argumentation (within the framework of rationality of reason) is called for in other cases as well; these cannot be dealt with here. However, one particular case merits examination, not because of its frequency but because in this case rationality of reason entails certain propensities of rationality of intellect, even though only *in nuce*. Here I have in mind the use of rational argumentation for and in good judgment. Now, rational argumentation does not always occur *in fact* if one applies 'norms-and-rules' to specific situations and events with good judgment. But the process of deliberation *could* take the form of rational argumentation, even the form of rational discourse with a real or imaginary interlocutor (in the latter case we enter into discourse with ourselves). Regardless of whether or not rational argumentation (once again, real or imaginary) precedes an act that is in keeping with good judgment, the act itself can always be *reconstructed* by rational argument. It stands to reason why this kind of rational argumentation entails the propensities of rationality of intellect *in nuce*. What has to be explained is rather the stipulation *in nuce*. Such arguments are still within the sphere of rationality of reason if the 'norms-and-rules' applied by good judgment are taken for granted. The rationality of such arguments *does not depend* on the reasons given being in accord or discord with reasons given in *other* situations, with the application of *other* 'norms-and-rules'. This is because the various 'norms-and-rules' are not subordinated to a value (or a number of values) with normative force. In terms of rationality of reason, one can argue that X *should not be* forced to marry against her will or inclination. Nonetheless, again in terms of rationality of reason, one can argue that the same X *should be* forced to stay with the husband she no longer likes. If both arguments take recourse to the 'norms-and-rules' of the given society, no one will question the rationality of the two arguments on the grounds that 'force' was rejected in one argument and accepted in the other. If the 'norms-and-rules' of a society take a lenient view of personal inclinations before marriage, but are very strict concerning the 'sanctity' of marriage, then the meeting of requirements for the rationality of reason will not result in a contradiction between the rejection of force in the first case and the acceptance of force in the second case, for *there will be no contradiction*. However, there will indeed be a contradiction from the standpoint of rationality of intellect. This form of rationality, in order to really become rational, has to reject one of the two 'norms-and-rules'.

At this stage I need briefly to return to the critique of 'vivisection of rationality'. In relation to this, it is clear that 'vivisection' will not do in the case of 'argumentative rationality' either. If rational argumentation takes recourse to 'norms-and-rules' which are being taken for granted, the rationality of argument hinges on whether or not this argument takes a successful recourse to these 'norms-and-rules' without contradiction. On the other hand, if an argument takes recourse to a norm, the rationality of *one* argument will be dependent on the *other* arguments used by the same person (or group of persons) in different relations and situations: the 'norms-and-rules' themselves will be tested regarding their consistency. If there is an inconsistency, certain 'norms-and-rules' will be rejected. Thus, again, the *form* of any single argument does not itself make an argument rational, for the simple reason (and this question will be examined more closely later) that the argument of rationality of reason can be judged as irrational by the rationality of intellect, and vice versa.

Sociological intermezzo

Rationality has been defined as acting according to reason. Reason has been defined as the faculty of discriminating between good and bad, good and evil, sacred and profane, useful and harmful, and the like. Rationality of reason has been defined as competence in acting according to the 'norms-and-rules' of a particular life-world (or institution of objectivation 'for itself'), because 'norms-and-rules' embody the positive 'aspect' of the categories of value-orientation, either in an imperative or optative manner. Rationality of intellect has been defined as competence in observing a norm (or a number of norms), norms which equally embody the positive 'aspect' of one or the other category of value orientation in at least *one* objectivation 'for itself' of the historical period in question. By observing this norm, rationality of intellect *devaluates* certain 'norms-and-rules' of the life-world or of institutions which do not stand the test of consistency when viewed from the standpoint of the norms observed.

Rational argumentation of rationality of reason is a simple and *everyday* procedure. It is fair to assume that it belongs to the empirical human universals. It is not a *continuous* procedure, for it is only needed when something is 'out of order'. But should people deliberate on an issue together, and should each person give his own opinion about the problem of how to act in this case in harmony with 'norms-and-rules', the speech act is undoubtedly a case of rational argumentation. Argumentation as a speech-act in the everyday setting is related to action proper. The question is always that of which action should be taken, or which action can be justified retrospectively. At this point I cannot enter into the analysis of theoretical attitude. Yet I believe, even if I cannot verify my hypothesis within the framework of this chapter, that rational argumentation in theoretical issues has developed much later than rational argumentation for action. More importantly, however, I wish to emphasize the following: if I use rational arguments in theoretical discussions, I do not necessarily shift from rationality of reason to rationality of intellect. If rational argument is the 'norm-and-rule' of an objectivation, and I keep with it without questioning or testing any other 'norm-and-rule' by this argumentation, I remain within the attitude of rationality of reason.

This last statement seems to be odd, even though it necessarily follows from all my previous assertions. It follows because I have continually emphasized that keeping within the 'norms-and-rules' of any objectivation 'for itself' allows one to remain within the attitude of rationality of reason (in so doing one practises competence in observing the 'norms-and-rules'). But I have *also* stated that, in the last instance, rationality of intellect is the attitude of *rationalism*, and if observing 'norms-and-rules' *includes* rational argumentation, this should already be indicative of the procedure of rationalism of *intellect*. How can I then possibly state that the procedure of rationalism can be attributed to rationality of reason, when it was precisely the rationality of intellect that, in the last instance, has been defined as rationalism?

Nevertheless, in stating that rationality of intellect is the *attitude* of reason that one rightly calls rationalism, I have not implied that *all procedures of rationalism* are performed by 'rationality of intellect'. It was precisely rationality of intellect that *established* the 'norms-and-rules' of rationalism, as I tried to show in my short historical digression. But once established (by the attitude of rationality of intellect), the 'norms-and-rules' of rationalism can be observed by rationality of reason. That modern science must employ rational argumentation is due to rationality of intellect, which has devalued all the constraints of religious world-views and released the cognitive surplus, as well as advocating the liberating view that we should accept a certain kind of knowledge as true if it is proved such. But once this deed has been accomplished, *rationalism as a procedure* can carry on its work without being accompanied by rationalism as an *attitude* of reason (rationality of intellect).

This distinction has very important *social* implications. The rationality of the argument of rationality of intellect depends on whether a person (or a group of persons) can take recourse to a norm-for-action in a contradiction-free manner. This norm cannot be a concrete norm (the latter is always a 'norm-and-rule'). It can only be an abstract or a universal one. Given the norm to which the argument takes recourse is either abstract or universal, it is also essential that the concrete argument for an action should not contradict other concrete arguments supporting other actions undertaken by the same person (or group of persons). In other words, all arguments either for or against a particular action should equally take recourse, without contradiction, to the same supreme norm (or norms). The restriction 'for the action taken' is very important. Rationality of intellect does not require that the person (or group) should apply the same norm (or norms) in situations having no relevance either for their life-world or for any of their actions. Put simply, acting and arguing according to rationality of intellect does not presuppose an all-embracing world-view that is void of theoretical and normative self-contradiction, because it does not presuppose an all-embracing world-view at all. Of course, such a world-view, in the framework of which all explanations and interpretations take recourse to the same supreme norm (or norms), could be envisaged as the 'pure model' of rationality of intellect *if* all *possible* actions and all *possible* judgments were to coherently take recourse to the same norm. I will return to the problem of whether the 'pure model' of rationality of intellect can be regarded as *exemplary* in every mode of its application. For the present I will focus on the problem suggested by the stipulation 'if' ('if all possible actions and judgments were to take recourse in a consistent manner to the same norm').

In this century the task of creating meaningful world-views has increasingly become the prerogative of professionals. Thus the *fundamental (socio-economic) classes* of modernity have ceased to produce meaningful world-views. Indeed, both the working class and the progressively 'flawed' class of the bourgeoisie have become thoroughly *pragmatic*: the members of these classes think contextually, and do not construct a transcontextual framework for their actions (and judgments). The intellectuals of the nineteenth century had nearly always been *organic* intellectuals of the bourgeoisie, and the working-class movements had produced organic intellectuals of their own. (I use the notion 'organic intellectual' in Gramsci's sense of the term.) Now there are almost no organic intellectuals at all. Present-day intellectuals are classless and thus 'inorganic'. Their profession is directed towards thinking transcontextually and providing meaningful world-views for the actors of various social classes. In the main, they produce such world-views for the establishment of every colour, but occasionally they speak for the oppressed. As their social function is not direct action but the production of meaningful world-views, intellectuals are inclined to over-identify with social classes (or with the 'nation' as such) while *imputing* consciousness to them.

Alvin Gouldner correctly pointed out that intellectuals are the people well-versed in CCD (culture of critical discourse): they are the ones who learn how to argue within a transcontextual framework (I analysed this problem in my review of Gouldner's book *The Power of Knowledge, Revue Internationale de Sociologie*, II Series, vol. XVII No. 1, April 1981, pp. 3–22). But from this the conclusion should not be drawn that intellectuals are, because of this propensity of their profession, more able and more ready to act according to 'rationality of intellect' than are other members of society. To illustrate this I am, perhaps, entitled to relate my own personal experience. My personal observation is that intellectuals who employ rational arguments in their theories, and who achieve consistency in explaining and interpreting all facts in a social theory, do not subsequently observe *norms* in their *personal actions* any more consistently than do other people. Moreover, being well-versed in CCD makes it far easier for intellectuals to *rationalize* (in the Freudian meaning of the term) their actions and judgments *retrospectively*; to ostensibly eliminate incoherence and self-contradiction with sophistication. I do not claim that all intellectuals do this. Still less would I suggest that intellectuals are incapable of acting according to the rationality of intellect. I simply mean that their profession is not conducive to their acting in this manner.

Today, the specific function of intellectuals does not reside in any alleged capacity of acting in greater harmony with the rationality of intellect. Rather, they provide norms and world-views for the latter. Indeed, they are able to do this precisely because they live in the same life-world as non-intellectuals, and are therefore confronted with more or less the same life-problems. The greater the extent that an intellectual utilizes and relies upon these shared life experiences, and the more crucial these experiences become, the more powerful are the valid norms and interpretations the theory thus conceived can offer to the actors whom the intellectual addresses. One devaluates 'norms-and-rules' from the standpoint of norms not *because* one is well-versed in CCD, but one devaluates them in CCD because one has already devalued them in life experiences shared with others. This is why I will reconstruct the 'switch' from rationality of reason to rationality of intellect not from the perspective of CCD, not even from the point of departure of rational argumentation of intellect, but from the viewpoint of *disobedience*. I do not wish to suggest thereby that in any particular case disobedience and rebellion precede *empirically* the attitude of rationality of intellect. I will only construct a *typology* of the switch. I would not even suggest that individuals go through all these phases in their 'pure' forms. But as any example can be understood from the vantage-point of these ideal types, I will neglect the 'impure' ones.

From disobedience to rationality of intellect

(a) I am going to call the *act of disobedience* the conscious rejection of observing a 'norm-and-rule' of the sphere of objectivation 'in itself', or the 'norms-and-rules' of an institution, with an equally conscious reference to other 'norms-and-rules' provided by the same sphere of objectivation. The 'norms-and-rules' to which the disobedient person refers are taken for granted. One can argue for the act of disobedience prospectively, though it can also be argued for retrospectively. This is why the act of disobedience is rational. But any argument for disobedience must differ substantially from the type of argument we have already analysed in conjunction with the analysis of rationality of reason. The allegedly cowardly soldier did *not* reject the *'norm-and-rule'* of military conduct; he only suspended it. Rejection, not mere suspension, of at least one 'norm-and-rule', can be the first step in the change of attitude towards rationality of intellect (under given conditions). Whether the change really takes place depends mainly on the reaction of the repositories of rationality of reason to the act of disobedience, as well as on the availability of objectivations 'for itself' and/or universal norms for the disobedient actor. Children are very often disobedient because they simply do not grasp the rationality of one or another 'norm-and-rule' (and sometimes very understandably so), and thus do not take them for granted. They question *why* something should be as it is, and it takes some time before they accept the frequent and obviously unsatisfactory answer, 'Because it should be so, and don't ask silly questions.' But such silly questions often indicate a rationality superior to that of self-indulgent adults. I would make the theoretical proposal that *rationality of intellect* (at least *in nuce*) is a human universal to the same extent as rationality of reason, and it is only extinguished by rationality of reason. This assertion is but the reconfirmation of the theoretical proposal to attribute 'practical reason *in nuce*' to all human cultures before the emergence of practical reason proper. No wonder then that philosophy, the only objectivation of rationality of intellect, has always raised precisely the childish questions: why is something the way it is; why should something be the way it is (see *For a Radical Philosophy*). Here it is appropriate to return briefly to the problem of 'cultural surplus', and to my criticism of Freud. The disobedience of children and 'childish questions' both indicate that one of the major human resources and capacities that is suppressed by the appropriation of 'norms-and-rules' of the sphere of objectivation 'in itself' is precisely the rationality of intellect. This can make us 'discontent' not with civilization generally, but with the 'taken-for-grantedness' of civilization. Thus disobedience can be sublimated through the ascent into higher objectivations. But perhaps sublimation is not the correct word, as what is being redirected into non-everyday channels is in itself one of the most sublime human propensities.

The gesture of disobedience is obviously not restricted to childhood. As mentioned, childish disobedience is mostly extinguished by rationality of reason, though this does not always occur, and may leave an imprint if it does. There are paradigmatic routes leading from childish disobedience towards rationality of intellect. Lukács related to me that as a child he always refused to greet visitors, a form of behaviour very common in children. Yet the young Lukács gave a reason as well, telling his parents, 'I do not greet strange visitors *because* I did not invite them.' This is indeed a paradigmatic example of argumentation on behalf of disobedience in everyday life. To invite visitors is a *custom* (it is not proper to come uninvited). And those who have done the inviting are bound to engage in the act of greeting. But those who have not, are *not* bound, the childish disobedience suggests. And why would they be? The next step followed quite naturally from this gesture of disobedience. Lukács started to read very early, and these initial influences, Homer and Cooper, led him into *an entirely different world* from that of 'normal' life. The act of 'irrationalization' inevitably followed from this: the world of books became for him 'real life', that of his parents 'unreal'. Thus the child counterposed objectivation 'for itself' to the objectivation 'in itself' of his own life-world, and devalued the latter from the standpoint of the former. The life-world which had been rejected by the child as 'phoney' was later rejected by the young man, and already from the perspective of *norms*. In a way, rationality of intellect had organically emerged from childish disobedience. This is clearly an extreme case, yet it is indicative of the entire general syndrome. In his work *The Divided Self* Laing made the remarkable observation (in connection with Ophelia) that overly obedient children often develop a tendency to schizophrenia. In other words, without at least *some* kind of rational disobedience, character will be susceptible to mental illness. The Ophelia syndrome is admittedly an extreme phenomenon (even more extreme than the very different one analysed above). Usually, childhood disobedience becomes, in the adult, mental experiments in disobedience, and is often 'irrationalized' by the mental experimenter himself. But even a mental experiment of this kind can become the point of departure for the emergence of rationality of intellect, although it can lapse into deviance pure and simple, or remain ineffective.

(b) The *rejection* of observing a 'norm-and-rule' of the sphere of objectivation 'in itself', or eventually of an institution, without taking recourse to any other 'norm-and-rule' of the same objectivation, and without actual or possible argumentation, I will term an *act of rebellion*. The act of rebellion (speech-act included) is a *gesture*. It can also be *explained*, but only by taking recourse to the *need* or *desire* (or to the absence of need or desire) of the rebellious person. Since the *presence* (or *absence*) of the gesture of rebellion is not subject to argument, this gesture is *self-explanatory*, yet it is also *irrational*. By the term 'self-explanatory' I do *not* mean that reasons for the gesture cannot be given. Also, in using the term 'irrational' I do not mean that the gesture cannot be justified. By 'self-explanatory' and 'irrational' I simply mean that the gesture of rebellion stands for itself and that the rebellious persons do not justify the rebellion in any other way but via the presence (or absence) of needs and desires that they express by the very act of rebellion. The act of rebellion is irrational from the perspective of rationality of reason *and* from the perspective of rationality of intellect: from the former, because it does not take recourse (contrary to disobedience) to *any* 'norms-and-rules'; from the latter, because it does not take recourse, via argumentation, to any valid norm.

When viewed by the rationality of reason, rebellion is always *deviance*. It is a malaise which should be treated. If it cannot be, either with punishment or with persuasion, the rebellious person will be written off as incurably mad, as a lost soul possessed by dark, devilish powers, as a neurotic – the label dependent on the current vocabulary of rationality of reason. However, from the standpoint of rationality of intellect, rebellion is never attributed to 'deviance'. This is understandable. One can only 'deviate' from 'norms-and-rules', not from the observance of norms one has not yet accepted. From this angle rebellion is not regarded as an illness either. Instead, it is seen as a *symptom* of the devaluation and immateriality of the 'norms-and-rules' the person has rebelled against. Consequently, rationality of intellect 'irrationalizes' rebellion only in a *relative* manner. It also rationalizes rebellion in so far as rationality of intellect understands rebellion as an *adequate* or *inadequate* (not as a 'sick' or inscrutable) response to the exigencies of a problematic set of 'norms-and-rules'. If a particular act of rebellion (be it private or public) rejects those same 'norms-and-rules' which are critically rejected by the arguments of the repositories of rationality of intellect, the act of rebellion will be directly transformed by the repositories of rationality of intellect into a *rational argument* against the rationality, viability and normative validity of the 'norms-and-rules' rejected by the gesture of rebellion. Gestures of rebellion are, then, inexhaustible sources of arguments for invalidating the 'norms-and-rules' of a particular life-world, or of any institution for that matter. However, if a particular act of rebellion (again, private or public) rejects a 'norms-and-rules' which induces the observance of the supreme values (norms) of a person (or persons) representing the rationality of intellect, these repositories of rationality of intellect will reject the rebellion as evil. But even the 'criminalization' of a gesture of rebellion implies the relative 'rationalization' of its irrationality, and from at least two aspects. First, the 'evil' rebellion will be viewed as a symptom (in the case under examination) of the weakness and decay of 'norms-and-rules'. Secondly, full responsibility will be attributed to the person in rebellion, as it will be assumed that this person could have rebelled in a way that he *should* have – in a manner whereby the rebellion could be retrospectively justified with the arguments of rationality of intellect.

Rebellion can be, even if it not always is, the decisive step towards rationality of intellect. If we examine rebellion from the perspective of rationality of intellect (and in philosophy we cannot do otherwise), the relative rationality of this irrational gesture will immediately be apparent. But because *radical rejection*, if it does not run counter to the ideas of goodness and truth of our chosen philosophy, is the antechamber of *radical acceptance*, philosophies are obliged to present their norms to the rebellious with the conviction that they will accept the norms because they should accept them. And philosophy has to be indefatigable in this pursuit, though it may suffer many setbacks due to the stubbornness of the irrationality of rebellion.

It is possible to illustrate the various types of action analysed so far with one example. The model will be the traditional nuclear family and single 'norm-and-rule' of this everyday institution: the wife has to prepare dinner for the husband every evening. Let us suppose that the husband returns from work and finds that the wife has not yet even started cooking the dinner. 'Why isn't the dinner ready, what happened to you?' he asks. There are four distinct *types* of answer. First, the wife may reply, 'I fell sick, I have a high fever, I simply could not make it.' This is a clear cut argument *within* the framework of rationality of reason. The wife has not rejected the 'norm-and-rule' of cooking dinner for the husband every evening. But in this case of sickness, this 'norm-and-rule' is actually suspended by another 'norm-and-rule' of the same sphere of objectivation 'in itself': the sick person should stay in bed and should not work (Type 1). Secondly, the wife may answer, 'I don't want to cook your dinner and I won't do it. You only come home to eat. You spend all your time with your lover, so she should cook for you. I am not your servant.' In saying this the wife has rejected one 'norm-and-rule' (that of cooking dinner for her husband), but she argued for her rejection by taking recourse to another 'norm-and-rule' of the traditional family. This is disobedience proper (Type 2). Next, the wife can reply, 'I do not want to cook your dinner and I will not do it any more.' To the next question put by her husband, 'But why, for heaven's sake?', she can answer in the following way: 'I don't know why, I am sick of cooking dinner, I simply do not want to do it, I cannot cope with this life any longer.' In so doing, the woman takes recourse to her own feelings, needs and desires alone, and not to the 'norms-and-rules' of any sphere of objectivation. This is rebellion (Type 3). Finally, she could answer: 'We are equally free persons, don't you think? Why should it be the permanent arrangement that you go out and do something which interests you while I am confined to the four walls of a kitchen throughout my whole life? If we are equally free, and I am damned sure that we are, then I should have my own life just as you do. I want to study. I have no objection to cooking the dinner as long as you don't see it as something which is taken for granted. Anyway, you can cook a dinner just as well as I can.' This is an argument from the standpoint of rationality of intellect (Type 4).

Hopefully, this example makes clear the specific character of rationality of intellect. If a 'norm-and-rule' is rejected by rationality of intellect, the rejection can only be substantiated by a *full argument*. This is so because the argument invites the interlocutor not only to change his or her *behaviour*, but also to change his or her *values*; that is to say, to accept a *norm*-for-action that one has not observed hitherto, either because he or she has not accepted this norm at all, or because he or she applied it with discrimination, incoherently and especially *not* to the case under dispute. From this it follows that both disobedience and rebellion can be transformed into a position acceptable to rationality of intellect only under the condition that the disobedient or rebellious person transcends the stage of disobedience and rebellion by taking recourse to *norms* from the standpoint of which he or she can '*rationalize*' with the use of full arguments, his or her own disobedient or rebellious actions.

Full argument has a double function. On the one hand it simultaneously 'rationalizes' and supersedes disobedience and rebellion. On the other hand it invites interlocutors to take the stand of rationality of intellect. The person representing rationality of intellect who is already capable of substantiating his or her action with full arguments has to assume that rationality of intellect is present, at least *in nuce*, in each and every human being. But this person *cannot* assume that the norms he or she takes recourse to will be observed by the same interlocutors. Further, there is no reason to suppose that the interlocutors recognize *any* norms superior to the 'norms-and-rules' of rationality of reason; or, if they do, that they are ready to abide by them.

It is appropriate at this point to recall the remarks contained in our intermezzo. Even if rationality of intellect proper is argumentative, and even if it employs *full arguments*, this does not imply either the theoretical ability or the learning to participate in CCD. It stands to reason that although the wife may be able to provide a *full argument* in order to reject the 'norm-and-rule' of cooking dinner every evening whilst her husband earns the money, she still might not be able to take equal recourse to the norms of 'freedom' and 'equality' with a full argument when departing from all other particular situations. In fact, she might be completely unfit to work out an all-embracing social theory; or, if she has accepted one, she might be unfit to enter into theoretical discourse over it and defend the theory against competing ones. However, she is fully able to do what she did; to reject one 'norm-and-rule' with a full argument, and to defend her decision rationally against everyone who holds a contrary view concerning this 'norm-and-rule'.

I have defined the 'public domain' as the field on which everyday actors have *direct* access to objectivations 'for itself' (universalized values included), and which is characterized by a continuous oscillation between life experiences on the one hand and objectivations 'for itself' on the other. Objectivations 'for itself' participate in the public domain only in so far as they remain sensitive to life-experiences *and* turn towards everyday actors with their theories or works of art. This does not mean that they should speak *exclusively* to everyday actors but that they should *include* them in this act. If someone is well-versed in CCD but addresses fellow-professionals alone (within an institutionalized framework), this person does not participate in the public domain, though of course his or her theory may be translated by someone else into the language of the public domain. But those well-versed in CCD *can* participate in the public domain, and if they do so, if they address themselves to everyday actors and provide them with theories for self-reflection and self-understanding, they can promote the shift from rationality of reason to rationality of intellect. Whether or not they do so depends on how sensitive they are to the problems of everyday experience.

I have distinguished between the 'repositories of rationality of intellect' and 'the repositories of rationality of reason' chiefly for the sake of simplicity. I did not have in mind two distinct clusters of people where Cluster A would encompass repositories of rationality of reason and Cluster B would encompass repositories of rationality of intellect. In everyday life (and beyond), most people take certain 'norms-and-rules' for granted whilst rejecting other 'norms-and-rules' from the standpoint of a given norm. Thus in one compartment of their lives people think and act according to rationality of reason, whereas in another they do so according to the rationality of intellect. As noted, people in rebellion make manifest their needs (or the absence of certain needs) alone, without being capable or ready to argue rationally for the rejection of any 'norm-and-rule'. But even people who are ready and able to do so, and can do so from the vantage point of a norm, mostly do so because of the presence of a need (or certain needs) which they cannot satisfy by complying with the 'norms-and-rules' which are taken for granted. A need like this may be strictly personal, but it can be morally motivated as well (for instance, by having in mind others in need). Whatever the case, people normally do not feel the need to question *all* 'norms-and-rules' simultaneously.

EVERYDAY LIFE AND RATIONALITY

Our knowledge of human nature teaches us that people who consistently criticize as cowardly or unadventurous the observance by others of 'norms-and-rules' taken for granted from the aspect of a norm, easily fall prey to self-deception should they turn the same criticism against themselves. It is only in rational discourse that this human weakness can be counteracted, for the reciprocity of criticism helps to overcome this inclination for self-deception. In my book on radical philosophy I presented the image of an 'ideal' discourse. I called it 'philosophical discourse'. I meant by this a type of discourse in which *all* debating parties argue exclusively from the position of rationality of intellect (even though I did not at that time employ the term), and all parties take recourse to a common ultimate norm. But given that philosophical discourse does not occur in everyday life, I have to put aside this version of discourse at this juncture. All real discourse that we engage in varies between everyday discussions about the proper application of 'norms-and-rules' which are taken for granted to the discourse between people who all argue from the position of rationality of intellect but *only from one vantage point*. However, it is usually the case that in a given argument one person adopts the position of rationality of intellect whilst another adopts the position of rationality of reason, with the roles often being reversed in future arguments. Clearly, some people are better than others in being *more consistent* in observing the norms they have accepted as legitimate. And they are able to maintain this consistency in various *life-situations* and when viewing issues from *various perspectives*, even though they may occasionally err. When speaking of 'repositories of rationality of intellect', I have exactly such people in mind.

It should be assumed that the repositories of rationality of intellect have to argue for and with the repositories of rationality of reason, for and with rebellious actors, and that this process of argumentation cannot be conceived of without the *intention* of persuasion. Not all good arguments are equally persuasive. A persuasive argument might also be *argumentum ad hominem* in a *specific sense* of this term. It has to refer to life-experiences of the people one wants to persuade. It has to pinpoint facts hitherto unknown to the interlocutors. One has to be aware of the force of tradition and of the weight of vested interest which make people persevere in their action patterns. Further, one has to comprehend that *if* rational arguments have already been presented, the best remaining argument is life-experience itself. Life-experience can make us sensitive to the message of objectivations 'for itself'.

This message might be powerful enough to liberate rationality of intellect from the bondage of mere rationality of reason, but arguments presented by the repositories of rationality of intellect can accelerate this process and stabilize it. Rationality of intellect should enhance the *self-knowledge* of the interlocutor. This is all the more decisive in that self-knowledge is one of the most important preconditions for the contradiction-free employment of norms by the repositories of rationality of intellect themselves. One should not forget that 'know thyself' is the postulate of practical reason, and rationality of intellect is the supreme form of practical reason.

The response of rationality of reason to disobedience, rebellion and rationality of intellect

The typology of the shift from rationality of reason to rationality of intellect has not yet accounted for the *response* of the repositories of rationality of reason to this shift, even if certain allusions have been made about the importance of the response to the challenge. Obviously, disobedience, rebellion and the argumentatively underpinned action of rationality of intellect do challenge, if in different ways and with different radicality, the self-indulgent 'taken-for-grantedness' of a world. And when I say 'world', I mean just that. Infringement of the 'norms-and-rules' itself does not undermine the 'taken-for-grantedness' of a world as long as the 'wicked ones' submit to punishment, or at least as long as they accept the validity of the 'norms-and-rules' for *others*, and recognize themselves as the exception. The thief who is outraged when he himself is robbed, the womanizer who censures the 'sin of flesh' in the case of his neighbour: the reactions of these people subserve the 'taken-for-grantedness' of their world in just the same way as does the behaviour of the meticulously conscientious accountant or the rigorously chaste young man. But disobedience is *disquieting*, rebellion is *startling* and the *rational rejection* of norms by the intellect is *alarming*, for these actions imply the generalization, or at least the generalizability, of the act of rejection, though they do so in different degrees. The disobedient child who raises the question of whether something should be the way it is, and why it should be so, is implicitly generalizing, because he or she is not attempting to create an exception to the rule, but is questioning the rule itself. So is the disobedient adult. The tendency to generalize is even more explicit in the case of public disobedience. Although in rebellion the presence (or absence) of needs and desires (to which the rebellious person takes recourse) can be purely idiosyncratic, *the gesture of taking recourse* to needs and desires as against norms implies generalizability, for by this very gesture the rebellious person does not even *pretend* to recognize the 'norms-and-rules' he or she violates; instead, the gesture calls for the recognition of those needs and desires that recourse has been taken to. To this point, 'generalizability' does not mean that one can generalize the act of disobedience or rebellion itself. It means that one could generalize the *rejection* of the specific 'norm-and-rule' the disobedient person does not abide by, or that one could generalize the gesture of taking recourse to the presence or absence of needs and desires if it comes to the question of the observance of a 'norm-and-rule'. To bring up arguments against the observance of a 'norm-and-rule' from the perspective of a norm implies, however, a *double* generalization. It implies the generalization of the rejection of the criticized 'norm-and-rule' on the one hand ('everyone should reject it!'), *and* the generalization of the procedure of testing 'norms-and-rules' by the rationality of intellect on the other hand ('every 'norm-and-rule' should be tested!'). It stands to reason then that disobedience is only disquieting, while rebellion is startling, and the critical employment of rationality of intellect is alarming – from the position of rationality of reason.

How a challenge will be responded to by the repositories of rationality of reason depends on various factors. These cannot all be analysed here. I will only put the *typical* responses under scrutiny.

In the case of disobedience the response can be:

(a) *Persuasion*, during which rationality of reason takes *recourse to the meaningful world-view* of the sphere of objectivation 'in itself', and thereby accounts for the validity of the 'norm-and-rule' (for example, 'this is God's will'). If the disobedient person shares this world-view the argument will be accepted as rational, and disobedience will disappear. If this does not occur, we are already confronted with situation (b).

(b) *The simple restatement of the 'taken-for-grantedness'* of the 'norm-and-rule' (in the case of the example just given the answer would now be 'it is so because it should be so'). It may be that disobedience then disappears, but only together with the disappearance of 'the rationality of intellect *in nuce*'. Also, stubbornness may result, along with a hardening of the original position. Stubbornness can lead to rationality of intellect or it can be stabilized in perpetual resentment.

(c) *The use of force*. Disobedience may disappear in the wake of force, but this time not only with the disappearance of 'rationality of intellect *in nuce*', but also with the 'defects' in rationality of reason: a greater incapacity to make good judgments is normally the outcome. Disobedience can also become stubborn. This stubbornness may lead to rebellion (and thus perhaps to rationality of intellect as well), though it can also be stabilized in perpetual hatred.

(d) Rationality of reason *accepts the challenge*. If the instances of a similar act of disobedience are not numerous, acceptance of the challenge may happen only through *love*. Love of a person can be stronger than the inducement of a 'norm-and-rule' of rationality of reason. The loving person identifies with the beloved, thus the disobedience of the beloved will shine in the light of truth and right. But the loving person can only remain rational if he or she enters into discourse with the beloved to decide whether or not the infringed 'norms-and-rules' are still relevant. Love implies the readiness for such a discourse.

If similar instances of disobediences are numerous, the act of disobedience already contains rationality of reason *in nuce*. This is usually the means by which 'norms-and-rules' *change*. Finally, the roles can be reversed. Holding to outmoded 'norms-and-rules' can indicate stubbornness perpetuated by resentment, misanthropy or simple nostalgia.

In the case of rebellion the response can be:

(a) *Force*. Given that rebellion is completely irrational from the standpoint of rationality of reason, the argumentative arsenal of rationality of reason cannot provide an answer to the challenge. The rebellious person has to be punished, the rebellion crushed. Should the rebellious person be in fact crushed by force, he or she will conform to the 'norms-and-rules' only with resentment and hatred. Rebellion may also be maintained via *indignation*. Here, the person meets force with *violence*: force is to be crushed by violence. If the rebel instead rises to higher rationality (of intellect), he or she will abandon the use of violence, but not necessarily force. Force used in this context can only be rational in so far as it aims at the *enforcement* of rational discourse with the repositories of rationality of reason; in other words, if the force used results in the latter renouncing the use of force on their part.

(b) *Isolation and marginalization*. This too is force of a kind, though of a subtle nature. It may appear through the physical isolation of the rebels or via their isolation through the mobilization of public opinion. When the wife refused to cook dinner, the husband might have turned to the family or the neighbours, to put the pressure of public opinion on her. Even when persuasion is resourceless, the *unanimous animosity* of those held in regard can crush the resistance of the rebel. Should the rebellion be crushed in this way, the one-time rebel might turn out to be completely subservient, even to the point of complete *indifference* (the gradual extinction of emotional life). The person can respond to the conflict with psychic disturbances, genuine madness and the like. However, rebellion can only be isolated if it is fundamentally idiosyncratic.

(c) Rationality of reason *can accept the challenge*. This can only be done by *love* as *empathy*: more precisely, by *love entailing empathy*. The work of love differs here from the work of love in disobedience. Since disobedience is rational, if one adopts the position of the beloved and disobedient person, then a rational position is occupied from which one can immediately enter into discussion, assuming that the other person might have been right and might have acted justly. But the rebel cannot give valid reasons for his or her rebellion; his or her act is thoroughly irrational from the perspective of rationality of reason. Love can accept the challenge only through the *recognition of the needs and desires* of the rebel: this is understandable when we bear in mind that the rebel takes recourse exclusively to these needs and desires. Clearly, the recognition of needs and desires is not tantamount to the recognition of rebellion (rationality of reason cannot legitimate an irrational act). But since love as empathy recognizes the needs and desires to which the rebel takes recourse, people capable of love as empathy can enter into a discussion with the rebel regarding the *circumstances* the recognized needs and desires sprang from. Psychoanalysis through love has a far greater history than the psychoanalysis of Freud. Its outcome may be exactly the same as the intended result of modern psychoanalysis: the 'indirections' of the needs and desires of the rebel can be corrected, changed for the better, through the rebel becoming aware of their genealogy. Thus the source of rebellion will be cut off, the rationality of reason restored. Yet in this particular quest for meaning the opposite may well be the result. The person expressing love as empathy may well discover reasons for not merely recognizing but *justifying* the needs the desires of the rebel. This act of *justification* is tantamount to the *rejection* of the constraints the other/s had eventually been subjected to. Thus love as empathy can lead again to rationality of intellect. The same love as empathy also aids the rebel in transcending the irrational gesture of rebellion and moving towards rationality of intellect.

Rationality of reason can respond to the challenge of rationality of intellect:

(a) With *offensive argumentation*. This may happen by taking recourse to the dominating world-view of the sphere of objectivation 'in itself' and/or by the mobilization of an indignant *sensus communis* of rationality of reason. Offensive argumentation not only *'irrationalizes'* but also *criminalizes* rationality of intellect. It is the subtle method of using force. The response of rationality of intellect to the offensive arguments of rationality of reason can be *self-humiliation* (the conversion of the black sheep), *perseverance* in observing the norm of rationality of intellect (stoicism), or the *total rejection* of rationality of reason due to an inflated consciousness of *superiority* (elitism).

(b) With *defensive argumentation*, by taking recourse to the traditionality and viability of 'norms-and-rules' that are taken for granted. The defensive argumentation of rationality of reason *'irrationalizes' rationality of intellect without criminalizing it.* Defensive argumentation expresses anxiety and the need for stability. The reaction of rationality of intellect in such arguments and to the anxiety of rationality of reason can take the form of either *entering into discourse* with rationality of reason, or perseverance in the inflated consciousness of *superiority*, or *force*. I will return to this particular problem shortly.

(c) *With force pure and simple*. Here I have to state once again that, 'primitive' societies excluded, the social division of labour implies the social division of the the sphere of objectivation 'in itself', and that the dominating-meaningful world-views are, by definition, world-views of domination. Thus observing 'norms-and-rules' *ipso facto* implies force. But normally domination is legitimated, and subsequent force does not take a naked form. One does not have to enter into the interpretation of the Weberian notion of domination and legitimation to recognize that if rationality of reason cannot cope with rationality of intellect via offensive argumentation, but instead has to use plain force, then at least some of the 'norms-and-rules' have lost their legitimacy, or are very near losing it. It is not only self-delusory but also self-contradictory to believe that one can silence the voice of rationality by decapitating a group of people who represent this voice or by burning the works that embody it. The rationality of observing 'norms-and-rules' the validity of which can only be defended in this way becomes highly suspect. The response of the repositories of rationality of intellect to force pure and simple can take more than one form: it may appear as the *'rationalization' of rebellion*, or the *resistance of pure morality*. It may even be a *surrender to force*, accompanied by *hatred* against the force surrendered to *and* against all those who have *not* surrendered to it.

(d) *With accepting the challenge with cognitive love*. Cognitive love also accepts the challenge of rationality of intellect, though not in the same way as understanding love accepts the challenge of disobedience, and love as empathy accepts the challenge of rebellion. Cognitive love is disinterested love in every respect; it does not express the need for reciprocity, not even the need for recognition. Repositories of rationality of reason can love with cognitive love repositories of rationality of intellect, even if they *do not understand* their argumentations; or even if they cannot, and do not want to, follow the repositories of the rationality of intellect in their acts. They might even view these 'knights' of the rationality of intellect as 'dreamers' who reach out for the impossible. But they assimilate all these pursuits with cognitive love because, even if they do not understand the arguments, or they believe that all these efforts comprise a castle in the air, they grasp that rationality of intellect is the search for the supreme cognitive value: truth. The observance of norms by men of rationality of intellect will appear for men of rationality of reason as the iridescence of supreme humaneness. The cognitive love of rationality of reason will thus accept men of rationality of intellect as 'sacred fools': it will 'irrationalize' their *goals* but not their attitudes.

The response of rationality of intellect to cognitive love can be *intellectual love*, both of the essence common to all human beings and of reason, normally combined with the resolution to 'live up to the promise' of entering into *discourse* with rationality of reason about the *viability* of goals set by rationality of intellect. It may eventually include a kind of *contempt* for the much too *pragmatic* and therefore *immature* attitude of cognitive love. In discourse, cognitive love can be transformed into intellectual love. But as cognitive love is an unselfish attitude it will not lose momentum even if it is met with contempt. If the goals of rationality of intellect are not realized it will still not lose momentum, as the object of this love is not the goals set by the repositories of rationality of intellect but their counterfactual pursuit of norms. But if rationality of intellect runs amok and cuts the umbilical cord with rationality of reason, cognitive love will turn into (unselfish) *cognitive hatred*.

Before proceeding to the 'dialectics of rationality of intellect' (see the analysis of the 'cunning of practical reason' in 'The Power of Shame'), I should comment on at least one of the lessons that may be drawn from the foregoing analysis.

Love appeared in this analysis as an aid and a prompter of rationality of intellect: it appeared not only as cognitive love felt for the repositories of rationality of intellect, but also as understanding or empathic love. At first sight this is an astonishing conclusion. Feelings are rational from the perspective of rationality of reason if they evolve in, or react to, situations in keeping with 'norms-and-rules' (expectations and habits) of a particular life-world. (For instance, the love of children for their parents, and vice versa, is considered a 'rational feeling' by the 'norms-and-rules' of the majority of life-worlds.) If love is – again in terms of the prevalent 'norms-and-rules' – considered to be the precondition of a good marriage, but the same 'norms-and-rules' also prescribe that a person must marry someone of his or her own rank, then obviously the love of a young man for a girl of his own social rank is considered to be a rational feeling, whereas love for a girl of lower social status is considered to be an irrational feeling. Even if the syndrome that X falls in love with Y and no one else can never be completely 'rationalized', if Y belongs to the stratum of socially eligible persons, the feeling is regarded as rational. Love is irrational from the perspective of rationality of reason if the pursuit of love infringes 'norms-and-rules'. But one property of rationality of reason, good judgment, can relatively 'rationalize' or 'irrationalize' the choice of Y in this example. One can criticize lovers because their emotional choice runs counter to good judgment, or approve of this choice as an expression of good judgment. But the choice can only be 'rationalized' on the precondition of its not having infringed the prevailing 'norms-and-rules'. Even if love is no longer related to 'conventions', it can still be related to the norm(s) of rationality of intellect. In this case, 'keeping with the norm' and good judgment tend to coincide, and it is the choice of the person (or a cause) alone as the object of love that can be (relatively) 'rationalized' or (relatively, and eventually absolutely) 'irrationalized'. If love is related neither to norms nor to conventions, it is, by definition, *irrational*.

From the perspective of rationality of reason, neither the understanding love for the disobedient, nor empathic love for the rebel, nor even cognitive love of the repositories of rationality of intellect, can be defined as rational love. But these forms of love cannot be defined as irrational either. They include *love for those* who do not abide by 'norms-and-rules', and from this aspect are irrational. But they also include the *love of those* who, on their part, abide by the 'norms-and-rules', and from this aspect they are rational. It is commonsensical knowledge that in ordinary love each loving person seeks his or her own satisfaction, and this is why 'norms-and-rules' are often infringed by them. In understanding, empathic and cognitive love, just the opposite happens: the loving person seeks exclusively the satisfaction (and understanding) of the *beloved*. Meaningful world-views have to find a place for a love of this kind in their universe, and have to provide actors of everyday life with guidelines to cope with such an extraordinary and worrying phenomenon. Christianity has found a simple and apposite solution of the problem. Love which seeks the exclusive satisfaction and understanding of others is called *goodness*. Goodness *transcends* rationality and cannot be learned. It is not a virtue but a merit surrounded with the aura of sanctity. This conception carried with it the limitation that both loving and beloved had to be good Christians, a limitation not applicable to a pluralistic universe. But some other limitation is, and should be. As mentioned, if rationality of intellect cuts the umbilical cord tying it to rationality of reason, cognitive love turns into (unselfish) cognitive hatred. Should this fail to happen, should affection persist for a type of rationality of intellect turning radically against rationality of reason, we are confronted with the love of evil behind the mask of goodness.

The dialectic of rationality of intellect, or the cunning of reason

To begin with, I must recapitulate two previous assertions:

(a) Rationality of intellect is competence in minding norm(s). Viewed from the perspective of such norms, certain 'norms-and-rules' of the sphere of objectivation 'in itself' or of other objectivations are criticized and rejected. It is the common denominator of both types of rationalities that their arguments must take recourse to some *evidence*. Rationality of intellect has to argue for the rejection or criticism of 'norms-and-rules' and thereby must take recourse to a norm which is taken for granted.

(b) The response to the challenge of rationality of intellect by rationality of reason can be offensive argumentation, defensive argumentation, cognitive love or plain force.

Normally, the rationality of intellect is confronted with all four responses *simultaneously*. This is a result of there being dominating classes and dominated classes, various interest groups and age groups, two sexes, etc. Similarly, there are various systems of needs with various possibilities for satisfaction, and various amounts and kinds of vested interest in various social structures. There are always those 'norms-and-rules' which are observed, and others which appear to be observed and yet infringed. In *individual* cases, repositories of rationality of intellect can be confronted only by plain force. Socially, this can never be the case, for the simple reason that the use of naked force is an expression in itself of a legitimation deficiency of a structure of domination and its dominating world-view.

To employ rationality of intellect in a proper manner means to prove via argumentation the devaluation and immateriality of certain 'norms-and-rules' from the perspective of at least one particular norm. It follows that rationality of intellect must always take up the challenge of rationality of reason in each and every case where the latter offers an argument of *any* kind. I have already pointed out that when being confronted by offensive argumentation by the rationality of reason (a subtle form of force), the subjects of rationality of intellect can themselves use force only in order to make the other party listen to counterarguments. In the case of defensive argumentation by rationality of reason, rationality of intellect is morally bound to bring up its own arguments without an accompanying force of *any* kind. And given that the repositories of rationality of intellect have to presuppose the existence of this kind of rationality, at least *in nuce*, and in their interlocutors as well, they must listen themselves to the arguments of the repositories of rationality of reason. Thus, according to its own definition, *the discourse aiming at enlightenment and self-enlightenment is the proper use of rationality of intellect.*

If rationality of intellect addresses itself only to the disobedient and the rebellious, its arguments become self-curtailed. This stands to reason, because under such circumstances these arguments will not criticize any 'norms-and-rules' *rationally*, and indeed they need not and cannot do so, for the 'norms-and-rules' have already been rejected by the disobedient and the rebellious. Here, the repositories of rationality of intellect argue exclusively *for* the acceptance of their norms, an action which does not meet the full definition of rationality of intellect. It is not only the norms taken recourse to that are now taken for granted, but also the non-validity of one or other of the 'norms-and-rules' of rationality of reason. It is still a process of enlightenment, though a restricted one. The argumentation thus curtailed does not aim at discourse but at the *recognition of the norms* of rationality of intellect by those who have already become 'enlightened'. Should the subjects of rationality of intellect, armed with the same curtailed arguments, turn not only towards the disobedient and rebellious, but also towards the advocates of rationality of reason, the argumentation of the former will become *offensive* and will entail a subtle use of force. To simply pinpoint the non-validity of certain (or perhaps all) 'norms-and-rules' for those who still believe in their validity, and who can bring up arguments, on the level of rationality of reason, on behalf of their validity, means to contradict the definition of rationality of intellect. By so doing, 'norms-and-rules' are simply *declared* to be non-valid without being proven so, and all those who still abide by them are suspected by insincerity, of defending their vested interests, or other selfish motives. In this way rationality of reason is not merely 'irrationalized' but is *criminalized* as well. This is the *dogmatic use* of rationality of intellect. In this mode of use, rationality of intellect already contains the element of *irrationality* of intellect. If rationality of intellect is used in a dogmatic way, then its 'irrationalization' by the rationality of reason, a normal feature of social life, cannot remain the mere *temporary* phenomenon that it does in the case where discourse is initiated. In discourse, 'irrationalization' loses momentum and gives way to increasing 'rationalization', whereas with the dogmatic use of rationality of intellect, 'irrationalization' is being stabilized as a just punishment. Burning books is not an argument, nor is contempt or insinuation. But as long as rationality of intellect observes norms and is ready to apply these norms without contradiction to all situations – in other words, as long as the subjects of rationality of intellect take recourse by these norms consistently in their deliberations and options, even if they do not care about arguing for their options with the subjects of rationality of reason – then the rationality of intellect nonetheless preserves its *rationality*, even in its dogmatic or intolerant forms.

But the tendency to dismantle traditional 'norms-and-rules' can go even further. Rationality of intellect can escalate in criticizing and rejecting 'norms-and-rules' of everyday life and of stabilized institutions. Its repositories can turn the weapon of intellect not only against 'norms-and-rules' but also against norms, and finally against *all* values and norms. In so doing rationality of intellect completely severs the tie with rationality of reason, for it waives the argumentative procedure common to both rationality of reason and intellect. It cannot take recourse to any value or norm which is 'taken for granted', and no evidence whatsoever remains. Rationality of intellect thus becomes self-contradictory. In terms of its own definition it ought to observe norms, but if these norms are devalued it cannot do so. It can only pursue goals which are now stripped of their value-content. But as people simply cannot live without observing at least some 'norms-and-rules', the repositories of rationality of intellect will observe some of them without acknowledging their validity: they will use 'norms-and-rules' or norms as mere *means* for their goals; they will become void of any value. I call this phenomenon the *perverted intellect*. It preserves the *form* of rationality (rationalism) while actually being *irrational*. Shakespeare presented a gallery of the repositories of perverted intellect: Richard III, Iago, Edmund, and several others. Rationality of reason might be the hearth of hackneyed traditions, the seat of domination, even a prison (a source of permanent discontent), but it can never destroy life and the meaning of life in as absolute a manner as can the perverted intellect. No mad passion, no sin of the flesh, no irrational impulse or desire, as long as they remain impulse and desire, can be as harmful as the perverted intellect. It is destructive in the highest degree, since it *aims at destruction*. Should perverted intellect establish itself as a social power (or domination), it becomes the *evil intellect*. Evil intellect no longer appears in the disguise of 'norms-and-rules' of rationality of reason (as does perverted intellect): it introduces its own 'norms-and-rules', which can no longer be rationally observed, as they cannot be rationally argued for and are not traditional. (In 'The Power of Shame'), I indicated that both Nazism and Bolshevism were offsprings of perverted reason, and that they both established irrational 'norms-and-rules'.) This is the dialectic of rationality of intellect. Even the most sublime human intellectual propensity, the supreme form of rationality, can become the source of absolute irrationality if the umbilical cord with rationality of reason is cut. Rationality of reason is the fundament of all rationalities, and so it will remain.

The category of rationality has been discovered and constituted by philosophy as the category of practical reason. Practical reason is reason in deliberation *for* action and *in* action. Not every human act has a direct ethical implication: there do exist ethically indifferent acts. The *form* of a single action or a single type of action does not indicate the rationality of action. Every particular action (or type of action) is located in a series of actions. The rationality of this series of actions depends ultimately on the ethical content of the actions. By 'ethical content' I do not mean *moral* content, the will to good, etc., even if this is normally included in the 'ethical content' of an action to a greater or lesser degree. Of course, the will to good that is inseparable from rationality of reason and the supreme will to good of rationality of intellect must be clearly distinguished from one another. The latter can be termed (as with Kant) morality. Though I cannot here enter into a discussion of ethical questions proper, it should be repeated that rationality *is*, in the end, an ethical problem. Viewed from this angle, it stands to reason *why* I have called the *transcensus* of intellect *perverted* intellect and *evil* intellect.

When I say this, what I have in mind is the transcensus of *practical* reason: the transcensus of theoretical reason has no bearing whatsoever on our problem. A might 'prove' God's existence and B 'disprove' it, but both A and B can be repositories of rationality of intellect in its most sublime form if, for example, both of them consistently observe the norm of 'alleviation of all human suffering', and reject those 'norms-and-rules' and institutions which cause suffering whilst arguing for their rejection. The assertion that transcensus in the practical use of intellect does not evoke transcensus in the practical use of intellect, does not imply the severance of theoretical and practical discourse. Even the most mundane practical discourse is prompted by a world-view. If this were not so, 'good judgment' would be inconceivable. The theoretical aspects of the argument need extend only far enough to provide a practical decision with sufficient knowledge about this decision. It is only when two meaningful world-views confront each other that the theoretical aspect of the discourse comes fully into its own. In other words, this happens when a particular rationality of intellect enters into discourse with a different rationality of intellect: when the conflicting parties abide by different norms, or interpret the same norm in a diverging or perhaps even contrary manner. In such cases it will not suffice to provide a theoretical foundation for the particular action taken; one must also argue for a theoretical foundation for all actions taken. This can only be done if rationality of intellect engages in a discussion *regarding values*, and if it dismantles the values or the interpretation of values of the other party (see *For a Radical Philosophy*). But the primacy of practical reason still prevails, because all theoretical arguments are presented in order to devaluate 'norms-and-rules' legitimated and supported by the world-view that is under attack.

VI The rational personality

On our mental and emotional abilities

The distinction between different forms of reason goes back to the beginning of philosophy. Often, if not always, these different forms are attributed to different *mental faculties*. It is in this vein that *Verstand* and *Vernunft* became two distinct faculties for Kant. Despite his vitriolic criticism of the 'compartmentalization' of mind, Hegel too considered *Verstand* and *Vernunft* as two distinct faculties, even though 'dialectically interconnected' ones. Hegel argued for the absolute superiority of *Vernunft*, and his spell has lasted into our century. The juxtaposition of analytical reason to dialectical reason, instrumental reason to dialectical reason, metaphysical reason to dialectical reason, and all similar configurations, reformulate the same idea in various ways. In all of them, humans have two mental faculties of 'reason', and the second, the 'dialectical' form, is superior.

Whatever the extent of my debt to these great philosophers, the distinction between rationality of reason and rationality of intellect has, on the whole, very little to do with their tradition. In my conception 'rationality of reason' and 'rationality of intellect' are not seen as two mental faculties. I have only treated rationality as the proper use of *all our mental abilities* when making practical decisions, and my main concern has been to understand how we *discriminate* between good and evil, right and wrong, true and false, useful and harmful, and so on. My conclusion is that we can discriminate between them in two distinct ways; either we develop the readiness to observe 'norms-and-rules', or we develop the readiness to observe norms. I have not conceived of 'rationality of reason' and 'rationality of intellect' as two faculties but as two *attitudes*. It was a presupposition of the theory that we utilize exactly *the same* faculties in both attitudes, only in different combinations, contexts and the like. When I insisted that the childish questions 'Why is that so?' 'Why should it be so?' are the expressions of rationality of intellect *in nuce*, I did not allude to any specific mental ability.

It is obvious, however, that the propensity we call *curiosity* is an empirical universal, and it emerges as such in entirely heterogeneous types of thinking and acting, from problem-solving to gossiping. Speaking about 'rationality of intellect *in nuce*' in respect of childish questions refers to an attitude in which a (dominant) ability is inherent. Curiosity is here extended to knowledge and expectations which should be taken for granted, and which are indeed taken for granted, by adults. The *function* of curiosity *here* is *not* to accept the 'taken-for-grantedness' of a world one is born into by chance. If I need a forerunner and a fountainhead for my conception, I would again refer to Descartes, to the Cartesian *bon sens* or *lumière naturelle* which is *equally* divided amongst humans, with the obvious difference that within my theory *bon sens* is intersubjectively constituted by the appropriation of the sphere of objectivation 'in itself'. As has been mentioned, *bon sens* means proper discrimination, and all our mental abilities – perception, memory and recollection, imagination, judgment, curiosity, argumentation and most of all, logical thinking – participate in proper discrimination. Given that feeling is involvement in something, all mental abilities elicit feelings of various types. Rational emotions are the result of proper discrimination, but they can also be the forces motivating it. I have already spoken of three types of love which can propel the ascent from rationality of reason to rationality of intellect.

Yet the rationality of intellect is not less intersubjective than the attitude I have called rationality of reason. A lower degree of intersubjectivity (or even none at all) is nothing other than a mere appearance due to the circumstance that rationality of intellect challenges the 'taken-for-grantedness' of a world and is represented by a minority, and eventually only by a very few. But the challenged 'norms-and-rules' have to be in the world, otherwise they could not be challenged. The negation of the intersubjective belief is always intersubjective. Moreover, objectivations, 'for itself' which provide norms for repositories of rationality of intellect are not less intersubjective than the 'norms-and-rules' of the sphere of objectivation 'in itself' or the 'norms-and-rules' of institutions. Not the absence, but rather the *general–universal character of their intersubjectivity*, makes their use as norm-providers possible.

An analysis of the various mental capacities would be all the more stringent, because this approach has been neglected due to the *misuse of paradigms*. The constitution of intersubjectivity via the paradigm of language is a powerful tendency in modern philosophy and sociology. But understanding each and every mental, structural and social phenomenon as 'language' does not follow perforce from the paradigmatic use of 'language'. Should everything be regarded as language, epistemological questions, including the examination of mental abilities, are simply ushered out of philosophy. It was Hannah Arendt's great deed to return to the problem of judgment, and that of Castoriadis to raise the problem of imagination, though so far they have not found many followers. I am aware of the gap I have left on my map of reason by neglecting a question of highest importance, and I will return to this in a later study. And though my presentation is incomplete, I must nonetheless state my conclusion: that all mental abilities perform tasks *in relation to discrimination*. Thus the act of discriminating between good and evil, true and false, beautiful and ugly, successful and unsuccessful, pleasant and unpleasant and the like is *not* the accomplishment of one particular mental faculty, but of *all* mental faculties, rational feelings and emotions included. Here we may recall what has already been said in the second chapter of this study. The appropriation of the sphere of objectivation 'in itself' (in all three aspects: ordinary language, customs and the use of man-made objects) develops the ability of discrimination (*bon sens*) in humans. This is why all our mental abilities have to be already developed to some degree at this stage. The subject of everyday life is the *human-as-a-whole*. *Bon sens*, that is, reason, and rationality (acting according to reason), comprise the attitude of the *human-as-a-whole* to his or her *world-as-a-whole*. It depends on the *human-as-a-whole* and its relation to *world-as-a-whole*, and not on one or another single 'mental ability' of this human, as to how far and to what extent he or she can be called a 'rational being'.

The loss of human wholeness

Aristotle was the first to attribute rationality to *human character* (*heksis*). The virtuous person *is* the rational person because it is *logos*, the form, which transforms all propensities of *alogon*, the matter, into the *formed matter* which is virtue. *Alogon*, the prerational part of soul, does *not* disappear in the character and actions of the rational person, since *logos* does *not* simply *subject alogon*, does not *dominate* it, but *forms* it. Pleasures, enjoyments, desires, dreams, fears, belong to the life of a rational (virtuous) person as well as to the life of the non-rational. But in the case of a good (rational) person, nothing is wrong with these prerational elements. Further, being rational (virtuous) means being rational throughout one's whole life. The non-rational character of a *single* action of the virtuous person does not curtail the rationality of *character*. It is the overall tendency, the 'whole', that really matters. Rationality is thus a form of life: it is the 'good life'.

Even though I subscribe to the Aristotelian understanding of rationality (given certain modifications), the difficulties in revitalizing this simple but monumental idea must be faced. Rationality of reason and rationality of intellect were distinguished in Aristotle's time (we know already that philosophy was born by making precisely this distinction), but they did not contradict one another. The 'norms-and-rules' of the city-state were not rejected; they were reinterpreted by rationality of intellect. Identical main virtues and values were accepted as valid by the *sensus communis* and by the repositories of rationality of intellect: the latter only juxtaposed an idiosyncratic interpretation of the commonly held values to their everyday interpretation. In modernity, the life-basis of commonly held values has diminished. Science has gradually become the dominating world-view, and rationalization seems to be the royal road to rationality. Due to all this, modern interpretations of rationality contradict the Aristotelian conception rather than reinforce it. Rationality is not attributed to the human person-as-a-whole but to the specialized human who acts within rationalized institutions. With the emergence of capitalism the traditional and particularistic values (and virtues) have been increasingly dismantled, and success has become the indication of goodness. The ideology of success-orientation has been more suited to understanding rationality in terms of 'character' than the ideology of science. As Hirschman has shown in his magnificent book, *The Passions and the Interests*, pursuing our interest throughout our whole life is a defence against the dominance of prerational feelings and passions. Thus perseverance in self-serving calculation has been identified with 'rational character'. But if pursuit of interest is identified with rational character, the latter becomes quite a different thing from Aristotle's conception of rational character. Practical reason (where good comes first) becomes calculative reason, for good is identified with successful. Further, if rational character is understood as the pursuit of interest throughout our whole life, every human propensity which does not serve our best interests is excluded from the rational character – propensities such as pleasure, enjoyment, dreams and the whole domain of prerational feelings which Aristotle included in the rational character (the virtuous person) and his life (the 'good life'). Finally, though the emergence of democracy has led to the universalization of certain values, these cannot be observed in either institutions or as *norms* in everyday life because the latter is designed and shaped by calculation and rationalization. The increasing hostility of rationality of intellect to the 'norms-and-rules' of rationality of reason is historically founded. The mutual 'irrationalization' of rationality of reason and rationality of intellect is thus deeply rooted in our history. The Weberian distinction between value-rationality and goal-rationality adequately expresses the *factum* of modernity without considering the relativity of this duality and the efforts to overcome the schism.

But the increase in *irrationalism* is equally due to this schism. Of course, irrationality is not a modern phenomenon (where there is rationality, there is always irrationality), but lionizing irrationality as superior to rationality is a thoroughly modern tendency. This may appear to contradict my previous assertion that madness has often been regarded as sign of divine blessing. But it was regarded as such only if the 'possessed' spoke or acted *in accordance* with the dominating world-view. It was not irrationality that was lionized, but the sacred order revealed via the tongue of the possessed. Besides, minding the 'norms-and-rules' of the sphere of objectivation 'in itself' was considered not only good but normal, since competence in so doing was a general social presupposition of normality. In premodern eras, when everyday rational action was always surrounded by the aura of prerational and postrational elements, and where rationality of intellect, if it surfaced at all, was more or less considered 'devilish', or at least evidence of transgression, rationality of reason was far less problematic than it is in modernity. From several perspectives, modernity is far more rational than all histories have been hitherto. But since modernity destroys the prerational and post-rational 'aura' which has always surrounded the actions of a more or less rational human-being-as-a-whole, this loss has to be made up by an increase in irrationality, its glorification included. In explaining why this has happened I cannot avoid certain repetitions.

Science is the dominating world-view of modernity. It is an extremely intellectual objectivation 'for itself'. Its appropriation is not based on reception but on understanding; moreover, on a cumulative understanding. It produces cognitive surplus and it can be learned. References made to science as a 'rational world-view' are not entirely correct, but they are certainly more than a figure of speech. Above all, this is so because the truth of scientific hypotheses is proven via rational argument and demonstration, even if the scientific discovery has been made by intuition. Thus the acceptance of any scientific statement occurs rationally in the strictest sense of the term 'rationality of intellect' (rationalism). The aura of the prerational and post-rational can still be efficacious in the discovery, but the scientifically rational action (speech-act) *per se* should be kept quite distinct from this aura. A 'charismatic' scientist is a charlatan. More precisely, if a scientist is charismatic, this aura can only be attributed to the personality, not to the scientific achievement.

To avoid any misunderstanding, I repeat that I regard the 'disenchantment of the world', in so far as it refers to the intellectualization of the dominating world-view, to be a gain rather than a loss. As long as religion determines the dominating world-views of societies, the distinction between knowledge and belief cannot be generalized, even if this distinction is normally performed under everyday conditions. But given that knowledge and belief coincide in the religious world-view, they can, and often do, also coincide when it comes to the explanation of natural and social phenomena. Christianity has never been able to eliminate magical beliefs and practices, the so-called 'superstitions', not even with the use of force. However, belief in witchcraft, in 'spells' or talismans, has by and large been eradicated by science without the use of force. I emphasize that by witchcraft I mean here practices that did *not* belong to the 'norms-and-rules' of a particular society: practices which were regarded as 'superstitious' even in their original setting. Science, as an intellectualized and meaningful world-view, decreases human credulity by its very existence. Although these facts are well-known, the term 'disenchantment of the world' evokes in us a feeling of loss. People know very little about previous societies, but usually know a great deal about their own. Even those who are knowledgeable about previous societies examine them with the experiences of the present one on their mind, and thus read something 'into them' which they then contrast with the 'deficiencies' of our age.

Of course, it is clear that there are deficiencies. The intellectual and meaningful world-view of science does not help us to discriminate between good and evil, only between true and false knowledge. Besides, everyday actors cannot contribute to science. They are merely informed about it. The imagination, the intuition, the emotional world of the everyday actor are laid bare vis-à-vis this meaningful world-view, which views them as simply useless (except when it comes to enchantment by the 'miracles of nature', which is not a scientific–rational attitude). Acting properly within rationalized institutions brings a loss of the same kind. The specialized subject must act in such a way that the personality *should not be* expressed in actions. The more 'impersonal' he or she is, the better he or she can cope with the observance of specialized 'norms-and-rules'. The action becomes neither an expression of the human person-as-a-whole nor that of human wholeness. Thus the human reason at work here is *minima ratio*: it is rationality which resembles a dry leaf; it is cut off from the totality of life, from the personality, from the prerational and post-rational aura of action. Let us again remind ourselves of Aristotle. Rational character (*heksis*) is created via rational–virtuous actions. But actions performed by *minima ratio* cannot involve a feedback to human character. One can rationally and continuously observe rigid 'norms-and-rules', yet these actions may still not result in a rational human character. The same holds true of the rational pursuit of true knowledge in science. Whereas the virtuosi of religion (to use a Weberian term) have transformed their character by their action, the 'virtuosi of science' hardly do so. A scientist in pyjamas does not differ from a stockbroker in pyjamas. He can, of course, develop a rational character, but to no greater degree than can the stockbroker.

Developing a rational character by pursuing one's own interest throughout the whole of life, and thereby overcoming passions, was the project of the early bourgeoisie, the declaration of independence of the private subject. In order to carry it out, the subjects had to strip themselves not only of moral and religious values, but also of the prerational and post-rational aura of their actions and of every feeling which might have impeded the pursuit of interest. This was unmistakably the general tendency that gained momentum with the development of capitalism. However, this was not a one-way track. Interest is a very vague term. It is open to various interpretations. According to at least one viewpoint, prevailing mainly in the period of the Enlightenment, the 'pursuit of interest' meant the development of all individual capacities. Rationality was believed to centre around the development of these abilities: the harmony of reason and the emotions was posited as the supreme ideal. The revival of the Aristotelian image of the rational personality was the greatest promise of the Enlightenment. But this image had to be remodelled to meet the exigencies of modernity. The almost insurmountable difficulties involved in putting the ideal into practice did not remain hidden from the advocates of the theory. From Diderot to Goethe, there was clear awareness of the crippling effect of increasing specialization.

Even the third option of rationality (besides science and the pursuit of interests), rationality of intellect, has contributed to the elimination of the prerational and post-rational aura of human actions. The observance of norms, along with the rejection of 'norms-and-rules' of rationality of reason, presupposes conscience as the ultimate arbiter in the judgment of human behaviour. As involvement in practical reason, conscience blames all the failures of the person of conscience on 'nature'; in other words, on emotions and feelings (see 'The Power of Shame', pp. 28–9). Thus the contrast between reason and emotion is reinforced. The only emotion beyond suspicion is abstract enthusiasm, a passion the source and object of which are the values and norms themselves (see *A Theory of Feelings*, Part Two). In spite of all this, in modernity it is those who observe norms throughout their whole lives who still stand the best chance of developing a rational character. Yet their chances are far greater in the sphere of everyday life than in that of public life, let alone within rationalized institutions, a paradox which had already been discovered by Rousseau.

In sum, the increase in the rationality of single actions does not lead to an increase in the rationality of human character. Single actions taken within various rationalized frameworks have no feedback into the character: if you act in accordance with such frameworks, you do not act from within your character. The single action generally takes the form of appearance, which has nothing to do with the whole person as an 'essence'. But rational character is supposedly the net yield of rational actions stemming increasingly from one's 'essence'. If this cannot and does not happen, 'essence' seems to be something *hidden* rather than expressed by appearance. And if appearances are 'rational' actions disconnected from one another and from the personality, the person becomes an *id*, a 'something' which cannot be expressed, and therefore irrational. Essence is thus incognito. It is supposed to be 'deep' because it does not surface; it is supposed to be 'timeless' because it does not reveal itself in 'actions in time'; it is supposed to be 'non-spatial' because it does not reveal itself in 'actions in space'; it is supposed to be 'authentic' because actions (appearances) which do not express the self are by definition inauthentic. Personally, I would strongly deny that there is any particular depth in the chaos of the unexpressed self. But where I do not perceive depth, I do perceive suffering; the mute suffering stemming from alienated rationality. I do not recognize any other interpretation of 'dialectical reason' but this one: to guide home alienated reason. The Hegelian dream about the self-recognition of reason is one of the most valiant ideas ever formulated. The home of reason is the person of *bon sens*. There is no other home for reason but the human person-as-a-whole, the fountainhead of rationality of all kinds.

Despite the resolute rejection of irrationalism (the glorification of irrationality), one cannot deny that it defends something that is highly important, and worthy of defence. All three types of alienated reason are responsible for irrationalism, both in theory and practice. Irrationalism is the well-deserved revenge of the human person-as-a-whole on alienated reason (the statement of this is a fair point in Lukács' otherwise one-sided and misconceived book, *Destruction of Reason*). As the sole authority in the judgment of human behaviour, conscience (practical reason) directly constitutes irrationality, for it 'irrationalizes' emotions as 'mere nature'. Additionally, the pursuit of interest on the one hand, and science as the world-view of domination on the other, reinforce irrationalism indirectly. If our actions do not throw roots down into our character as a whole (which state is *heksis*), we are bereft of soul, and life slips through our fingers without having been lived at all. Anxiety from nothingness is anxiety of nothingness. Irrationalism offers something we are in deep need of: the belief in the substantiality of our chaotic internal experiences, the projection of our nothingness into rationality of reason, or at least the acceptance of our nothingness as the universal human fate. Beside, irrationalism restores our prerational and post-rational feelings and propensities to their rightful place. What I have in mind are all those feelings and propensities which can be interwoven in a rational way of life but which are ousted and banished by alienated reason: dreams, hopes, fear, pleasures, playfulness, imagination, intuition, mystical contemplation, unrestricted self-expression, the right to weep, cry, touch, to shut our eyes when the light is harsh, self-abandon to excitement, to the feeling of nirvana, the capacity of an idiosyncratic (if not private) language, as well as of the language of gestures, of 'being-together', of listening to 'purposeless' voices and embracing 'purposeless' beauty, and so on. Irrationalism is a bad counsellor to a just cause, for it employs rational means in defence of irrationality. Dialectical reason would make a better counsellor: it would employ rational means in defence of its just cause while making a plea for all these feelings and propensities and idiosyncrasies before the democratic grand jury of reason, so that they could be acquitted of the charge of irrationality, since they all occupy a legitimate place in the good life of a rational individual. The homecoming of alienated reason involves the recognition of all human needs in so far as their satisfaction does not presuppose the use of any human person as mere means (see 'Can true and false needs be posited?'). Thus the non-rational is recognized as a vital element of human ipseity.

The disenchanted world of modernity is the world of alienated rationality. Prerational and post-rational feelings and propensities are blocked in all the specialized actions we perform within a rationalized framework. If these actions do not carry the imprint of character, or, in case of the rationality of intellect, if they are not fed back into character as a whole, prerational and post-rational feelings and propensities are *de facto* 'irrationalized'. But since prerational and post-rational feelings and propensities cannot be eliminated, they build up and unexpectedly burst out in actions that we cannot understand at all. Modern rationality would label these actions as 'neurotic' or 'hysterical'. Thus we speak of 'mass neurosis' and 'mass hysteria'. Politicians are experts at unleashing these 'feeling attitudes' by catering for prerational and post-rational feelings and propensities. The striking contradiction between a rationalized world and the ease of unleashing irrational feelings and attitudes *en masse* makes even the veritable 'man in the street' believe in the inborn irrationality of human character. Interestingly, even Max Weber, that sceptical rationalist, believed that 'charisma' is by definition irrational, and that people are easily carried away by charisma due to their irrational propensities. But 'charisma' has only become irrational in modernity because 'being charismatic' contradicts the rationality of science, the pursuit of our own interest, the observing of 'norms-and-rules' within specialized institutions, and because it cannot be explained by any of them. Modern charisma releases prerational and post-rational feelings and propensities *against* the expectations of modern rationality: this is why it is indeed irrational. One might refer to innumerable counterexamples taken from premodern histories, but it will suffice to mention two cases, very different in character: the 'charisma' of Socrates, and that of the god-anointed kings. There was indeed nothing irrational in the charisma of a god-anointed king. In fact, just the contrary was true, for being god-anointed was necessary for the king's deeds to appear in a light of sublimity which, in turn, was necessary for ruling. Consequently, total devotion to such a king meant simply acting in accordance with 'norms-and-rules' (which is my definition of rationality of reason). On his part, the ruler acted in accordance with 'norms-and-rules' as well. A great number of prerational and post-rational elements were at work in the devotion of subjects to the king. Here, all prerational and post-rational elements combined to constitute the 'aura' of rational actions in the sense of rationality of reason.

Socrates may figure here as an even more striking example, as he had not carried any traditional (institutional) aura. Nonetheless, he became, at least in Plato's presentation, the carrier of a post-rational and prerational 'aura'. He had his entourage and followers. His spell consisted, first of all, though not exclusively, of his rationality, of his rational philosophy. But the very fact that he did not only teach, but also *lived* his philosophy, contributed considerably to his influence. Following his teaching and following him up the ladder to Truth were *identical* acts. However, both Socrates and his followers were repositories of rationality of intellect, and in the attachment of the followers to the master there was no element of irrationality. It was the rationality of the master's *character as a whole* that appealed to them, and they turned to him as to human 'wholeness'. This is why the prerational and post-rational aura has not been eliminated from this attachment: it included eroticism, gesture, intuition, imagination, the joy of being-together, self-abandon, and several other factors. If a personality is rational and the person acts rationally (either in terms of rationality of reason or in those of rationality of intellect, which are capable of shaping the whole character), there is absolutely nothing irrational in charisma. Perhaps a special term is needed for the accurate denotation of this non-irrationalist charisma, though terms do not really matter. A representative life (and character) emanates a prerational and post-rational aura, not because of any inherent irrationality but because such a life is the good life incarnate, the embodiment of supreme rationality.

It cannot be stated with certainty that rational charisma has completely disappeared from modern life. But due to the alienation of reason, charisma has become problematic in a very real way. The specialized subject has to act in accordance with specialized 'norms-and-rules'. Should human *wholeness* enter this game, then an irrational element is introduced which is external to the institution itself. This could disrupt the functioning of rationalized institutions, and could cause dismay and confusion in defying the 'division of labour' between human faculties. This can be seductive and can become a source of injustice. The charisma of repositories of rationality of intellect can also be seductive because people are ready to accept their arguments without understanding them, simply out of fascination. Seduction of this kind can become very dangerous if the target group of the repositories of rationality of intellect exhibits an overwhelmingly irrational attitude (as in the case of rebels). The practice of enchantment in a disenchanted world can prepare the soil for irrational seducers. A preference for holy mediocrity in contrast to great characters is not entirely unfounded, but mediocrity is not an antidote against the danger of enchantment. There would be no 'seduced' if everyone could work out a rational character for themselves; if every action were surrounded, more or less, by the aura of the prerational or post-rational. And if there exists no 'seduced', there is no seducer either.

The recognition of human wholeness in love

There is only one niche in modern life in which post-rational and prerational feelings and abilities have the green light: *amour passion*, the passion of love. Passionate love is by definition great; so is every person in love. Nothing is more democratic, and at the same time more generous, than love. Everyone is, or at least can be, in love: love lends sublimity to everyone. This is the only personality experience which we share with all fellow-creatures. At the same time, this is the only form of *recognition* of our personality, of our 'being-as-we-are', of our ipseity, or our *wholeness*, which is open to us. Everyone who has been loved by someone has felt the joy of being recognized not for a specialized ability, performance, success, but in his or her human existence. Love is not irrational even if it can be: we can *understand* love. Also, love motivates understanding; *it is understanding*. The person in love wants to understand the other in his or her entirety, in his or her motivations, desires, wishes, projects, thoughts. The actions of love are surrounded by a vast aura of prerational and post-rational feelings and abilities, and at least here they are accepted (not 'irrationalized'). This is also why the love of *others* (in life or in an art work) has an irresistible fascination for us. Kant referred to enthusiasm as to a feeling rooted in reason because it inspires disinterested actions. Something similar can be said of love. The mere sight of people in love, be they known or unknown to us, stirs feelings in us, pleases us, gives us enjoyment without interest of any kind. Protecting lovers is a tempting, if disinterested, act of everyday life. Of course, there is the sarcastic interpretation which treats the 'disinterested involvement in love' as the sublime act of the *voyeur*. Nor is it difficult to represent enthusiasm as sublimation. However, such reductionist explanations are rooted in a most fragmented image of reason, in the image of vivisected rationality, of rational actions stripped of their prerational and post-rational aura. It is a redundant argument that sensual satisfaction cannot be disinterested due to its being pleasant. It is also an inconsistent one, as it implies that sensual dissatisfaction can be disinterested because it is painful, even though 'pleasure' and 'pain' are of the same feeling quality. If 'pain' is accepted as an element of the aura of rationality, pleasure has to be accepted in much the same way.

Each beloved person has a charisma for the loving. *Imputing charisma to the beloved one is infatuation.* Love is said to be blind. But so is poetry, and justice is regularly portrayed blindfolded. The blindness of justice and the blindness of love are opposite in kind. Blindfolded justice expresses impartiality; the blindness of love indicates partiality. The blindness of poetry and the blindness of love are similar in kind: both of them *see* something invisible to the average eye. Poetry can transform the invisible into the visible for everyone; love does not fare so well. This is not identical with the statement that an infatuated lover is simply a fool. The infatuated person can be a fool, as with Shakespeare's Titania. And a fool's love is indeed irrational. But imputing charisma to the beloved is not outright folly, or if it is, it is a blessed one. 'Imputing charisma' to character means in this case to see *actualities* where there are only *potentialities. Assuming that there are not far more potentialities in a person than actualities is a greater folly than assuming the contrary.* There are all manner of reasons for believing that people in our world cannot live up to the maximum of their abilities and potentialities: that they have not developed a character as harmonious as they could have developed under more favourable circumstances. Love, this poetry of life, is the recognition of the beloved one in his or her human wholeness. Infatuation is the recognition of an invisible wholeness, of a promise never kept, of an opportunity lost. It is not a lie, not a simple mistake, nor is it mere self-delusion: it is a dream. This dream can eventually come true; sometimes the character is pulled together under the spell of love. But this is certainly exceptional. The great moments of love are *utopian*. However, this utopia contains at least one element of the utopia of the 'good life'.

In a world in which the character as a whole is only recognized in love, loss of love means the *total* loss of recognition. The common human feeling that *everything* is lost when love is lost, is more than a subjective fancy. The loss of recognition is the loss of the meaning of life. The more insecure the character of the lover, the more he or she seeks for 'life insurance'. To be loved by *many* seems to be a life insurance of this kind. If one love is lost, others still remain.

Actions in love are rational actions with an emphatic aura of post-rational and prerational feelings and propensities. However, should they not be reciprocated, the entire aura becomes *irrational*. Othello desperately complained of the 'chaos' which threatened to return should Desdemona be unfaithful. 'Chaos' of this kind can lead to irrational acts: to that of Othello, or, in more innocent cases, to acts of hatred. Hatred is not necessarily an irrational feeling. It can be an adequate response to 'norms-and-rules', or just norms. But now that freedom has become a universal value idea, hatred felt because of the other's withdrawal of love is irrational indeed. That this irrational hatred is largely a reaction to our total loss of recognition can be easily proven. A new love, a new total recognition, usually extinguishes the irrational hatred against the former loved one.

Should love be continuously reciprocated it does not lose its rational propensity, yet it increasingly loses its prerational and post-rational aura. The unique miracle of the mutual recognition of the human as-a-whole slowly dissipates in the routine of daily life. Mutual property relations are substituted for mutual relations of human recognition. Even if the beloved does not disappoint the lover in any demonstrable way, the latter will feel disappointed because of the loss of an aura, of an enchantment. Irrational recriminations will follow, as if the beloved had been responsible for this loss of enchantment. Seeking for a new love might seem to be a recompense. But in every new love the story will repeat itself. Love, even if it contains the element of the utopia of the 'good life', *cannot be a substitute for the latter*. However, it is not love that should be blamed for its defeat, but rather the world of alienated rationality – the world where rational character is a mere exception, where prerational and post-rational feelings and propensities are blocked in all specialized rational actions, where personality as a whole cannot obtain recognition.

Substantive rationality

It is a commonplace and even tautological statement that only individuals are endowed with reason. In the wake of a 2,500-year-old philosophical tradition I defined rationality as 'acting according to reason'. From this definition, two conclusions follow. First, that attributing 'reason' to any historical development, historical tendency, to historical 'laws' and 'necessities' and the like, is sheer mythology, and mythology of a far more obscurantist nature than attributing supreme intelligence to God. God is still a person, whereas 'world-spirit', in all its variations, is not. Secondly, the stating of rational world-views, institutions, norms, rules as such, makes no sense at all unless it is meant as a shorthand formulation standing for a far more elaborate position.

World-views can be classed as 'non-rational' and 'rational' from the standpoint of rationalism. One can label a world-view as rational if the actions related to and instigated by this world-view are carried out via testing the validity claims of values and the truth claims of statements about facts. There is really nothing novel in this specification. Anyone who speaks of 'rational worldviews' implicitly means this. My interpretation of 'rational institutions' is far more idiosyncratic. Normally, 'rationalized' and 'rational' institutions are identified in the discourse, and at least from one aspect correctly so, for the action patterns within rationalized institutions are determined by the rational world-view (science). But this identification can also be rejected, from the viewpoint of rationalism. Given that if one acts within the framework of these institutions, one takes its 'norms-and-rules' for granted, rationalized institutions require the same kind of action as any other (non-rationalized) type. In other words, from the viewpoint of a conclusive action theory the former are neither less nor more 'rational' than the latter. If we take the problem of rationalism seriously, and intend to proceed conclusively – put otherwise, if we want to apply exactly the *same standards* to institutions that we have applied to world-views – then we have to reserve the denotation 'rational institution' for those that can be maintained and reproduced via actions taken from the standpoint of rationality of intellect. To put it simply, from the viewpoint of a conclusive action theory, only *democratic* institutions can be termed rational. Finally, one can distinguish between 'rational' and 'non-rational' 'norms-and-rules' from the perspective of rationality of intellect, and hence call 'rational' the 'norms-and-rules' which have been tested by reason, 'non-rational' the ones which have not been tested by reason, and 'irrational' the ones which have been tested by reason and rejected.

In other words, in speaking of 'rational' world-views, institutions and 'norms-and-rules', one is not employing a figure of speech, but rather an *evaluative* statement. This statement comprises both a confession and a commitment. Rationalism is here identified with rationality, and only actions of rationalism are regarded as matching the *idea* of rationality. I have challenged this conception throughout the whole of this study without concealing my ultimate commitment to rationalism. But even this ultimate commitment does not mean the 'irrationalization' of rationality of reason, since it is, and will remain, the foundation of rationality of all kinds, rationality of intellect (or rationalism) included. Should one take this position seriously, then referring to world-views, institutions and 'norms-and-rules' as rational, as against others called 'non-rational', is indeed simply a figure of speech. Only actions can be called rational, and they can *equally* be called rational whether they are performed via the competence in minding 'norms-and-rules' or the competence in minding norms. No world-view or institution or 'norms-and-rules' 'possesses' an intrinsic rationality (or irrationality), nor does it 'carry' rationality *per se*. Rationality is a category of *relation*.

But if this be so, rationality of *character* has to be understood as a category of relation to the same extent. And though it is indeed a category of relation, it is an *all-embracing* one, by which I mean that it has two distinct features. 'Rational character' is all-embracing because it encompasses *all* rational actions taken by the same subject (all *possible* rational actions included). On the other hand, it is all-embracing because it is conceived of *independently* of the particular (contentual) character of the 'norms-and-rules' the subject is related to.

It may appear that I am caught in my own trap. Earlier I rejected the 'vivisection of rationality'. I argued that no formal criteria of an action defines the rationality of action because the rationality of any single action depends on the rationality of the *series* of actions in which the former is embedded, and it is finally the *content* of the series of actions that makes the single action rational or irrational. It is obvious that if I assume 'rationality of character' to be the all-embracing category of rationality, I again reject 'vivisection of rationality', only this time from a different standpoint. But by so doing, I am going to *abstract* this concept of rationality from all historically changing *contents* of 'norms-and-rules'. Should one look at the notion of 'rational character' from this angle, it will obviously prove to be a highly *formal* concept. Yet it is simultaneously a *substantive* concept, for human being as 'substance' is to be described as *rational* in its relation to 'norms-and-rules', whatever content the latter might contain, imply or mediate.

The term 'substantive rationality' has been coined by Weber, and he applied it as a main category in his theory of law. There, 'substantive rationality' was counterposed to formal rationality.

Weber meant by substantive rationality roughly the same relation that I had in mind when referring to the substantive elements of an action which make this action, in the last instance, rational, whatever form the action might take. It is well known that Weber, at least as far as legal action and thinking was concerned, distinguished clearly between formal (procedural) and substantive rationality. However, there is no strong indication that Weber made the same distinction within the framework of a general action theory. In defining the main categories of a general action theory, Weber distinguishes between purposive (goal) rationality and value rationality; a division which, in my view, differs substantially from the division of 'formal' and 'substantive' rationality. An interpretation of Weber's theory is not really appropriate to this study. I mention this problem in order to make my position clear, and so that I may explain my own use of the category of 'substantive rationality'. These two matters I will now briefly deal with.

In the section on the 'vivisection of rationality' I argued on behalf of the following: that the rationality of *any* action depends also on the content of the action. A single action is rational only in so far as it is embedded in a series of actions taken 'in accordance' with 'norms-and-rules', or least in accordance with one norm. Further, an action is rational *within a concrete historical context* and by virtue of the *regard* of actors, if the latter express at least certain elements of the historical consciousness of a given epoch (time and space). As a result, the same action can be rational or irrational depending on the regard. I have formulated this thesis within the framework of a general action theory. This theory of rationality was not meant as a denial of the relevance of the distinction between various forms of actions (instrumental, pragmatic, communicative, etc.). It only implied that even if one defines (and classifies) the *forms* of these actions, one has not yet defined their *rationality*. One can exemplify this via the use of formal rationality in legal procedures. Formality in legal procedures can be called *rational* because our *regard* makes it such; because it is a consensually accepted *norm* in modernity that legal procedures *should be formalized.* Consequently, the application of formal procedures is 'in accordance with norms'. The formal is rational because the content makes it rational, or at least codetermines its rationality. In societies in which the formalization of legal procedures is *not a normative requirement*, simply because the norm 'equality before the law' has not yet been born, and the problem of 'how this equality can be put into effect' cannot even be raised, if the category of the rational has already emerged, formal legal procedures cannot be considered rational. Or, it is *our* normative system that makes rational argumentation the supreme form of rational action.

It is easy to understand why I have not used the notion of 'substantive rationality' in its Weberian meaning. First, Weber only applied this category in a conclusive manner to his theory of law, whilst I have concerned myself with a general action theory. Secondly, the assertion that contents of action codetermine the rationality of action is no less true in relation to the actions referred to by Weber in his theory of law as 'formal'.

Certain theorists interpret this category in the following way. A person or a group of persons set a concrete (substantively defined) goal. All actions must aim at the realization of his goal. Here 'substantive rationality' does not refer to one type of action but to a cluster of types of action. Within this cluster, all actions are purposive in so far as all of them are directed towards realizing the substantive goal, but the *form* of these actions does not fulfil the criterion of purposive rational action. Actors do not deliberate on the proper means themselves for they have already been evaluated by the substantive goal. On the other hand, within this cluster of actions all actions are value-laden because they have been evaluated by the substantive goal, but the *form* of these actions does not fulfil the criterion of value-rationality because the observance of values has been identified with the realization of the substantive goal. This particular interpretation of 'substantive rationality' applies to the action patterns in Soviet society. The proponents of this interpretation argue that the *modus operandi* of the Soviet type of society can be understood as the realization of substantive rationality. I cannot put this theory under closer scrutiny here. I have already made a critique of it in conjunction with the analysis of Soviet political structure (see F. Feher-A. Heller-G. Markus: *Dictatorship Over Needs*, Part Two) and at this point I must be satisfied with a brief summary of the conclusions of that work. Even though 'substantive rationality' so interpreted serves as an auxiliary mode of legitimating the Soviet type of society, it could never become the main legitimating ideology. This is so because of one perfectly simple reason. Were substantive rationality really to be set into practice, it would sooner or later reintroduce certain patterns of action (or speech acts) which are incompatible with the actual *modus operandi* of Soviet societies (criticism of means and criticism of values and the like). In all this it has not been meant that substantive rationality, as defined above, *cannot* become the actual *modus operandi* of any *modern* society, I simply mean that this is not the case in Soviet societies. Again, it is not the subject of this study to ponder on the possibility of a conclusive employment of substantive rationality in modern society.

An entirely different notion of 'substantive rationality' is also possible, and if I am going to speak of 'substantive rationality' as a quality of human *character*, I use the category only in this second sense. There is some evidence that Weber too has occasionally this second interpretation in mind. For instance, when he speaks about 'substantive rationality' in relation to *kadi*-justice he implies that the rationality of judgment does not depend on the application of any rational 'rule' of justice but on the rational character of the judge (the *kadi*). The latter passes rational judgments because his rational (and just) human character is the source of these judgments. But it would be somewhat lax to rely on Weber's authority in this issue. I will offer my own theory instead.

Person and personality

In my book on everyday life I distinguished between two types of character: the 'particularistic person' and the 'individual person'. For the sake of ease I will refer to the same types in what follows as 'person' and 'personality'. They are ideal types in the Weberian sense of the term. (In *Everyday Life* I analysed both character types in detail. Here I have kept strictly to the special problem under scrutiny, namely the problem of rationality.)

Both person and personality make use of *bon sens*, but their attitude in using it is different. The person uses it as rationality of reason, the personality uses it as rationality of reason *and as* rationality of intellect. I call the rationality of the person 'rationality in itself' and the rationality of personality 'rationality for itself'. This distinction is a very real one. It indicates that the *person* is rational *in relation* to the sphere of objectivation 'in itself', as well as *in relation* to the 'norms-and-rules' of objectivations 'for and in itself', which the person takes for granted *as if they were* 'norms-and-rules' of the sphere of objectivation 'in itself', whereas the *personality* is *rational* also *in relation* to the *sphere of objectivation 'for itself'* (universalized values included).

The person observes the 'norms-and-rules' of the sphere of objectivation 'in itself': they are taken for granted, they are not reflected upon, their validity is not queried. The person does not become *distanced*, not even relatively, from the 'norms-and-rules', even though there may be an occasional 'exemption' from observing them. Keeping within the 'norms-and-rules' is the precondition of smooth, potentially conflict-free reproduction of the person. Their infringement normally happens under the proviso that it remains hidden from the eyes of others. Knowledge of this presupposes the use of reason as 'calculation', which by no means implies a conscious and reflective relation to 'norms-and-rules', but rather something else. It indicates that the person has no conscious and reflected relation to its own self either. The person identifies with the 'norms-and-rules' of its environment on the one hand, and with its own particularistic self on the other. The 'norms-and-rules' are accepted by the person as 'nature'. It does not distinguish between 'constant' and 'variable' elements in this respect; but it takes its own particularistic propensities as if they were also mere nature, and again, does so without any kind of distinction between 'constant' and 'variable' elements. Should it come to a conflict between 'norms-and-rules' and particularistic nature, then two 'constants' are conflicting with one another. And so the person either submits his or her own 'nature' to the other constant (the 'norms-and-rules'), and suppresses the former in order to remain in harmony with the latter, or it becomes 'deviant'. But as deviance endangers the smooth reproduction of the person, it is perforce exceptional. Normally, the suppressed particularistic feelings and propensities are 'irrationalized' without being transformed. However, occasionally they can burst out as well, or be redirected by the sphere of objectivation 'in itself' into permitted channels. In case of the redirection of irrationalized feelings and propensities, the rational action taken will be surrounded by a far more intensive and extensive prerational and post-rational aura than other actions taken by the same individual. If the sphere of objectivation 'in itself' cannot redirect the irrationalized feelings or propensities, they may eventually be absorbed by a certain objectivation 'for itself', or they may remain irrational.

If the person learns to manoeuvre between the two 'constants', that it is to say, between the network of 'norms-and-rules' and its own self, he or she develops character patterns which in time become more or less stabilized. The person will act in accordance with expectations in two respects: it will act according to the general expectation of 'norms-and-rules', and also according to the expectations of all other persons it interacts with in face-to-face relationships. To predict whether the person will score lower or higher in one or the other performance in the future is only possible if rationality is attributed to the character in question. Eventually, a prediction of this kind can prove false, but if the person-as-a-whole performs in interaction with, and before the eyes of other persons-as-a-whole, grave mistakes are not frequent. The Popperian criterion of rationality, *predictability*, can easily be applied to the rational character. If a person constantly observes 'norms-and-rules', one normally assumes that the person has learned to manoeuvre between the two constants (the 'norms-and-rules', on the one hand, and his 'nature' on the other). One also assumes that its character patterns have been stabilized. Every partner in regular interaction with him will be able accurately to predict what he will do, how he *will* act in the future: they can rely on this knowledge and direct their own behaviour accordingly. The less a person succeeds in channelling prerational and post-rational propensities, the more irrational they become, the more *unpredictable* will the person's further actions be. In the traditional everyday setting, where persons-as-a-whole are *seen* by other persons-as-a-whole, distinguishing between rational, less rational or irrational characters is not a difficult task. People usually know, almost without fail, whether a person is 'predictable' or 'unpredictable'. Making judgments about the rationality of a person's character has always belonged to the mode of procedure of everyday thinking, and it has always been a sign of good judgment if all these predictions (or almost all of them) have come true.

Our modern age confronts us with a far more complex pattern. It is far more difficult now to develop a rational character 'in itself' than it has been hitherto. Consequently, it becomes almost impossible to predict all possible future actions of a person on the grounds of observations drawn from his or her everyday behaviour. I have already argued that the actions of a *specialized subject* have no feedback at all, or only a very feeble one, to the subject's character-as-a-whole. The more specialized a person becomes, the smaller are the person's chances of stabilizing a rational character 'for itself'. The person will not learn how to manoeuvre in a *network* of 'norms-and-rules' and the person's own self, for the very simple reason that there is no such network except within the family. The expectations of specialized institutions are specialized expectations; the persons expecting something from someone else are specialized subjects as well. They will thus be unable to predict what any person would do in relationships of different kinds; and anyhow, this is not their concern. Within the family, where the network of interconnected 'norms-and-rules' still persists, the rationality of the character of the person is curtailed as well. The person cannot be completely a human person-as-a-whole within the family, if his or her main life activities lie outside it. No wonder then that in modernity women have been able to remain relatively more rational than men, and that they are, at least generally speaking, far less ready to resign their wholeness even within the framework of rationalized institutions. This explains why heroines were more frequent in bourgeois tragedies than heroes, a phenomenon analysed extensively in the second part of *A Theory of Feelings*. In addition, the family is the sphere of intimacy in modernity. This is why the families network of 'norms-and-rules' has lost its impersonality (regarding child/parent relationships, see 'The Power of Shame', pp. 17–18). Hence the person's incapacity to learn satisfactorily how to manoeuvre between 'norms-and-rules' and their own self. Within the family, one's absolute identification with one's own self becomes preponderant and outweighs the requirement of observing 'norms-and-rules'. The person can easily forget about the eyes of others because the 'family regard' is an intimate eye. One can forcefully identify with one's own Ego and not bother about being seen. As long as 'the neighbours' do not hear or see anything, suppressed irrational feelings can be freely released.

I called the character of a person rationality 'in itself'. The more the sphere of objectivation 'in itself' regulates the whole life of a person, the more rational the person may become. To put it simply, if the person has acquired a *way of life*, it develops a more or less rational character 'in itself'. The qualification ('more or less') refers to the 'irrationalized' feelings and propensities, never completely eliminated from the character of the person. However, the less the sphere of objectivation 'in itself' regulates the whole life of a person, the less rational the *person* may become. Its acts do not spring from its character, and as a result these acts are not indicative of the person. Increasingly, rational actions have very little to do with the rationality of character. The person cannot attain self-knowledge either. 'External' and 'internal' life are completely divided and internal life is experienced as the chaos of irrationalized feelings and propensities. True enough, the rationality of the character 'in itself' is never completely nil, for the person still develops the competence to cope with various 'norms-and-rules'. But since the latter are atomized, in so far as the heterogeneous 'norms-and-rules' are no longer interconnected in an all-embracing network, the rationality of the character 'in itself' is destabilized, and a slight impetus is enough to push it into irrationality. In the main, it was Marcuse's and Fromm's major achievement to shed light on the dangers of this instability even though they offered different accounts and remedies for it. But whatever the explanations might be, they make us aware of the frailty of alienated rationality. And alienated rationality is indeed frail if the bearers of reason can only develop *minima ratio*: it is frail, indeed, if the rationality of character hangs by a thread alone.

It is due to a vast increase in rationality, even if produced by its alienated version, that our world is not entirely god-forsaken. As I have spoken about this increase from several angles, it suffices to refer back to the previous analyses at this stage. Due to the possible generalization of rationalism, the chances of developing a higher type of rational character, *a rational character 'for itself'*, are far better than they had ever been in premodern societies. To become a *personality* rather than a person has been more or less possible in all societies, but rather 'less' than 'more'. Ancient democracies were a great exception in this respect; no wonder, then, that the image of rational personality was first designed in Athens and in the Ionian democracies. But once this image was designed it was never forgotten. The ideal of the rational personality outlived the societies from which it had sprung. The continuity of Stoicism and Epicureanism bears witness to this never-fading memory. In addition, the image of the rational personality is not exclusively embedded in the European tradition. Similar ideals of personality had been developed in Eastern traditions such as Buddhism and Taosim. But the rational character 'for itself' has never stood a chance of becoming generalized; it has not even had the opportunity to become widespread. Apart from ancient democracies, rational personalities were exceptional; highly exceptional access to learning and to 'exercise' marked their way. They were not even in strong need of the smooth functioning of society; rationality 'in itself' sufficed to this end. One can rather say that persons accomplished the task of reproducing society far better and more efficiently than did personalities because of the former's complete identification with the 'norms-and-rules'. Even a relative generalization of the personality's attitude would have proven fatal in traditional societies. The wheel has turned in modernity. The future-directedness of society, where 'norms-and-rules' quickly decline and are replaced; the loss of ways of life; the increase in (alienated) rationality; the universalization of a few values – because of all these things – personality, as against mere person, simply had to gain momentum. Yet the shift from person towards personality has been both relative and one-sided, and it could not substantially counterbalance the loss in rationality 'in itself' (of the person). To answer the question of why this has happened in this way, I must focus on how the qualities of rational personality emerge in the first place.

In contrast to the person, the personality has a *reflected* relationship in both the 'norms-and-rules' of its environment and to its own self. Personality does not take the network of 'norms-and-rules' of its environment simply for granted. Personality uses its *bon sens* as rationality of intellect *as well*. It observes one or several norms and from the standpoint of these is able to test the validity of 'norms-and-rules' of its environment. 'Testing' of this kind does not always imply the rejection of certain 'norms-and-rules'. It can result in the elaboration of an idiosyncratic *hierarchy* among 'norms-and-rules'. As a hierarchy of this kind has been constructed from the standpoint of a value, acting in accordance with this hierarchy is *binding* for the personality. Since at least the hierarchy of 'norms-and-rules' is changed by the personality, this network of 'norms-and-rules' cannot be accepted as if it were 'nature'. The network is conceived of by the personality as more or less constant; *therefore*, as more or less variable. Thus the personality does not submit itself without further ado to 'norms-and-rules'. On the contrary, where it observes them they themselves become engraved with the indelible mark of personality. If the personality does not merely observe them, but changes them, this process occurs to an even greater degree. Indeed, the personality consciously contributes to the validation and devaluation of these 'norms-and-rules'. Here, rational action does not simply mean minding 'norms-and-rules', but rather the recognition of our *own reason* in the 'norms-and-rules' thus minded. By so acting, the personality to some extent fuses intersubjectively constituted rationality and subjectively constituted rationality. Intersubjective becomes consciously subjective, and vice versa. But we know that personality has a reflected relationship to its own self as well. It views its own self from the standpoint of the observed value(s) and these 'norms-and-rules', and it does not take its own self as simply granted either. The personality puts the inducement of the Delphi oracle ('Know thyself') into effect. Its 'self' is not accepted as mere nature but as 'more or less' constant and 'more or less' variable: as *potentiality*. This potentiality must be transformed with the guidance of reasonable 'norms-and-rules'. Moreover, the hierarchy of 'norms-and-rules' is worked out in a twofold way: it has to be consonant with the supreme norms observed, as well as with the potentialities of the self. The personality does not simply pursue its own preservation, it pursues its preservation *and* its own unfolding *as* a personality. The life of personalities is a *good* life; to simply live is something that has no merit for them. Certaintly, human dignity is regarded by them as an essential part of life.

The actions of personality spring from the character: they express and reinforce it. These actions have a post-rational and prerational aura of their own. Since the personality does not submit to the quasi-nature of the network of 'norms-and-rules', it normally does not 'irrationalize' prerational and post-rational feelings and abilities either, but gives vent to them. Personality as a rational character 'for itself' is capable of successfully coping with its non-rational feelings, impulses and propensities. It does not yield to 'norms-and-rules', and redirect these feelings and impulses into 'permitted' channels. It is personality that gives the red or green light to its own non-rational impulses: it is in charge and they are under control. It can do this because it knows these non-rational impulses well. This is why irrationalized impulses, propensities and feelings do not *unconsciously* accompany the actions of the rational character. Personality need not 'rationalize' its own actions, for they *are* rational. Rational character 'for itself' is familiar with dreams and hopes, fears and pleasures, playfulness, imagination, intuition, mystical contemplation, unrestricted self-expression. It does not relinquish the right to weeping, crying, to touch, to shut the eyes when the light is harsh, nor does it resign the ability of self-abandon, of excitement, of nirvana, of idiosyncratic (if not private) speech, of the language of gestures, of being-together, of listening to 'purposeless' voices and embracing 'purposeless beauty', and so on. Only the 'when' and 'where' and 'how' is regulated by the personality in order that the non-rational does not impede the observance of norms and of 'norms-and-rules', the hierarchy of which constitutes the hallmark of personality.

To this brief catalogue of the constituents of the rational character 'for itself', two remarks have to be added. First, the fact that the rational character 'for itself' presupposes the use of *bon sens* as rationality of intellect does not imply that everyone who uses *bon sens* as rationality of intellect is, or will become, a rational character 'for itself'. By definition, rationality of intellect means the observance of one (or a few) norms along with the critical rejection of at least one 'norm-and-rule'. But the use of *bon sens* as rationality of intellect does not necessarily involve a reflected relation to our own self, even less the intention to develop the possibilities of one's own 'nature'. The claim that not every repository of rationality of intellect elaborates on its own 'wholeness' is an understatement. The 'intolerant' use of rationality of intellect can turn against themselves with the same intolerance they show towards the repositories of rationality of reason.

Becoming a personality, a rational character 'for itself', has very little to do with so-called 'great achievements' in any specialized field. Great achievements in a special field express strength of character but not necessarily its rationality. If the achievements are beneficial, the strong and accomplished person deserves praise. But the personality, the rational character 'for itself', deserves high praise even if no spectacular achievement is connected with it. The rational character 'for itself' is the happily anticipated vessel of the homecoming of reason.

From modernity to Aristotle, from Aristotle to modernity

Rationality of character is not an inherent quality but a possible result of the appropriation of 'norms-and-rules' and of norms, of social relations and human relations, by series of actions. If it comes about, it does so through learning processes, acts of objectivation, interactions, communication. To quote Aristotle once again, it is in *praxis* that *hexis* is established. But once it has been established, *further* praxis (and *theories*) is rooted increasingly in *hexis* itself. When I speak of 'substantive rationality' I mean *hexis* as the source of all actions. No single action can therefore be called 'substantively rational', for no single action is the source of all actions. The same can be stated of the series of certain actions.

At first glance there might seem to be a flaw in these introductory remarks. The assertion that the human character is the result of action and that the established character then becomes the source of all actions taken in the future, and the assertion that the established character is 'substantively rational', in so far as it becomes the source of all actions, are two very distinct matters. One might object that irrational characters too are sources of all their actions. But this is not so. One need not be familiar with the analyses of Spinoza's *Ethics* in order to know that the actions of an irrational character are always determined 'from outside', by ephemeral objects, which trigger *passions* that cannot be controlled or directed. A person (a character 'in itself') is irrational if it accepts the judgment of others concerning the validity of 'norms-and-rules', but is unable to observe these 'norms-and-rules' because external phenomena trigger impulses and passions which it cannot resist. A personality (a character 'for itself') is irrational if objects affect it in such a way that it will repeatedly act *against* its own conscience. An irrational character is *unpredictable*, in regard to itself as well as to others. It can resolve most strongly not to continue to act against its will, yet it will do so. The irrational character is therefore *unfree*, as Spinoza put it, whilst the rational is free, and is so precisely because it is the source of all its actions. For this reason it is entirely correct to speak of 'substantive rationality' in so far as the character is the source of all its actions.

It is obvious that characters are neither completely irrational nor completely rational. They are either more rational or less rational. Substantive rationality is a regulative idea rather than an empirical fact. But it is correct to speak of 'substantive rationality' if the personality in question regulates its behaviour by this idea. And this is far from being counterfactual.

In respect of the person we speak only of 'substantive rationality *in nuce*', because here practical reason is still *in nuce*. In respect of the personality it is legitimate to speak of 'substantive rationality proper', for the practical reason at work here is practical reason proper. As I have already shown that the rational character 'in itself' (in other words, the rational person) has lost its life-foundation to modernity, in what follows I will concentrate on the analysis of the rational character 'for itself'; on the substantive rationality of *personality*.

The rational personality (just like the rational person) is a possible result of the active appropriation of intersubjective knowledge in accordance with the categories of discrimination (value-orientation). It is only thus that it becomes the source of all its rational actions. Clearly, intersubjective knowledge and subjective knowledge (intersubjective knowledge appropriated by the subject) never coincide. What is meant by the personality as the 'source of all rational actions' is *not* the coalescence of intersubjectivity and subjectivity, which would produce (if it could come about, which is another matter) only self-contained atoms like the gods of Epicurus. What I have in mind is a subject who is ready and able to cope with intersubjective relations rationally out of the intrinsic quality of its socialized subjective nature. *It is not intersubjectivity and subjectivity that coalesce but the two types of 'wholeness': human person-as-a-whole and the whole human*. It is appropriate here to recall Lukács' distinction between these two kinds of wholeness. Human person-as-a-whole is the subject of everyday life, whereas the subject who rises to the sphere of objectivation 'for itself' via the suspension of everyday activities becomes a whole human. The coalescence of these two kinds of human wholeness does not imply the continuous involvement in a homogeneous sphere of objectivation 'for itself', but rather the *homogenization* of every human activity by the human person-as-a-whole. Thus the heterogeneous activities of the life-world and of the specialized institutions do not remain separated. Instead, each and every one of them becomes the (self) expression of a *homogeneity*: the homogeneity of personality.

I have made it clear that my image of personality as 'substantive rationality' is shaped after the Aristotelian design of the 'good' (virtuous) man. But I also hinted at the difficulties one might face when applying an ancient solution to a modern question. I referred to the fact that Aristotle still took the main virtues of his age for granted, and that he could therefore depict the rational personality as the person able to practise these virtues throughout his entire life. But if no virtues are consensually accepted, and if we do not define the rational personality as the one who practises virtues, our rational personality will not be identical with the 'good man' (good person). However, rational personality is an incontestable asset only if the personality is 'good' or, to use a modern expression, if it is a *moral* personality. Moral personality presupposes personality, but being a personality is no guarantee of being moral.

Here I will only list three conditions of personality's becoming a moral personality. First, it must recognize the personality (or the person) in all human beings. This implies the recognition of all human needs, excluding those that can be satisfied only by using other human beings as mere means (see *For a Radical Philosophy*, 'Can True and False Needs Be Posited?'). Secondly, the personality must be willing to enter into rational discussion with every standpoint which, for its part, is ready to enter into discussion. Thirdly, the personality has to recognize the validity of at least one universal norm (besides the recognition of other personalities and the norm of rational discourse), and endorse it in practice. I agree with Apel and Habermas that there is no modern moral personality without readiness for rational discussion, but I do not accept their thesis that it is precisely rational discourse that constitutes morality. Only the rational (and good) personality guarantees the rationality of discourse to come. On the other hand, rational discourse is only one form of expression of the moral personality. To account for the first of these statements, two remarks are necessary. We enter into discussions with our passions and interests, and only those who have a reflected relation to their own self are aware of these passions and interests, and can thus suspend them, if need be, in the process of discourse. Also, openness to the arguments of others presupposes the recognition of the other's personality, his or her needs included. In relation to the second statement, two additional remarks have to be made. To come to agreement with others regarding the interpretation of values or proposals for action does not in itself create the moral personality. Speech act is action indeed, but it does not replace action proper. Coming to agreement does not necessarily imply acting according to the agreement unless the character of the interlocutors is rational. Only if the speech act and action proper spring from the same substantive rationality, from the homogeneous human-as-a-whole, will the action be adequate to the decisions of discourse. The action taken by the individual is not 'residual', something which should not be reckoned with in the theory. It is precisely the individual action which is the bearer and expression of morality. Moreover, no good argument impresses the interlocutor if it is not supported by the actions of the personality who is doing the arguing. One cannot abstract the personality as the agent of discourse from the personality as a whole. The personality interacts as a whole personality with others. His or her prudence and good judgment play a decisive role in these interactions. The prerational and post-rational feelings and propensities which are not 'irrationalized' by the rational character 'for itself' contribute to his or her moral substance. There are supreme ethical qualities which are not open to discussion at all but which are all-important in action: tactfulness, delicacy, liberality, humour, intuition, sympathy, empathy and the like.

Here I must repeat what has been said of the primacy of practical reason – that it is not only an Ought, but an empirical fact as well. My whole argument against the 'vivisection of rationality' has been led by this conviction. However, it needs to be made clear that the primacy of practical reason as an Ought and the primacy of practical reason as an empirical fact are different in kind. I will now exemplify this matter from the perspective of the problem under scrutiny; that of substantive rationality.

Practical reason has been defined as the ability to discriminate between good and evil, true and false, useful and harmful, successful and unsuccessful, beautiful and ugly, and the like, according to their hierarchical position (good coming first). The ability to discriminate was said to be the preconditon of human social life. If the individual has to learn only what has been discriminated in the sphere of objectivation 'in itself', practical reason is purely passive, and is not yet a relatively independent agent. It will become independent only if the learned discrimination has to be applied individually, selectively and critically.

In most human histories practical and pragmatic reason had not been distinguished. Modern capitalism and industrialization had to appear before this distinction could be made. More precisely, the development of modern capitalism and industrialization *created* this distinction. Here I must again refer back to Aristotle, as he was the first to distinguish between 'goal-rationality' and 'value-rationality', though in a way totally different from that of Weber more than 2,000 years later. Aristotle assumed the all-encompassing unity of values and goals, and the hierarchy of values meant for him the hierarchy of goals. Every goal shared by a cluster of human persons is good, but supreme good is the goal shared by every one in conjunction and separately. Two supreme goals in this respect are happiness and the goodness of the state, both of which rest on virtue (and of the good man and the good citizen, see 'The Good Man and the Good Citizen', 'Rationality and Democracy'). 'Value-rationality' and 'goal-rationality' are only distinguished within this framework. They are structurally different, in so far as for 'value-rationality' action and goal *do not differ*, since action is the 'end of itself', whereas in the case of 'goal-rationality', end is *outside* the action. Thus if the end is achieved the action stops. Action of the first kind is *energeia* (both praxis *and* theory). Action of the second kind is *techne* (crafts, arts, sciences and even drawing up and implementing a new constitution). The analysis of *techne* in its own right played a highly important role in the philosophy of Aristotle (see my *The Ethics of Aristotle and the Ancient Ethos*, Barcelona, Edicions Peninsula 1983). But *techne* was regarded as *techne* (and not an inferior type of work) only if the person who practised it *shared* in goodness, only if the person was, or at least *could* be a good person and a good citizen (he had to own property, he had to be independent of others). In short, in Aristotle, rationalities of all kind were purposive and all of them stemmed from the 'substantive rationality' of the good person and the good citizen. But the *social precondition* of becoming rational personalities had also been made clear: personal freedom, the relative equality of wealth, a state in which everyone can rule and be ruled in turn, and proper education (education of the person as a whole). I will return to these preconditions later.

What does an argument of this kind have to do with our problems, with modernity, where practical and pragmatic action have split, and remain sundered? Undoubtedly, the fact that Aristotle made a case for the factual primacy of practical reason is no evidence of such primacy in our age. I must therefore return at this point to the problem of why the factual primacy of practical reason and its primacy as an Ought have today become so different in kind. I will assume to begin with that this factual primacy has not completely vanished into thin air.

The *recognition* of a person as a person depends on their ability to discriminate between good and evil, true and false, and the like, according to the standards set by society with an eye to the social status of this person. Up to modernity, it was only in a special sense that one could speak about the recognition of persons *per se*, as they were mainly recognized as members of the social cluster they belonged to. Aristotle formulated this in the following way: a slave can be recognized as a person to the degree that he is a good slave, a woman to the degree that she is a good wife, and so on. It cannot be emphasized enough that the unconditional recognition of the person as a person, and not as a member of a particular social cluster, is a fundamental achievement of modernity. The universalization of certain values and the (possible) radicalization of democracy rest precisely on this achievement. However, the more closely we examine the matter the more we realize that in modernity persons are recognized as such if they learn how to discriminate between good and evil, and the like; that is to say, they are recognized on the grounds of their use of practical reason. As Hegel put it, *mutual* recognition is the foundation of modern civil society. Mutual recognition of persons as persons is the mutual recognition of each other's practical reason, of each other's *bon sens*, with which they discriminate between good and evil, etc. This is precisely what Kant called the release from the self-incurred tutelage. And it is not only completely irrelevant, but also contradictory to all our personal experience, to think that people today act purely pragmatically because they allegedly have become wholly indifferent to the recognition of the ethically 'correct' quality of their persons. Should one be called a scoundrel, the degree of offence is not less now than it was in pre-modern times. We all need at least a few people who will testify that we have properly discriminated between good and evil, and that everything we have done we have tried to do for the sake of good. We might even appeal to posterity, hoping that future generations will recognize our *merits* (and not only our *results*). We would not rationalize our actions (this time in the Freudian sense of the word) if practical reason did not still maintain its factual priority. What has been lost is not the ability to discriminate, and the right to claim that what we have done has been done properly, but the *standard* of goodness, and what has not yet emerged in the standard of goodness which might apply to everyone. This is why we can rationalize all (or almost all) of our actions, which we could not have done in times when the standards were fixed. To sum up: the primacy of practical reason is still a fact of life, but an *empty* fact (it must be empty if almost all actions can be rationalized as good). Primacy of practical reason as an *Ought* is the utopia of the revindication of at least one absolute norm the infringement of which *cannot be rationalized* by any person under any circumstances. But there is no such universal norm in modernity. If there were, the primacy of practical reason as the absolute yardstick for discriminating between good and evil would not be counterfactual (would not be an Ought). I have already mentioned that the few universalized values have no universal *normative* power. It is only the Ought of the primacy of practical reason that constitutes their normative power. And this involves discriminating from the position of rationality of intellect.

Before proceeding any further, certain of my conclusions require recapitulation. Every human being acquires *bon sens*. *Bon sens* is mobilized in the attitude of rationality of reason and, occasionally, in the attitude of rationality of intellect. Every healthy human being is able to appropriate the 'norms-and-rules' of the sphere of objectivation 'in itself'. The subject of the sphere of objectivation 'in itself' is the human being-as-a-whole. In modernity, where science has become the dominating world-view, these 'norms-and-rules' are more or less emptied of their ethical content. Increasingly, the subject becomes a specialized subject, and, as a whole, can encounter other persons as wholes only in the sphere of intimacy, particularly in love. Under the impact of capitalism the life-strategy of the pursuit of interest has become widespread. Under the impact of democratization (in the modern democracy) persons are recognized as such, and the attitude of rationality of intellect has become equally widespread, not only from the standpoint of objectivations 'for itself' but also from the standpoint of universalized values. The position of rationality of reason can make the character rational 'in itself', but not rational 'for itself'. Adopting the position of rationality of intellect may transform the character into rational character 'for itself', but it does not necessarily do so. The primacy of practical reason as a fact persists, but it is empty. The primacy of practical reason as an Ought is the position of the rationality of intellect. Universal values are not universal norms – they only have normative power for the repositories of the rationality of intellect who in fact observe them. Their universalization is not conceivable if the repositories of rationality of intellect turn against the repositories of rationality of reason. Rationality of reason is the foundation of rationality. If it is repressed, irrationality takes the lead. Thus the repositories of rationality of intellect must have a discursive relation to the repositories of rationality of reason on the basis of mutual recognition. But only personalities (rational characters 'for itself') are able and ready to enter into discourse. Further, one can only hold a conclusive discourse if at least one value (or norm) is shared by the interlocutors, and is taken recourse to by all of them. Only universalized values are held in common between repositories of rationality of reason and those of rationality of intellect. Thus it will not suffice if the repositories of rationality of intellect are personalities. In order to enter into rational discussion with the repositories of rationality of reason, they must be *good* personalities as well. If they are rational, all their actions will be embedded in rationality. If they are good, not only their rational actions, but the prerational and post-rational aura of their actions will be good as well. Thus we have arrived back at Aristotle again: humans who lead a good life are the fountainheads of rationality. All the specialized actions of these people are embedded in two 'wholenesses'. One of them is human wholeness as the coalescence of the human person as a whole and human wholeness. The other is supreme good, which is the supreme end and purpose: decent action led by at least one norm as an end 'in itself' throughout the whole of life.

I cannot see any other *theoretical solution* to the main problem of modernity, a problem which has been described as the primacy of practical reason losing its spell. As I share the commitment to the primacy of practical reason, my theory is formulated with a practical intent. But theory cannot transform life, not even theory that has practical intent. It may be a consolation that theory belongs to *energeia*. It is thus – and it would be hypocritical to deny it – also a purpose in itself.

Second sociological intermezzo

Let me recall once again that Aristotle listed the following social preconditions for the rational personality to be generalized: personal freedom, the relative equality of wealth (property), a state in which everyone can rule and be ruled in turn, and proper education of the person-as-a-whole. Of these preconditions, only the first is met today – at least, in certain parts of the world. Therefore, even if one thinks in terms of the Aristotelian theoretical framework, one must realize that the good life as a way of life (open to all) is beyond reach. In addition, modern society is *dissatisfied society*, where the feeling of general dissatisfaction is shaped by the same values as the democratic attitude, that is to say, by universalized values. This fact confronts us with further difficulties, because general dissatisfaction is an immense impediment to the good life as a *way* of life. But if one means thereby that rational character 'for itself' cannot emerge out of this situation, the Ought of the primacy of practical reason would cease to function as a regulative idea in our actions. Let me formulate this the other way round. As long as the Ought of the primacy of practical reason does not disappear as a regulative idea, the emergence of rational characters 'for itself' is not excluded. True enough, a rational way of life is not open to personalities of our time. But *a rational conduct of life* still is.

The Aristotelian conception of the good life might, in a modified version, inspire us to design the utopia of a radicalized democracy (I have undertaken this controversial attempt in *For a Radical Philosophy* and in 'Rationality and Democracy'). However, as far as our 'here and now' is concerned, it does not offer us a model we can cope with. We should rather turn to traditions which are far more relevant to our tasks and possibilities. I have in mind the Stoic-Epicurean tradition. This is precisely a tradition offering us a blueprint for good conduct of life in dark times. When speaking of this tradition, there is no need to add the qualification 'in a modified version', as the tradition itself allows for constant modification according to the exigencies of the moment. The element that is constantly alive in both Stoicism and Epicureanism is just this of a rational conduct of life. Changes in the theoretical reconstruction of the world, in the attitudes of theoretical reason, even substantial changes in the social structure and in the understanding of these structures, have had no impact on the relevance of the *core* of Stoicism and Epicureanism. This core always was and has remained relevant, from the ancient Greeks to Rosa

Luxemburg. Stoicism and Epicureanism suggest an *ethics* which meets the exigencies of our age because it makes a plea for the rational character 'for itself' as the source of all our actions.

At first glance it may not seem justified to introduce the problem of Stoic-Epicurean ethics into a study which has raised the issue of everyday life and rationality. So far I have offered a social theory, or more precisely, a general action theory, conceived from the perspective of the paradigm of the sphere of objectivation 'in itself'. In doing so I have taken recourse to interpreted facts only in so far as they prove the *relevance* of an ethics of this kind. I cannot have recourse, at least not as to an interpreted fact, to the very *existence* of such an ethics, and certainly not to its widespread existence. Moreover, if a Stoic-Epicurean ethics is relevant to our times, what exactly does this mean? Here, the notion of 'relevance' includes a *recommendation*, which could be read as follows: Those having the strong will to live a good life under present-day circumstances can still do so *if* they are ready and able to organize their lives according to the common normative elements of a Stoic-Epicurean ethics.

Stoic-Epicurean ethics

Stoic-Epicurean ethics involves a commitment to the value of personal freedom. Personal freedom is interpreted as rational character 'for itself'. The more that all actions spring from such a character the freer the person becomes. The value of personal freedom and the interpretation of personal freedom as rational character 'for itself' both fit very well the field of action and behaviour of modernity. Freedom has become a universal value, and as such is open to any interpretation. Personal freedom is one legitimate and generalizable interpretation from among many. In the age of rationalism, where rationality of intellect has a fair chance to develop, and where, although the rationality of the person is fragmented, the rationality of personality has more scope without encountering social barriers than in previous histories, Stoic-Epicurean ethics seems to be more appropriate than ever. Further, the only concrete *virtue* democracy has developed so far, namely, civilian courage, presupposes a *resoluteness* of character very much in accordance with Stoic-Epicurean ethics. Finally, such an ethics suggests elaborating a conduct of life in a world where there is no longer any 'way of life'. This loss is exactly the human condition of the present that we have to cope with.

To all this, three objections can be raised (and all three were in fact raised repeatedly during public discussions after the presentation of my theory in 1982). First, that a Stoic-Epicurean ethics might be adequate to the *problems* of our age, but is not viable because of the specific features of our *social structure*. Next, that this ethics might be adequate to the problems of our age but its generalization contradicts *human nature*. Finally, even if this ethics were viable and generalizable in our age, *it could not cope* with the major problems of this age because it is not an ethics of *responsibility*. These objections are both grave and substantial, and merit individual answers.

(1) For Stoics and Epicureans of previous societies the option of withdrawing from every social action had always been possible. An option like this is now neither open nor desirable. Present-day Stoics and Epicureans must work as specialized subjects in both economic institutions and those of power. They must perform actions which do not spring from their characters but are imposed on them by the division of labour. Only the privileged few who perform only such actions as spring from their character have any chance of living up to a Stoic-Epicurean ethics. Of course, there is another possibility: that of performing all imposed tasks with *indifference*, without involvement. This lack of involvement can mean two things: lack of involvement in the activity itself, or lack of involvement in the recognition of one's individuality through the activity performed. The former implies complete separation of body and intellect, as well as of body and 'soul'; the latter entails disinterestedness in success or failure. In earlier historical periods it was far easier to make a plea for disinterestedness in personal success, promotion or public recognition than in this age of general dissatisfaction.

However, at least a relative disinterestedness is not completely out of reach. It is also badly needed, since self-esteem which is dependent only on external signs of recognition (public opinion, promotion, social prestige and the like) is self-made unhappiness. But this is easier said than done. Even if we become relatively disinterested in *external* signs or symbols of recognition, we cannot become disinterested in recognition itself. Epicurus had a 'garden', a community of friends in which everyone was recognized according to his merit, as a personality. No thorough appraisal of the generalizability of a Stoic-Epicurean ethics is possible without reference to 'gardens'. Today, it is the nuclear family alone wherein persons can be recognized as 'whole'. But the quest for communities is still present. This quest is indicative of a need for the establishment of the framework in which Stoic-

Epicurean ethics may be possible. Whatever their social objectives might be, modern social movements express, among other things, the strength of a need like this.

(2) The second objection to the generalizability of Stoic-Epicurean ethics refers to human nature in general, but especially to modern human nature.

The first argument related to this objection runs as follows. Even if the rational conduct of life is no longer the privilege of a social elite, it is still the privilege of a *genetic elite*. Otherwise we could not explain why it is that even under favourable circumstances only an elect few are able to become personalities (rational character 'for itself'). The second argument adds to this that under present-day circumstances human nature is mutilated and distorted to the degree where it cannot take the first step towards human wholeness. Thus the proposal to follow a Stoic-Epicurean ethics is nothing but a daydream.

This objection, which I have stated in only a brief manner, does in fact expose a gap in my theory of substantive rationality. I stated that the personality has on the one hand a reflected relation to his or her world, its 'norms-and-rules' and norms, and on the other hand has an equally reflected relation to his or her own self. Yet although I analysed in detail what 'norms-and-rules' and 'norms' are all about, I have said very little about the self, and especially about *psychological character*. This neglect was of a dual nature. Some of our potentialities are inborn, and this is true not only of our physical constitution but of certain psychological propensities as well. Even very simple biological patterns like the over- or under-production of our thyroid glands or our higher or lower blood pressure may influence the psychological character. So do the idiosyncratic patterns of our new brain. Secondly, the society in which we happen to be born starts to shape and model our psyche long before the emergence of our moral consciousness, even before we learn to speak, and it depends not on our will or resolve but on simple good or bad luck, as to what kind of influence our environment exerts on the development of certain basic patterns of our psychological character. How much protein we get as small children, whether we are loved, hated or treated with indifference, the social status we are 'allocated' to upon birth, what type of fear we have to cope with; all this and much more leaves the deepest marks on our psychological make-up. This is why the elaboration of a rational character 'for itself' is very easy to accomplish for some people, and very difficult or even impossible to accomplish for others. The emplacement of prerational and post-rational feelings and propensities within a rational conduct of life goes on smoothly if the psychological character is harmonious. Should the psychological character be torn, internal conflicts of a serious nature are unavoidable. If the person makes every effort to know his or her own self and reflect upon it, the conflicts can still be perpetuated, or else he or she may pay for moral resoluteness and rationality with the impoverishment of emotional life. We are morally free only to the degree that no initial good or bad luck fundamentally determines our moral character. But even morally, we are only *relatively* free to the degree that the initial good or bad luck is very likely to influence our fate throughout our whole life. Even if decency and honesty may be within everybody's reach, a happy disposition and success in handling problems may not be. Aristotle hit the nail on the head when he remarked that happiness can be achieved via virtuous activity throughout the whole life, but that complete happiness requires additional 'goods of luck'. Every rational character 'for itself' has an affinity with happiness, but substantive rationality does not in itself warrant happiness. However, 'affinity to happiness' is more than merely being 'worthy of happiness'.

The second argument concerning the second objection to the generalizability of Stoic-Epicurean ethics is even more puzzling. It claimed that present-day social circumstances mutilate and distort human nature to the point where it is almost impossible for the rational character 'for itself' to emerge. And so how can the mutilated person possibly make the leap to homogeneous personality?

To cope with the problem through taking recourse to a messianic tradition is an obvious (but facile) solution. One could say that the greater the humiliation, the closer one approaches redemption (or the greater the alienation, the more forceful the will to liberation). But I reject this 'dialectics'. If there is no redeemer, then it rests with the humiliated to lift themselves. Moreover, the humiliated and alienated might rebel, but it should be recognized beforehand that out of this rebellion may be born not only liberation, but a new servitude as well.

But when all is said and done, the second objection raised against the recommendation of a Stoic-Epicurean ethics can be raised against *every* ethics. All ethics confront *unequals* with *equal* norms. The norm 'You ought not to kill' is equally valid for people with strong aggressive impulses and for those who wouldn't harm a fly. Even if we reduced all moral norms to one single norm, namely *justice* (this cause being the pinnacle of so many present-day moral philosophies), we could still not circumvent inequality, because the psychological make-up of certain people makes it very difficult for them to act according to the rules of justice, whereas the character of others makes it easy and quite 'natural' for them to do so. The inequality of equal moral norms can only be mitigated in ethical judgments passed in *single cases*. This is one of the reasons why good judgment is so important in ethics. As far as Stoic-Epicurean ethics is concerned, moral judgment is very lenient. Since the good life based on the rational character 'for itself' is self-rewarding, empathy with those who are unable to achieve it is stronger than in any other ethics. True enough, empathy can turn into contempt (and this should be avoided), but it can never turn into hatred. Consequently, this strongest of all the emotions which might impede the implementation of the norms of justice is not at all present in a Stoic-Epicurean character. It is easy for this character to recognize all human needs, in accordance with the long-standing Epicurean tradition, while excluding from recognition those needs the satisfaction of which requires the use of other persons as mere means (as rational character is conceived of as a goal 'in itself'). Therefore, even if Stoic-Epicurean ethics involves inequality (because it is not *equally* difficult or easy for everyone to observe its norms), the judgments passed from the standpoint of this ethics take better account of the inequality of human needs and psychological characters than other ethics do.

(3) The third objection of Stoic-Epicurean ethics questions not only its generalizability, but its relevance for our time. The argument boils down to the following. If the merit of a Stoic-Epicurean ethics lies in its capacity to help us make sense of our lives in a darkening world, and in this alone, then it is an ethics of escapism. Additionally, if it is also an ethics the acceptance of which might bring us closer to the radicalization of democracy (socialism), then it leads us back to the hackneyed idea of goodwill (benevolence) as a social agent, as well as to the fated illusion that social problems can be solved through ethical improvement. But as this is not the case, and as the solution of social problems is our main *obligation*, it is precisely this type of ethics that is irrelevant to our age. The very suggestion that *energeia* (virtuous action through our whole lives) can be considered as an end in itself, even if only relatively, is outrageous, since it undermines the resolve with which we fulfil our supreme duty: the pursuit of social goals *beyond* our activity. However, it is argued, a pursuit like

this implies using ourselves, and incidentally others as well, as mere means for the realization of such goals.

I have stated that Stoic-Epicurean ethics is the ethics of substantive rationality. When the category of 'substantive rationality' was first introduced I referred to the *formal* capacity of a rationality of this kind. One can become a rational character 'for itself' on the grounds of the acceptance of entirely different norms and values which, for their part, involve quite different goals. It is exactly the formal propensity that explains the longevity of Stoic-Epicurean ethics, and its 'resistance' to change in concrete and abstract norms, values, and goals. Stoic-Epicurean ethics has sometimes meant escapism, sometimes just the contrary. (Rosa Luxemburg, for instance, may be claimed as a representative Stoic-Epicurean, yet was anything but an escapist.) Moreover, Stoic-Epicureans are the most reliable and trustworthy actors when it comes to social and political action. They stand for social justice and political freedom because 'standing for them' – that is to say, *activity* itself – springs from their character. They never use socio-political actions as mere means to achieve power, prestige or wealth. Because hope and fear does not motivate them, they will not lose faith through defeat. Because their faith does not require illusions, they will neither experience empty illusions nor fall prey to disillusion. No one is more prepared for rational argument than Stoic-Epicureans, who do not need to rationalize actions or convictions (in the Freudian sense of the term). If they are wrong, they will admit it. They do not have to defend a weak self which might collapse upon admitting failure.

But what happens if, under given circumstances, no social action can spring from a rational character 'for itself'? What happens if all possible social actions are judged and rejected by a personality as irrational? Cases like these might frequently occur if we allow that the alternatives for social praxis may eventually be very limited. In order to maintain their substantive rationality, rational personalities may in fact opt for 'escapism'. Here I should distinguish between two types of escapism. In the first type direct action is replaced by speech-acts (persuasion, argumentation, discussion, enlightenment) in order to widen and change the alternatives of action. This is not withdrawal from, but continuation of, social actions with other means, where the means (the speech-acts) spring from the essence of personality. 'Escapism' of this kind is not only rational. It is far more adequate to the norms of democratic politics than the determination to stay in the mêlée, notwithstanding that there is a price to pay for it, sometimes in the form of loss of face and resoluteness. But even allowing for this, it might be suggested that there are stronger moral commitments than acting in accordance with substantive rationality, or commitments that are at least equally strong. Yet here I would remind the reader that the rational character 'for itself' emerges by taking the attitude of rationality of intellect: the norms which are continuously observed comprise the kernel around which the rational character is crystallized. It might happen that the supreme norm can only be observed if the action does not spring from the rational character as a homogeneous whole. In such a case the person must choose between a single value-rational action and an action which springs from substantive rationality. Rosa Luxemburg died for a cause she believed to be widely unsupported, in other words, irrational, but she observed the value of solidarity. Since we act with others, we cannot avoid making compromises. If people only signed a petition of protest if every word of it was to their liking, in all probability no petition would ever be signed. But it is obvious that signing a protest the contents of which outrightly *contradicts* our conviction, is an improper compromise.

Then there is the second form of escapism tantamount to total withdrawal from social action in order to preserve the rationality of our character: this is the celebrated option of cultivating our garden. Contrary to one of the objections to my theory, I would not say that this is always a wrong option: what is good cannot be wrong. Neither would I say that an option like this is completely impotent, for it can exert influence by its very existence. But in formidable times, times of evil and danger, it is guilty of inaction.

Thus I take the point of the third objection. There are borderline situations where even our 'substantive rationality' might be sacrificed for the sake of a single value-rational action. Compromises must be made if we engage in actions which do not contradict our convictions but do not spring from our character either. It is the task of our awareness of our 'situatedness' in our age to be aware of the limits to substantive rationality. Stoic-Epicurean ethics has to deal with 'situatedness' in so far as it designates good judgment as the arbiter in deciding the degree of elasticity admissible in the pursuit of common goals. Good judgment can be prospective and retrospective. A rational personality can judge his or her previous actions as overly elastic or insufficiently elastic, and a retrospective judgment like this may influence prospective judgments.

This same objection to the relevance of Stoic-Epicurean ethics makes a strong case for self-sacrifice. Clearly, Stoic-Epicurean ethics does not exclude *self-sacrifice*, even if it most emphatically excludes the *sacrifice of the self*. It is exactly Stoic-Epicurean ethics that has always reflected on borderline situations and made the recommendation that if an action robs you of the chance to live a good life, choose death instead. In this case the choice of death can be understood as self-sacrifice, but not as the sacrifice of the self; indeed, just the contrary is true. Borderline situations aside, the same holds true of less spectacular circumstances. There are very common forms of temptation that a rational character 'for itself' resists, and there are very common types of fear that a rational character 'for itself' overcomes, and this is done not in spite of, but in fact because, he or she considers the good life as an end 'in itself'.

I do not want to pass judgments on singular cases, for there might really be singular cases where the sacrifice of the self as a form of self-sacrifice is authentic. But I protest strongly against ethics which view such cases as exemplary (for example, the theory of 'moral sacrifice' by Lukács exemplified by the tyrannicide of the biblical Judith). This rejection is not only supported by the arguments I have hitherto presented, but also by my conviction that the sacrifice of the self as self-sacrifice is, as a rule, inauthentic, and is mostly a form of rationalization performed by the particularistic person, a rationalization of another sacrifice: the sacrifice of the self on the altar of a self-seeking power. I do not think that Dostoevsky's inquisitor was anything but an inquisitor.

One problem has remained undiscussed, at least in an explicit manner: the accusation that to recommend a Stoic-Epicurean ethics tacitly implies another recommendation as well; the solving of social problems via ethical improvement. This latter recommendation is not part of my position, though the objection is not completely irrelevant.

It is easy to understand why I do not identify with the above position. Substantive rationality is a goal in itself. Rational characters 'for itself' who meet the standards of Stoic-Epicurean ethics have a good life here and now, irrespective of the success or failure of the cause they are committed to. In addition, the notion of ethical betterment or 'moral betterment' is in itself misleading. We have no common yardstick to measure and compare moralities and ethics of various cultures *in toto*. Fundamentalists of all kinds would regard Stoic-Epicurean ethics as a form of ethical degradation rather than the reverse because it does not prescribe particular norms that everyone must observe (like chastity, humility, etc.).

Yet I repeat that the objection above is not completely irrelevant. I have made it clear that I consider the rational character 'for itself' to be the *model* of the *democratic character*. And since I openly profess my commitment to radical democracy, as socialism, the recommendation of a Stoic-Epicurean ethics and my commitment to the radicalization of democracy are truly interconnected, and the sooner this is understood the better. But to characterize *democratic character* as a possible prompter towards the radicalization of democracy is not to say that social transformation comes about via moral improvement. Rather, this structure was conceived using the analogy of Weber's celebrated theory of the Protestant Ethic as a prompter of capitalist development. Of course, it is always safer to offer explanations for past history than to make suggestions about interrelations in the present (the future of the present included). But it is still not theoretical bravado to assert that a radically democratic society cannot come about unless there are people who so act that it could come about, and only people can so act whose personality patterns are radically democratic. I have interpreted modern Western society as the unique combination of three distinct logics: capitalism, industrialization and democracy. I have also asserted that because the dynamics of these logics have become increasingly contradictory, one of the dynamics – and all of them do indeed *exist* – will limit the dynamics of the other two, and eventually establish itself as dominant. I do not pretend to know which of the three logics will in fact break through. It cannot be denied either that our history may end in the self-destruction of human culture, and even of the human race. I have only suggested that *if* the existing dynamics of democracy indeed break through, *then* the ethics of democratic personalities will contribute decisively to this outcome. My conception has nothing to do with the creed that goodwill is the path to salvation. This is especially so considering that rational character was said to be the source of rational *actions*, and not simply of rational will.

Everyday life, rationality of reason, rationality of intellect – viewed from the perspective of substantive rationality

The category of 'basic character types' has been reintroduced into social theory by the culture and anthropology school. While investigating tribal societies these people have discovered that the appropriation of specific 'norms-and-rules' is concomitant with the appropriation of a 'social character' or a limited number of social characters. If one examines premodern art, one arrives at the conclusion that the same thing, or at least something similar, applies to all societies where the appropriations of the sphere of objectivation 'in itself' alone defines the scope of action of persons. The human *types* represented by these art works are not individual types, but social character types, 'masks'. Here, rationality of reason (competence in acting according to 'norms-and-rules', according to reason) means 'fitting into' *the* social character, or one or the other social character type. What I called rational character 'for itself' (rationality of the person) is not something which can or cannot come about: it simply *must* come about. Persons must 'fit into' the social character type(s). Should they fail to do so, the character of the person will be *irrational*. Rationality of character is not a rationality which I have introduced into the discourse or constructed for the sake of a value, or in order to criticize the 'vivisection of rationality'. I simply use this notion to refer to a human universal.

In as far as the sphere of objectivation 'in itself' *still* performs the work of socialization, one can *still* detect traces of social character types. If one says that X is a typical English worker, Y is a typical English aristocrat, one refers to these character types. However, the chief characteristic of modernity, the causes of which have already been scrutinized, is the progressive elimination of social character types. Persons become far more idiosyncratic (individualistic) on the one hand, and far more conformistic on the other. By 'conformism' I do not mean that all characters are similar to, or identical with, one another; I have in mind the decreasing rationality of character structure. Riesman coined the term 'outer-directedness' when referring to conformism, and this expression suits my theory well. If someone is completely outer-directed, his or her character is irrational because his or her actions do not spring from the character. Nonetheless, complete outer-directedness is a very extreme case; it is more fitting to speak about the tendency towards outer-directedness. Moreover, outer-directedness cannot be a social character type, because it is not a character type at all. The very fact that the tendency to act in an outer-directed manner has become widespread indicates that acting according to rationality of reason alone does not suffice to stabilize a character structure in our age.

Acting solely according to the rationality of intellect in a *continuous* way is simply impossible. Questioning the validity of 'norms-and-rules' from the standpoint of a norm or a few norms is an epistemological shift. The attitude assumed in the course of this shift can become our lifelong attitude, but one cannot question 'norms-and-rules' every single day, and in particular, cannot question the validity of all of them, because if one does not abide by at least one (and preferably several) of them, it is not possible to keep living. The rational character 'for itself' has been defined as the homogenized unity of the human person-as-a-whole and human wholeness, and this implies the reconciliation of rationality of intellect and rationlity of reason, a reconciliation achieved with the guidance of rationality of intellect.

Rational character 'for itself' is an individual character, and the notion of *personality* refers to the *uniqueness* of such a character. But it is a *social character* all the same. It is our age that has seen the attitude of rationalism become widespread, it is our age that highly values the uniqueness of personality. Consequently, if one succeeds in combining human person-as-a-whole and human wholeness, rationality of intellect and rationality of reason, and is successful in homogenizing one's person into a unique personality, one fits adequately into the patterns of 'social character' of modernity.

Social character types are *the* rational character types in every culture and in every age. Substantive rationality proper is the only social character type of the post-traditional era: it is *the* rational character type of this era. This is why the theory of our complete outer-directedness is nothing but a *negative utopia*. Of course, it is equally true that the theoretical design of a world in which everyone becomes a homogeneous and substantively rational personality is nothing but a *positive utopia*. In reality, the present confronts us instead with three characteristics combined. The first is the increase in outer-directedness. The second is the stabilization of at least some rational personality traits. The third is the return to premodern, conventional 'norms-and-rules', which more or less stabilize the rational character 'in itself', the rationality of person. But from the *regard* of substantive rationality proper (the rationality of personality), the retreat to the character 'in itself' (the rationality of person) is *irrational*; it is *regarded* as a regression into irrationality. And since substantive rationality proper is *the* rational (social) character type of our post-rational era, one cannot impute 'false consciousness' to a perspective which 'irrationalizes' the traditional and particularistic character types. Even though the three tendencies listed above are normally displayed by different persons, movements and social groups, they may coexist in differing proportions within these same entities as well. It is easier for fundamentalist movements to recruit followers from more outer-directed persons than from stabilized personalities because the loss of way of life, which is experienced to a greater degree by the former than by the latter, has not been counterbalanced by any – even a weaker or less consistent – conduct of life, thus making these people susceptible to *any* way of life, even to one which is 'irrational' from the perspective of substantive rationality proper.

At this point it is appropriate to provide a further reason why such importance should be attributed to the strengthening of substantive rationality proper, to the generalization of a more or less democratic character. The notion 'democratic' might to some extent be misleading if one identifies democratic with political action, democratic behaviour with a quality of political behaviour. By the term 'democratic character type' I only meant that the substantively rational character is essentially democratic when it comes to socio-political action. But if one refers to the conduct of life of a personality, and the particular conduct of life built around a Stoic-Epicurean ethics, one has not only political action and behaviour in mind but life as a whole, everyday life included. And it is precisely in everyday life where the conduct of life is of the highest importance. But the reference to a character type as 'democratic', even in the everyday setting, is not simply a figure of speech. Recognition of the needs of others, respect for the personality of others, readiness to employ rational argumentation, as well as resolution, good judgment, objectivity combined with emotionalism and empathy, the ability for self-reflection without self-abasement: all these attitudes, actions and abilities are of the highest importance in a humane everyday life, even if they can justly be called democratic. The unity of the human person-as-a-whole and of human wholeness is tested in the first instance in everyday life. One should not forget that the human person-as-a-whole *is* the subject of everyday life.

It is possible to raise a serious objection in relation to the final conclusions of my theory. In this theory I have made certain theoretical proposals, which can be stated thus: (a) Substantive rational character proper *is the* rational character type of modernity (it is a *social* character type). (b) Modernity is characterized by three constituents which develop independent logics and finally collide with one another: industrialization, capitalism and democracy. (c) Capitalism and industrialization both penetrate everyday life and rationalized institutions to a greater depth than the attitude of democracy. (d) Substantive rational character proper is the democratic character. Given these proposals, the objection concerns the claim that although they may be interrelated, they are certainly not highly consistent, and that the conclusion does not follow from the propositions. In short, it is suggested that a fairly bad logic prevails throughout. Yet I cannot accept this claim.

True enough, industrialization is a major component of modernity. But I have already analysed in detail *why* industrialization cannot provide modernity with *any* character type. In fact, industrialization tends eventually to destroy traditional character patterns, or at least contributes to their destruction. In addition to being responsible for creating the specialized subject who has lost its human wholeness, it bequeaths to this individual the ruins of a way of life. On the other hand, if values are not simultaneously universalized, industrialization can proceed whilst leaving intact traditional and particularistic ways of life which have been 'irrationalized' from the standpoint of rationalism, or it can establish new and irrational character types. Thus we can legitimately neglect industrialization when we speak about the 'social-rational character pattern' promoted by modernity.

The same does not hold true of capitalism. The conclusive pursuit of our interest throughout our whole life has stabilized a rational character type, that of *rational egoism*. Not only democracy, but also capitalism, places a premium on personality, on 'substantive rationality'. In this sense Riesman was justified in speaking of 'inner-directedness' when he referred to the character type promoted by early capitalism. But even though early capitalism subscribed to the 'inner-directed personality', I do not believe – as Riesman does – that it could realize such a personality. If the rational character is being realized through the value of the pursuit of interest, success or failure are the sole sources of happiness or unhappiness. But happiness or unhappiness also depends on something which is not within, but outside, the person: the individual's life still depends on chance. Even if one does not pass moral judgment on the rational egoist, but only examines how substantive his or her rationality is, one must conclude that it is fairly limited. Of course, all actions of a rational egoist spring from his or her character, and to this extent the character is substantively rational, but this substantive rationality is fragile because it is dependent on external circumstances. If bad luck is encountered, the character falls apart.

Indeed, substantive rationality is the social character type of modernity, because it has been shaped by both capitalism and democracy. The third constituent of modernity always was, and still is, incapable of offering any character pattern. This is why I called substantive rational character proper *the* rational character type of modernity. I have not yet substantiated my proposal to call this character type *democratic*.

Capitalism raised the idea of substantive rationality proper, but rational egoism has been unable to live up to the exigencies of this idea. But the democratic character can successfully live up to the exigencies of 'substantive rationality' proper. Where a democratic character is concerned, not only do all possible actions of the personality spring from the character, the goals and objectives of any possible action do so as well. These goals and objectives are raised in accordance with universal or generalizable values, the observance of which has been 'built into' the character. It is on these grounds that one is entitled to say that, in the last instance, the rational character 'for itself' is equal to its idea only in the democratic character.

Truly democratic characters are fairly exceptional. The enormous obstacles to the generalization of the democratic character, the everyday pressures which can crush the democratic personality structure *in statu nascendi*, and push us back into emptiness or make us seek refuge in neo-fundamentalism, as well as outer-directedness and rational egoism, have been examined from various perspectives. There is no single 'big leap' from the mutilated and distorted person to the rational character 'for itself'. As far as character structure is concerned, such leaps are impossible anyway. Furthermore, radical democracy is not an institution which can be established by a decree. If it comes about at all, it will only do so via a lengthy process in which increasingly democratic institutions are established, and ancient ones revitalized, and with the active contribution of an increasing number of democratic personalities. If radical needs and universal values could meet, the *social barriers* to the generalization of the rational character 'for itself' could be very much reduced, if not completely eliminated. But all this tends to lead us away from our present and further and further into that realm of regulative ideas we call 'utopia'. The regulative idea under the guidance of which my theory of rationality has been presented, is the utopia of the 'homecoming of reason'.

CHAPTER 4

Rationality and Democracy*

The moral maxims of democratic politics

The relationship between politics and morality, at least in recent times, may be formulated in the following, contradictory, assertions and theoretical propositions.

(1) Politics is a form of *techne*. In political life we do not follow ethical norms, but technical rules. The success of any kind of politics depends on the skilful application of a number of basic rules. These rules can be learned. To an extent, their skilful application demands a special talent. It is also partly a matter of experience. Any form of politics which is not based on adherence to a set of technical rules will fail to achieve its objectives. The assertion that politics is a *techne* is also to be understood as a postulate: politics should be practised as a *techne*.

(2) Politics is in practice learned and applied as *techne*. It *should*, however, be founded on morality. The real task of politics is not simply to seize power or strengthen one's hold on power but to improve mankind and the world. The merits of any system of politics depend on the strength of moral purpose of those who believe in it and act in accordance with it. Any system of politics which does not adhere to some moral norm must be wrong, simply because it sets no high moral goals and is, moreover, incapable of generating any enthusiasm for achieving them.

Despite the contradictions between the norms they establish,

---

* The first part of this chapter was published as 'The Moral Maxims of Democratic Policies' in *Praxis International*, Vol. 1, 1981. The second part was published as 'Rationality and Democracy' in *Philosophy and Social Criticism*, Vol. 8(3), 1981.

both propositions agree in stressing that in practice politics follow technical rules and not moral norms. We shall now go on to question the truth of this assertion and examine how far either or both of these norms can be justified.

The assertion that politics only follow technical rules and not social norms can only be true in one particular case, namely, when all political decisions are taken by just one person and that person is above all social laws and controls – either an absolute monarch, a charismatic leader, or a despot. It is no coincidence that Machiavelli recommended the Prince to adopt his political *techne*. If an individual stands above all social rules, then it follows that he does not have to conform to them. At the same time, however, his power depends entirely upon the spectacular success of his political and military decisions. Neither his goals nor the means by which he achieves them presuppose a consensus; a false consensus, motivated by fear, is guaranteed anyway. It must be acknowledged, however, that unlimited political power is characterized not by its stability but by its liability. If a statesman's freedom of action is prescribed and limited to some extent, then the population is much more tolerant of his failures than if he enjoyed unlimited power. Furthermore, the human psyche is not adapted to wielding unlimited power. The consequences of all this are easy to appreciate. Although politics can only be practised as *techne* as long as the statesman is above all social rules, under those circumstances its practice is de facto rarely governed by rational consideration. When power is unlimited, politics generally loses all trace of rationality. This is a minor point which is repeated here only in order to dispel the preconception that politics is nothing but *techne*.

Apart from this one case, politics could never be practised as pure *techne*, and that still holds true today. Tradition, on the one hand, and laws on the other, considerably restrict both the choice of goals and the means of achieving them. Moreover, these social norms not only prescribe the limits which cannot be exceeded without arousing disapproval, but they also contain more or less definite rules for just conduct. There are, of course, various restrictions and rules governing behaviour within individual countries and relationships with other states (both allies and enemies). The conduct of politics as pure *techne* is more customary in the latter than in the former case, but even there there are exceptions. The argument that the rules are frequently violated, particularly in the sphere of foreign politics, is irrelevant. Moral norms are frequently violated without losing their validity.

There are, of course, technical rules in all forms of politics. 'Politics' as such, however, has no general technical rules, for differing social norms determine the nature of the rules operating in different societies. For example, the technique of vote-catching can only be employed in a state where elections are held at all. Whether someone plays a major or a minor role depends no less on the rules of a society than on its parliamentary methods.

In a modern state where the rights and liberties of the individual are protected by law, its social norms are formalized in its constitution (whether written or unwritten). No political technique is officially permitted to infringe the constitution, although in practice of course it may. But as well as legal controls, there are also numerous purely traditional rules which have to be taken account of in the mechanics of politics.

Social norms are *binding* on those active in politics. Whether an individual accepts them as binding on himself or conforms to them purely for pragmatic reasons is another question. From this point of view the attitudes of politicians are of minor importance. As long as they do not infringe the society's political norms and conduct their political affairs within this framework, it does not matter whether they are motivated by concern for the prosperity of their country or by the pursuit of power. As Kant pointed out, the norms of politics have nothing to do with morality. They are legal norms reflecting social, not moral, values.

In countries where human rights are constitutionally guaranteed, politicians must accept them as defining the limits on (and opportunities for) their own actions. They function as the moral framework for all political activity. This does not mean, however, that human rights also have the status of moral maxims governing this activity. Those engaged in politics are not *compelled* to take into account whether or not their decisions promote the liberty, equality, etc., of every citizen. All that they need to consider are simply the reactions of those who elected them, of their supporters, and of other power groups, together with their possible counteraction. They must, that is, take into account whether their decisions will provoke protests which make it impossible to put them into effect and which might jeopardize their own positions of power. It is clear, therefore, that the moral norms expressed in a bill of human rights can be accepted as maxims of wise political conduct, and that they are in fact usually accepted as such. One may suspect that in countries where human rights are guaranteed, political morals are in a much healthier state than in those where this is not the case. However, it cannot be inferred from this that political morality is in an equally healthy state. This can be seen most clearly in the field of foreign politics. Despite the fact that every member of the United Nations has committed itself in writing to respect human rights, the majority of states have today still not constitutionally recognized the existence of human rights, still less enacted legislation to guarantee them. It is not surprising, that these empty gestures, which commit countries to nothing, have failed to lead to the provision of agreed social norms in international affairs. Even in democratic states, where the recognition of human rights imposes moral restrictions inside the country and has made possible the formulation of maxims of wise political conduct, no such maxims can be applied in the sphere of foreign politics because of the lack of any social morals which could result in a similar commitment. Consequently, the democratic regulation of foreign politics by maxims of wise conduct is inconceivable at present. Only when politics is prepared to follow moral maxims will there be any likelihood of introducing truly democratic politics in the field of international relations. It will, however, be necessary to assume here that foreign and domestic politics cannot be completely separated from one another. We can, moreover, take seriously Marx's dictum that an oppressed people cannot be free. In the same spirit I should like to put forward the following theoretical suggestion: a consistently democratic form of politics is not characterized solely by the fact that a state recognizes human rights as constituting social norms, and chooses its maxims for wise conduct accordingly. It must also conduct its political affairs in accordance with a set of moral maxims.

We have assumed that both our contradictory suggestions about the relationship between politics and morality agree in asserting that politics today is simply *techne*. We have rejected this assertion as false. We have concluded that, with some exceptions, political activity is governed by social norms and that its technical rules must also be compatible with these norms. In acknowledging that constitutional guarantees of human rights define moral norms and the legal status of democratic politics we also refuted the suggestion that politics should simply obey technical rules. We also made the theoretical suggestion that a consistently democratic form of politics should accept certain moral maxims. Accordingly, it would seem that we share the view that politics should be founded on morality. However, this is not the case.

RATIONALITY AND DEMOCRACY

A moralizing form of politics has the aim of improving mankind and the world. If one wants to improve mankind, one must have a clear conception of what true virtue is. True virtue relates to mankind as a whole, all aspects of man's behaviour both in public and in private life. Moralizing politics opts for a particular way of life and is prepared to demand its general adoption, at least within a given country or political movement. Modern society, however, is characterized by its heterogeneity. It contains a multiplicity of customs and individual options, which is increased further by the various cultural traditions within a country. Moralizing politics is antagonistic towards all cultures, movements, classes, even individuals, with divergent life-styles. It can, therefore, only achieve its goal – of improving mankind in accordance with its conception of virtue – by resorting to force. Moralizing and oppression go hand in hand in politics. The history of puritanical political systems, and particularly of Jacobinism (which openly declared its belief in morality and in terror), speaks for itself.

Moralizing politics has two distinct traditions. One upholds a conception of virtue and a way of life founded on religion, and is pre-enlightenment, even though it has re-emerged in our own time (in, for example, forms of politics based on Islamic teachings on virtue). The other crystallized out in the course of a series of revolutions (as a reaction against Liberalism) and can be characterized as a retreat from enlightenment. In this second case it can also happen that the morally evil, in Hegel's use of the term, functions as the basis of politics. If one looks at the slogans of the two most destructive dictatorships of this century – 'Honour is loyalty', 'The party is our reason, our honour, our conscience' – one can understand immediately how morality and terror can be associated. Moralizing politics is certainly no less cruel than Machiavellian politics. The proposition that the end justifies the means is part of its ideological arsenal rather than part of the mechanics of politics (which does not recognize 'sacred' goals, only 'advantageous' ones). If one were faced with the choice between political *techne* and moralizing politics, it would certainly cause less suffering to human beings if one were to choose the former.

It is clear from what has been said so far that any theoretical proposal that one accept certain moral maxims for political conduct is far from being a plea for all politics to be founded on morality. But before we begin analysing what moral principles a form of politics *not* founded on morality might have, we must first examine carefully another area of political activity.

In politics, one can either follow certain laid-down principles or act in a purely *pragmatic* fashion. These two possibilities can also be combined in various ways. Pragmatic politics is the politics of *adaptation*. It involves skilful manoeuvring on the part of several power groups or lobbies, each attempting to safeguard their own position of power. Programmes and objectives must be regarded here purely as instruments of power. A pragmatic politician will never voluntarily retire from office simply because he cannot push through his policies; instead, he will give his support to some other policy. Pragmatic politics is often termed, with justification, 'empirical' (since it responds with great sensitivity to experience). Sometimes it is even called '*bureaucratic*' (since it risks nothing and develops no new initiatives). However, this label is inapt. Nowadays, all types of political activity require some form of bureaucratic apparatus, pragmatic politics no less than politics motivated by principles.

'Principled' politics sets out to put into effect programmes, plans, and aims that have been conceived in advance. A politician committed to certain principles will resign if he cannot achieve his objectives, and will wait until the time is ripe for their achievement; in a state which does not recognize liberal values, he will simply achieve his objectives by force, if he can. The political principles themselves can differ greatly, not simply in kind but also in scope. They may include the complete restructuring of economic or foreign policies or changes in party policy, or they may relate to a single specific objective or decision. This does not mean, of course, that 'principled' politicians are indifferent to power, only that they always regard power as 'power to achieve something'.

It is open to debate whether pragmatic or principled politics is 'better'. Viewed strictly from a standpoint of a morality based on individual conscience, principled politics is preferable. Which of the two kinds of political action proves to be better depends probably on whether the politicians live in a democratic or an undemocratic state. In an undemocratic country, principled politics may cause more harm than pragmatic politics. If one poses the question of how politics could be regulated by moral maxims, however, one is forced to come down on the side of principled politics. But it must always be borne in mind that principled politics is not necessarily superior to purely pragmatic politics. The principles which a politician should be encouraged to adopt as moral maxims are, therefore, those which can in general ensure the superiority of principled politics over purely pragmatic political action.

When we examined principled politics we were talking about *political* and not *moral* principles. Principled politics has just one moral implication – loyalty to a chosen set of principles. The principles themselves are not moral in origin. If it were possible to formulate universal political principles which were capable of acting as principles in all forms of democratic politics (however diverse their individual goals) and which could function as maxims of a universal morality *as well*, then, *theoretically* at least, our problem would be solved. It is easy to see why.

If politics is founded on morality, it is open to it to use any means to achieve whatever desired 'improvement' in mankind it sets as its aim. But no single way of life (no system of moral values) is universal, even if it claims universality. Accordingly, its political principles are *ideological* and essentially *undemocratic* simply because it generalizes particular values and therefore prevents, if it can, the expression and representation of all other value systems. Indeed, it excludes and suppresses them. However, if it is not a particular value system that is (wrongly) universalized, but the political principles themselves, then those political principles become binding on all men, whatever their value system or way of life. Political principles can only be universalized if they assume a plurality of value systems and ways of life. In order for political principles to function as moral maxims, they must accord in form (though not in content) with all moral decisions.

What does it mean to follow universal principles (as moral maxims)? Certainly not (or not only) to declare one's belief in them. It means rather: (a) to consider whether political decisions are in accord with those principles, (b) a readiness to base one's arguments for any political decision upon those universal principles, and (c) to brand as illegitimate all political decisions taken by individual citizens (or nations) if it is proved that they contradict those principles.

It seems as though we have worked out something quite abstract, utopian and hypothetical. This is not so, however. All we have done has been to reconstruct, albeit with some modifications, a procedure that has been in existence and put into practice sporadically for more than 200 years. It would be more accurate to say that we were arguing in the spirit of a democratic *tradition*.

A glance at the *Declaration of Independence* will be sufficient to make this clear.

The *Declaration* begins with the statement that the political decision which it represents requires a reasoned justification. The way this is expressed, however, makes it relevant to more than just this one political decision. It has something to say about *all similar* decisions: 'When in the course of human events, it becomes necessary for one people to dissolve the political bonds . . . a decent respect to the opinions of mankind requires that they should declare the causes. . . .' The *Declaration* goes on to list the *universal principles which are also valid as moral maxims*. All governments should safeguard the three 'unalienable' human rights, as well as life, liberty and the pursuit of happiness. If this does not happen, then 'it is their right (that of the people), it is their *duty*, to throw off such government and to provide new guards for their future security.' It is clear from the reference to 'duty', which cannot mean political duty since it calls for the overthrow of the existing political order, that the three universal political principles were also conceived of as moral maxims. However, since the *Declaration* goes on to list the grievances of the American colonies against the English Crown and these turn out all to be political in nature, it is clear that they were devised primarily as political principles. The nature of the colonies' grievances confirms that the Crown had persistently violated all universal political principles. That is sufficient to justify the specific political act proposed here. And the conclusion reads: 'We, therefore . . . solemnly publish and declare that these United Colonies are, and of right ought to be, free and Independent States.'

This is a masterpiece of political deduction, without a trace of ideological demagogy. Of course, the argumentation depends on the truth (correctness) of the initial premise. However, the truth (and correctness) of the initial premise requires no justification. It reads: 'We hold these truths to be *self-evident*, that all men are created equal, that they are endowed by their creator with certain inalienable rights, that among these are life, liberty and the pursuit of happiness.' It was appropriate in the *Declaration* to assume the universal principles of politics (which also have the status of moral maxims) as self-evident, not simply because it restated a view which was already widely held at the time or because such a *Declaration* could not concern itself with philosophical problems, but also for more profound reasons.

One could criticize the text of the *Declaration* on the grounds that its starting-point is wrong. First of all, the assertion, that all men are created equal and with inalienable rights, to life, liberty and the pursuit of happiness was by no means self-evident at the end of the eighteenth century. It was only self-evident within the context of a particular view of the world. It is, moreover (according to our view), a false assertion as it stands. We shall return to the second point later. As for the first point, however, I believe that it is impossible to improve substantially upon the views expressed in the *Declaration*, still less to evade them. It is true that the political principles of the initial premise are only self-evident with a specific political world-view. Clearly, however, it becomes impossible to formulate any general principles of political conduct at all as soon as one starts looking in detail at all possible forms of political conduct. In speaking at all about universal principles, one can only mean a form of politics which can be related to universal political principles. The title of this essay is: 'Moral maxims of *democratic* politics'. In fact, it is anything but *self-evident* that politics must be democratic; but within the framework of this analysis it is assumed to be so. It is the axiom of our argument. So here too I am following in the footsteps of those who drew up the *Declaration*. And I believe that the idea of replacing the initial formulation, 'sacred and undeniable', by 'inalienable' in the final version of the *Declaration* involved a similar insight on the part of its authors and that the fundamental reason for it is to be found in the axiomatic validity of the principles.

In proposing universal principles for a democratic system of politics, I must re-emphasize that they are only reformulations of traditional democratic principles. But one can only reformulate principles which have already at some time been regarded as self-evident, if only within one particular world-view. They have to be reformulated in order to make them more plausible in the context of contemporary philosophy and, by so doing, to be able to acquit them of the charge that they are 'wrong'. At the same time, the principles can only be reformulated in the spirit of contemporary philosophy if they are subjected to some form of social radicalization.

The principles are as follows:

(1) Act as if the personal liberty of every citizen and the independence of every nation depended on your actions. This is the moral maxim and political principle of *liberty*.

(2) Act in accordance with all the social rules and laws, whose infringement, even in the case of just one citizen (or one nation) you would disapprove of. This is the moral maxim and political principle of (*political*) *equality*.

(3) In all your political dealings assume that all men are capable of making political decisions. So submit your plans for public discussion and act in accordance with the outcome of those discussions. If you cannot do so, resign all your positions of power and set about convincing others of the correctness of your opinions. This is the moral maxim and political principle of (*rational*) *equality*.

(4) Recognize all human needs, as long as they can be satisfied without coming into conflict with the maxims of liberty, political equality, and rationality. This is the moral maxim and political principle of justice.

(5) In all your dealings support those classes and nations which are enduring the greatest suffering, as long as this does not conflict with the other maxims of political conduct. This is the moral maxim and political principle of *equity*.

These are in my view the universal moral principles of democratic politics. They are, at the same time, moral maxims, since they can act as guide-lines for all moral decisions. Using these maxims we can also formulate the *basic law* of democratic politics:

Act in a way which allows all free and rational human beings to assent to the political principles of your actions.

This basic law assumes the possibility of a *consensus omnium*, not a consensus in all political decisions but a consensus about the political principles of such decisions. Simply because free and rational human beings assent to the principles of decisions and actions, this does not prevent them from questioning, criticizing or even opposing an individual decision or action. A *consensus omnium* will be the exception rather than the rule. If individuals were forced to reach such a consensus, this would establish a norm which would be firstly unrealizable, secondly unnecessary from the point of view of democratic politics, and thirdly undesirable. Firstly, there can often be not just one but several decisions which are in accord with the first, second, fourth and fifth principles, and in a society with many heterogeneous ways of life and different needs and desires it is highly improbable that everyone would arrive at the same decision. Decisions are in any case always taken under pressure of time. The third principle of democratic politics enjoins that in cases where there are several options and time in pressing, the decision of the majority as it emerges through discussion should be accepted. The principle of majority rule would often be criticized, but there is no way of avoiding it completely. This can be unpleasant and frustrating for the minority, but whenever decisions have to be taken quickly one has to say: *vox populi vox dei*. In practice, a *consensus omnium* assumes homogeneity and does not leave room for discontent or trial and error, a state of affairs which is far from desirable. However, if all that is required is a *consensus omnium* that the political principles must be obeyed, then unanimity and disagreement need not be thought of as mutually exclusive.

To avoid misunderstandings, it should be emphasized that the basic law is not meant to be a legitimizing principle in the stricter sense of the word. The requirement that one act in a way which allows all free and rational human beings to assent to the political principles of your actions is not only binding on governments but on all those engaged in political activities, that is, it is formulated in a spirit of absolute reciprocity. If all men can and should act legitimately, that is, in accordance with the basic law, there can be no legitimation in the narrower sense of the term, namely the legitimation of domination. And then there is no such thing as domination.

It may seem as if we have become lost in daydreams and tangled up in contradictions. We were talking about politics, about a form of action in which power is the overriding factor. But at the same time we assumed the existence of a basic law of political conduct which precluded domination of one group or individual by another. We have also generalized the concept of legitimate political conduct in such a way that it can apply to all those engaged in political activities. In Max Weber's classical formula, however, control is identified with legitimate power. I should like to suggest here that Weber's third form of legitimation of domination, namely legitimation by laws, is highly ambiguous, and can be interpreted in accordance with our own analyses.

'Domination' describes a relationship between ordering and obeying. If all men obey the laws (or just one single law) equally, then the word 'domination' is simply a metaphor without any social content. In saying this, I in no way wish to deny that domination cannot be legitimized by laws, only to emphasize that legitimation by laws does not necessarily mean the legitimation of domination.

In our analysis of the universal principles (moral maxims) of democratic politics nothing was said about the structure of any society. It goes without saying that universal principles and the basic law can only *in practice* act as guidelines for conduct if all men (and all nations) have an equal opportunity to participate in the decision-making process. If this condition is not fulfilled, they function *only as moral maxims*, which are binding only in the consciences of some individuals. It is an old truth that property relations determine whether men are *equal enough to enjoy equal freedom*. Aristotle regarded (relative) equality of wealth as the first prerequisite for equality of freedom. It is tempting to contrast *'being'* and *'having'* as the two possible forms of human existence, but only birds can be free without owning any possessions, and then only in the realm of allegory. I have discussed in detail in another article the proposition that all men must be property-owners in order to be free, and merely repeat it here. In the modern industrialized world, universal ownership of property is only conceivable in the form of collective ownership, of self-government. If no single individual enjoys such overwhelming economic power that he can force his political will upon others, and if everyone enjoys sufficient economic power that they can direct some of their energies towards the political decision-making process, then one is only 'obeying' laws, not another individual or group, and then it becomes conceivable that one is obeying the universal political principles and the basic law. The result is a society without a ruling elite.

This does not mean, however, that there exists such a thing as a society without power. It would be attractive to imagine a society in which power did not exist, but this would also be a society without politics.

If one defines power as the ability of some individuals or social classes to impose their will upon others, then one cannot speak of power in a society in which universal political principles are binding on everyone. But this is too narrow a definition of power. It is still power when some individuals are empowered to refuse to others the right to act in accordance with their own will or to satisfy their needs. And in this sense the universal principles are not in any way inconsistent with the exercise of power.

If after public debate it is agreed that a decision may be reached on the basis of majority opinion (in accordance with the third general maxim), then the minority is forbidden to assert its will (in accordance with the first maxim). The fourth maxim enjoins the recognition of all human needs (as long as their satisfaction is not inconsistent with any of the other maxims), but not the satisfaction of all these needs. The relative priority of the needs of different social groups is also a matter for public discussion. So at any given time, there must be some groups whose needs cannot be satisfied. This means, on the one hand, that power is decentralized, and on the other hand that power conflicts are resolved by rational discussion (in Habermas' sense of the word). It certainly does not mean that there is no longer any such thing as power.

Moreover a system of politics committed to universal political principles (moral maxims) excludes neither pragmatism nor political *techne*. The ability to propose rational compromises acceptable to all concerned during the course of a discussion demands certain pragmatic skills. And once a decision has been reached in accordance with the principles, certain learnable rules must be obeyed and abilities brought into play when putting it into effect. These may with justification be described as the technical skills of politics. What a system of politics based on these principles does exclude are *ideological* and *moralizing* politics, since adherence to these principles makes it impossible to set up any individual way of life or goal as an absolute, 'the general good' or 'all that is desirable'.

The theoretical proposal that univeral principles be accepted as binding moral maxims for a democratic system of politics, therefore, does not seem utopian at all, even less so since the principles themselves have been worked out in the course of a long tradition stretching back more than 200 years. It is also clear, however, that today they can only have force as purely moral maxims founded on individual conscience, since the preconditions for their universalization as political principles are lacking in society. They do not exist even in liberal-democratic countries where human rights and liberties are respected, as a result of property relations in them, and they are completely absent from the various forms of despotism, where no trace of such principles has yet emerged. In foreign affairs, the establishment of the principles present many difficulties. The inequality in property relations is even more striking here than within individual states. Political power is more centralized too, and liberal-democratic states are confronted more frequently with despotic states than with other liberal-democratic ones. Neither from a philosophical nor a political point of view can we simply acknowledge the fact that liberal-democratic states are impotent. Although, on the one hand, it would be suicidal to urge that force (that is, the power to compel others to do something) should be eliminated from the arsenal of present-day political strategies, it would on the other hand be even more suicidal to abandon the norms represented by universal political principles and by so doing aid and abet the enemies of all democratic traditions.

You cannot force anyone to be free. You can, however, force them into a situation in which they *have* to listen to rational arguments and meet them with counterarguments. If one forces others into a situation where they have to share power equally for a short period, the way is then open for rational argument. This is not a new procedure; it occurs every day when striking workers force employers to listen to their grievances. From the point of view of democracy, however, power that has no other purpose than the destruction or suppression of another group cannot be tolerated. Within a liberal state which respects human rights and liberties, it is by no means impossible to introduce the above procedure into all political affairs. The same procedure is much more difficult to apply to foreign affairs. There is, however, no alternative as long as one is determined not to give up hope that democratic politics can become universally established, and if one does not want to see the world edge nearer the catastrophe of a third world war. The principle of such a system of politics would not, of course, be identical with the basic law of democratic politics nor with its principles. It would be: in all your political decisions and activities strive for a balance of power which can bring about the universal acceptance of the political principles (as moral maxims). From the point of view of democratic traditions and the democratic ethos, the acceptance of such principles would not only be honest (principled), but would also make good pragmatic sense. By 'good pragmatic sense', I mean that all other options can only lead to the self-destruction of all democratic traditions.

The good person and the good citizen

In the first part of this study ('The moral maxims of democratic politics') I have argued for the following theses:
 (1) Politics should not be based on morality.
 (2) Democratic politics can only be universalized if every member of a given body politic accepts political principles that also serve as moral maxims for all political argumentation, decisions and actions.
 (3) These principles, few in number, should be accepted consensually. But a *consensus omnium* concerning every particular decision and action is neither possible nor desirable.

It is obvious that these three propositions imply a theory of ethics, and in what follows I wish to elucidate this implication. For this purpose I will assume that a consensus regarding the principles of a democratic politics has already come about. The analysis of an ideal situation serves to illuminate basic ethical problems that we have to cope with here and now.

If political principles are consensually accepted, they function as valid norms for every political decision and action. Yet even if people come to a voluntary agreement regarding the standards of right decisions or actions, it is far from certain that they will decide or act in keeping with them. Although the ideal case of a *consensus omnium* presupposes the coalescence of external and internal authorities of human conduct – in other words, the state wherein valid social rules are endorsed and maintained by the companion of practical reasons – it is clear that self-interest and passion can still motivate people to ignore the obligations imposed by this concordance. The acceptance of a few political principles is therefore not the final stage in the establishment of a truly democratic political ethics, but is rather its precondition. The genuine ethical dilemma is neither automatically nor entirely solved by the ideal case of a *consensus omnium* regarding the principles: the constant task of observing these principles and applying them to all particular cases of action and decision equally belong to this complex.

That the universal principles of a democratic politics should also serve as moral maxims, and yet that politics cannot and should not be based on morality, are proposals implying that political ethics is only the tip of the iceberg of ethics in general. But whether the universal principles will be applied or infringed is something not entirely independent of accepted moral values and forms of behaviour practised in the non-political sphere. Pluralism is the hallmark of world-views and modes of conduct, and it always will be. Even if such universal political principles were consensually accepted, this multiplicity of values would never wither away, and any belief that it could is totally unfounded. Moreover, the pluralism of life-conduct and the consequent pluralism of ethical codes should be recognized as a value in itself, its being coterminous with the principles of freedom and the recognition of all human needs. The utopian model of a radical democracy envisages a world-citizenry educated in various value systems. In principle, one thing must be common to all divergent value systems, namely that their attendant socialization processes must ensure as much as possible the observance of the universal principles of a democratic politics. By this I do not mean to say that there cannot and should not be universal values other than the moral maxims shared by each particular avenue of life-conduct. I will come back to this matter later.

In order to find a theoretical solution to our general problem, it is imperative that we turn away from the various paradigms of modern moral philosophy. Neither the formalism of Kant, nor the theories of moral judgment, communication and utilitarianism can account for the two levels of moral behaviour so different and yet not independent of each other. In the same way, in several other areas we can find a reliable guide in an ancient theoretical approach, in Aristotle's ethics and political philosophy.

The Aristotelian paradigm of ethics concerns the *good man* or the good person. Aristotle is the only philosopher to distinguish clearly between the good man and the good citizen. He writes:

> the aim of all citizens, however dissimilar they may be, is the safety of the community, that is, the constitution of which they are citizens. Therefore the goodness of the citizen must be goodness in relation to constitution; . . . On the other hand we do say that the good *man* is good in virtue of one single perfect goodness. Clearly then it is possible to be a good and serious citizen without having that goodness which makes a good man . . . since it is impossible for all the citizens to be alike, there cannot even be one goodness of citizen and good man alike. For the goodness of the good citizen must be within the reach of all; only so can the state itself be really good. But it is impossible for all to have the goodness of the good man. . . .

Disregarding the Aristotelian distinction of good ruler and good citizen, as it has no bearing on the social model delineated here, we can turn to the definition of the good citizen, which reads as follows: ' . . . the goodness of the . . . citizen [is] to be good at both ruling and obeying.'

The Aristotelian distinction between good man and good citizen obviously does not entail the contrast of public and private morality: the less so since it is well-known that for Aristotle a man cannot be good at all without being a good citizen at the same time. Moreover, only free citizens are able to attain the perfect goodness of a good man. No one who is dependent for his or her livelihood on another person (slaves, women, wage labourers) can have the goodness of the good man. Instead of dividing morality into private and public, Aristotle regards a person as a totality of various moral qualities, all of which are exercised in human activities, although to different degrees and in different forms. Even though, in contrast to Plato, Aristotle distinguishes between the private, the intimate and the public spheres, they are not set up against, but are interconnected with each other via the moral person, the good man. If we have in mind the ideal of various self-managed societies constituting a future world-citizenry, we can subscribe to the Aristotelian theoretical proposal, with one modification. We can safely subscribe to it because in a model of self-management those decisions concerning commonly held property would obviously take place in a sphere which is simultaneously private and public. The modern abyss between private and public morality is thus bridged by a ladder, the rungs of which lead progressively from the intimate to the public sphere. The modification, suggested by the same idea, is the universalization of the citizenry, which in other words means that no one will be dependent for his or her livelihood on another person. This is why I substitute the notion of 'the good person' for the Aristotelian 'good man'. Objections may, of course, be made to the revitalization of the concept of 'the good man' (or the good person), given that our common Christian tradition stamped this concept with a very specific meaning, a connotation not easy to get rid of. This is why I must make it very clear that by the notion of 'the good person' I simply mean one who leads an honest life. But I wish to emphasize too that I have revitalized the notion for a purpose. Goodness is the orientative element in morality, and anyone who leads an honest life has a good character regardless of occasional moral blunders. Consequently, if someone has a good character, he or she has to be called a 'good person'. There is no proper substitute for the term.

I have formulated the fundamental law of democratic politics in the following way: act in such a way that anyone could give his or her consent to the principles of your action. The precondition of realizing this fundamental law is a citizenry comprised of *good citizens*. The good citizen observes this fundamental law continuously and gives his or her consent only to actions and decisions that harmonize with the universal principles of a democratic politics. It is doubtless a foolhardly assumption that everyone will be a good citizen even if the universal political principles were consensually accepted, but the ideal of the good citizen has to be binding. Only this ideal can successfully regulate the various actions and decisions taken in a democratic society. It follows from this that all the various ethical systems and types of life-conduct based on them have to have one ideal in common: the ideal of the good citizen.

However, the issue of how different ethical systems can share this common ideal of a good citizen was not raised by Aristotle.

He assumed, since he had accounted for a great variety of constitutions, that the ideal of a good citizen is different in a monarchy, an aristocracy and a democracy. What is common to all good constitutions is rather the ideal of the good man. Although Aristotle discussed a variety of forms of life-conduct as well, the latter were restricted in number (three, to be precise) and hierarchically ordered. What he never questioned was the value system and the value hierarchy of the city-state in general: he took them for granted. He universalized the mores of a particular society and drew up the features of the 'good man' in keeping with it. This is why, despite the acceptance of the Aristotelian distinction, I have to reflect upon the relationship between the good person and the good citizen from a different angle.

I have suggested that we accept the Aristotelian distinction of the good person and the good citizen, but I have not yet argued for it. It is therefore necessary briefly to discuss this matter.

If we are acting in an institutionalized public sphere, we cannot act in our capacity as human persons without further qualification, but must do so as 'this' person or 'that' person, to use Lessing's qualificatory formulation. We are men and women, we have acquired different skills and trades, we represent various communities in various capacities. Politics is the sphere of power. Even if power no longer included domination or exercising power against others, but instead meant, in the truly democratic sense of the word, 'being empowered' by a community or a body politic, it would still be an area of one-sided interaction. Of course, there are various levels of public life, and the representative of some of these is precisely the 'whole man without qualification'. This is primarily true of face-to-face relationships. But an all-embracing democracy has to transcend the level of direct democracy and face-to-face relationships in many respects: institutionalized interactions are inconceivable without set rules of behaviour. For example, if someone is empowered by a community to represent its opinion or carry out its will in regard to an item on an agenda, the person thus empowered cannot enter with the totality of his or her personality into the decision-making process: in fact, it is imperative that he or she must not. The adversary in the discussion may be one's best friend, but the person in question does not have the right to act and behave in the capacity of a friend and sacrifice the mission assigned to him on the altar of friendship. He has to carry out the will of those who have empowered or delegated him. Even if I do not think that bureaucratic behaviour is a necessary condition of a democracy, I do agree with Weber on one basic point: the entirely personal handling of public business contradicts the principles of democracy. Furthermore, several human qualities of a good person have no relevance at all for the good citizen. Their presence or absence, so important in personal contacts, is completely extraneous in public performances. One can be a good citizen without being capable of loving or of sharing generously: even 'keeping a promise' does not characterize the good citizen in this sense. The good citizen of a radical democracy does make the promise to observe the universal principles of a democratic politics, and he or she is bound to keep that promise completely. But whether or not he or she has kept the promise to be faithful to a lover has nothing to do with being a good citizen.

This ideal of the good citizen of a radical democracy is far from identical with that of a 'law-abiding citizen'. Let me refer to Aristotle again: a good citizen has all the capacities of ruling, not just of obeying. In the model outlined here ruling proper would mean the reassertion, validation and application of the universal principles in such a way that their interpretation is adequate to the particular situation. The ability to rule is not a natural propensity but an acquired capacity. According to Aristotle, it is a special kind of mental ability called *prudence (phronesis)*. Aristotle writes:

> There is a certain faculty called 'cleverness' . . . which is the ability to do the things . . . as contributory to the end we have set before us, and so to achieve that end . . . Cleverness is not the same as prudence, though prudence contains an element of cleverness. On the other hand the 'eye' of the soul . . . cannot acquire prudence or sagacity unless it has first acquired virtue. . . .

If we follow Aristotle on this, then the continuous application and interpretation of the universal political principles to any particular situation presupposes prudence. Prudence is a partnership of value-rationality and goal-rationality; of practical reason and cleverness. It enables us thoroughly to scrutinize a particular situation and to choose the proper means to achieve the proper end while observing the universal principles of a democratic politics. It stands to reason that prudence is the supreme virtue of a good citizen. All citizens who have acquired prudence can argue for decisions which on their part combine value- and goal-rationality. *Thus the supreme virtue of a good citizen is a rational virtue.* I wish to emphasize again that prudence, too, like all other virtues, is acquired. It is gained through an *educating* for prudence, as well as practice in decision-making. Since education (in the original sense of the Greek concept of *paideia*) and practice in decision-making are rooted in various forms of life and pluralistic moral systems, different as they may be, all of them should equally develop the quality of prudence, even if they do so in very different ways.

All this is far from being a matter of mere speculation. Everyone knows what prudence is, and we normally appreciate someone who is able to apply valid principles with prudence to particular situations, not only in the public but in all spheres of life. We esteem the teachers and colleagues who have firm principles (provided that we share or at least respect them), and who are able to consider the particular situation, time, place and persons, and thus the foreseeable consequences of their proposals, decisions, and actions. What has been described here as the main merit of the good citizen is only the universalization of an already existing human quality.

It is a serious theoretical fallacy to limit the problems of ethics to the realm of politics and to assume that once public life is rational and democratic, all moral questions will be properly solved. It is a no less serious fallacy than that of drawing the borderlines of ethics within the private sphere, especially within the family. I have already hinted at one aspect of the insufficiency of this and similar solutions: that even though it is not mandatory for a good citizen to be a good person in respect of all human qualities, given that the qualities of the citizen constitute only one aspect of human behaviour in general, there is for every one of us an undivided human personality. In short, an evil person cannot be a good citizen. One could object to this that the respective categories of 'good' and 'evil' would have absolutely no relevance if only one ethics (namely the public) existed. But such a conception presupposes a complete break between public and non-public life, a break even deeper than the present one. At any rate, one cannot imagine that people brought up in the spirit of 'do as you like' would accept the universal principles and observe the postulate of rational argumentation the moment they entered the public sphere. Further, the question of the desirability of such a dichotomous and fragmented life-style has to be raised. Without direct personal contacts, life would not be worth living. To be sure, no one can be obliged to develop such contacts, but the realm of the morally good is, in all the relevant philosophical perspectives, far broader than the realm of 'Ought'. Even several positivists allow for two types of moral judgment: good-judgments and ought-judgments. Further, if one enters into such direct personal relationships, one thereby accepts certain binding norms as well, depending on the character of the relationship in question. What is more, there are several situations in every person's life where no political principles, universal or otherwise, can be applied. We have to face death and illness; that of loved ones, and of ourselves. We are often in need of personal and sincere advice, and only the advice of a good person can be good advice. The deeply existential problems which concern us most cannot be resolved by public discourse and cannot be annulled merely by being good citizens. We need different norms and moral practices, and it is the task of pluralistic moral systems and forms of life-conduct to generate just these norms. Present-day moral systems fall short in this respect. People are abandoned to themselves in their misery and suffering, and eventually seek institutionalized help, an anomaly we are so well aware of.

At this point I can turn to the issue which must be raised within the framework of my model, but which Aristotle did not deal with. How can various forms of life, various expressions of morality, meet in harmony in public life? Equally, how can various types of good persons become good citizens in harmony?

The following conditions are prerequisite to this state of affairs.

(1) No particular values of a specific life-style should contradict the universal principles of a democratic politics. If they do, the universal political principles cannot serve as the moral maxims they are supposed to be.

(2) All moral systems, and what is equivalent to this, styles of life, have to acknowledge prudence as a virtue within their particular frameworks. Moral norms of any kind, different as they may be, should not function as mere external authorities of human conduct, but should be applied and interpreted according to the situation, time, place and persons concerned. Put differently, it is practical reason that has to make the proper decisions in harmony with the accepted values and norms. Here I am again following in the footsteps of Aristotle, who considered prudence as the main rational moral authority in particular decisions.

(3) One of the principles of a democratic politics enjoins the recognition of all human needs (excepting those the satisfaction of which involves the use of other human persons as mere means). Since needs are used in value systems, observing this principle

also implies the recognition of all human values and norms (again with the former restriction). While the imperative of recognizing all human needs here and now generates a regulative idea of the satisfaction of all human needs, the recognition of all human values here and now does not generate a regulative but a constitutive and practical idea: the idea of *respect for all human values*. We can respect all human values without having to share all of them. Only if we are capable of respecting all human values (even the ones we do not share) can we respect, to use Kant's terminology, 'humankind in ourselves'.

Let us suppose for the time being that these three conditions are met: that is, that no moral norm contradicts the universal principles, that every moral system exhibits the virtue of prudence, and that all human values and norms are respected by everyone. It is clear that even here good citizens will interpret the universal political principles via their own moral systems. As a result, the discussions concerning a particular practical decision may be value discussions. Value discussions are not normally discussions about values: the latter could very rarely be settled at all. Rather, the conflict involved here is related to which of the several values is chosen as the mediator in between the universal principles and the decision in a given situation. All citizens participating in any kind of discussion must explain their reasons for preferring to mediate and interpret the universal principles with one set of values instead of another. These and similar discussions can in principle be settled if none of the discussants is obliged to deny the validity of his or her value, though he or she should refrain from its applications where good reasons for the application of the value cannot be given. (This is so because the mutual respect of values is a methodological presupposition here.) However, this and similar discussions can only be settled if each participant can refer to at least one commonly held universal value universally accepted as ultimate. Even though I assumed (within the ideal presuppositions) that no value system contradicts the universal principles (the moral maxims) of a democratic politics, such a contradiction is not impossible if the value systems are applied to decisions which concern people who lead various life-styles. The mutual elimination of such contradictions from the position taken by the partners is one of the major procedures of all value discussions.

It is common knowledge that there are certain values – which can be referred to as 'ultimate' or 'absolute' values – the validity of which we are either not ready to support or are not capable of supporting with arguments. This is why certain positivists and 'critical rationalists' normally refer to values and norms as irrational factors in human decisions. I would formulate this problem exactly from its obverse. People can, and often do, give reasons for their value decisions, thus they are in principle capable of settling value discussions *since* there are a few values, or at least one single value, which they recognize as absolute and ultimate. The validity of these few ultimate values (or maybe of even one ultimate value) which cannot be questioned at all is the precondition of every value discussion and value rational discussion. If such ultimate values did not exist, we could give no reasons for decisions or judgments on behalf of *any* value. Also, if this were the case there would only be one type of rationality left: mere instrumental rationality.

Yet the reduction of rationality to instrumental rationality is the negative utopia of positivism. What is more, it is simply impossible in any relevant social intercourse. No special goal is pursued according to mere instrumental reason. Of course, one can substitute success for good, as normally happens in modern societies, but success is equally a value, even if it is not primarily an ethical one. But should we substitute success for good, then even here normative regulation will not cease to exist. In this case we would approve of success and disapprove of failure, but approval and disapproval are intrinsically ethical judgments. This is how we conceive of disapproval if we are ashamed of being unsuccessful. The external authority of human conduct does not cease to exist in this case either; it will rather be reinforced. Conscience becomes calculative and pangs of conscience appear in the case of a wrong calculation. If the norm of success can homogenize the behaviour of social actors, the norm itself will no longer be queried and success would become an ultimate value beyond reason. If the norm of success cannot homogenize the whole society, people will act and behave according to different norms, and they will question not only the validity but also the rationality of the norm of instrumental reason. Human beings can never act without observing certain norms. This being the case, and if we can account for our value decisions only with the aid of recourse to one or several ultimate values, then the acceptance of these ultimate or absolute values cannot be described as an irrational act. The foundation of any kind of value rationality cannot be regarded as 'irrational'.

Let me repeat: we can only give reasons for our evaluations and we can only settle value disputes if we share certain common values which we accept as ultimate: values which are so utterly self-evident that, if they are questioned, cause us to throw up our arms in a gesture of despair. If there are no commonly held ultimate values accepted as self-evident with a gesture, no value dispute can be settled at all. Were the validity of all our values abruptly suspended, no value debates with the slightest chance of consensus could come about. However, *there are* values which are accepted as valid. Their universal validity is not an ideal but a simple fact. I call them 'value ideas'. Value ideas are all those values the opposites of which cannot and do not have validity. It is precisely for this reason that they can be recognized with a gesture and that all value debates can have recourse to them. In my book on philosophy, I singled out the idea of freedom as just such a universally accepted value idea. Other value ideas may be justice or the alleviation of human suffering. There is no question but that people do oppress others and do deprive others of their freedom; that they do commit injustices and cause suffering, often without alleviating other sufferings, but it is equally certain that they would not *choose* unfreedom, injustice or suffering as valid values. We can safely recognize valid values with a gesture as ultimate. Such a gesture is not an irrational act, for it merely evidences the fact that on such matters there is really no choice at all. I would rather use the Kantian category, and term the validity of value ideas '*the fact of practical reason*'. This is why one is entitled to regard all those not recognizing the validity of value ideas as 'morally insane'.

I have raised the question of how a world citizenry could settle value disputes given the existence of heterogeneous systems of values and forms of life. I have come to the conclusion that value debates can be settled – even though they in fact not always are – if there is at least one commonly shared universal and absolute value that every participant can revert to. Here I have to add that not only commonly held values (value ideas) can serve as *ultimate* values in various value systems, types of life-conduct. Each value system may involve, even if it does not necessarily do so, one or another ultimate value of its own. Max Weber's well-known example was that the salvation of the soul can be – and generally is – an ultimate value for a religious community, but it is obviously not shared by every moral system of a world-citizenry. This is why I have to add the following restriction to my model: if public matters have to be settled between various communities with different life-styles and value systems, the participants in discussion can only make recourse to those ultimate values which are shared by the whole citizenry; in other words, to universally valid value ideas.

Here it is appropriate briefly to return to the universal principles of a democratic politics. Some of these principles make recourse to value ideas in a particular interpretation (for example, to the principle of freedom or justice); others, however, fall back upon values that are not yet accepted as value ideas. The recognition of all human needs is not a value idea, and the same holds true of equality. It follows from this that the universal principles of a democratic politics can only be accepted consensually as a result of the *prior* existence of a few value ideas to which these principles can make recourse without any internal contradiction. Were there no value ideas shared in common, consensus regarding the principles of a democratic politics would not only be utopian (as it actually is) but a sheer impossibility.

I stated earlier that the image of the 'good person' varies according to different value structures and there is no reason to assume that this will be different in the future. However, I have also argued that in a radical democracy *prudence* should be appreciated as a virtue in all paths of life. Prudence involves the individual application of the binding norms and values to particular situations according to everyone's personality structure. Thus the value of prudence accounts for the great variety of moral personalities within each distinct moral system. In this way it implies the possibility of observing the valid norms by *all* persons regardless of their physical, mental and emotional constitution. Were prudence accepted as a universal value, one would be entitled to assume that it would be within everyone's reach to become a more or less good person, the more so since moral systems are not conceived of in terms of organic ties. Various persons can choose various paths of life according to their inclination and become 'good persons' by observing norms which best suit their personality. Even if I began from the assumption that the good person and the good citizen are not identical, and that someone can be a good citizen without being a good person, I may conclude that it is not beyond anyone's reach to be both. It is obvious that the statement 'to be a good person is within everyone's reach', does not authenticate its counterpart that everyone will indeed be a good person. It means that social circumstances, the struggle for survival and the operation of alienated ethical norms, do not limit the moral autonomy of persons.

A further step is now necessary. There exists a type of human goodness which is no less transcultural in the present as are the value ideas. In order to distinguish this goodness from the idea of the 'good person' I am going to term it 'the transcultural good person'.

The 'transcultural good person' is not a theoretical construct either, because we are perfectly familiar with it from our life experiences. We have all met people whom we can call good persons in a *transcultural* sense.

It was Paul Edwards, in *The Logic of Moral Discourse* (1955), who argued that people with quite different moral systems and world-views, people who would never find a common denominator in the assessment of any political decision or action, quite easily agree if it comes to the qualification of a person as 'good'. Should we state about X that she had never been envious and vain, that she had sacrificed everything she had in order to help people in need, that she had always volunteered to care for the lonely, the ill or the dying, and that her sense of humour and her courage helped others overcome the ordeals of their lives, no single person, whether conservative or leftist, religious or atheist, would deny that she was good. In this and similar cases people never argue about values, only about facts. One can object that 'X is not good because X did not do A, B, C', but one will simply never say that X is not good even if A, B, C, is the case. Lukács once recounted the story of a Hungarian writer who, in the years of the great terror, invited to dinner a child of a victim every week, and sent, also every week, a parcel containing food and clothes to unknown people in the concentration camps. A bag containing his essentials had been his pillow for several years, so certain was he that one morning he would be arrested by the secret police. Lukács added to this story: 'he had lost all his convictions and principles, he had no belief in any cause, but he was a good man; yes, a very good man.' Personally, I would describe him as a hero; others, perhaps, as a foolishly overconsiderate person, but I am sure that no one would challenge Lukács' judgment that 'he was a very good man'.

No imperatives can be addressed to human beings to be 'good' in the transcultural meaning of the word. After all, it was Weber again who noted that the *virtuosi* of a particular religion never made up its church. But where the idea of 'transcultural goodness' is concerned, I would even object to the notion of 'virtuoso'. Transcultural goodness does not require, nor is it constituted by, daily exercise. A transculturally good person is rather a genius of morality. Even if this goodness is related to inherited moral laws (for example, the ten commandments), there is a streak of natural empathy in it for which no law can account. Just as an artist cannot normally be assessed by the standard of a genius, so ordinary human goodness cannot be measured with the yardstick of a moral genius. The latter has to be, and is, accepted with a gesture. The more so since the moral genius too communicates with gestures. Sending parcels to unknown people in concentration camps, inviting their children to your table in times of raging and indiscriminate terror, giving all you own to those in need, volunteering to dress the wounds, physical and mental, and being willing to hold the hands of those dying in agony: all these are gestures. Transculturally good persons normally cannot even give good reasons for why they do what they do. At any rate it is not argument, but only the gesture, that has relevance. The gesture is generally understood as intrinsically good.

To repeat, it is inappropriate to measure ourselves with the yardstick of the moral genius. It is sufficient to be a good person, to live an honest life. But there is still a difference between the artistic and the moral genius. It is foolish to attempt to imitate the artistic genius, while it is far from being foolish to imitate the moral genius. The latter action is not mandatory for the good person, but it is at least possible.

It has been mentioned that being a good person has relevance for being a good citizen. This is so even though the two are far from being identical for the perfectly simple reason that the good person is good 'at prudence', and without prudence no one qualifies for being a good citizen. But we may wonder whether the existence of the transculturally good persons and their possible imitation (given the impossibility of their universalization) has any bearing at all on the life of a radically democratic sphere.

It is easy to grasp that in times of extreme violence and terror, gestures of a transcultural goodness are at the same time political gestures. Everyone who gave shelter to fugitives in Nazi Germany acted politically. But in liberal or democratic countries transcultural goodness does not enter the political sphere. This is why it is not considered in political discourse, and leftists in liberal countries normally regard references to such goodness as pious and moralizing drivel that only endangers the common cause of political radicalism. It is, of course, very true that transcultural goodness will not change society, if only for the simple reason that it is transcultural. But this mundane fact cannot diminish the relevance of this concept for a radical democratic society.

One of the universal principles of a democratic politics is the recognition of all human needs. Given the fact of relative scarcity and the impossibility of satisfying all recognized needs simultaneously, priorities in need satisfaction must be decided in public debate. If it happens that several needs have equally just claims, priorities between them must be decided nonetheless. In this and similar debates, transculturally good people, and all those imitating them, may consent to satify the needs of others as a first priority with a gesture of charity. Without this gesture of charity (which does not imply self-sacrifice because for a transculturally good person the need for being good is more powerful than all others), a functioning radical democracy is not at all imaginable.

I have described two types of rationality, communicative rationality and prudence (the latter being a combination of value-rationality and goal-rationality), and both are equally necessary in any kind of radical democracy. We have to enter communication with prudence, and we have to apply the principles agreed upon whilst using prudence even in cases in which discourse is excluded (for example, where a decision must be taken immediately). I have also suggested that discourse implies value discussions as well, discussions which can be settled by making recourse to universal value ideas, and that this settlement about need satisfaction priorities might also presuppose the gesture of charity. I would like to make the basic message of this summary clear: these two types of rationality (communicative rationality and prudence) stretch between two boundaries (value ideas and the transcultural good person) to which neither of them actually applies. I have already stated that value ideas cannot be suspended and proven rationally via discourse – and in this sense they are not irrational but beyond reason – because no rational discourse is possible without the prior acceptance of their ultimate validity. The same can be said of prudence. It is value ideas that guide us in our prudent decisions and arguments because at all times when we act and decide with prudence it is exactly these value ideas that we interpret. But observing value ideas has nothing to do with prudence. Aristotle remarked that prudence refers to changing things and situations, never to the eternal. Value ideas are situation-free because they are ultimate and absolute. The same holds true of the transculturally good person. We do not question whether the goodness of the transculturally good person is 'genuine'; we accept it without reflection in the same way as we accept value ideas. Prudence cannot play the part of the rational authority judging the transculturally good person either. The moral genius is not prudent, for this person stands beyond prudence. If I earlier described the rejection (non-recognition) of the value ideas as 'moral insanity', I am entitled to describe the rejection of the goodness of the transculturally good person as 'moral blindness'.

If my thesis is correct, and neither a value idea nor the goodness of the transculturally good person is and ought to be made the subject of argumentation, nor should prudence be related to them, one has to conclude that not even the radically democratic ethic can be completely rationalized. But all those who share partiality for reason, if they are confronted with the limits of rational communication and prudence in ethics, with the value ideas on the one hand and the transculturally good person on the other, should not draw sceptical conclusions. I have already referred to the former as the fact of practical reason. I can refer to the latter as the fact of human nature indeed. Should someone state that all our ethical endeavours are in vain because our species is evil by nature, we can safely point to the transculturally good persons and to the fact that their goodness is recognized (even if not universally imitated) as goodness transculturally. These two facts (the facts of practical reason and of human nature) are the foundation, the source and the resource of all rational ethics.

Returning to Aristotle again, let us take his argument that we cannot apply prudence to eternal things. This granted, it is nevertheless true that these same eternal things can be subjected to theoretical-philosophical speculation. What I have termed value ideas and the transcultural good person can also be made the subject matter of philosophical speculation. Some would explain them through the commandments of God, others by the existence of Platonic ideas, others again by history. Even if I subscribe to the historical explanation, I do suggest, as far as practical–ethical behaviour is concerned, that theoretical explanations do not at all matter. What matters is the gesture. But, unimportant as it may be from the perspective of practical reason, I owe a brief explanation on this.

Histories of civilized humankind have been histories of murder, looting, plundering, human suffering – and they still are. If we examine histories they appear as bedlam rather than any march of progress, reason and freedom. The only crutch inherited from (certain) histories that we can rely upon is that of value ideas, all usually infringed, and the moral genius, always exceptional. If we can legitimately call anything 'reason in history', this title should be reserved for the value ideas and the transculturally good person alone, because we have to revert to them in order to gain any conception of a rational ethics and a good life. But since value ideas have always been infringed, and the transculturally good person has usually proved impotent, reason in history is at the same time unreason in history. Only where there is reason can there be unreason. It is by definition unreasonable to violate value ideas and sneer at the good person, and it is precisely because such actions are unreasonable that they are normally rationalized, in the Freudian sense of the word. However, rationalization cannot mitigate the feeling of guilt, which people efface by means of mass neuroses and mass hysteria. No one can safely foretell whether or not unreason in history can be overcome; whether our species will be the victim of its reason *and* unreason or whether the former will break through and tame the latter. This is above all why the gesture pointing to value ideas and the transculturally good person is the gesture of planetarian responsibility. True, this gesture is meaningless without a real commitment to communicative rationality and prudence, the idea of the good life. But the primacy of practical reason necessitates the primacy of this very gesture.

Up until now I have referred to the Aristotelian distinction of good man and good citizen. But Aristotle also distinguished a third modus of the good human character: being 'good at something'. This notion applies to *techne*, to goal-rational activity. *Techne* encompasses political *techne* plus free arts and crafts. Creating a good constitution was conceived of as *techne* by Aristotle, as was playing a musical instrument well, or being a master-builder. Here, people can be good at something only if they have a clear picture of the goal, have acquired certain technical rules via knowledge and exercise, and have the ability to apply these rules to particular tasks or issues. The latter ability, that of choosing the means adequate to the goal, is also a kind of prudence, and is called technical phronesis. In what follows I will apply the notions of being good at something, being a good man and being a good citizen, to the model of radical democracy whilst disregarding the Aristotelian analysis of their interconnection.

If all citizens are supposed to participate in the production of material and cultural wealth, it is obvious that everyone has to be good at something (or at least at one thing) apart from having the ability to participate in public affairs. This proviso does not only mean that everyone has to acquire the ability of acting in keeping with goal-rationality, for goal-rationality is no less a human universal than value-rationality. The appropriation of a sphere of objectivation which encompasses the use of language, the observation of social norms, and the use of man-made objects is the mode of socialization of every healthy specimen of our species. 'Being good at something' involves more than the proper use of man-made objects; it is a more or less specialized goal-rational activity pursued in the service of *social utility*. It is work in the broadest sense of the notion. One of the principles of democratic politics is the recognition of all human needs, which on its part involves the regulative idea of the satisfaction of all human needs. Consequently, in order to observe this principle, everyone has to contribute something to the material or cultural wealth – whether we are speaking of the wealth of a society, group or single person. This is what is meant by 'being good at something'. But, and this must be emphasized, work has been viewed here as goal-rational activity. Should individuals no longer have the freedom to choose and realize their own goals, and to select the proper means to this end themselves, and should the mental and manual aspects of work be divided (as they now normally are), then work changes from being a goal-rational to a merely instrumentally rational activity. The latter term signifies such an impersonally rationalized work process. It is impossible to imagine a society wherein all universal principles of a democratic politics are continuously observed without such behaviour generating a radical change in the very character of work. Goal-rationality reclaimed implies self-management on the one hand, new technology on the other. If one envisages a future with a variety of life-styles, one should envisage not only one type of new technology but several. Time will not permit elaboration of this problem, yet the conclusion must be drawn. Since in terms of the model of a radical democracy no one could be a good citizen without being good at something, and since no one could be a good person without being a good citizen (even if the converse is not necessarily the case), one may conclude that every good person has to be good at something.

I have already stated that I consider the rigid line of demarcation between the sphere of politics and all other human spheres incompatible with a radical democracy. Even though within the political sphere *sensu stricto* a certain degree of depersonalization of invididuals as totalities seems to be unavoidable, there are other levels of discourse and decision-making at the juncture of the private and the political (for example, within a self-managed factory) where such a depersonalization may be less necessary or desirable. On the level of direct democracy and in face-to-face intercourse the good person can function as a good citizen without any, or only with a slight degree of depersonalization. Since everyone participates in decision-making and discourse at various levels, such depersonalization at the strictly political level should not lead to fossilized bureaucratic behaviour. But this does not exclude or render irrelevant the institutionalization of rationality either, at least in the public affairs of any huge body politic. Rationalized institutions implementing public decisions would consist of people who properly support the goal they are working towards, and who are also good at their job. There is nothing wrong with the rationalization of activities if the goal or task is shared. We readily accept such authorities if they are better at organizing a common endeavour than we are.

It is a widespread idea, and strongly supported by Hannah Arendt and others, that the public–political domain is the supreme field of human action and that thematizing political issues is the noblest form of human speech. I would make this claim with greater reservation. In one respect it is beyond doubt that Arendt is right: good and rational political institutions are the preconditions of the good life. Still, they are not identical with it. I would rather say that even though political activity and discourse are, from this viewpoint, the highest types of activity and discourse, they represent at the same time its lowest-ranking types as well. The good life is the life of the good person, not of the good citizen. The more a type of activity engages the good person and gives voice to that person's totality, the higher this activity stands; and it is *usually* not in the sphere of politics that this happens. The discourse and the intercourse is more humane and of a higher quality if simply being together is a goal in itself. Moreover, the personal ties that bind people to one another; that involve the totality of persons in their capacities as friends and as lovers; that signify relationships in which we do not refer to others as 'this' or 'that' person; in other words, the bonds whereby we perceive people not as embodiments of socially determined roles but as persons only, as the self-determined individuals that we consider ourselves to be – these ties represent the supreme good that humans can achieve. These contacts alone can arouse in our souls the feeling of brotherhood and sisterhood, a feeling which binds us invisibly to our fellow-creatures in a manner no less strong than the visible ties of any body politic. This feeling of brotherhood and sisterhood is not identical with the emotion and friendship, even if friendship may imply this feeling as well. The feeling of brotherhood embraces people we do not even know and transcends the boundaries of our value system, our conduct in life. Having no restrictions in time and space, it is unlimited, and can embrace even past and future generations. This is the very feeling which motivates us to imitate the transculturally good person: this feeling itself becomes transcultural.

Reflection and speech are obviously not restricted to the public sphere; they are present in every sphere of human life. Even in the Athenian city-state that Arendt has such preference for, not only public affairs were subject to discussion, but so were friendship, love, art, work, nature – and above all, human nature. To regard all issues of human life as problems, in other words, to philosophize, is an activity that cannot be restricted to public life, even less to politics. Its customary *locus* is the contact between friends, and sometimes it takes place between two friends. In this latter case, reflection, speech and gesture are so interwoven that they are hardly distinguishable. The quest for truth in common may even have an erotic dimension, but this dimension tends to intensify rather than diminish rational reflection. Philosophy is a love of wisdom, and love always has an erotic dimension.

I do not see why work, creativity or anything else belonging to the sphere of goal-rational activity, the sphere of *techne*, should be ranked lower in the hierarchy of activities than political discourse and action. True, work and creativity abstracted from their social setting have no moral implications, and it is always social evaluation, norms and rules, that defines the types of goals pursued in work. It is also true that in the process of creation we are abandoned to ourselves, a single mind and a single body concentrated on one task. But what is wrong with being alone in one of our life activities? What is wrong with concentrating on the task which, if performed successfully, fills us with joy and happiness? What is wrong with the structure of the only performance which makes us comparable to the gods of our imagination? The idea of the deification of Man through social intercourse is the temptation of evil, for no single person should place himself or herself outside the bonds with his or her fellow-creatures. But as creation is value-indifferent from the moral point of view, we can become as gods because we can *create*.

I doubt that the various gods of a radical democracy would confront us with an 'either or'. Zeus, Prometheus, Athene and Eros can all have a role in the lives and concerns of human beings. In this respect I completely subscribe to the Marxian idea of human individuals rich in needs, universal in their praxis. One is not even entitled to list these gods in a hierarchic order, the less so since people have different characters, desires, values, ideas and talents and so need to create their value hierarchy accordingly. If one prefers Zeus, one will be completely absorbed by public life: for such an individual, a good citizen and a good person will be identical. All others can perform their duties as good citizens and may be good persons under the guidance of their own major deity. In this respect, the utopia of a radical democracy points towards the present also. There were times in leftist discourse when everyone was fully dedicated to Prometheus. Then there were other times when Zeus became the ample god of the socialist Olympus. Nowadays Athene and Eros seem to occupy the privileged place. But there is no reason whatsoever for thinking that political action exclusively, or work exclusively, or rational communication exclusively, or friendship, gesture, bonds of brotherhood exclusively, should be regarded as the sole and royal road to a future that may be equally designated as radical democracy, socialism or autonomous society. For a better future can never come about without political action, without rational communication, without changing the structure of work, and without developing new qualities of life. Of course, in social theory and philosophy we normally choose one paradigm. But this paradigm has to be elaborated on that it offers meaningful answers to all the major issues on which the other paradigms rest. Only if this condition is met can we imagine a society in which every human being can make sense of his or her life. *And making sense of our lives is what rationality is all about*: goal-rationality in work and creation, communicative rationality in speech, prudence in action, all of them making recourse to the two levels of absolute values with a final gesture, all of them together constituting radical democracy as an all-embracing form of life at all levels and in all forms of human intercourse. This must be the goal of our human endeavour. If we are successful, this imaginary world would become re-enchanted, not with myths but with meaning. This image, as a utopia, can be employed, first, as a regulative practical idea for action, communication and life, and secondly, as a regulative theoretical idea from the standpoint of which, based on the reason we have already acquired, the unreason of the present can be criticized in all its forms and expressions.

CHAPTER 5
Can 'True' and 'False' Needs be Posited?

The familiar division of needs into 'true' and 'false' contains three different aspects of understanding and/or assessment of needs. To analyse the legitimacy and limitations of the critique of needs, these three aspects must be considered separately.

The ontological aspect

The categories of 'true' and 'false' as applied to needs mean the confrontation between *real* and *unreal* (imaginary) needs. In this conception, the conscious needs of a part, eventually those of the majority, of present society cannot be regarded as 'real' since they are but derivatives of the fetishism of social being or of the manipulation of needs. When the individuals who consider these types of needs to be relevant for themselves and who seek the satisfaction of such needs attain the level of 'correct consciousness', 'imaginary' needs are replaced by 'real' ones.

The above train of thought suffers from the theoretical deficiency that it places the judge (the theoretician) outside the world to be judged. The mere gesture of separating 'real' needs from 'imaginary' ones forces the theoretician into the position of a god passing judgment upon the system of needs of society. One can separate real needs from the imaginary only by assuming that one *knows* which are the 'real', the 'true' ones. When the non-reality of needs is explained by the theory of manipulation, the knowledge of the theoretician passing judgment can only originate from the fact that his consciousness is not fetishized, that it is 'the' correct consciousness. But how does the theoretician know that

CAN 'TRUE' AND 'FALSE' NEEDS BE POSITED?

his consciousness is 'the' correct one? If the theoretician assumes that society is being objectively fetishized, he disqualifies his own knowledge as being 'the' correct one since his consciousness, too, is a product of society. As a consequence, the division of needs into 'true' and 'false' proves to be nonsensical. If the theoretician does *not* depart from the above assumption, his consciousness *may* be the correct one. The consciousness of every individual expressing different systems of needs may similarly be correct, however, and the whole division again becomes meaningless. To avoid this vicious circle, none of the advocates of the theory of 'true' and 'false' needs seriously faces the question of how one knows if one's consciousness is not a fetishized one. Or if they do face it, they do not proceed in a consistent manner. Such is the case with Lukács in *History and Class Consciousness* when he concludes that the proletariat by virtue of its social position is capable of expressing true (correct) consciousness. Lukács' inconsistent treatment of the problem is visible from the fact that he declares the empirical (factual) consciousness of the proletariat to be false consciousness and simply imputes 'true consciousness' to the Being of the class. By doing so, Lukács places himself outside society, even outside the class allegedly representing 'true consciousness'. All division of needs into true and false ones based on the theory of fetishism assumes that the position of the judging persons transcends the society in question.

Of course, there are empirical types of classifications (of 'true' and 'false' needs) dividing the *particular* needs themselves into real and unreal ones. For instance, one can contend that the need for food is real, but the need for meat is imaginary; the need for meat is real, but the need to eat meat every day is imaginary; or that the need for one winter coat is real, but the need for two is imaginary. In such cases, the basis of division is naturalistic. It neglects the circumstance that needs are developed historically and that each particular need is historically determined in each particular instance. In the above examples the value constituting the division is egalitarianism, indeed in its most primitive form. Everything that exceeds the bare minimum for survival is, from the point of view of the judging person, degraded to the level of 'imaginary' needs. Since human needs are historically determined, they do not themselves provide the objective criteria for dividing needs into 'real' or 'imaginary' categories.

Apart from its theoretical deficiency, the concept of 'true' and 'false' needs has its inherent practical danger, too. Whenever it is no longer the isolated theoretician but a system of social institutions that arrogates the right to distinguish real needs from imaginary ones, the dictatorship over the needs comes about. The power structure allows the satisfaction of only those needs it interprets as being real. It does not produce satisfaction for any other need and oppresses all aspirations for it.

To break the theoretical deadlock and to avoid this dangerous practice one must avoid equating 'true' and 'false' needs with 'real' and 'unreal' (imaginary) needs. All needs felt by humans to be real must be considered as real. These include needs of which they are aware, which are formulated by them, which they seek to satisfy. As there is thus no difference between the needs with regard to their reality, it ensues from this that *every need must be acknowledged.*

Dividing needs into 'true' and 'false' not only involves denying acknowledgment of needs considered to be unreal but means, too, that the demand for their satisfaction is irrelevant. Advocates of the 'true' and 'false' needs concept believe that the unreal needs should not be satisfied. It is precisely this type of argumentation that founds every dictatorship on deciding people's needs.

If, however, the standpoint is adopted that all needs should be acknowledged since all of them are real, can we adopt the standpoint, too, that all of them should be satisfied? Consistency would urge it. Failure to do so would, in a concrete way, reinstate the division that has just been rejected.

But is the satisfaction of all needs possible? No doubt, there are always more needs in present dynamic societies than can be satisifed by society under given conditions. This is true even when disregarding the social inequalities of existing societies, some of which are blatant. As a consequence, a system should be created which at any given moment gives priority to the satisfaction of certain needs at a given point in time over the satisfaction of other needs.

If, however, we depart from the acknowledgment of all needs and the legitimacy of their satisfaction, then the determination of priorities presupposes a system of social institutions different from the one dividing needs into real and unreal ones. The system best suited to determining such priorities is one which institutionalizes the decision itself by way of a public-democratic debate. In such debates the social forces representing equally real needs decide (always repeated by way of consensus) what types of need satisfaction should be preferred to the satisfaction of other – equally acknowledged – needs. Thus the establishment of priorities in no way conflicts with the democratic principle of consensus.

CAN 'TRUE' AND 'FALSE' NEEDS BE POSITED?

The ethical aspect

The conclusion that since all needs are real, then all needs should be acknowledged and satisfied, neglects the problem of moral judgment. This second aspect of the division into 'true' and 'false' needs does not distinguish between 'real' and 'imaginary' needs but between *good* and *evil* ones. Should we discard the latter differentiation as well, we ought to assume that whatever is real is at the same time good in ethical terms, or at least value-indifferent and by no means morally condemnable.

Such a thesis cannot be assumed. Say, for example, that a need to oppress others is undoubtedly real, similarly the need to humiliate or exploit others. If people insist on the acknowledgment and satisfaction of all needs without any kind of moral restriction on the grounds of their being real, then the need to exploit and oppress others must be acknowledged and satisfied. The acknowledgment and satisfaction of these needs would, however, contradict the first thesis according to which all needs should be acknowledged and satisfied. Their acknowledgment and satisfaction conflicts with the acknowledgment and satisfaction of the needs of all others, primarily the real needs for being liberated from exploitation and oppression.

The central inconsistency of equating 'good' with 'real' now becomes clear. Without the division of needs into 'good' and 'evil', the acknowledgment and satisfaction of all needs is practicably unrealizable. At the same time, the evil needs should not be acknowledged and satisfied. Therefore the demand for the acknowledgment and satisfaction of all needs is theoretically untenable.

Let us make an attempt at the division of needs into 'good' and 'evil' ones. We depart from the fact that the division had actually been accomplished by norms in all concrete social systems. Some particular needs had been condemned as evil, others exalted as good. Once it was the need for the erotic, at another time the need for the seclusion from society, in other cultures either the need for physical work or the emancipation from physical work; once it was the need for the free choice of vocation or of a mate, again in other times it was the religious need that had been condemned as an 'evil' need from the viewpoint of the system of social norms.

As a consequence, the above needs remained unacknowledged, or more precisely, were the ones whose satisfaction was considered to be a sin or wrong-doing. In the process of the evolution of bourgeois society, simultaneously with the disintegration of the fixed hierarchies of values, the division of good and evil needs became ever more questionable and less viable with regard to the concrete quality of needs. This holds true even if later developments (in Europe as well) brought about systems of social institutions which reintroduce the concrete subdivision and sustain it by coercion.

In principle we could avoid the above anomie if we proposed a new moral roster. Here, however, the question arises: what is our justification for it? And again: in whose name? And the question implies the answer as well. By elaborating a moral roster we would get into the same position as the theoretician who *knew* that his consciousness was the only correct one as confronted with the false consciousness of all others. The only modification here would be that we and only we know which particular needs are 'good' and which are 'evil', whereas others live in ignorance with regard to the moral good. This would again mean a position that transcends the society to which we belong. In so far as our moral roster would be accepted anywhere (speaking, of course, in a hypothetical manner), it would lead anew to a dictatorship over needs, to the oppression of all particular needs that our moral roster had deemed to be evil.

Nevertheless, another solution remains. Those needs must be excluded from acknowledgment which prevent all needs from being acknowledged and satisfied. Is there, however, an *ethical norm* on the basis of which that exclusion can be made theoretically and practically without relapsing into the already rejected standpoint of the division of particular 'good' and 'evil' needs?

There is such an ethical norm, and it was formulated by Kant in a crystal-clear manner as one of the formulae of the categorical imperative: man ought not to be a mere means for the other man!* This norm is *formal* inasmuch as it neglects the circumstance during the satisfaction of what particular needs man becomes or may become a mere means for another man. It is at the same time a *substantial* one, too, since the forms of need-satisfaction in which a man fulfils the role of a mere means for the other can always be grasped and recognized from a content point of view.

---

* 'Handle so, des Du dic Menschheit, sowohl in Deiner Person als auch in de Person eines anderen, jederzeit zugleich als Zweck, niemals bloß als Mittel gebrauchst.' Immanuel Kant, *Grundlegung zur Metaphysik der Sitten*, in Werke (Akademiker-Ausgaese), vol. 4 (Berlin, 1903).

CAN 'TRUE' AND 'FALSE' NEEDS BE POSITED?

Kant himself spoke of three 'thirsts' (*Süchte*), each of which presupposes the use of the other as a mere means. They are the thirst for possession, the thirst for domination and the thirst for ambition (*Habsucht, Herrschsucht, Ehrsucht*). These 'thirsts' are obviously forms of alienated needs. The man driven by the 'thirsts' does not strive for the satisfaction of one or the other of his particular needs since all his particular needs are multiplied by the 'thirst' itself. In principle, all concrete qualitative needs are satisfiable, but the quantified system of needs is unsatisfiable *ex principio*. One cannot possess power that could be regarded as sufficient or so much property that one would not hunger for more. Accepting the Kantian imperative according to which man ought not to be a mere means for the other excludes – from an *ethical* point of view – all those needs that are not concrete qualitative needs, that is to say, excludes sheer quantitative alienated needs. In this way three different but interconnected problems are solved.

First, the Kantian categorical imperative provides a criterion for the distinction between 'good' and 'evil' needs on the grounds of which one can disregard the divisions of *particular* needs into 'good' and 'evil' ones. Second, the exclusion of quantitative needs which are unsatisfiable *ex principio* makes relevant the previous requirement according to which all needs should be satisfied. Third, we have broken the above mentioned deadlock. All those needs that created a dilemma with respect to overall need-satisfaction belong to the category whose satisfaction requires that man become a mere means for the other, for example, exploitation or oppression. If we use the Kantian categorical imperative to exclude them from acknowledgment and satisfaction, the acknowledgment and satisfaction of all other particular needs become immediately relevant.

Let us then formulate the thesis by rejecting the division of needs into real and unreal ones and by accepting the guidance of the moral norm. In that case it would run as follows: All needs should be acknowledged and satisfied with the exception of those whose satisfaction would make man into a mere means for the other. The categorical imperative has, therefore, a restrictive function in the assessment of needs.

CAN 'TRUE' AND 'FALSE' NEEDS BE POSITED?

The political aspect

Discussion has thus far focussed on two types of interpretation of the division of needs into 'true' and 'false' ones. The first interpretation, which understands the terms 'true' and 'false' as a dichotomy between 'real' and 'unreal', has been rejected as irrelevant. The second, which sees the distinction in terms of 'good' and 'evil', has been accepted in a concrete way. The next question is whether or not this differentiation conceals some 'third' problem left unanalysed until now. Does the rejection of 'evil' needs in the Kantian sense mean that all the needs not excluded are at the same time 'good' or, more precisely, *equally* good?

The acceptance of the concept of 'good' and 'evil' needs in a specific interpretation was deliberate. The first and simplest reason is that we opt for the acknowledgment and satisfaction of all needs with the exception of the excluded ones. Another reason is that we regard as irrelevant all moral rosters in the assessment of concrete needs. Practically, this is equivalent to the statement that the division of needs into 'good ones' and 'less good ones' can play no role at all in the institutionalized democratic debate on priorities in need satisfaction. It is self-evident that the acknowledgment of all needs must be equivalent to the *equal* acknowledgment of all needs. For in a debate about priorities in need-satisfaction, the assessment of their needs as 'better' or 'less good' ones would also imply the assessment of their reality. The demand for satisfaction of those needs being evaluated as 'less good' could not be acknowledged seriously, and the debate on priorities would be degraded into a pseudo-debate, and not even the relative conclusion of the debate could lead to consensus since the promoters of the needs degraded into being allegedly 'less good ones' would withdraw their agreement. With a detour, we would arrive again at the dictatorship over the needs.

What individuals are aware of to be their need, actually is their need. It is real, it has to be acknowledged, it has to be satisfied. But *is one entitled to wish* that they have other or additional needs? Is it possible, is it reasonable to interpret the division into 'true' and 'false' needs as a division between preferred and not preferred needs? Is an interpretation possible and reasonable that is not identical with the division into 'good' and 'evil' (for it does not condemn anything in a moral sense) but which nevertheless has options?

The existence of options of that type is not our concern here since it is obvious that they exist in all time. The question is of their rationality and function. The most important thing is that the options do not order concrete needs into any consecutive series. If the question should be raised as to whether it is the need for food or for creative activity, the need for friendship or for hygiene that is 'more important', we would get entangled into entirely meaningless debates, for all these needs appear in the most different aspects of human life and activity. The preferences, however, do not order the particular needs into a consecutive series, they refer to the *system of needs*. It is the way of life that is reflected in the system of needs. The options taken within the system of needs mean, then, the preference of one or more ways of life to others.

However, the preference of a way of life is always guided by values. Since in modern societies the values are pluralistic, the preferences for different ways of life are pluralistic as well. Moreover, among the values there are contradictions, too, which are tied to conflicting interests or to divergent types of *Weltanschauung* or to both. Consequently, there exist competitive or contradictory options for ways of life and options for needs, too.

The various options for needs claim to fulfil the same function of need-satisfaction, but actually they cannot. The claim can be formulated as follows: the system of human needs should correspond to the system of needs opted for by people. It is the *influence* upon the development of systems of needs, eventually their direct guidance, furthermore the critique of systems of needs not corresponding to the preferred one that fulfils this function.

There is an actual and a pseudo-form of the fulfilment of the function. The pseudo-form consists of the imputation of needs.

The imputation of needs means that one ascribes to persons or groups of persons needs of which they are not aware as their needs. This can take place in two forms, first by questioning the fact that the needs the given persons seek to satisfy are their real, authentic needs; second, by giving voice to the assumption that people have other needs, too, of which they are unaware (but – should they be aware of them – their systems of needs would differ from the present ones).

Before any further analysis, let us separate the two ways of need-imputation from one another. It has already been demonstrated that the previous one (declaring the conscious needs to be inauthentic ones) is theoretically untenable and practically dangerous. It is possible to maintain, however, that whole groups of persons have – apart from the needs of which they are aware

CAN 'TRUE' AND 'FALSE' NEEDS BE POSITED?

– other, unconscious needs whose rendering conscious would modify their whole system of needs?

We departed from the assumption that needs are conscious, that only a need of which a person is aware can be considered to be his or her need. At the present moment our question centres on the problem of whether the level and the form of awareness are homogeneous.

Sartre suggested a very important distinction with regard to the forms of consciousness of needs. According to him there exist needs as *manque* (deficiency) and needs as *projet* (plan). The first is only the *awareness of the existence* of a need, the second is the *awareness of the forms of satisfaction* of needs and a conscious activity with regard to the need-satisfaction. If someone is aware of being lonely, he feels that life is senseless and aimless; even this is the formulation of a conscious need: that for community or for others in general, the formulation of the need for a meaningful conduct of life. Should such a feeling appear in people *en masse*, it may be assumed that the need in question exists in a general form. What does not exist is the activity aimed at the satisfaction of the need, the consciousness with regard to the satisfiable character of the need or to the form(s) of its satisfaction.

One may ask why that consciousness and that form of activity is missing. The answer is unambiguous. The reason is that the social objectivations, goals and institutions are missing which may guide the satisfaction of the need, in other words, could transform it from deficiency (*manque*) into a plan (*projet*). And this is a reasonable assumption.

What does imputation mean in this case? The need itself is not imputed since it is posited in the form of a *manque* as existing. It is the following hypothesis that is imputed: if the objectivations guiding the needs existed, a *manque* type of need would turn into a *projet*, and in the wake of this, the human system of needs would be transformed. This is undoubtedly an imputation since no one is capable of making true assertions with regard to the future. No one can know with *certainty* that the assertion will *actually* be realized even if all preliminary conditions are met. But undoubtedly the imputation is reasonable. Notably, the value under the guidance of which people prefer a system of needs can point out existing needs in present society whose satisfaction *may* at least lead towards the preferred system of needs.

If we admit that the second form of need-imputation is reasonable, we have to raise the question anew of why we regarded the imputation of needs in both of its forms as the pseudo-form of

CAN 'TRUE' AND 'FALSE' NEEDS BE POSITED?

the guidance of needs. The reason was that ideas and values – whatever type they should belong to – cannot fulfil this guiding function by themselves, or if they can, only temporarily, in the 'great moments' of social boiling points. Even the representatives of the second, reasonable form of need-imputation have to admit that it is counterfactual. It can only become an actual force in transforming needs if it is embodied in objectivations, institutions, in social life itself. True enough, ideal objectivations (in the given instance: theories) can represent sufficient power to transform the structure of needs of particular persons according to their ideas. But even if this change in the need-structure is democratic in its content, it's of an elitarian character and precisely for that reason mostly vanishing. A new structure of needs should be deeply rooted and has to offer a real social alternative in order to become generalizable.

I am going to return to the initial problem that the various options for needs claim to fulfil the same function but actually cannot. The power structure of every present society – regarding production and social coexistence – contains inherently the preference of concrete systems of needs. The various power centres are, however, capable of what those partially or totally bereft of power are incapable of, namely, of bringing about systems of objectivation (products, institutions, etc.) that direct the needs and their forms of satisfaction. It is this direction of the systems of needs through objectivations and institutions that is called manipulation.

Of course, manipulation may take on various forms. György Lukács distinguished between two extreme forms of it. He called one of them brutal manipulation and the other refined. Brutal manipulation brings the first type of imputation to the fore. It declares existing needs to be non-existent, and it bans by arbitrary decision the emergence of objectivations serving the satisfaction of existing needs. It is precisely this that may be called the dictatorship over needs. In opposition to that, refined manipulation is effected through the acknowledgment of existing needs. At an ever-increasing pace, the system of refined manipulation produces and offers institutions for already existing and universal *projets*. What is neglected by it is need as *manque*. It does not produce for alternative ways of life; it does not create counterinstitutions. As a consequence, the *manques* which are not satisfiable (cannot be channelled) through *projets* accumulate, and their manifestation takes on irrational forms: those of neurosis and violence.

Both forms of manipulation accomplish, then (in either an overt or in a covert form), the division of needs into 'real' and 'unreal' needs. All types of manipulation of needs infringe the norm that all needs should be acknowledged, all needs should be satisfied with the exception of those which render one person a mere means for the other.

The alternative: radical needs

All that has thus been formulated on a more theoretical level achieves a social relevance here. It has been stated that unless one of the formulae of the categorical imperative is applied to restrict the acknowledgment and satisfaction of needs, the acknowledgment and satisfaction of all needs becomes *ex principio* impossible. The above formula of the categorical imperative excludes the need for degrading the other man into a mere means. Wherever social relations are based on subordination and hierarchy, wherever there are haves and have-nots with regard to power, wherever possession of property (the right of disposition) is granted to some but not to others, there exists the need of using another individual as a mere means. In these societies it is practically impossible to acknowledge all needs, let alone satisfy them. It also ensues from the foregoing, however, that the negation of the division into 'real' and 'unreal' imaginary needs was not real itself, that is to say, it did not stem from the empirical description of facts. On the contrary, it proved to be counterfactual itself, a value, a norm that can only be conceived together with the idea of abolishing social relations based on subordination and hierarchy.

However, the norm was formulated in a way that did not question the competence of every person to become conscious of his or her own needs (nor with regard to their being conscious already): it was precisely that competence that created the point of departure. The fact of needs-manipulation has not been related to the assertion of need-fetishism. We have not placed ourselves outside humankind. This needs further clarification.

According to Marx, those who transcend societies based on subordination and hierarchy are those who have radical needs. These are persons whose conscious needs cannot be satisfied by the society within which the needs were formed. To satisfy their needs these persons must transcend their given society by establishing the 'society of the associated producers'. The 'society of associated producers' ceases to be a mere speculative construction only when progressive forces create the social preconditions capable of satisfying their radical needs in continuous struggle against oppression and exploitation.

I tried to demonstrate in several of my writings that in the world – and its various structural forms – there exist radical needs and that new movements constantly emerge to meet them. I stated repeatedly, too, that my own concept of transcending relations based on subordination and hierarchy expressed an affinity to these existing radical needs. I would like to go a step further.

The movements centred and organized around radical needs represent a minority of people; at least they have until now. Yet these movements have always held that their aims and aspirations to transcend social subordination and hierarchy represent the values and needs of all humanity. The question is whether that consciousness is ideological and whether thereby the social utopia expressing an affinity to radical needs does not bear the traces of an ideological character.

There is no wall of China between radical and non-radical needs. The movements centred around radical needs also represent non-radical needs, that is to say, needs that are satisfiable within the given society. Even the need for radical movements can be satisfied in present societies which are democratic legal states. Further, radical needs can be articulated and often are articulated as well in all movements, parties, interest groups that do not order their needs around radical ones. Last but not least, if we assume that the acknowledgment and satisfaction of all needs can be realized only by transcending societies based on subordination and hierarchy, the following assertion is implied: the acknowledgment of *all* human needs is a radical claim, too.

Ascribing radical needs to all humanity is, then, not necessarily ideological, which does not mean that it cannot become ideological. It becomes ideological when the non-radical needs or the systems of needs that are not ordered around radical needs will thereby be declared 'false' or 'unreal'. Further, it will become ideological if it turns against the precondition of its existence, the democratic legal state.

More, however, we have to go back to the third form of the division of needs into 'true' and 'false'. Even if the radical movements reject the 'real' 'unreal' division of needs and posit themselves as non-ideological movements, they are nonetheless justified – on the grounds of their values – in preferring certain systems of needs and in influencing society accordingly. How can this be accomplished and what is its function?

To begin with, radical needs are themselves pluralistic. There is no such movement whose system of needs includes *all* radical needs. Different radical needs constitute the nucleus of the movement of self-management, of the revolution of way of life, and of feminist movements. As a consequence, they do not prefer the same system of needs; they do not want to exert influence upon society from the same perspective. There is, however, one trait in common in all their options, and that is what makes them radical movements: all of them exclude from the preferred system of needs the ones oppressing or positing the use of an individual as a mere means of the other.

When speaking about radical needs striving for the influence upon system of needs, it is assumed that the guidance itself is pluralistic, too, since it is accomplished from the viewpoint of different models of way of life. Pluralistic influence is not in a position to become manipulative. This would in itself, however, be only a negative characteristic. The negativity will be turned into positivity when radical movements live their own options to the limit of their potential, which would exclude manipulation from the very beginning. Whenever they cease to do so, whenever they do not exclude those needs that make one individual a mere means for the other, they cease to be movements representing radical needs *regardless* of the radicalism of the ideas they advocate. To put this simply if a radical movement intends to make people happy against their will, it ceases to be radical in the meaning of the concept delineated here.

Clearly, the option for alternative systems of needs can exert influence in only one form – by creating such objectivations and institutions which include the counter alternatives of the existing ones and grant a possibility thereby for the needs existing as a mere *manque* to become *projets*. At the same time the result of the choice cannot turn against the existence or relevance of any objectivation or institution for which real needs exist or which satisfy existing needs (except for needs that make one individual a mere means for the other). It has to advocate, then, the gradual abolition of manipulation and a social division of power. Within this framework all needs – the radical ones, too – may appear as equal, with the objectivations (objects, institutions) satisfying needs being commensurate to various alternatives of way of life.

Coexistence

The fact that there is only one non-manipulative way of guiding needs, namely, the creation of the equal chance for qualitatively different needs and systems of needs in the form of objectivations, in no way means giving up the right and duty to *criticize* certain systems of needs. The public form of such a needs-critique, however, cannot be a democratic system of the institutions in which decisions will be made on the priority among equally legitimate needs. The critique of needs must be of a personal character. The term does not refer to a strictly person-to-person exchange; public life can be the channel of the critique of needs, too. Rather, it is meant to convey the non-coercive character of the critique. For instance, it is legitimate for a heterogeneous educational system to prefer the forms of education compatible with the way of life which that system serves. It is legitimate to argue privately and publicly on behalf of that form of education, and there is nothing wrong with criticizing other forms of education in trying to convince opponents. But no one is justified in demanding the abolition of an institution for which there is a need. Critique and argumentation must focus only on modifying the need so that the need for the criticized system of objectivation will finally wither. This is also the norm for the directly personal needs-critique. The norm must never be the refusal to satisfy needs but must be the appeal to others. If our brother, for example, spends his days in idleness while the family works hard to survive, we shall not appeal to the paternal authority not to sustain him, instead we appeal to our brother. We try to convince him that his behaviour is not democratic and we try to arouse his interest in types of activity for which he has talent, in which he may gradually find pleasure. A preference for a way of life and a critique of needs do exist in this case, but they are not coercive.

Not even the democratically pluralistic state and its system of institutions can be the source of the elaboration of new systems of needs and new ways of life. Moreover, it *should not* become their source. It can only establish a framework to all this. Eliminating the needs that make one individual a mere means for another is a long-lasting process; it is *democracy as labour*. The trend of this labour is to make it possible for all individuals to participate in social decisions and to decentralize power.

It is in this process that individuals should implement the norm of acknowledging and satisfying needs according to agreed priorities. But it *contradicts* this labour if the options for different ways of life, the transformation of the way of life or the system of needs, are endowed with power.

The function of the transformation of the way of life, the need-options, and the critique of needs is the formation of social coexistence. In other words, the function is reciprocal education, both in its individual and communal forms. This can, however, only take place when democratic states and institutions receive feedback from actually transformed needs. Of course, this does not exclude – indeed, it even presupposes – that the new system of needs and the new ways of life should possess new objectivations. The more objectivations there are for new needs, the greater is the chance that these needs will be acknowledged and satisfied.

CHAPTER 6
The Dissatisfied Society

Let me start with a flagrant truism: the structure of needs of our modern Western world markedly differs from the structure of needs in previous societies. But as an immediate addition to this truism it has to be mentioned that in the most recent debates, the unique character of the developmental pattern of the modern structure of needs is, in the main, identified with two of its most conspicuous features: with the cancerous growth of the production of material goods on the one hand, and with the ever-increasing demand for more and more new commodities on the other. Industrial growth produces new forms of satisfaction for material needs and, simultaneously, creates new needs; the rapid diffusion of new demands further accelerates industrial production. Criticism of the modern structure of needs tends to focus all attention on these two conspicuous features. Consumerism is blamed for all the ills of contemporary society. Modern man is identified with man the *consumer*, for the assumption is that capitalist, or in another vocabulary, industrial society has in fact reduced people to consumers. Some critics specifically blame the mass media for spreading dangerous consumerist need-patterns and make advertisements responsible for the so-called 'manipulation of needs'. They seek a panacea that will identify 'true' needs and eliminate 'false' needs, or they advocate central control of the evolution and satisfaction of needs by a world-wide authority which will impose a scientifically established 'limit to growth'.

But the crux of the matter is that the tendency for needs to expand indefinitely characterizes our modern structure of needs *as a whole*, not just man as consumer. In order to understand man the consumer, we have, first, to understand the system of needs of modern man as a symbolic structure. It will then become apparent that the remedies suggested by the critics of consumerism are either ineffectual or positively poisonous.

The classical sociologists, Marx, Tönnies, Weber, Simmel, have provided a far deeper understanding of the modern system of needs. In precapitalist epochs, so Marx suggested, the development of needs was limited by a set of norms of conduct. The individual's system of needs could develop only within these fixed boundaries. This is why 'great individuals' were only apparently great whereas in fact they were narrow-minded (*borniert*): they accepted their confinement to the boundaries of a particularistic world of symbolic meaning as their 'natural' limitation. Only after capitalism had dismantled all particularistic systems of conduct, could the individual system of needs expand unimpeded. If the modern individual is superior to the premodern one it is because his or her self-development is *unlimited*. The general dissatisfaction engendered by the dismantling of all limits to individual development is the very precondition of communist society. Weber described modernity in roughly the same terms as Marx, though without any utopian perspective. In his view the modern individual no longer dies 'satiated with life' as his ancestors could. In analysing science as a vocation, Weber stressed the unlimitedness of modern scientific knowledge. All discoveries and theories of today will be falsified and surpassed tomorrow. It is no longer possible to know enough. And given that our life is a limited enterprise, we not only live, we also die, in dissatisfaction. The Weberian 'disenchantment of the world' describes the same tendency as that hailed by Marx as the transcendence of all 'sacred limits' – even if with a fair amount of doubt and scepticism.

It is following in the footsteps of both Marx and Weber that I call modern society the dissatisfied society, and the modern individual the dissatisfied individual. It is in their spirit that I emphasize the *all-encompassing* character of dissatisfaction. But I must add some considerations of my own to this.

Marx attributed dissatisfaction to the universal diffusion and socially dominant character of commodity production – especially under the conditions created by capitalist manufacturing industry. Weber attributed it in the main to rationalization. I would suggest that the social epoch characterized by 'modernity' can, and should, be grasped as a unique combination of three different, and by no means necessarily interconnected, tendencies – capitalization, industrialization and democratization. Each of these three tendencies has a logic of its own, and the development of each can, and often does, contradict the other two. Commodity production alone, whatever intensified forms it may assume, does not bring about 'dissatisfied society'. Democratic values have to exist, at least as regulative ideas, for this to come about. Lasalle, contemporary with Marx, still had to complain about the 'damned contentment' of the German workers. And contentment in an outrageous world is even now far from exceptional among the damned of the earth in capitalist countries lacking in democratic social imagination. This is precisely why I am going to disregard in what follows both the system of dictatorship over needs in the Soviet societies and the capitalist states without democratic movements and institutions.

But even if capitalism, industrialization and democracy have logics of their own, and even if each has developmental tendencies contradicting the others, so far as the problem under scrutiny here is concerned, they rather amplify each other. As a result, the most dissatisfied societies are those which combine all three of them. The reasons for this seem to be obvious.

I have already referred to the modern structure of needs as a symbolic structure. This is, of course, no *differentia specifica* of our epoch: all need structures have always been, and still are, symbolic structures, in other words, they are shaped by the systems of values of their respective societies. A natural drive, for example hunger, is not a need; hunger for something (involving the exclusion of something else) is. This is because the 'something' needed and the 'something else' excluded are defined by the norms and rules of the social unit the human being has been born into. Needless to say, the symbolic character of the need structure does not imply a complete homology of the value-structure and the need structure in any complex society which allows for a variety of individual need systems. But at least the *clusters* of needs are evaluated, in a positive or negative sense. Patterns of individual need development are shaped according to the social values attributed to particular kinds of action, attitude, behaviour, things. What we need *become goods*. And obversely: only the things and activities are 'goods' which are evaluated as such in any given society. When Marx emphasized that only *use values* can have exchange value, he hinted precisely at this interconnection.

The needs of modern man are insatiable because our values *define* them as such.

In the following analysis of 'dissatisfied society' I am going to construct an ideal type. I intend this ideal type to depict various aspects of modernity without claiming that it covers every need structure characteristic of our epoch.

Simultaneously with the dismantling of traditional norms of conduct, several norms and values have gradually become universalized. Particularistic integrations no longer serve as uncontestable points of reference for dignified, honourable or virtuous behaviour. The idea of being a 'Man', instead of being a 'good citizen' or a 'good Christian' or a 'good servant', gains ground vigorously. Establishing one's self-identity with the emphatic sentence: 'I am a Man', 'I am a human being', by renouncing allegiance to every organic, traditional bond and institution, this representative gesture of the Enlightenment which has not been radically challenged since then, is based on two interconnected value commitments. One of them is a commitment to *humankind* as to the only binding integration, the other is the commitment to the *uniqueness of human personality*. All universalized values like freedom, equality, fraternity, scientific knowledge, alleviation of suffering and so on have recourse either to humankind or to the unique personality or to both. Neither capitalism nor industrialization alone can bring about a new structure of needs characterized by the *unlimitedness* of human demands. It was precisely the trend towards the new universalization of values that reshaped the system of needs. Capitalist development cleared the way for such a universalization which, in its turn, helped to accelerate the general diffusion of capitalist industrial production. The system of symbols of modernity induced individuals to conceive of their needs as insatiable.

If the value of freedom has a concrete and limited meaning and if this meaning is defined by the norms of conduct of any given society, the need for freedom is equally concretely defined, thus limited. For example, it was self-evident to Aristotle that the 'free man' is the citizen eligible for office in a city-state. No one could be 'more free' than being a free citizen; the granting of this status completely satisfied a person's need for freedom. It was equally self-evident to him that women cannot be free for reasons of principle; this is why, in terms of this theory, they cannot have a need for freedom at all. Contrary to this concrete and limited value of freedom, the universalized form does not specify what freedom really *means*. In principle, universalized freedom can cover everything from free trade to the free development of all human abilities. On the other hand, the universalized value of freedom does not attribute freedom and the need for freedom to any particular social group or class: every human being can claim, and have the need for, freedom. But given that freedom is not defined, it has no limitation either. Each step towards liberation tends to a new restriction, a new constraint which has to be overcome, and once overcome, another new constraint is felt. Measured by the yardstick of the universalized value of freedom everyone is *unfree*. We cannot be satisfied with the particular quality of freedom we eventually enjoy, and we die dissatisfied.

Modern man is indeed the Faustian man; yet he does not implore the present moment to stay unchanged as it is so beautiful. Nothing should remain as it has been. Achieving something is not fulfilment: one immediately reaches out for the next thing. Should we cherish the hope that by achieving something, we shall alleviate our suffering from 'wants', such a hope evaporates the moment we actually achieve the thing desired, as we feel another want, *ad infinitum*. Bearing our lot as 'naturally given' or as being designed by Providence has become an outrageous notion. We are always dissatisfied with our lot because we compare it with the unlimited possibilities beyond our reach in fact but not in imagination. The hunger for ever-newer ways of satisfying need drives people not only in their capacity as consumers. Nor are the creation and quick dissemination of new needs restricted to consumption: the needs for independence, for education, for satisfying work are only a few of the possible examples. Everything thought, done, sought for in modern society is similarly related to the same symbolic structure of needs. The worker who strikes for higher wages, the woman who struggles for recognition within the family or for sexual liberation, the radical who aims at transforming the whole world in the redeeming act of a total revolution, the scientist who desires to explore the universe or to eliminate all diseases, are children of the dissatisfied society to the same extent as man, the consumer who is dissatisfied with the material goods at his disposal. What is grandeur in one respect, can be pettiness in another. But both grandeur and pettiness are nurtured at the same source. If something is 'out of joint' about 'dissatisfied society' the problem has to be faced in its entirety. The question to be raised is whether or not the dissatisfied (modern) individual should be considered an uncontestable value in himself; whether or not the same type of individual could develop in a satisfied society; whether or not 'satisfied society' is possible at all, and if so whether it is desirable as well; whether or not any limitation to any satisfaction would hamper indivudal self-development. Later I am going to return to these problems. For the time being, certain further characteristic features of 'dissatisfied society' have first to be put under scrutiny.

Kant attributed three insatiable drives to the modern individual: the lust for possession, the lust for fame and the lust for power. Interestingly, the lust for lust (pleasure), the desire on which most of the social ills were blamed in earlier societies, does not figure in this catalogue. It stands to reason why this is so: lust is satiable. Firstly, because it is limited by our organism: one can be satiated by pleausre up to the point of indifference, even of disgust. Secondly, because it is limited in time: death puts an end to all pleasures. However, fame is immortal, and in that sense unlimited; power and wealth can be inherited and, at least in principle, endlessly increased and multiplied. In that sense the latter are equally unlimited in space and time. Of course, lust for power, for fame and wealth is not specific to the modern individual and because it is not, certain philosophers, for instance Hume, could derive the lust for having from the 'acquisitiveness' of human nature. But it is easy to comprehend that the three Kantian 'lusts' essentially differ from the desire of *possessing something*, from the love of being *honoured for something* or from the lust for *being powerful in and for something*. A knight might have wished to gain distinction by becoming the finest swordsman; by defending the Christian faith, he might eventually have desired to plunder the cities of the pagans to satisfy his greed, but it could never have occurred to him to seek distinction as a merchant and accumulate wealth by commerce. Thus his lust might have been violent but it certainly was not unlimited. In all precapitalist societies it was certainly the dominant value system that *defined* the particular types of power, wealth and fame worth achieving *and* the proper means of achieving them. Even the hierarchy of fame, power and wealth was shaped by various value systems; the distinction between honourable and unruly passions was set by them as well. Moreover, the division of labour was sanctified in so far as entirely different optimal objectives of power, wealth and fame were attributed to all those participating in it. The lowest-ranking estates were normally excluded from the pursuit of power, fame, sometimes even of possession. A slave in the Ottoman Empire could not achieve fame of any kind unless by joining the Janissaries.

In modern times the picture became increasingly modified, even though the change was slower in countries with a feudal background than, for example, in the United States. But in the world of today the basic motivational patterns of dissatisfied society have become fairly generalized. The need for fame is no longer the need to gain distinction in one particular field with the adequate means: one can gain distinction in *everything* and the means to this do not really matter. Winning a gold medal at the Olympic Games is just as good as becoming a well-known actor, scholar, businessman, general, beauty queen, politician, designer in *haute couture*, writer, adventurer, revolutionary leader, explorer, guru of a new sect, big-time criminal. Specific fame is no longer the objective but *fame as such*, and similarly power as such, wealth as such. No kind of fame, power or wealth is beneath the dignity of modern man.

It is appropriate here to recall the proud statement of the Enlightenment: I am a Man, I am a human being and nothing else. The unspecific character of the lust for power, fame and wealth had been shaped by this construction of self-identity in more than one aspect.

First of all, the value of personality became the supreme value; as Goethe put it: 'Höchstes Glück der Erdenkinder sei nur die Persönlichkeit.' As human character no longer develops in keeping with the strict norms of estates, dignity pertains to individual personality alone. As Marx put it: to be born into, to be a member of, a class is regarded as accidental. Or, to formulate the same statement the other way round: social classes, as contrasted with estates, are characterized precisely by the accidental relation of the individual to the place he occupies in the division of labour. The individual has become the sole master of his or her achievement, accomplishment and fate, if not in reality, at least in the dominant imagery. Making, creating, doing something hallmarked by *uniqueness* is now the expression and the repository of individual dignity.

'I am a human being', and everyone else is equally a human being. If fame, power and wealth can be sought for in anything, all of them can be achieved by *anyone*. Everyone can embark towards any kind of fame, power and wealth: nobleman and commoner (as long as this distinction exists at all), man and woman, rich and poor. Napoleon, the self-made man who brought the hereditary monarchs of Europe to their knees, was the symbol of times to come.

'I am a human being' implies something else as well: the substitution of humankind for any local and limited integration. Achieving something within the framework of a local community is worthless if we compare it with achievements on a world-scale.

No one can deny candidly that the proud statement: 'I am a

THE DISSATISFIED SOCIETY

human being', in its capacity of pointing to our universal as well as unique existence, is dear to us. I am going to make the statement more personal: It is dear to me and to everyone who does not wish to revoke Enlightenment. And I wish to have no ambiguities regarding the fact that, despite all its malignant side-effects and consequences which I am going to analyse at their point, I do consider the universalization of certain values as the only ethical progress achieved in the history of humankind. I also reject all neo-fundamentalist movements aiming at de-Enlightenment as the embodiments of regression. But this resolute stand does not prevent me from facing the fact that something went wrong with our value system and with the system of needs it shaped.

There was only one Napoleon but there were millions of young men dreaming of becoming one. There were very few self-made business tycoons but there were millions who cherished the dream of becoming one of them while toiling in factories or small shops throughout their whole lives. The mass media have undoubtedly a corrupting effect, not because they advertise electric knives but because they advertise the universal yardstick of fame, power and wealth. But so do the lists of citations and international awards: all of them contribute to general dissatisfaction. No fame is sufficient if compared with that enjoyed at the top, no power is sufficient if compared with that wielded at the top, no wealth is sufficient if compared with that accumulated at the top. And even those few at the top cannot be satisfied because they can very easily be overtaken by others in the world-wide race.

Man the consumer can only be understood from this perspective. And I even venture the unorthodox view that consumerism is the most democratic form of the three major lusts.

If a salesgirl is watching the Marilyn Monroe story on TV, the gap between her own situation and her dreams of becoming a famous actress is absolutely unbridgeable. But should she be concentrating on the dress, rather than on the career, of the actress, it is not in principle out of her reach to buy such a dress, at least similar in colour and in style, for herself. If one's ambition is not related to power or fame, but to consumables, dissatisfaction as a basic emotional background feeling will not disappear, but one can, at least for a few moments, feel like a queen or a king if one uses the same brand of soap as Sophia Loren, the same necktie as Rockefeller or the same cap as Lenin. If human dignity is linked up with fame, power and possession, where should human beings look for dignity if not to the sphere which is, at least to some extent, open to all? Consumerism is an *imitable* reducer of dissatisfaction in modernity. It is an attitude which may offer some chance of dignity for everyone within the all-embracingly frustrating dissatisfied society. But it is not the only one.

The lust for fame, power and wealth can be projected into the 'we-consciousness'. In this case the person 'shares', so to speak, the achievements of a collective subject, be it nation, class, race, cultural elite, party and the like. If my country soccer team has won the World Cup, the glory is mine as well. At first glance, there is nothing new about this. Moreover, it seems as if the increasing identification of 'we-consciousness' with a *particularistic* collective imagery invalides my previous assertion about the increasing universalization of values in modernity. But, as the example of the soccer team might have suggested, the lust for collective fame, power and wealth (the imagery of 'we-consciousness') can be just as unlimited (related to *everything*) and measured by the yardstick of humankind to the same extent as in the case of the individual. The crux of the matter is that because of this new form of 'we-consciousness' dissatisfaction is not solely individual. We are dissatisfied not only with our personal lot but with that of our nation, class, party, cultural elite, race and the like. I am going to restrict my analysis to the most sublime example of the dissatisfaction of this type: to the one related to the value of *progress*.

Of course, the very idea of progress has emerged in dissatisfied society. The motion implies not only perfection but also an unlimited and increasingly accelerated development in direction of what is 'higher', 'better' and 'more'. When viewed from the vantage point of the idea of progress, the present state of affairs is transitory. Present-day affairs mediate between the previous 'lower' stage of development and a future on a 'higher', 'better' stage. The motion of universal regression has emerged simultaneously with that of universal progression, simply as the reverse side of the coin but as a philosophical theory rather than a popular and all-embracing imagery. However, the idea of progress has occupied a place in the pantheon of universalized regulative ideas: ever since, it has regulated action, behaviour, imagination. As Feuerbach put it: Captain Forward became the scourge in the hand of the god of modernity. The newest is always considered the best. But the society in labour cannot take delight in the newborn since it grows old whilst still in the cradle. Permanent progress keeps society permanently in labour. But what is being born in this process?

THE DISSATISFIED SOCIETY

The idea of progress is as undefined as the universalized values (freedom, equality and the like) on the one hand, and the three Kantian 'lusts' on the other. And this is why the idea of progress can be related to both, and in various combinations. Progress can be measured in terms of power, possessions and fame, or in terms of the realization of freedom, equality and the alleviation of suffering. These two yardsticks do not necessarily present a dilemma although they can and increasingly do so. Progress can be mainly or exclusively measured by the yardstick of the development of production and the creation of ever-changing wants, the satisfaction of which becomes more and more costly. But it can be measured also by the progressive realization of freedom, equality of all human beings and the alleviation of the suffering of humankind as a whole. Given that our need structure is a symbolic one shaped by our system of values, we have to come to the conclusion that the idea of progress can bring about *two different* patterns of needs, both represented symbolically by the same idea. One of them is a need structure which seeks for and stimulates increased production, increased consumerism, increased power and domination, and the other is a need structure which is aimed at and promotes an increase in freedom, equality and the alievation of suffering. But, should we cast a further glance at these two new need structures, we shall realize that they are completely interwoven: in fact, they constitute one structure of needs with an internal contradiction. The latter expresses the tension between the developmental logic of capitalism and industrialization, on the one hand, and the developmental logic of democracy on the other. The idea of progress implies in both cases *dissatisfaction* but it propels the actors in two different directions.

Here I have to return to a problem touched upon previously. I have suggested that the 'consumerist attitude' is still the most democratic channel through which the three lusts can operate; I could have added that it is the least dangerous safety valve for any lust as well. By buying ever 'newer' goods we do harm to no one, whilst just the opposite holds true of actions motivated by the lust for power, and eventually also of actions motivated by the lust for fame. But this more democratic, or even innocent, propensity of consumerism circumscribes a negativity (a lack of destructive passions) rather than any positive quality. Consumerism is innocent in that it is infantile: it is a behaviour without moral implications, and thus without any kind of responsibility. And if we view it from the point of view of progress towards 'radicalization of democracy', the relatively more democratic character of consumerism, as compared with the implications of the other lusts, will prove deficient in democratic *values*. Everyone who takes seriously the values of freedom, equality and the alleviation of suffering in regard to humankind as a whole, will judge consumerism in a tiny part of the world to be an outrage against those who die of famine, suffer from regular malnutrition on an earth we share. How can we proudly assert: 'I am a human being', if we do not care for human beings? And when asking this question, one should be aware of the fact that general dissatisfaction which includes all protests against suffering, humiliation, oppression and domination is the offspring of the same culture, of the same value system, of the same progress which it criticizes, rejects and tries to overcome. Dissatisfaction with dissatisfied society belongs to that same society.

Given that the modern system of values as a symbolic structure is shaped by universalistic values, the supreme values shaping them, precisely because of being universalistic, cannot constitute *any particular way of life*, as earlier particularistic and hierarchical value systems could and did. The process of rationalization described by Weber and the universalization of certain values are two sides of the same coin. The 'disenchantment of the world', as Max Weber put it, or the dismantling of all traditional normative systems as Karl Marx formulated it, on the one hand, and the process of rationalization, on the other, open up an immense gap between the normative regulation of life and the subordination of persons under mere rules. The latter takes place within the framework of various institutions from the school to the factory, the office building, the market, the political institutions and the like. All these institutions have different set of rules which their 'members' have to comply with, and there are either no values to be observed or only completely emasculated ones. It is only family life that may provide a few norms for human behaviour as a whole but if it does, 'primary socialization' makes persons unfit rather than fit for 'adult life' within highly rationalized institutions.

The rash application of the Aristotelian notion of 'the good life' to modernity is fairly misconceived. The distinction between 'life' and 'good life' only makes sense as long as a distinct type of 'way of life' can be established in keeping with a set of values and practised continuously. In its original, and very reasonable, meaning 'the good life' was identical with the happy life human beings could primarily achieve by practising virtues. The systems of needs in life, pure and simple, and in 'the good life' were qualitatively different from each other. Life was satisfaction through pleasure, 'the good life' was happiness through virtue. No quantitative increase in satisfactions of 'life' can lead to the happiness of 'the good life'. It stands to reason that this distinction between life and 'the good life' cannot simply be applied to modernity. In modernity, it is success that people normally seek. The lusts are oriented towards the 'more' of the 'same': more power, more fame, more wealth. As there are no consensually accepted virtues to achieve or to practise, there is no 'way of life' at all, and the qualitative difference between sublime and base is replaced by the quantitative difference of more or less success. Even the idea of progress does not perforce generate the possibility of 'the good life'. If someone is passionately involved in the growth of an enterprise or in the establishment of a health service or in a new scientific discovery, in other words, in some kind of progress, the involvement itself does not provide him or her with a normative set of 'virtues'. Since the projects of progress are being implemented within the framework of a particular institution, involvement does not imply, nor does it constitute, any framework or form of human intercourse as a whole.

It would be sheer romanticism to pinpoint the malignant effects alone of the above trend. One should not forget that the firmly established 'ways of life' belong to worlds in which the particular ways of life were attributed to particular estates and in which 'the good life' was ascribed only to the highest estate, the qualitative distinction between the system of needs in 'life', pure and simple, and in 'the good life' can appeal to us and provide us with a regulative idea only if the system of needs in 'the good life' is shaped by universalistic values which do not contradict, only interpret, universalistic ones. This is why neo-fundamentalist tendencies which try to revoke universalistic values cannot offer 'the good life' in any other way but through regression.

Radical needs, needs for a radical democracy, and non-radical ones are being shaped by the *same* universalistic value system, even though their ways of satisfaction are being sought for in opposite directions. But radical needs do not constitute a different way of life, even less 'the good life', by their very existence. They come about via *reflection* on universalistic values whereas other needs are only shaped by the latter without reflection on universalistic values. Reflection on universalistic values *can* provide people, if not with a way of life, at least with a *conduct of life*. By the latter I mean a coherent, idiosyncratic but imitable, life strategy based on the observance of obligations set by the interpretation of universalistic values. For the time being, 'conduct of life' is an aristocratic venture in the sense that it cannot be generalized. However, it is more or less inherent in movements which are organized around radical needs. Today only a 'conduct of life' can be called 'the good life' if we take the notion of 'the good life' seriously.

After a brief inventory of the need structure in dissatisfied society, it is appropriate to return to the questions unanswered so far as to (1) whether or not the dissatisfied (modern) individual should be acclaimed as an uncontestable value-for-itself; (2) whether the same type of individual could develop in a satisfied society; (3) whether a 'satisfied society' can come about, and if so, (4) whether it is desirable as well; and (5) whether any limitation to any satisfaction would hamper individual self-development.

Of these questions, the third and the fourth can be unambiguously answered in the negative. Marx's dreams cannot come true. We cannot conceive of the continuously expanding individual need structure and the simultaneous satisfaction of all human needs in the same breath, for several reasons. We can no longer believe what it was reasonable to believe in the nineteenth century, that the natural resources of our planet are unlimited, nor can we believe that even in the case of a continously expanding demand for material goods a state of complete abundance can ever come about. The objection to such a reservation, namely, that it is only spiritual, not material needs that will unlimitedly expand, is irrelevant. This is so, firstly, because even the satisfaction of the so-called spiritual needs presuppose a certain amount of material investment (it is not less expensive to produce books, pianos and especially equipment for scientific research than cars or food processors); secondly, and this is perhaps even more important, because each particular need is embedded in a structure of needs and a structure which contains several unlimited needs along with other limited ones is hardly conceivable. Thus complete abundance on the one hand, and unlimited need expansion on the other cannot be conceived of together. But the problem of whether or not a completely satisfied 'abundant' society is desirable at all should be raised. The simultaneous satisfaction of all human needs would put an end to *tension* in human life; it would make institutions for the solution of conflicts completely superfluous. But a democratic body politic is an institutionalized framework to solve social conflicts. In a radical democracy everyone could equally participate in the process of the solution of conflicts. And at this point I agree with Aristotle: a life without political activity, without a conscious engagement in the solution of conflicts cannot be a 'good life'. As a result, a society of complete abundance, a society satisfying all human needs simultaneously, cannot be a 'good society' because it cannot ensure 'the good life'. It is precisely for that reason that answering the second and the third question in the negative is not equivalent to striking a pessimistic note.

The answers to the first and last question are far more ambiguous.

I have already stated my partiality for the modern individual. But I have also emphasized that the insatiable lusts for power, possession and fame, the imagery of a quantifiable progress, the dissatisfaction in and with society, the radical needs – all this has sprung from the same source. One cannot deny that the destructive and self-destructive consequences of the imagery of unlimitedness become more evident day by day. But, and here I return to the major point, the outcry against the destructive consequences of unlimitedness is equally a self-expression of the modern individual, no less than the imagery of that same unlimitedness. The modern individual is aware of the embarrassing fact that something should be done about the modern individual who runs amok. But what *can* be done?

Preaching against 'false needs' is irrelevant. The theorist who does it simply 'wishes away' the difficulties, speaking in the name of the Father Christmas of History, a symbolic and non-existent entity. The other option, namely, organizing a world-wide authority in order to control all available material resources and to limit satisfaction in keeping with a scientific plan, has very dangerous implications, or, alternatively, it proves to be ineffectual. The first argument against it stems from Hannah Arendt who asked with gallows humour but with serious insight: if there were to be a world government, could we escape from its police? The second objection refers to the ineffectual character of such a global arrangement. Given that a world-wide authority with the assignment of controlling all material resources can only be a hyperrationalized institution, and given that the rationalization of institutions is not only coeval with the emergence of the dissatisfied individual but also the life element of the latter, by limiting material dissatisfaction, such a rationalized institution would in no way change the need structure. At best, it could only reorient the need for possession into other channels or the other two lusts: the lust for fame and, in particular, the lust for power. But we know that the latter two are less democratic and innocuous than consumerism. It is by no means impossible that something like this will happen but the prospect is sufficiently gloomy for us to prefer the world in its present problematic state.

Theoretically, the problem can be answered without assuming the role of the Father Christmas of History and without recourse to a merely institutional solution. The answer will, of course, be purely theoretical but not necessarily illusory. Modern needs are insatiable because universalistic values do not define them in any respect at all. Previous need structures were satiable, because they were shaped by various particular sets of norms. If one does not wish to revoke the universalization of values, one can at least imagine that several particular sets of values mediate between the universal values and the personal interpretations of those same values, between humankind on the one hand and personality on the other. For this to happen, various human communities with different life-styles have to be established, all of them being able to offer normative-moral patterns of 'the good life' but diverse ones. The divergent systems of values could define the system of needs in different ways, and each of them could have a unique quality. Individuals would be free to join and leave each community, to choose the one most adequate to their personality. Once again, the need for having could become the need for having *something*, the need for power for *something* (to execute a particular assignment), the need for being famous in *something* in harmony with the consensus regarding the quality of 'the good life'. If this were so, limitedness and unlimitedness could be conceived of together since the consensus regarding 'the good life' defines the limits, but the individuals are free to choose and rechoose the forms of living, and thereby to opt for unlimitedness. Moreover, as various particular value systems would define needs in divergent ways, no single need would grow cancerously on the level of humankind as a whole. Even though not all needs could be satisfied simultaneously, not even within the framework of one single form of life, the conflicts would not become insoluble. People could once again die 'satiated with life', without becoming 'narrow-minded' individuals in the Marxian sense of the word. 'Satiated' life would not mean that one has experienced, known, lived everything one could, but that everything one experienced, knew and lived was *meaningful*.

This is at least one of the options for the solution of the value conflict formulated by those who do not want to revoke universality; but precisely for that reason they conceive of our progress as scandalous. Whether this option stands any chance, I do not

THE DISSATISFIED SOCIETY

know. What I do know is that it stands no lesser chance than the establishment of any central authority in order to limit production and satisfaction. Anyway, if we dream, it is preferable to enjoy pleasant dreams than have nightmares. Furthermore, dreams, once they become widespread, normally contribute to their coming true, even if the outcome does not match the dream completely. Widespread dreams express values and value interpretations which, on their part, may contribute to reshaping of need systems as well. Of course, not all dreams, even if shared by many, come true, but at least some might. And making a dream public means taking full responsibility for its eventual realization.

Dissatisfied society makes individuals dissatisfied with society. Various types of dissatisfaction have brought about various structural changes in dissatisfied society over the last 200 years. Nor is it too far-fetched in the face of the present state of affairs to assert that the loss of a sense of life is generally felt, that we have become increasingly dissatisfied with living in a cultural limbo, amid mortal dangers that we are impotent to face, in an atmosphere of infantile irresponsibility, striving for ever more without achieving anything, and with the undefined feeling that things cannot go on for ever as they are.

Children and denizens of the nuclear age, we live in constant fear. We do not believe that humankind will survive if we do not do something about this fear. And to get rid of this fear might well be a stronger impulse than dissatisfaction.

The actor in Brecht's *Good Person of Setzuan* turns to the audience at the end of the play with the exclamation: 'There *has* to be an answer!' There has to be an answer to the dilemma of the dissatisfied society as well. And there can be more answers than one.

Index of Names

Adorno, 77, 79, 175
Aeschylus, 113
Anytos, 132
Apel, K.-O., viii, 151–3, 155, 160, 162–7, 174, 230
Arato, A., 120n
Arendt, H., viii, 16, 143, 204, 282, 283, 313
Aristotle, viii, 8, 34, 40, 59, 66–7, 205–6, 209, 228ff., 236, 240, 262, 266–9, 271, 278, 279, 280, 303, 310, 312
Arnason, J., 150n

Balzac, 36
Baudelaire, 112
Benedict, R., 2, 45
Brecht, B., vii, 315
Bürger, P., 126

Castoriadis, C., viii, 205
Cezanne, 79
Chardin, 79
Conrad, 26
Cooper, 184

Darwin, 5
Descartes, viii, 204
Dickens, 21
Diderot, 209
Dodds, 11
Dostoevsky, 28, 39, 55–6, 244
Durkheim, ix, 7, 51, 85, 88, 103, 122

Edwards, P., 276
Einstein, 132, 141
Epicurus, 229, 238
Euripides, 126

Feher, F., 120n, 126, 137, 220
Feuerbach, 308
Fingarett, H., 14
Foucault, 63
Francis of Assisi, 46
Freud, 2, 13, 19, 170–1, 176–7, 182, 184, 194, 234, 242, 280
Fromm, 225

Germanicus, 109
Goethe, 43, 209, 306
Goffman, 122
Gouldner, A., 182
Gramsci, 181
Greco, 79

Habermas, J., viii, 45, 71, 72, 77, 95, 100, 120, 129, 167, 174, 230, 262
Hartmann, N., 65
Hegel, viii, 33, 39, 45, 64, 104, 161, 162, 203, 210, 233, 255
Heidegger, ix, 79
Heller, A., 120n, 137, 220
Hirschman, 206
Homer, 184
Horkheimer, 77
Hume, 305
Husserl, 67, 81

INDEX

Kant, viii, 25, 28, 36–6, 53, 118, 162, 202, 203, 214, 233, 253, 266, 272, 274, 289–90, 291, 305
Kierkegaard, ix
Kissinger, H., ix
Kluge, ix
Koestler, 46, 49
Kuhn, 132, 172

Laing, 185
Lasalle, 302
Lessing, 268
Lukács, G., viii, ix, 56, 63, 65, 66–8, 78, 79, 93, 110, 175, 184, 211, 229, 244, 276, 286, 294
Luther, 28
Luxemburg, R., 237, 242, 243

Machiavelli, 252, 255
MacIntyre, A., viii
Marcuse, 225
Markus, G., 120n, 137, 220
Marx, viii, 57ff., 72, 140, 141, 145, 146, 162, 254, 295, 301, 302, 306, 310, 312
Masaccio, 2
Mead, M., 2
Montesquieu, 15
Mozart, 118
Mucius Scaevola, 30, 45

Napoleon, 45, 55, 306, 307
Negt, ix
Newton, 141
Nietzsche, 38

Ongka, 7

Paul (St), 145

Peisistrathos, 12
Perikles, 12
Piaget, 8
Picasso, 79
Plato, 16, 171, 213, 266
Polanyi, K., 145
Popper, 223
Poussin, 79

Rawls, J., viii
Rembrandt, 118
Riesman, 45, 246, 249
Rilke, 79
Rousseau, 42

Saint–Simon, 64
Sartre, viii, 23, 293
Schutz, A., 161
Shakespeare, 201, 215
Simmel, 301
Smith, A., 145
Socrates, 10, 12, 41, 42, 75, 132, 212–13
Solon, 12
Sombart, 147
Spinoza, viii, 108, 228–9
Stalin, 46

Themistokles, 12
Tintoretto, 79
Tönnies, 301

Weber, ix, 10, 12, 34, 43, 63, 64, 67, 75, 78, 114, 118, 144, 146, 150–1, 156, 160, 161, 162, 166, 172, 207, 212, 218–21, 232, 245, 261, 269, 274, 276, 301, 310
Wittgenstein, 81, 90, 121

For Product Safety Concerns and Information please contact our EU
representative GPSR@taylorandfrancis.com
Taylor & Francis Verlag GmbH, Kaufingerstraße 24, 80331 München, Germany

www.ingramcontent.com/pod-product-compliance
Lightning Source LLC
Chambersburg PA
CBHW071801300426
44116CB00009B/1166